The Traitors Circle

Also by Jonathan Freedland

NON-FICTION
Bring Home the Revolution
Jacob's Gift
The Escape Artist

FICTION (AS SAM BOURNE)
The Righteous Man
The Last Testament
The Final Reckoning
The Chosen One
Pantheon
To Kill the President
To Kill the Truth
To Kill a Man

FICTION (AS JONATHAN FREEDLAND)
The Third Woman

FOR CHILDREN
King Winter's Birthday (*with Emily Sutton*)

The Traitors Circle

*The Rebels Against the Nazis
and the Spy Who Betrayed Them*

JONATHAN FREEDLAND

JOHN MURRAY

First published in Great Britain in 2025 by John Murray (Publishers)

1

Copyright © Jonathan Freedland 2025

The right of Jonathan Freedland to be identified as the
Author of the Work has been asserted by him in accordance
with the Copyright, Designs and Patents Act 1988.

Maps drawn by Barking Dog Art

All rights reserved. No part of this publication may be reproduced, stored in
a retrieval system, or transmitted, in any form or by any means without the
prior written permission of the publisher, nor be otherwise circulated in any
form of binding or cover other than that in which it is published and without
a similar condition being imposed on the subsequent purchaser.

A CIP catalogue record for this title is available from the British Library

Hardback ISBN 978-1-399-81367-9
Exclusive Hardback ISBN 978-1-399-832342
Trade Paperback ISBN 978-1-399-81368-6
ebook ISBN 978-1-399-81370-9

Typeset in Bembo MT Pro by Palimpsest Book Production Ltd, Falkirk, Stirlingshire

Printed and bound in Great Britain by Clays Ltd, Elcograf S.p.A.

John Murray policy is to use papers that are natural, renewable and
recyclable products and made from wood grown in sustainable forests.
The logging and manufacturing processes are expected to conform
to the environmental regulations of the country of origin.

Carmelite House
50 Victoria Embankment
London EC4Y 0DZ

www.johnmurraypress.co.uk

John Murray Press, part of Hodder & Stoughton Limited
An Hachette UK company

The authorised representative in the EEA is Hachette Ireland,
8 Castlecourt Centre, Dublin 15, D15 XTP3, Ireland
(email: info@hbgi.ie)

For my sons, Jacob and Sam –
with the love of a proud, grateful father

Contents

About the Sources	xi
Author's Note	xiii
Cast of Characters	xvii
Maps	xx

Prologue 1

PART I: The Guests

1.	The End of Germany	11
2.	The Diplomat	26
3.	The Countess	30
4.	The Widow and Her Daughter	37
5.	The Headmistress	41
6.	In the Room	44
7.	The Circle	51
8.	The Night of Broken Glass	56
9.	Someone Must Tell the Truth	59
10.	The Detective	62
11.	Time to Die	65
12.	A Spy in Our Midst	70
13.	Trial Run	74
14.	A Secret Funeral	77

CONTENTS

15.	The Walk to Freedom	82
16.	Cast Out	86
17.	Present at the Creation	89
18.	The Path of Resistance	94
19.	The Blonde Poison	101
20.	A Bomb on a Plane	104
21.	Closing In	109
22.	A Secret Mission	113
23.	Go On, Shoot	118
24.	The Breakthrough	122
25.	An Invitation to Tea	128
26.	Agent Robby	132
27.	An Unexpected Guest	136
28.	Kindred Spirits	141
29.	A Traitor to the Circle	144

PART II: After the Party

30.	Secret Listeners	155
31.	A Mole at HQ	159
32.	Sixth Sense	163
33.	Be Warned	168
34.	Across the Border	173
35.	Double Bluff	177
36.	Silk and Lace	182
37.	Himmler Decides	186
38.	Dawn Raids	189
39.	Free No More	193

CONTENTS

PART III: Prisoners

40.	The Fall	201
41.	The First Round	206
42.	Ravensbrück	215
43.	Threats and Menaces	221
44.	Body and Soul	226
45.	The Fallout	229
46.	The Bridge of Love	233
47.	The Scourge of Guilt	237
48.	The Hands of God	242
49.	All But a Miracle	246
50.	Fate Has Intervened	251

PART IV: The Trial

51.	The Court	257
52.	The Hanging Judge	260
53.	In the Dock	263
54.	'Anti-State Person'	268
55.	Star Witness	273
56.	The Verdict	277

PART V: Punishment

57.	Killing Hitler	285
58.	'The Führer Adolf Hitler Is Dead'	289
59.	A Name on a List	292
60.	The Butcher's Hook	295
61.	Operation Swedish Furniture	300

CONTENTS

62. Death Row	305
63. The Murder Register	310
64. The Dead Centre	313
65. Indicted, Again	317
66. An Exquisite Deliverance	323

PART VI: After the War

67. Into the Daylight	333
68. Bearing Witness	339
69. Through the Generations	345

PART VII: The Traitor

70. 'The Defendant Is to Blame'	351
71. 'A Congenital Psychopathy'	354
72. 'Such Dirty Things'	360
73. 'Can You Sleep?'	365
74. Betrayal	368

Acknowledgements	375
Picture Credits	379
Notes	381
Bibliography	427
Index	439

About the Sources

THIS IS A work of non-fiction. Every detail on these pages is drawn from letters, diaries, testimonies and court documents, from the memoirs of those involved, from contemporaneous reports and historical accounts or from interviews with the surviving descendants of the central players. It is the product of scouring archives in Berlin, Munich, Karlsruhe, Koblenz, Lichterfelde, Lüneburg, Anklam, Jerusalem, Washington DC, Stanford and London.

Where there is direct speech, it is taken from that same documentary record. Barring the odd change to punctuation, the quotations appear untouched. The sources of those quotations and of the key facts are to be found in the endnotes, which are not numbered but arranged by chapter, matching the order in which they appear in the text. The endnotes are best used alongside the bibliography, which lists all sources, published and unpublished, in full, with URLs for material whose primary publication was online.

National spellings are the default, with a few exceptions, among them the German Eszett, which appears as a double 's' except in the case of family names.

Author's Note

I GREW UP IN a house where nothing German was allowed. No Siemens dishwasher or Krups coffee machine in the kitchen, no Volkswagen, Audi or Mercedes in the driveway. The edict came from my mother. She was not a Holocaust survivor, though she had felt the breath of the Shoah on her neck. She was just eight years old on 27 March 1945, when her own mother was killed by the last German V-2 rocket of the war to fall on London, a bomb that flattened a corner of the East End, killing 134 people, almost all of them Jews. One way or another, the blast radius of that explosion would encompass the rest of my mother's life and much of mine.

Of course, she knew that the bomb that fell on Hughes Mansions had not picked out that particular building deliberately. But given that the Nazis were bent on eliminating the Jews of Europe, she also knew how delighted they would have been by the target that fate, or luck, had chosen for that last V-2, how pleased that at twenty-one minutes past seven on that March morning it had added 120 more to the tally of dead Jews that would, in the end, number six million. And so came the rule. No trace of Germany would be allowed to touch our family: no visits, no holidays, no contact. The Germans were a guilty nation, every last one of them implicated in the wickedest crime of the twentieth century.

There were other Jews I knew whose parents followed the same prohibition, but few were as strict on the matter as my mother. And yet, though her practice was unusual, her underlying thinking was not. Far beyond the Jewish community, many shared, and perhaps still share, the assumption that I was raised on: that, with just a handful of exceptions, Adolf Hitler found a universally willing accomplice in the German nation. We know of the French resistance and of underground movements across Europe, but tend to hear little about opposition in Germany itself. If we think about it at all, many of us assume the dissidents were entirely swept away and rounded up as soon as the Nazis took power in 1933: *First they came for the communists* . . .

And yet that's not quite right. There were Germans who defied the Third Reich from the very start and throughout the Nazi dictatorship. In the immediate aftermath of the war, one Allied investigator estimated that, during the twelve long years of national socialism, some three million Germans had been in and out of prisons or concentration camps for crimes of dissent, sometimes punished for nothing more than a critical remark. There were 65 million German citizens in 1933, which means the vast, overwhelming majority, more than 95 per cent, did as they were told. They raised their right arm in salute and said 'Heil Hitler!' But quite a few did not.

What does it take to step out of line like that? What makes one person refuse when everyone around them obeys? And what compels them to do it when it would be so much easier to do nothing, when breaking ranks can only bring pain, hardship or death?

Anyone who has stared hard into the abyss of the mid-twentieth century has surely asked themselves versions of those questions, and one question above all: what would I have done? Most of us like to think we would have been one of the rebels or refusers, that we would have been brave. But the statistics suggest that most of us would not. Almost all of us would have stayed silent.

Several years ago I began work on *The Escape Artist*, the story of a Jewish teenager who escaped from Auschwitz. That book required me to contemplate the darkest parts of the human heart, the gravest evil of which human beings are capable. But while I was doing it, I stumbled across a different story from that same era, a tale of staggering bravery that, save by a few experts, had been almost entirely forgotten. It had its share of terrible cruelty, of course, but at its centre was something just as inexplicable: acts of radical, unnecessary, mortally dangerous good.

In pursuing that mystery, I learned that though none of those directly involved was still alive, some of their children and grandchildren were, several in their eighties and nineties. They still carried

AUTHOR'S NOTE

the memory of a group of men and women who were not consistent in their opposition to Nazism, still less perfectly heroic, who were instead flawed, often hesitant, sometimes fearful individuals who nevertheless dared to say no to a mighty and terrifying regime – and so found themselves engulfed in a drama that would exact a heavy cost and whose impact would be felt at the very top of the Nazi state.

The questions confronting those people pressed with a particular intensity in the Germany of the 1930s and 1940s. But those questions are not only of that time or that place. Some of them echo down the decades. Some of them reverberate especially loudly at this moment.

Cast of Characters

Hubertus 'Hubert' von Ballestrem (born 1910): count, military officer and second husband of Lagi Solf.

Albrecht von Bernstorff (born 1890): count; former diplomat, previously posted to London.

Marie-Agnes 'Anza' Braune (born 1893/1894): younger sister of Elisabeth von Thadden.

Wilhelm Canaris (born 1887): head of the Abwehr, German military intelligence.

Roland Freisler (born 1893): jurist and politician, president of the Volksgerichtshof, the People's Court.

Nikolaus von Halem (born 1905): lawyer and businessman; friend of Hubert von Ballestrem.

Hans Hirschel (born 1900): lover of Maria von Maltzan.

Otto Kiep (born 1886): former German consul general in New York, diplomat and lawyer.

Hanna Kiep (born 1904): wife of Otto.

Albrecht Kiep (born 1926): son of Otto and Hanna.

Richard Kuenzer (born 1875): former Foreign Ministry official.

Fanny von Kurowsky (born 1887): board member of the Patriotic Women's Association; daughter of a former Cabinet minister under Otto von Bismarck.

Herbert 'Leo' Lange (born 1909): lawyer and SS officer.

CAST OF CHARACTERS

Maria von Maltzan (born 1909): countess raised on one of Silesia's grandest estates, veterinarian and horsewoman.

Father Max Josef Metzger (born 1887): Catholic priest and pacifist.

Helmuth James von Moltke (born 1907): lawyer and friend of Otto Kiep whose family estate at Kreisau became a meeting place for a group of dissidents: the Kreisau Circle.

Herbert Mumm von Schwarzenstein (born 1898): diplomat; worked under Wilhelm Solf in the German embassy in Tokyo.

Hans Oster (born 1887): deputy head of the Abwehr, German military intelligence, and friend of Otto Kiep.

Paul Reckzeh (born 1913): doctor at Berlin's Charité hospital and son of one of the city's most distinguished physicians.

Anne Rühle (year of birth unknown): childhood friend of Anza and Elisabeth von Thadden; former model turned social worker; cousin of Friedrich Siegmund-Schultze.

Hilger van Scherpenberg (born 1899): diplomat specialising in Scandinavian affairs at the Foreign Ministry; son-in-law of Hjalmar Schacht, former head of Germany's central bank.

Inge van Scherpenberg (born 1903): wife of Hilger.

Bianca Segantini (born 1886): close friend of Elisabeth von Thadden; poet, living in the Engadine region of Switzerland.

Friedrich Siegmund-Schultze (born 1885): reforming cleric, educationalist and peace campaigner, exiled in Switzerland; cousin of Anne Rühle.

Johanna 'Hanna' Solf (born 1887): widow of eminent former German ambassador Wilhelm Solf and convenor of a political salon: the Solf Circle.

So'oa'emalelagi 'Lagi' Solf (born 1909): daughter of Hanna and Wilhelm, society beauty and wife of Count Hubertus von Ballestrem.

CAST OF CHARACTERS

Elisabeth von Thadden (born 1890): daughter of Protestant nobility and reforming headmistress.

Adam von Trott zu Solz (born 1909): lawyer and diplomat; friend of Helmuth James von Moltke and Hubert von Ballestrem.

Erich and Elisabeth Vermehren (born 1919 and 1911): dissenting couple, posted to Istanbul by the Abwehr, German military intelligence.

Joseph Wirth (born 1879): former chancellor of Germany in the Weimar era, exiled in Switzerland.

Elisabeth Wirth (year of birth unknown): close friend of Elisabeth von Thadden; no relation of Joseph.

Arthur Zarden (born 1885): former senior mandarin at the German Ministry of Finance.

Irmgard Zarden (born 1921): daughter of Arthur and his late wife, Edithe.

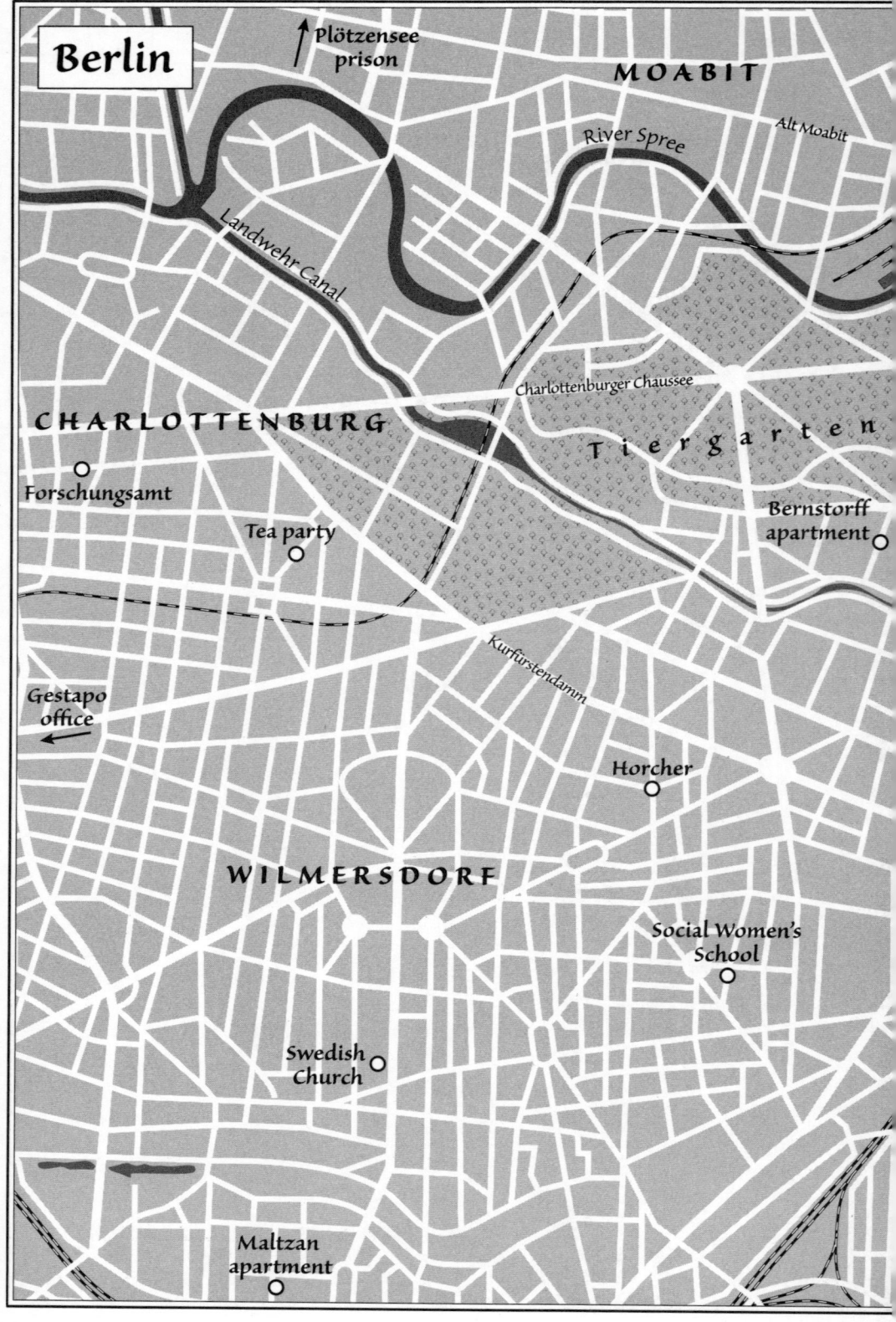

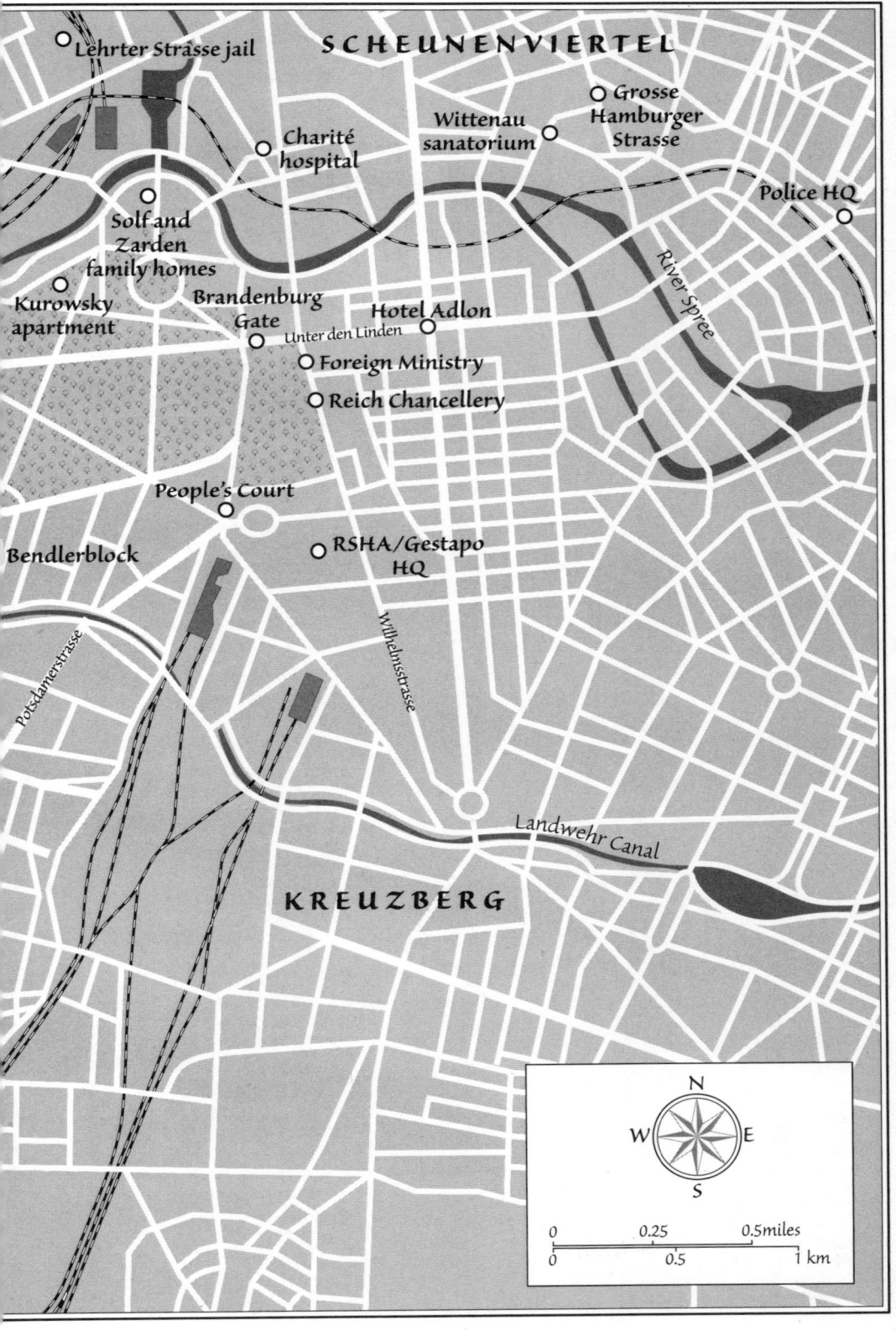

PROLOGUE

12 January 1944

ON A CRISP January morning in 1944, seven Gestapo officers, two of them detectives, pulled up outside a cottage in a small Alpine town in southern Bavaria. It was the middle of the week, a Wednesday, and it was wartime. A few years earlier, this would have been peak skiing season, the snows around Partenkirchen pristine and perfect. But this trip was strictly business.

Led by the detectives, both of whom were women, the Gestapo did not wait for the door to be opened. Instead, they forced their way in and found their target right away.

She was a woman in her mid-fifties, short and slim with a head of unmissable white hair. Usually, she would be in Berlin, where she had long been a fixture at some of the city's most prestigious tables as well as a much-admired hostess in her own right. Her address book was filled with the names of ambassadors and intellectuals, scholars and politicians: anyone in Berlin she didn't know was scarcely worth knowing. She had only relocated here, to this far-flung mountain hideaway, a few weeks earlier, after her house in the capital had been bombed out, her chosen refuge the home of her unmarried sister. But it was no refuge now. The Gestapo were ordering her not to move a muscle.

She did as she was told, frozen still while the officers turned over the two-room apartment where she had been staying. The search continued for a full hour. It was early and she was not yet dressed, but they did not allow her to excuse herself. Instead, she had to put on her clothes in the presence of the Gestapo, who continued their search. She watched them while they watched her.

PROLOGUE

Before long, the secret police moved to the house next door, as she knew they would. Sheltering there was her daughter, the slim, beautiful countess who had been turning heads at Berlin parties since her late teens. She was recuperating from a serious operation that had left her bedridden, the result of an injury she had sustained when the family house in Berlin was bombed. She was a volunteer firefighter and had tried desperately to put out the blaze – air strikes always started fires – which she had feared was about to devour her home. Injured or not, sick or not, she was also to be arrested.

So too would be the two others present that morning: the unmarried sister and the housekeeper who had been working for the family since 1911, when she went into service as a chambermaid and nanny. The Gestapo wanted all of them: that way this dawn raid would remain a secret, with all those who had witnessed it remaining safely mute in custody. The police took the four women away in three separate cars.

On that same January morning, in the town of Meaux in Nazi-occupied France, three SS men arrived at a convalescent home for injured soldiers. The patients were men of the Wehrmacht, but the centre was administered by the German Red Cross. Among the nurses and medics was a woman raised on a grand Pomeranian estate, a daughter of the country's Protestant nobility. She had gone on to excel in her professional field; a few years earlier, her expertise had been sought by some of Berlin's most eminent citizens. It was her the SS men were after.

Her features strong, commanding even, she was eating breakfast in the dining room ahead of a planned railway trip to Paris, to consult with her superiors about her next move in the organisation. The SS knew all about that. When they strode in, apparently full of breezy good cheer, they called out to her: 'You don't need to take the train to Paris. You'll be picked up by car!' They seemed to find that hilarious.

She understood right away what was happening and moved quickly. She turned to the bursar of the soldiers' home, someone she trusted, and asked him, doubtless in a discreet whisper, to take care of a folder of hers containing personal letters. She told him exactly where in her room he would find it.

PROLOGUE

But she had left it too late. Earlier she had considered an attempt to cross the border, fleeing Germany for Switzerland, but there was no chance of escape now. The SS trio frogmarched her to the room, watching her every movement. She stood as they pulled open the drawers, examined the bed she had slept in, inspected every inch of the furniture. Inevitably, they found the folder with the letters, one of which was a message of farewell, written because she had known this day would come.

She could do nothing but look on as they rifled through a room that, until a few minutes before, had been a private space, the rough hands of the state handling objects that had been intimately hers. What she had, they took.

Throughout she felt the eyes on her, not only of these men, but also of those who, until that moment, had been her colleagues. They were now spectators to the arrest, looking through the windows of the building that faced into this room. She sensed no sympathy for her, or pity. Nor did she detect any anger at the SS for what they were doing. Instead it was the sentiment that filled so many Germans as they saw a sometime neighbour or workmate taken away by the authorities: a blend of relief that it was not them and fear that they would be next.

At that same hour, in one of Berlin's more sedate neighbourhoods, there came a knock on the door at the home of a former official who had risen to hold one of the most powerful offices of the German government. Bald, his features distinct, he would once have been instantly recognisable in Berlin's ruling circles, admired as a particularly urbane mandarin. The knocking did not stop. He knew what it meant and he went quietly, even as the men bundled him into a car and drove him to the offices of the Gestapo, the Secret State Police, at Kurfürstendamm 140, on the long, wide avenue that Berliners liked to think of as their Champs-Élysées.

On her way to work at that very moment was a woman of twenty-two who had once been among Germany's richest young heiresses and who had already inherited the sweet, wide eyes of her mother. She had grown up in an apartment on the banks of the River Spree so vast that every room was the size of a decent flat. She had been walked to school by a butler, had travelled first class to Rome, Paris and across the Atlantic while still a teenager, and had partied with debutantes and their beaus in London, staying with friends off Berkeley Square for the last great 'season' before the war.

She had an office job now. Getting to work involved a walk through the park towards the subway station. Suddenly, and without warning, several men stepped out of the bushes and faced her. They wore the unmistakable long leather coats of the Gestapo and they asked her to come with them. Seeing a car idling nearby, she did as she was told, and they drove her away.

Elsewhere in the city, another woman, older, was bundled into a *Grüne Minna*, a Black Maria prison van.

It all happened within a few swift hours, the men and women of the Gestapo and SS fanning out across the Reich with quiet, co-ordinated efficiency. By lunchtime, they had almost all their chosen suspects in custody. Two more would remain out of reach for a few more days. But before long, the Gestapo would have them too.

Those involved knew there was nothing routine about this work. For one thing, the warrants had not been authorised by a mere desk officer, but by Heinrich Himmler himself, Reichsführer-SS and commander of the Nazi security state.

That was in part because of the gravity of the accusation and in part because of the identities of the accused: who these men and women were and who they were not. They were not the usual suspects. They were not communists or street agitators. They were not members of despised categories that the state had long ago deemed genetically or racially inferior. With one tenuous exception, they were not Jews.

Instead, they were drawn from the upper reaches of German high society, from the world of grand townhouses and country estates, of nights at the opera and embassy balls. They had titles and jewels and impeccable contacts. They were the last people to be subject to an arrest at dawn.

And they were not a random collection of individuals, coincidentally picked up on the same January day. They were a group, made up of people who had secretly opposed the Nazi regime for the best part of a decade, meeting and operating in the shadows, spreading the word, combining their unique talents, saving lives. But

PROLOGUE

now they stood accused of the crime regarded as the gravest possible offence in Hitler's Germany: treason. They were branded traitors to the Third Reich.

Their fates had become intertwined some four months earlier, when they came together for what, to an outsider's eye, would have looked like a wholly innocent gathering: an afternoon tea party to celebrate the birthday of a friend. But that single event would eventually expose them to the hangman's rope and the guillotine's blade. Its reverberations would reach all the way to the top of the Reich, even altering the way Germany would fight the war against its Allied enemies.

And watching it all unfold, drawing a particular satisfaction from the arrests on that winter morning, were two people who, between them, had made this moment happen. They had plotted it and engineered it. One was among the Third Reich's most ruthless men, a leading player in the darkest chapter of the twentieth century. The other was someone who had been a guest at the tea party, who had sat with the group as a comrade and ally, someone who had convinced the others that they were bound together in a common cause. For the group had been undone by a great act of deceit and betrayal committed by a person they had believed was one of their own – and by the simple human failure to see that not every danger comes from without, that sometimes the most deadly threats come from within.

Who was that betrayer? And how did a group of brave, principled rebels, who had successfully defied Adolf Hitler for more than a decade, come to fall into such a lethal trap?

PART I
The Guests

I

The End of Germany

30 January 1933

A DECADE BEFORE THEY took tea together, each one of those who would be invited to gather on that fateful day – and those who would be watching them – were forced to adjust to a new German reality. Several of them witnessed for themselves the shift, the moment in January 1933 when their country, and the world, seemed to tilt on its axis. For some, the understanding of what had changed would take months or even years to arrive. But for others, it was in that moment, on that torchlit night in Berlin, that they fixed the resolve that would govern their actions for the next ten years or more.

Hanna

One of those who grasped the shift instantly could hardly do otherwise. She was at the side of a man whose view of the matter was unbending. He was seventy-one years old and had given his working life to the service of Germany. He had done it all, acting as a colonial governor in multiple corners of the far-flung German empire, including in the South Pacific, and sitting around the Cabinet table in the final days of the Great War. Indeed, by the end of 1918, he was serving as the last foreign minister of Imperial Germany, though it took him some time to realise he had acquired that distinction. Still, it was in that capacity that it fell to Wilhelm Solf to send the telegram on behalf of a defeated empire to President Woodrow Wilson requesting the armistice that would end the war that had raged since 1914.

In the Weimar years, Solf had kept on serving, spending most of the 1920s in Tokyo, where he was a well-liked and well-connected ambassador. At his side was his wife, Johanna – everyone called her Hanna – twenty-five years his junior and his most devoted ally.

Whether in Samoa, where her husband was the white-uniformed governor already in his fifties when they married, or later in Asia, German East Africa, India and Britain, Hanna had always been a partner in Wilhelm's work. It was a joint decision, for example, to make their home a salon for political conversation and the open, convivial exchange of ideas. This was not mere entertaining, with Hanna in the role of young society hostess, but a more serious project. Both husband and wife were equally convinced that a forum where those of opposing views could meet was a prerequisite of a free country. Once he was back home, Wilhelm soon realised how badly such a place was needed. He had returned to a Germany that he scarcely recognised.

The rising force in German politics was an entity that had not existed in Wilhelm's day. Its name was the Nationalsozialistische Deutsche Arbeiterpartei, or NSDAP, the National Socialist German Workers' Party, and it alarmed him. Its loutishness, its prejudice, its contempt for democracy, its threat of violence. But the party kept rising, until the day came, on 30 January 1933, when Wilhelm Solf saw the brownshirts march under the windows of his home in the Tiergarten district, celebrating their installation as Germany's governing party. The Nazis, as they were nicknamed, were in power now. With a deep and baleful conviction, Wilhelm Solf declared out loud to those watching with him: '*Finis Germaniae*'. The end of Germany.

Maria

At the other end of the country, a young countess had arrived at a rather different conclusion. Maria Helene Francoise Izabel von Maltzan, Baroness of Wartenberg and Penzlin, was only twenty-four, but she had long had her eyes and ears open. All but banished from the family seat in Militsch in rural Silesia, where she had been raised by English nannies and French governesses in a castle of domed halls and medieval galleries, she had been making her own way in Munich since not long after she left boarding school.

There, she watched the rise of the Nazis with incredulity. She read Adolf Hitler's writings, *Mein Kampf*, 'My Struggle', and *Die nationalsozialistische Bewegung*, 'The National Socialist Movement', and found them poorly written, littered with grammatical errors and unambiguously clear in revealing the author's intentions for Germany. Equally plain was the fervour this man could inspire. As a student in Munich, she once dined at the Osteria Bavaria, a favourite haunt of Hitler's. She had scarcely arrived when the door to one of the back rooms opened and the future Führer marched out, trailed by a phalanx of aides and disciples. Maria watched as a woman at the next table rushed over to the chair where Hitler had been sitting and promptly covered the seat with kisses.

Later that year, 1932, she witnessed a grand parade staged by the Nazis in Munich: the boys of the Hitler Youth and the young women of the League of German Girls, or Band of German Maidens, marching down Leopoldstrasse in formation, followed by the brownshirts of the Sturmabteilung, or SA, the Storm Division or Storm Troopers who functioned as the paramilitary wing of the Nazi party, the Nationalsozialistisches Kraftfahrkorps or Motor Corps, before, finally and in black, the men of the SS.

Maria found the cult of national socialism visually impressive, occasionally frightening but, above all, ludicrous. She did not alter that view even after the Nazis took power a few months later. When, in early 1933, she returned to the castle in Militsch to find her brother, Carlos, in full Nazi uniform, she told him immediately that he looked as if he were in fancy dress. Was there a carnival somewhere, she wondered, from which he had become separated? He was enraged. Now that their father was dead, Carlos was the head of the family, with the power to cut off Maria's allowance – which he promptly did.

Her father's death more than a decade earlier had left her with no protector. He had always looked out for her, the youngest of his eight children, encouraging her to voice her opinions when others expected a little girl to keep her mouth shut. He took it upon himself to instil in Maria the ancient patrician principles of the nobility, teaching her early that her duty was to protect the most vulnerable. When she reported that the parents of her nanny had lost their farm in a fire, her father promptly ordered her to empty her piggy bank and hand her savings over to the luckless family. 'You have to look after your people,' he told her. From the start, she was a defender of the weak and even the reviled, taking pity on the animals of the estate that others despised. When Carlos, who was terrified of snakes, had a number of them killed, it was seven-year-old Maria who exacted revenge on the reptiles' behalf – pushing the boy off a paddle boat and holding him by the legs so that he could not get his head out of the water, releasing him only when their father intervened.

But that was long ago and now Maria was without allies. There was no point in Maria appealing to her mother who, Maria was convinced, hated her, preferring her eldest daughter because she was more beautiful, and Carlos, the sole son whom she treated like a crown prince. For Maria, there was only a series of maternal edicts: among them, a prohibition on studying veterinary science because 'if a doctor, then better a human doctor', and an order never to marry a Jew. Later Maria would joke that she found it easy to resist Nazi authority because she had defied her mother's authority first.

Arthur and Irmgard

There was one thing Arthur Zarden knew with certainty that night of 30 January 1933. The arrival in power of the Nazi party of Adolf Hitler was a moment of history, one that, as a good father, he wanted his only child to witness for herself.

It would mean a slight change of plan, but nothing too onerous. That evening, he and his wife were due to be guests at the Press Ball, where they would savour yet another evening of elegance and glamour among Berlin high society. Zarden may not have obviously looked the part but he fitted right in. Then word came that the ailing president, Paul von Hindenburg, had named Adolf Hitler as chancellor, in deference to the latter's position as leader of the largest party in parliament. The national socialists were to celebrate by staging a torchlight parade through Berlin that would end at the

Chancellery, where Hitler would greet his followers, standing on the balcony to receive their devotion.

This, Zarden understood, was something his twelve-year-old daughter ought to see. The chauffeur was called and ordered to get as close as he could to the Brandenburger Tor. And so, seated in their Maybach motor car, the Zardens watched as the brownshirts sang and marched in unison, proclaiming their new mastery of Germany.

Until that moment, the family had lived a charmed life. The closest they had come to disruption was in 1932 when they had moved out of a ten-room apartment on the banks of the Spree into a twelve-room one around the corner. Their days were marked by uninterrupted luxury, waited on by a staff that included house dressmakers and that was headed by a husband-and-wife team of butler and cook, the latter giving way now and then during the winter season, when dinner parties required reinforcements, to two chefs, each wearing a white toque. Little Irmgard would be brought in to say hello, curtseying for the forty guests seated at a single, long table in the dining room. The place was so vast, with a private lift that opened directly into the entrance hall, that Irmgard would cheerfully navigate her way around the flat on a scooter.

The wealth that made this life possible had not come from Arthur, who was a civil servant, but from his wife, Edithe. She was the daughter of Benno Orenstein, a Jew who had dragged himself up from nothing to establish a scrap-metal business that had eventually grown into a global industrial corporation, producing locomotives and railway equipment. By the beginning of the First World War, Orenstein was one of the richest men in Germany, with 20 million gold marks to his name, a personal fortune so great that not even the hyperinflation of the Weimar years could destroy it.

The reward was a seat at the country's highest tables. On their tree-lined street, Alsenstrasse, they had foreign embassies for neighbours; lunch guests might include a visiting Dutch prince. Among Irmgard's fellow pupils at school were the daughters of the British ambassador, dropped off in the morning and picked up in the afternoon by a Rolls-Royce. When Irmgard had a birthday party, the entertainment was a treat then almost unheard of: a private movie screening, the girls giggling with delight at the sight of Charlie Chaplin twirling his cane or Harold Lloyd dangling from the hands of a giant clock.

She was utterly at home in this world, unfazed by the footmen who would greet her at a friend's apartment in Ruritanian knee breeches, announcing her as 'Fräulein Zarden' before ushering her into a ballroom that was a replica of the Hall of Mirrors in the Palace of Versailles. She had dance classes in that room, watched by one Annelies von Ribbentrop, whose two children were also in the group. At that point, the Nazis' accession to power was still a distant dream: Annelies's husband, Joachim, was not yet foreign minister of the Third Reich, but rather a salesman in his father-in-law's Champagne firm.

They all knew so little of the future then. Frau von Ribbentrop's hostess in the Versailles-style palace, Frau von Friedländer-Fuld, did not know that within a few years she would have to leave Germany because she was Jewish. Benno Orenstein did not know that when he and his wife bought a large house by Lake Wannsee, they were moving within striking distance of the place where, before long, the upper echelon of the Reich bureaucracy would agree on 'the final solution to the Jewish question'. The Zardens did not know that their neighbours in the apartment building at Alsenstrasse 9, the former diplomat Wilhelm Solf and his wife, Hanna, would soon be hosting a group of secret dissidents against a tyrannical regime. All that was to come.

There were clues, of course, but, like most in their circles, the Zardens did not see them. Life seemed to be gliding along as it always had, smoothed by wealth, as it always was. They continued to summer at Heiligendamm, a resort on the Baltic Sea, and did not allow their day to be unsettled when, one morning in 1931, they found the courtyard of their hotel crammed with people who looked not at all like guests. Someone explained to Irmgard that Adolf Hitler, then a rising star of the political opposition best known for his street clashes with the communists, was on a campaign tour through Mecklenburg, accompanied by two lieutenants. Before long, Hitler emerged, wearing his trademark brown shirt, flanked by Hermann Göring and Joseph Goebbels. What struck Irmgard, not yet ten years old, was that Göring was fat, Goebbels had a clubfoot that made him limp and the crowd went wild. Mothers held their children aloft, as if they were witnessing the Second Coming and hoped for their young to be caught in the divine glow. The commotion did not die down till the three men had been driven away. But what Irmgard told her mother was that the Nazis had looked rather ridiculous in their brown shirts. Surely no one could take such people seriously.

Arthur Zarden learned soon enough that that was a mistake. His career had only ever headed upwards before that torchlit evening in January 1933. At the age of forty-seven, he had risen to become secretary of state, the most senior official, at the Ministry of Finance, second only to the finance minister himself. His office stood across the street from the Chancellery, looking out on Wilhelmsplatz, and he was chauffeured to work in that Maybach, the highest of high-end marques. Arthur Zarden was rich, successful and at the height of his powers.

The new government was scarcely in place when he was summoned to meet his boss, the finance minister. Zarden knew that his lifestyle had always attracted the envy of his colleagues: he may have been the ministry's leading expert on tax, and the inventor of a tax credits scheme that allowed the government to create jobs, but what rankled was that he lived less like a civil servant than one of the Reich's largest taxpayers, a group with which he mixed freely. The minister did not like this contact between his secretary of state and Germany's richest. But that was not what was on his mind now.

Instead, it was something more basic and less amenable to remedy. There was no way to put this delicately, but Zarden's wife was a Jew and Zarden himself was rumoured to have some Jewish ancestry. Given those immovable facts, the minister suggested that his senior official ought to apply for retirement.

For all the polite semblance of a choice, Arthur knew this was anything but optional. He had no desire to serve the new Nazi government, but could not deny that this was an involuntary exit, even if custom dictated that the departure of a man of his rank would be marked by a farewell meeting with the new chancellor himself. Zarden's last day of work was 31 March 1933, drawing to a premature close what had been a stellar administrative career. The Führer sent a letter, reiterating his thanks for Arthur Zarden's valuable service; Zarden's place was taken by one Fritz Reinhardt, a loyal and ardent national socialist who would go on to play a leading role in the plundering of the territories invaded and occupied by the Third Reich and in the thorough, systematic project to steal every penny that could be taken from the Jews: the homes they lived in, the businesses they had built, the gold in their teeth, the hair on their heads. The Nazis were barely in, but Zarden was most definitely out.

Elisabeth

Elisabeth von Thadden was not too dismayed by the appointment of Herr Hitler as chancellor. On the contrary, she was initially quite well disposed towards national socialism. Like Maria von Maltzan, she was a daughter of the landed aristocracy. She had grown up at Trieglaff, the huge Pomeranian estate that belonged to her father in his capacity as district administrator, though her growing-up had been accelerated. After her mother's early death, and as the eldest child, the nineteen-year-old Elisabeth was handed responsibility not only for the upbringing of her younger siblings but for the running of the entire household and estate, which employed some fifty people. Still a teenager, she became its chatelaine, its organisational, economic and social centre, and continued in that role throughout her twenties. The expectations on her were clear. She was to tend not only to her family but to the social needs of the villagers too. She was to embody those virtues by which the Protestant aristocracy liked to define itself: duty, reliability and selflessness.

But then, just as suddenly as those responsibilities and sense of purpose had come, they were taken away. In 1920, after more than a decade as a widower, her father announced he was to marry again. There would be a new mistress of the house, and she was five years younger than Elisabeth. Overnight, and at the age of thirty, Elisabeth had lost the core of her work and her life.

She found a new mission, one that had captured her interest since the outbreak of the First World War, if not before. She would devote herself to a practical form of the Christianity she held so dear: caring for starving children and families who had nothing.

She already had a mentor, in the form of the Berlin pastor Friedrich Siegmund-Schultze and his Soziale Arbeitsgemeinschaft, or Social Work Organisation, admiring especially his double commitment to the poor and to peace. She had met him at Trieglaff in 1916, when her father invited him to give the harvest festival sermon, a bold move considering Siegmund-Schultze was something of a social radical. He had famously traded the role of court preacher, with a pulpit whose congregation included members of the Imperial family, for a ministry in a working-class district of east Berlin. His was not a mission from on high: the shepherd lived among his flock. All of which deeply impressed Elisabeth, who resolved to walk in his footsteps. She now set about inviting malnourished children from the city to spend time at Trieglaff. She wrote to Siegmund-Schultze, asking him to recommend a book on trade unions, social democracy and the like – so long as it was 'not too rambling'.

But Elisabeth was no leftist. On the contrary, she hewed to the Prussian aristocratic tradition in which she had been raised: she believed that landowning families like hers were responsible for the peasants on their estates, just as they had been in the days of her ancestors. The difference now was that that tradition was endangered, thanks to a world changed utterly by the Great War. If the aristocratic ethos of patrician generosity was to survive, it would have to accept reform.

That conviction combined with both her faith and a new creed then taking shape. Her late mother had asked a question that would capture an important aspect of the age: 'Where is a woman with spirit to begin?' The women's movement was in its infancy, but Elisabeth von Thadden was drawn to it and especially its insistence that every human being should be able to fulfil their potential; that, no matter whether they were man or woman, they should be able to reach a position that matched their gifts and achievements. That struck Elisabeth as not so much a political imperative as a deeply Christian one.

The clearest exponent of that view, the educational reformer Alice Salomon, now became a second inspiration to the young Elisabeth, who studied under Salomon at the Soziale Frauenschule, the Social Women's School, in Berlin. Education became Elisabeth's vocation. She soaked up new ideas, went to hear the philosopher of alternative education Rudolf Steiner speak, absorbed it all. For two years, she taught at Salem Castle under Kurt Hahn, the innovator and future founder of Gordonstoun school in Scotland (among whose early pupils would be a Greek prince by the name of Philip, later the consort of Queen Elizabeth II).

But her true calling was education for young women. She was against co-education, which she believed shortchanged women, and by 1927 she had established her own school, the Evangelical Rural Education Home for Girls, in an eighteenth-century manor house in Wieblingen just outside Heidelberg. The location was perfect. If she had imagined the ideal Christian boarding school for girls, and she had, this was it. The first cohort consisted of sixteen pupils in two classes; after the summer holidays she added ten more.

The school believed in faith, in homeland and in 'loyalty to duty, order and cleanliness'. It blended traditional Christian, patriotic principles with the latest progressive thinking on teaching methods, all of it directed towards a thoroughly modern mission: to produce educated, fulfilled women.

Whether because of her years running the family estate or her physical appearance – tall, strong and stately – or both, Elisabeth was a figure of easy, natural command. She had a clear authority, and the sincerity of her faith, her piety, was obvious to anyone who met her. But she was no pursed-lipped scold. She ran the school like a family household, with herself as a maternal figure who understood that plenty of her pupils had not chosen to be in Wieblingen, but had been sent there. She allowed for homesickness and unhappiness. She wanted the girls to feel safe in their school, so, once a week, she would host a 'common evening' in her private living room. She might tell a story or read aloud while the girls did handicrafts and listened.

She did not demand Victorian conformity; she did not require her pupils to suppress their emotions. On the contrary, she encouraged talent and individualism: there was no uniform, but rather a dress code that left scope for the girls to choose their own colours and fabrics. Elisabeth was determined to produce young women who would appreciate the beauty of nature and high art. Before long she was taking her students to chamber concerts and lectures, and arranging visits to the Mannheim National Theatre. She might rent a bus and lead a tour of Venice or visit the World's Fair in Paris. On one occasion, as a surprise gift for two members of staff who had got married that day, she rented a boat to sail down the Neckar, with the girls dressed as water spirits. Word soon spread that Director von Thadden was doing something special in Wieblingen. Prominent families, including those based abroad, began sending their girls. The school expanded. Within a few years, the student body numbered nearly a hundred.

Elisabeth herself cut quite a dash, usually in a hurry, always with some new titbit to pass on, designed either to provoke anger or prompt laughter, yours and hers. It helped that, like Countess Maria von Maltzan, but unlike most German women of the age, she could drive. Around Wieblingen you might see her, sporting a bright straw hat and sleek sunglasses, at the wheel of her open-topped car, her very mobility a statement of female daring. She had no money to speak of – she was a woman, so none of the family fortune had passed to her – but she had panache.

The school had been up and running for six years when the new government arrived in 1933. Elisabeth did not fear it. She was, after all, a conservative and a nationalist. She let all the compulsory symbols of Nazism be displayed in the school, made some changes to the curriculum and allowed the creation of a branch of the League of German Girls, the young women's version of the Hitler Youth. She even published a newspaper essay explaining the role schools like hers might play in building 'the new Germany'. She believed they were especially well placed to produce 'German comrades, fully conscious members of the national socialist state'. As if to demonstrate her commitment to the new order, she travelled to Karlsruhe with her pupils to hear a speech by the Führer himself. To the naked eye, Elisabeth von Thadden was looking and sounding like a loyal Nazi.

Otto

For so many Germans, those weeks after the elevation of Adolf Hitler were a moment of decision. Even those an ocean away could not escape it.

Take Otto Kiep, a seasoned diplomat then serving as Germany's consul general in New York. Fluent in English, thanks to a childhood spent in Scotland as the son of an expat German businessman, with a kindly, genial expression on his face and a young, attractive wife at his side, Otto had proved a great success in the United States.

The work was uncomplicated, the social life delightful. Summer brought invitations to the country houses of the New York elite, whether on Long Island, in Connecticut or New Jersey: long, languid days of tennis, horse riding, swimming and sailing. But the news from home would not leave him alone. He had grown ever more alarmed at the rise of extremism, on the left and right, which only accelerated after the Wall Street Crash of 1929 and the mass unemployment that followed. From the comfort of his townhouse at 55 East 77th Street, a block away from Central Park, he could see what was happening. The surging waters of national socialism were beginning to seep in, even under his door.

German-Americans who visited the consulate were sounding more and more like the pages of *Mein Kampf*, one of the books that had accompanied Otto when he made the Atlantic crossing to take up his US post six years earlier. These expat patriots were making impromptu speeches on the need for Germany to rise from the ashes of 1918, to stand up to the world, to insist on the superiority of Germany 'with blood, if necessary'. And so, when word came of the death of the Weimar Republic and the birth of a new government in Berlin, installed on 30 January 1933, Otto might have been dismayed or fearful, but he could not claim to be surprised.

And then, a matter of weeks later, a letter arrived addressed to him. Inside it was a single sheet of paper bearing one of the world's most famous names. Otto may not have realised it at the time, but that letter would change everything.

Hilger, Paul, Fanny, Anne and Anza

Hilger van Scherpenberg at least had the benefit of distance. He was working as *Legationssekretär*, or second secretary, at the German embassy in London when the new government of Adolf Hitler arrived. Not that that cooled his judgement. On the contrary, it only seemed to harden his disapproval of the new regime.

As a member of the Sozialdemokratische Partei Deutschlands, or SPD, the Social Democratic Party, he was already predisposed against the Nazis. At the embassy he was surrounded by fellow internationalists, each ready to reinforce the views of the other. Eventually seven of the nine career diplomats who staffed the London mission wrote a joint letter to Hermann Göring, expressing their collective dismay at the Nazi seizure of power. One of the two to refuse to sign the letter was Prince Otto von Bismarck, grandson of the Iron Chancellor and Hilger's immediate superior. Adding his name was probably not Hilger van Scherpenberg's best career move.

For nineteen-year-old Paul Reckzeh, 1933 had already brought one major change: he had left school and become a medical student, ready to follow in the footsteps of his father, one of Berlin's most eminent doctors. But on the first day of May, there came another change. The Nazi party had established itself as the new power in the land and the teenage Paul decided he should play his part: he joined up, becoming party member 2,878,897.

His timing was good. Had he left it even a day later, he would have fallen foul of a ban on new members that came into force after 1 May, imposed partly in response to pressure from party veterans who feared that the NSDAP's ideological purity was being diluted by the huge influx of newcomers who had rushed to join in the spring of 1933. Paul had got in just under the wire.

In years to come, he would not describe himself as lucky. He would take his place at a table filled with critics of Hitler and Nazism and lament the decision made by his younger self, reserving a special ire for his parents. He had been a boy when he had signed up, still in his teens; if only they had stopped him.

In her mid-forties in January 1933, Fanny von Kurowsky was born in the age of empire and was still living there: her home was at the edge of the Tiergarten, the former Imperial hunting grounds. She might have been expected to recoil in horror at a vulgarian such as Hitler ascending to the first rank of the German government. But she was a strong German nationalist, the long-serving second deputy chairwoman of the national board of the Vaterländischer Frauenverein, the Patriotic Women's Association. The group organised everything from kindergartens to first-aid training, as well as clubs for wounded soldiers, of whom there was a ready supply in the years following the Great War. Some of the new government's rhetoric would have struck a chord with her. In 1932, she had written an article in the German Red Cross magazine about the role of women in confronting the economic crisis in Germany. 'Nothing but a revived spirit of sacrifice and community spirit in the German people will save the German people from the looming crisis of despair,' she had pronounced. Hitler and his men would have warmly agreed.

Anne Rühle might well have shared some of Fanny's instincts when it came to the new regime. Yes, she had studied social work under the progressive thinker Alice Salomon, but that had only exposed her to some of the pressing problems then besieging Berlin and the country, the very problems that Hitler insisted only he could solve.

As for Marie-Agnes, or Anza, younger sister to Elisabeth von Thadden, she did not need to take a course to know the deprivation Germany faced. Her husband, a naval officer in the last war, was left without a job when the German navy was dismantled and its ships scuttled. Eventually money came from her father, who, unable to conceive of transferring money to a woman, even his own daughter, passed what would have been Anza's inheritance to her husband. But the couple divorced in 1923, leaving her with nothing. In 1933, she was forty years old and penniless. If there was talk of change under a new leader, that was surely for the good: after all, the status quo had brought only hardship and disappointment.

The Detective

While plenty of Germans greeted the ascent of the Nazi party with an open mind, Herbert Lange – his friends called him Leo – was positively delighted. Born north of Berlin in the small village of Menzlin, Western Pomerania, he had no attachment to the old order that this new movement promised to sweep away. He had been born into poverty, his father a jobbing labourer who struggled to feed his family. The Langes lived on a lively street, where Jews and non-Jews mixed easily – the Cohns lived next door and the Gersons were opposite – and the family scraped together enough money to send young Leo to the prestigious *Oberrealschule*. But life never stopped being hard.

In May 1930, he headed to Greifswald to study law, soon joining the Burschenschaft Rugia, a student association committed to defending the 'timeless values' of 'honour, freedom and fatherland'. By the time he dropped out of college two years later, his views were beginning to harden. He placed an early bet on national socialism, joining the Nazi party on 1 May 1932, when he was just twenty-two years old. When January 1933 came around, Leo could draw satisfaction that it had taken less than a year for his wager to pay off. Never mind that he had failed to complete that degree; now a different path to advancement had opened up. By March of that year, little more than a month into the new era, he was a member of the Schutzstaffel, literally the 'protection squadron', which served as the paramilitary arm of Nazism better known as the SS. He was on the inside and the only way was up.

Of course, none of these people knew what the next decade would bring, either for them or for their country. They certainly did not know that their paths, however distant from each other they were in 1933, would eventually converge at, of all things, an afternoon tea party – with consequences that would engulf them all.

2

The Diplomat

Otto, February 1933

OTTO KIEP'S DIARY was always packed. This was less a reflection of his own social charms, or even those of his young wife, than of the post he held. There were said to be twenty thousand different German-American clubs in New York City in the early 1930s and all of them seemed to need the presence of the consul general at this celebration or that anniversary banquet. Every day brought an avalanche of invitations. Even so, this one stood out. It was for a dinner in honour of one of the world's most admired men: Professor Albert Einstein.

The event was a joint fundraiser for the Hebrew University in Jerusalem – Einstein was a founder and had delivered the inaugural scientific lecture – and a news service, the Jewish Telegraphic Agency. It was scheduled for mid-March, but the planning had been going on for months, starting well before the Nazis had seized power. When the organisers first drew up the invitation list, it had been no more than simple courtesy to include Germany's official representative in New York. After all, Einstein was among the country's most distinguished figures. But by the time Otto Carl Kiep – O.C. to his friends – stared at the invitation on his desk, it had acquired an entirely new meaning.

For Einstein was now a symbol as well as a man. He was a Jew from a country that had turned on its Jews. A dinner in his honour would, inevitably, be a rally in solidarity with the beleaguered Jews of Germany and a protest against the new Nazi government that was persecuting them. If Otto attended, he would be standing with those protesters. In the eyes of his superiors in the Foreign Ministry in Berlin, he would be siding with the enemies of Germany. He would be a traitor.

And yet, if he were to refuse the invitation, he would be tacitly endorsing those who were hounding Einstein, both back home and here in New York. Otto had been told of an assassination plot against the scientist: a group of German exchange students at Columbia University were planning to attack and kill Einstein just before he boarded the ship that would take him back to Europe. The death threats from assorted German-Americans had been coming since the great man's lecture tour of the US had begun, but this one seemed serious.

As the situation grew more tense, it also became clearer, to Otto at least. To attend the dinner was to terminate his career in the foreign service. To say no was to become a servant of national socialism and the thuggery of its supporters. That was the choice.

He discussed it with his wife. She cursed the rotten luck of the situation. Why did this dinner have to be in New York? Why did it have to be Otto? The answer to the latter question appeared simple enough: the German ambassador to Washington had also been invited but had written quickly to the organisers to explain that, to his great regret, he could not make it, adding that he hoped the consul general in New York would be able to attend. The ambassador had left it to Otto's 'discretion' whether he should go or not, thereby dumping the whole impossible conundrum into his colleague's lap. O.C. was on the spot. There was no way out of it.

It was now 16 March and Einstein had arrived in the city. At the railway station, the scientist, mobbed by reporters, praised 'Germany's contribution to the culture of mankind' as 'so vital and significant that you cannot imagine the world without it' – which made it all the sadder that now 'the genuine exponents of this culture are receiving unworthy treatment in their own country'. If there had been any ambiguity over what a public embrace for Einstein from a German official would mean, a small grey area in which Otto might have found diplomatic refuge, it was now gone. He had to make a decision.

He resolved to do what he believed was best for the country he served and loved. His absence would confirm that all the accusations against Germany were true, that the state was indeed hostile to Jews. What's more, if Einstein were attacked or killed in New York, it would be seen as a reflection, or even result, of official German policy. For the sake of Germany's good name, and in the name of German decency, he wrote to the organisers to accept their invitation.

They replied by asking him to make a speech.

There was no dilemma this time. In making their request, the hosts had only followed protocol. He would be the highest-ranking German official present; of course they would want him to make a speech. Besides, he could see no point in half-measures. If he was going to risk his career, he might as well do it with his head held high, loudly and publicly. He began work on a short text.

The dinner was exactly what he would have expected of a gala night in Manhattan. Inside the Waldorf Astoria hotel on Park Avenue, the ladies wore gowns, the men white tie and tails, while a string quartet serenaded their arrival. Otto Kiep was shown to his place at the top table.

There were pleasantries and formal welcomes and then, at last, it was his turn to speak. In the hush, there was no mistaking the significance of the moment. As he rose to his feet, both speaker and audience knew that every word counted.

He began by paying tribute to Einstein for all that he had achieved for science and for humanity. He praised the United States for showing him the same welcome it had extended to other luminaries of German scholarship. Then, in what sounded like a coded reproach to his own government, he said it was the mark of all great nations that they were open to new ideas and refused to judge an idea by the nation or group from which it came.

Finally, he turned to the guest of honour. 'This company does not honour you, Professor Einstein. On the contrary, you honour this company, and I might say, every company of which you choose to make yourself a part.'

The ovation was long and sustained. Few present were surprised to read an account of what they had witnessed published on the front page of the next day's *New York Times*. Otto himself was similarly unsurprised by the report that appeared in Berlin a few days later in the house organ of the Nazi party. It noted that an official representative of the German nation had insulted the Third Reich in a room full of Jews. It did not take long for the order to arrive, demanding he return to Germany for 'consultations'. Among those doing the consulting would be Germany's new chancellor: Otto would have to explain himself to Adolf Hitler.

3
The Countess

Maria, 1933

SHUNNED AND DISINHERITED by Carlos, her Nazi brother, Countess Maria von Maltzan would have to make her own living. She soon picked up work on a Catholic weekly newspaper and its accompanying radio listings guide, printed in Innsbruck. What's more, it was through the paper that Maria met a key figure of the emerging anti-Nazi resistance, a Jesuit priest branded an enemy of the state as early as 1934: Friedrich Muckermann. Determined to ensure that the outside world would know what was happening inside the new Germany, he swiftly enlisted Maria's help in smuggling out of the country information that would be deemed critical of the regime, and therefore illegal.

The method was ingenious. The reports were written in code, formatted to look like the radio schedules that appeared in the listings guide. That way they could be sent to Innsbruck along with the rest of that week's editorial material. Maria's job was to type up the information.

She would do it at night. At the university, she was studying zoology with a particular focus on fisheries biology – and that gave her access to the Biological Institute. She got hold of a key and, after hours, when the place was empty, she would let herself in and use the office typewriter. Much better to use a machine that could not be directly traced to her.

Once the fake schedules were written, she was to take them to Starnberg station near Munich in a suitcase packed with other mail bound for Innsbruck. Except, on her very first trip, the station was crawling with SS men. Several approached and one asked what was inside the bag.

'Press mail for Innsbruck,' she replied.

'Open up, show me.'

She had to think fast.

'Take it easy,' she said, all charm. 'Every lock I open costs a schnapps.'

Now the men smiled. So began a drinking game, lasting several rounds. Maria held her own before making a great show of suddenly realising the time. Frantically gathering up her things, she said she needed to make the mail train if she was to keep her job. Anxious to assist a young woman in need, the SS men even helped her slot her post into the right letterboxes – all need for a search forgotten.

Unsurprisingly, the countess soon became one of the priest's most trusted aides. But Father Muckermann's activities were dangerous: his superiors in the church believed the Nazi authorities would not tolerate them, or him, indefinitely. His life was in danger. So they sent him into hiding, out of the country. Only seven people were given the password by which he could be reached at the Oldenzaal monastery in Holland – and one of them was Maria von Maltzan.

Steadily, she was getting noticed, including by the new powers in the land. The Gestapo hauled her in for questioning at their Munich headquarters repeatedly. She became adept at parrying their questions, at maintaining the hauteur that always served her so well. On one occasion, she gave full vent to her irritation, ordering her interrogator to telephone a prominent Nazi minister at once to explain to him where she was. The call was necessary 'because I am expected for lunch'. She would later brag that, when they finally let her go, she walked out carrying a little bag they had not searched and that would have confirmed her as a resistance operative if they had. The bag contained a small bomb.

Sometimes her inquisitors were less easy to fend off. One session turned violent, the men from the Gestapo leaving Maria with a broken jaw. But she was not deterred. Instead, she took steps to minimise the risk of a future arrest or worse. She inveigled her way inside Gestapo headquarters and, thanks to a duplicate key she had acquired – perhaps through comrades in the resistance – found the file the secret police had compiled on her. Which she promptly destroyed.

Still, the signs were clear. Munich was becoming too hot for the rebel countess. She accepted an offer from her editor at the Catholic paper to join him on a six-month road trip to Africa: they would make the entire journey in a Chevrolet. What followed was an adventure that seemed only to make Maria bolder, if not actually reckless. Sometimes it entailed nothing riskier than sleeping in a tent, cooking on a campfire and listening to Mozart and Bach on a portable gramophone. But it also saw her cross a desert for twelve hours, solo and on foot, in search of petrol when the Chevy ran dry; join a sheikh in a springbok hunt, which first required a ride of more than forty miles by camel; and take part in a Sinai patrol on the trail of a gang of hashish smugglers, a quest that would end in a shootout, the brigands taking cover behind the humps of their camels and bullets whistling past the young aristocrat's ears.

When she returned to Germany, it was clear how much had changed. Now if people talked politics, they did it in whispers. Her circle of friends in Munich had become smaller, limited to those who could be trusted. The cold hand of the state seemed to reach into every corner. Even on the family estate, the staff now greeted her with a 'Heil Hitler!', in accordance with instructions laid down by her brother. She met up with a former classmate, a friend in Militsch, and as they walked along the promenade, she casually, and with barely a thought, linked arms with him. He hurriedly pulled away, his voice full of fear. 'Don't! Please! I'm Jewish!' The dangers of appearing to be a mixed couple, in a country that would soon have a Law for the Protection of German Blood and German Honour banning *Rassenschande*, or 'race defilement', were clear enough to him, even if they had not crossed her mind.

But her resolve to resist was undimmed. If anything, it had grown stronger.

Officially, she now spent her time as an interpreter and freelance journalist, with a sideline in exercising the horses of the rich at local riding schools and working as a riding double at the film studios at Geiselgasteig, doing the horseback scenes for some of the leading actresses of the day. She had also fallen in love, joining the long line of daughters of well-born families attracted to men bound to draw disapproval – in this case, an artist, bohemian and thorough reprobate. He was Walter Hillbring, a cabaret performer and singer of banned songs with a devoted following in Munich who was, at forty, more than fifteen years her senior. Utterly unsuitable and therefore wholly irresistible.

His proposal, when it came, was hardly drenched in romance. 'Now that we've got on so well, I think I'll abandon the idea of remaining an eternal bachelor. I mean, we could give it a try.' Despite that, she said yes.

She had few illusions that her family would follow Maltzan tradition and organise a lavish wedding for her of the kind she had witnessed for her sisters: a two-day affair that involved a horse-drawn procession through the village, a twelve-course menu, with corresponding wines, and servants dressed in yellow velvet frock coats and blue satin knee breeches. She mentioned that the Maltzans saw nothing to celebrate in her impending marriage to a friend who immediately set about organising everything instead. No bridal carriage or staff dressed in gala uniforms or lace cuffs, but instead dinner and a visit to the Brennessel, a pub favoured by Munich's starving artists. The landlord allocated them a back room where an unwanted extra guest was present. There, on one of the walls, hung a portrait of Adolf Hitler.

Once the drink was flowing, the sense of being watched by the Führer grew oppressive. 'You shoot so well,' one friend said to the bride. 'Can't you shoot Hitler's eyes out?' Maria explained that she had come unarmed: a gun would have spoiled the line of her wedding dress. No matter, someone else had a weapon, promptly placing a revolver in her hand. Now, she was out of excuses. She stood up, took aim and shot out both of Hitler's eyes, one after the other. The party went on with the previously all-seeing Führer watching them no longer. The landlord, however, was distraught. What if the authorities were to come by and see that he had allowed the leader of the fatherland to be insulted so violently on his premises? He was placated only by the promise from one of the guests, a painter, that Hitler would have his sight restored by noon the next day.

Maria von Maltzan's defiance of the Third Reich continued after she and Walter moved to Berlin – he found Munich 'too brown', too Nazi – and after their marriage broke down, as it had by the end of 1936, thanks chiefly to his serial infidelity. Sometimes it would take the form of small, unnoticed acts of rule-breaking, such as striding up to the military checkpoint that was policing entry to the Berlin Olympics and, when asked for a ticket that she naturally did not have, replying with her trademark imperiousness: 'Don't you recognise me?' Once inside, the countess made sure to head straight to the best seats, planting herself close to Field Marshal Werner von Blomberg, the first minister of war in Hitler's government. She met his eye and he politely nodded back.

Of rather more value than these moments of audacity were her continued contacts with the Catholic resistance, especially those elements centred on Munich. The work she would do in this period, and the consequences of it, would serve as a kind of trial run for what was to follow. It would steel her for the battle ahead.

It was in early 1937 that she first turned her home into an unofficial refuge. She was asked to take in a former inmate of a concentration camp, a political prisoner who had just been released from detention in the German town of Sonnenberg. He was frail and needed somewhere to stay. Maria was shocked by what she saw. He had been beaten so badly that his entire back, from his neck down to his coccyx, was black.

Not long afterwards she would experience for herself how national socialism dealt with those it believed were engaged in action against the state rather than mere acts of disobedience. It happened thanks to a trip she made across the border to Czechoslovakia in 1938, when the talk was of an imminent German invasion. She encountered there a group of pro-Nazi Czech activists and, in conversation with them, her trademark confidence tipped into recklessness. She knew her brother-in-law was serving as a senior officer in the border area and she asked after him. It was a bad mistake.

The Czech fascists instantly assumed that a woman asking such questions could only be a spy and promptly handed her over to the German border police, who arrested her on espionage charges.

She was interrogated for eight days, held in the dark, two bright lights shining in her eyes, as the same questions came at her again and again. If she so much as closed her eyes from exhaustion, they threw a bucket of water in her face or aimed a truncheon at her head. Or they would try a different approach, more honey than vinegar: they would ply her with alcohol, gently nudging her to make the statement that would serve as a confession. She tried to repeat the trick she had pulled off when sending the coded radio listings to Innsbruck, when she managed to keep pace with the SS men, schnapps for schnapps. She held out for a while, but eventually collapsed.

Frustrated, one of her tormentors eventually led her outdoors where, in an open field, he aimed a gun at her. 'Admit everything,' he ordered. She replied that perhaps this kind of behaviour explained the German corpses that had been found at the border, which official propaganda blamed on the Czechs.

Her insolence was punished with a transfer to a labour camp: Patschkau. But the countess was not treated like a regular inmate. Instead, she was placed in a room in an administrative building and given two buckets of water and a paper, the *Völkischer Beobachter*, the Nazi party daily. She was able to give herself a thorough wash and, as for the newspaper, she used that to improvise curlers for her hair.

One of the camp commandants showed a personal interest in his aristocratic prisoner and Maria played along, even allowing him to take her away from Patschkau to a small hotel. They had a decent dinner and Maria regularly ensured his glass was refilled. He led her upstairs to the room he had booked for the night, a bottle of Slivovitz in hand and hope in his heart, and here too she encouraged him to keep drinking, pouring the contents of her own glass into a plant pot whenever he looked the other way. The man's speech was slurring when, at last, he muttered and murmured and fell fast asleep. Maria tiptoed over to the telephone and disconnected the cable. As she left the hotel, she stopped at reception, leaving instructions that the guest was not to be disturbed during the night or woken early in the morning. She left for the railway station, where she melted into the crowds of Czechoslovaks desperate to get out of the country before the German tanks rolled in.

She had got away, but she had not truly escaped. Once back in Germany, she learned that she was the subject of a 'Wanted' poster at German police headquarters. It would surely not be long before the Gestapo caught up with her and, when they did, she would be doubly accused: first, as a spy and, second, as a fugitive from justice.

Her response was, once again, the kind of move available only to someone armed with the supreme confidence of the governing classes. If people like Maria von Maltzan acted as if they owned the place, that was because they largely did – and had done so for several centuries.

And so, the countess headed to Alexanderplatz and Berlin police headquarters, where she strode in and loudly confronted the relevant SS man at his desk. She said it was an outrage that she should be a wanted woman, accused of engaging in espionage. The very idea was ridiculous. She insisted that all suspicion be removed from her immediately.

She got the impression that the man was hung-over. He yawned ostentatiously and seemed not to be listening to a word she was saying. She would need to get his attention. She duly picked up the inkwell that sat on his desk and hurled it at the wall.

She resumed, 'My freedom and my livelihood are at stake.' She would not be satisfied until he put an end to this bogus investigation.

An outrageous gambit, but it worked. The SS man summoned a typist, who took down Maria's statement, then dictated and signed his own document declaring the manhunt against Maria von Maltzan officially over owing to lack of evidence. She was free to go, her name cleared.

Others might have taken that as the cue for a fresh start: count yourself lucky, stay out of trouble from now on. Maria could easily have done that. She was beginning to bring in a tidy income as a writer of animal stories that she herself dismissed as 'schmaltzy, tear-jerker nonsense' – about cats and dogs, taken before their time – but which editors lapped up and which she published under an easily decoded pseudonym: Naztlam, which was Maltzan in reverse.

But if she now had a chance to keep her head down, Maria was not interested in taking it. She found a new apartment, above a shop in the Wilmersdorf neighbourhood of Berlin, drawn especially by its usefulness as a safe haven: its two rooms meant more space to harbour those who needed to be hidden. Among them would be the man who would soon become her biggest secret.

4

The Widow and Her Daughter

Hanna and Lagi, 1933

THE SOLF FAMILY grasped more quickly than most that they were living in a new era. Wilhelm Solf, the one-time governor of Samoa, had seen enough the night Hitler took power to declare *Finis Germaniae*: the end of Germany. He was especially appalled by the Nazis' persecution of the country's Jews, and resolved early on that he would not confine himself to an old man's grumbles. He wanted to act. He sought out Hitler's propaganda minister, Joseph Goebbels, to tell him the new regime was making a terrible mistake, adding a particular plea for those 'cultured Jews' who had proven themselves patriots and should be spared. Goebbels waved aside the elder statesman: 'That this poison has penetrated even you, Your Excellency, shows how dangerous it is,' he said.

Solf was unbowed, speaking openly of his fears, so much so that the British ambassador in Berlin would report back to London that plenty of leading Germans were ashamed that their country had, in launching a one-day boycott of Jewish shops and businesses on April Fool's Day in 1933, resorted to 'medieval methods'. Among those who felt 'the stigma on their land', he cited Dr Wilhelm Solf.

Now in his seventies, Solf did what he could to help those who were in the Nazis' sights, using what remaining influence he had. But the new masters found it easy to wave aside a man who had been at the peak of his powers in the days of the Kaiser. Solf soon concluded that, if there was no way of changing the policy of the new administration, he would have to work around it.

The most direct action he could take would be to help Jews get out. Here his contacts in Japan, coupled with his knack for the indirect language of diplomacy, were invaluable. Say he knew of a German Jewish musician, a flautist. He would write to an old chum at the University of Tokyo, recommending the musician as a world-class scholar of the flute who would make an excellent addition to the faculty. He would not write that the man was a Jew, and the recipient of the letter would not need it spelled out. But both would know. Soon the fortunate Jewish flautist in Berlin would receive a letter from Japan containing a job offer, which would also be his ticket to survival.

Solf kept on like that for the first three years of the new era, until his death in February 1936. But the work continued, the burden now carried by those who had been the former ambassador's comrades from the start: his wife and his daughter.

The prime task was spiriting Jews out of the country. That meant using a contacts book that had grown thick through the four decades Solf had spent in the foreign service. As soon as the threat to Germany's Jews became clear and incontrovertible, Hanna put those contacts to work. She drove almost every day to one or more of Berlin's embassies or consulates, seeking the visas or emigration affidavits that would enable Jews of her acquaintance to get away. It might mean the patient navigation of bureaucracy, with long hours spent waiting in line and filling in forms, or it might demand the quality she had acquired through years of cocktail parties and diplomatic receptions: charm. If legitimate passports or visas proved unobtainable, the great man's widow was not above acquiring forged ones.

The same went for the documents that would allow Jews not to leave Germany but to stay, in the open. A good set of Aryan papers was a precious commodity and, after her husband's death especially, Hanna was inundated with requests from those in need. The same rule applied: real papers if possible, forged ones if necessary.

But when legal emigration became blocked, with every escape route a dead end, and Aryan identity papers were out of reach, all that was left was lending a hand to those in hiding. Countless people, including those Hanna did not know and had never met, would ask for help. It might be Anni Schulz, living underground, or the Weyl family: Bruno, Marie-Louise and daughter Sabine. They were *Geltungsjuden*, those deemed Jewish under the strictures of the so-called

Nuremberg race laws which sought to separate Jews from German society, isolating them and stripping them of their rights – even though, of Sabine's four grandparents, one was born a Christian and the other three were baptised Jews. Hanna helped them out with money and food stamps. It was the best she could do.

All the while, her daughter was engaged in similar efforts, albeit half a world away. In those early years of the Reich, the younger woman, whose very name was a souvenir of the years the Solfs had spent in Samoa – she was So'oa'emalelagi Solf, though known to friends and family alike as Lagi – lived not in Germany, but in Shanghai. She was there with her husband, the man with whom she had eloped when she was twenty-two, infuriating both families and causing a minor scandal in Berlin society. Husband Wolfgang was in China working as an engineer for a German firm, so that Lagi found herself in Shanghai when that city became a sudden and precious refuge for Jews fleeing Hitler, from Germany at first but later from Austria and Poland too, until some twenty thousand had made the journey. It may have been half a world away, but Shanghai had one overwhelming attraction: no entry visa was required.

Some of the lawyers and doctors among the new arrivals opened for business, a few musicians set up orchestras, but others who arrived with next to nothing – they had spent all they had getting to China – struggled. Those Jews who had been there a while and were on their feet set up an aid committee, but early help came from the young, striking woman with an unusual name: Lagi Solf.

Her activities were much appreciated by the refugees; by the German expats, rather less so. For one thing, she defied social convention: her marriage broke up while she was in China and she rarely showed her face in the 'German corner', the favoured watering hole of the German fraternity in Shanghai. For another, they suspected Lagi of poisoning foreign diplomats and statesmen, most of them old friends of her father, against the Third Reich.

All of this caused trouble for her when she returned to Berlin in 1938, now divorced and still in her twenties. Her feet had barely touched German soil when she was summoned by the Gestapo for questioning. They wanted to know more about her 'political agitation' in China.

Had she opted for full disclosure, she might have said that, to her mind, her 'political agitation' consisted of nothing more than the free voicing of her own opinions. In response to the accusation that she had stayed away from the German corner, a truthful answer would have explained that she was more shunned against than shunning, that she had been ostracised by the expats for the sin of helping Jewish refugees from the moment they started arriving in Shanghai. As for seeking to persuade the diplomatic corps of the wickedness of Hitler, she might have replied that, in that enterprise, the Führer hardly needed any help from her: he was doing a most effective job on his own. Instead, she said little they could use against her and was released.

If the Gestapo hoped their summons might deter Lagi Solf, it did not work. She picked up where she had left off in Shanghai, only with more ardour. She found in Berlin a city that was, steadily but unmistakably, isolating its Jewish population, shutting them off from everyone else. Eventually, Germany's Jews would be confined to flats marked with what the official edict called 'a Jewish Star': it was to be 'in black print on white paper', corresponding 'in style and size to the one to be worn on clothing' and 'to be put up on the front door next to the nameplate'. Aryans were forbidden to visit those homes, no matter the circumstances. Lagi would visit anyway, not that she was fearless, because she was not; she was scared of getting caught. But she would go all the same. On these visits, she would ask the Jews within what they needed and come out with a shopping list: it might be a request for a newspaper for those starved of information from the outside world, or for fresh vegetables or something that was not yet subject to rationing. Carrying the shopping bags was no hardship. It had become her habit always to have a shopping bag loaded with laundry or vegetables in each hand. That way, she would be unable to give the now requisite Heil Hitler salute.

Somehow, in the midst of all this, Lagi found time to meet a man and fall in love. Like every other choice she and her fellow dissenters made in those years, that one would have grave implications, carrying her a step further towards her date with destiny.

5

The Headmistress

Elisabeth, 1933

ELISABETH VON THADDEN, headmistress to the daughters of the German elite, had approached Nazism with an open mind. But the reality of national socialism soon became unmistakable. First, some of the women Elisabeth most admired, Alice Salomon among them, lost their offices and had to close their institutions because of their Jewish origins. They were victims of the so-called 'Aryan paragraph', the clause that was now increasingly inserted into the statutes of organisations, institutions and professional associations, excluding Jews or other non-Aryans from those bodies and indeed from public life. The very idea was anathema to Elisabeth, who had considered it perfectly natural to organise a school trip to the synagogue in Heidelberg a couple of years earlier, arranging for the students to meet the rabbi and the cantor.

Next, Elisabeth saw what the Third Reich had in mind for Christianity, as it sought to create a new 'German church' that would be an arm of the all-powerful Nazi state and in which Adolf Hitler would outrank Jesus Christ. By November 1934, she had thrown in her lot with the dissidents of the Confessing Church, founded in part in opposition to the Aryan paragraph.

Now she had to play a subtler, cannier game, navigating between two mutually repelling poles. On the one hand, she wanted to stay true to her own revulsion at the direction the country was taking. On the other, she needed to keep her school open. And so she began to choose her battles carefully, tolerating much that she found intolerable and finding artful compromises on the rest.

In that spirit, rather than confront the authorities, she allowed her pupils to join the Bund Deutscher Mädel, BDM, the League of German Girls, and even for there to be a BDM association in the school. But she ensured it was staffed by the school's own teachers rather than outside Nazi officials or activists: that way, she hoped, she could manage, and restrict, the degree of indoctrination that would occur under her roof. And when Wieblingen got a new pastor, one whose Nazi convictions had led him to join the party in 1932, she might allow him to teach her students one hour a week, and then quietly fail to renew the arrangement.

It was a constant and careful balancing act, one that favoured practical action over the striking of heroic postures. Elisabeth would go through whatever motions the authorities demanded of her – say, displaying the NSDAP party programme at the school entrance – just to keep the place functioning. Without a school, she could not inculcate the next generation with the values of social responsibility and Christian piety she cherished. More concretely, without a school she could not take in the girls who needed a safe haven – a need that would only become more urgent.

Quietly, Elisabeth had been admitting pupils of 'non-Aryan' origin, among them one Irmgard Zarden, the senior civil servant's daughter who, as a curious twelve-year-old, had watched the brownshirts celebrate their seizure of power in January 1933 from the back seat of a chauffeur-driven car. According to the Nazi system of racial classification, Irmgard was a *Mischling*, a 'Jewish half-breed', of the first degree, because her mother was a Jew. When the state-run schools were closing their doors, the Zardens had heard that Wieblingen was 'Nazi-free'. Students noticed how new girls might suddenly arrive in the middle of the school year, only to disappear again soon afterwards. The obvious explanation was that they were holding out in Wieblingen while their families acquired the papers they needed to flee the country.

Elisabeth was turning the school into a discreet refuge, and not only for people. When Professor Max von Waldberg, who had once supervised the doctorate of a young Joseph Goebbels, felt the national mood darkening, he made an unexpected but prescient request. He asked Elisabeth if he could store his precious grand piano in her castle. She agreed at once, and an instrument that might otherwise have been smashed by the mob remained in one piece.

She would make a compromise here, a concession there, even as she sought to get away with as much as she could. So she might quietly drop the word 'Evangelical' from the name of the school in 1936, as state hostility to denominational schools and indeed to Christianity itself intensified, with the party increasingly drawn in its propaganda to what it imagined was an earlier, pagan Germany. But inside the bounds of the renamed Rural Education Home for Girls, neither staff nor pupils were required to give each other the so-called German greeting: there were no Hitler salutes.

She seemed to have found if not quite an equilibrium, then at least a modus vivendi. She had found a line she could walk that would keep her just the right side of the Reich, thereby allowing her to do what she could to defy it. The line held, until the day she slipped up. Of all things, it was a line from her cherished Bible that was to prove her undoing.

6

In the Room

Otto, 1933

HE WOULD NOT see the Führer straight away. First Otto Kiep would have to receive a dressing-down from the new head of personnel at the Foreign Ministry who, as the eldest son of Prince Friedrich of Waldeck and Pyrmont and Princess Bathildis of Schaumburg-Lippe, was entitled to style himself a prince. Not that that made Josias, Hereditary Prince of Waldeck and Pyrmont such a rarity in the upper echelons of Nazism. By one count, more than 3,500 princes from three hundred aristocratic families had joined the Nazi party even before Hitler had come to power. They were drawn, in part, by the promise of restoration: Hitler's pledge that the titles that had been abolished, the monarchies and dukedoms that had been swept away, the inheritances that had been lost with the abdication of the Kaiser and the establishment of the Weimar Republic in 1919, would all be returned to their rightful owners. Since the mid-1920s, the Nazi party had been allowing the denuded nobility of the kingdoms of Württemberg and Prussia, or the grand duchies of Baden and Hesse, to register as party members using their abolished titles, so that in the realm of national socialism at least, assorted grand dukes and princesses could be known as their forebears had been known. Which is how Otto Kiep came to be carpeted by a prince.

It was less a meeting than a rally for a crowd of one. Even though Otto was the only other person in the room, Waldeck delivered a speech, full of rhetorical fire, as if channelling the spirit of Hitler himself. The enemy, he thundered, was the Jews. The task before the German nation was to purify itself of 'the poison of the subhuman

Jews', he said, slamming his fist down on the desk, adding that 'Representatives of the Reich cannot allow themselves to drink at the poisoned well.' Which sounded like a reference to the ballroom of the Waldorf Astoria, where Otto had toasted Professor Einstein. If it was, it was the closest Waldeck would come to addressing Otto's offence in New York. He had bigger ideas to express.

'A new age has begun, demanding new things from us all,' he said. 'Nothing from the past, except our loyalty, can carry us forward. Adolf Hitler is our only law and our only morality.'

And then, just as suddenly, the demon that had seemed to possess the prince deserted his body, leaving behind a ministry official who started inquiring after the mission in New York, how the staff were working and what extra support might be needed. He walked Otto to the door and shook his hand. He did not fire him.

Which meant that, when Otto Kiep reported at the office of the Führer next day, he was still officially the German consul general to New York.

Hitler had not been chancellor long when Otto received his summons. It was almost an achievement to have crossed the master of the new Germany so soon after he had taken power. And yet here Otto was, being ushered into the holy of holies of the Third Reich, the private office of the chancellor himself, for what was surely going to be an epic dressing-down. He had dared defy the cause of national socialism and for that he was bound to be punished, even if he had not quite anticipated a scolding from the leader of the movement, the man who was its singular incarnation and Germany's new all-powerful ruler.

Adolf Hitler was taller than Otto had expected, but it was his eyes he noticed most. The Führer seemed not merely to be looking at Otto, but watching him. Hitler, he concluded, had the eyes of a thief.

Hitler did things in the reverse order from Waldeck: first came the questions. Was it true that Americans were 'disturbed' by Nazism? Otto replied that it was true, and that the disturbance was greatest in cities that were home to many Jews, with New York as the obvious example. That was hardly surprising, said the Führer, given that most American newspapermen were Jews. Otto could have nodded or done nothing. Instead, he chose to disagree with Hitler.

He said that he did not think that was true, though he did concede he knew a good number of Jewish reporters in New York.

That prompted a ten-minute reply, more a lecture than the full rally-style address offered twenty-four hours earlier by Waldeck. Hitler's theme was the future of the Third Reich. When it was done, Otto was shown out.

And that was the end of that. Against all odds, he had still not been fired.

Confirmation came that same evening when Otto was invited to a 'men's dinner' at the home of Franz von Papen, who had briefly been chancellor of Germany the previous year and who now served as Hitler's official number two. There, Otto talked into the early hours with no less than Hermann Göring, future head of the Luftwaffe, the German air force, who was then preoccupied with the creation of a new secret police, to be known as the Gestapo.

Göring laughed off Otto's anxieties about his job. The denunciations that had appeared in the Nazi press were just space-fillers, he said, written by ambitious reporters eager to do their bit for the party. Otto was admired by those who counted, Göring said. Germany was proud of him.

And so, Otto Kiep, the man who had sided with the world's most famous Jew against the Third Reich, returned to America and his job. He had survived. Though, he was bound to wonder, for how long?

After the Einstein episode, Otto inhabited a kind of limbo. He returned to his post in New York strangely unsacked, resolved to walk a line he had drawn for himself: he would serve as the representative of Germany, rather than its government. He would be the envoy of the German people, not Adolf Hitler. But it was barely sustainable.

On the one hand, there was a stampede of German Jews heading to the consulate, hoping for a safe harbour in the United States and looking for help. Otto might see a dozen such refugees every day. On the other, the Foreign Ministry in Berlin was sending regular, thinly coded demands that he become a louder advocate for national socialism. The Nazis had been in power for only three months when one of Hitler's most senior ideological lieutenants, Alfred Rosenberg, denounced Otto Kiep by name as 'politically undependable'. The tightrope walk was becoming ever shakier.

By the summer, it had become impossible. When Hitler banned all political parties except his own, Otto decided his time was up. He wrote a letter of resignation and it was accepted. He was out.

Once back home in Germany, he could see for himself how the Nazis were becoming ever more deeply entrenched, taking control of every aspect of life. The party was everywhere: its posters and banners hung in the streets, its messages were carried on the radio, in the papers and even in private conversation. People Otto knew and liked were full of praise for the new regime, brimming with talk of a Germany that was back on track, that had rediscovered its soul. His own younger brother, Max, always a devotee of the great outdoors, was excited by the Nazi enthusiasm for exercise, a return to the soil and a new generation of healthy minds in healthy bodies. Others told Otto to celebrate the fact that those who had been jobless before Hitler took power were now earning a wage. True, Otto himself was struggling to find work: he was not a party member, which put him at an instant disadvantage. But surely he could see that, for millions of others, things were looking up. After the lunacy of hyperinflation, money was worth something again. At what was now the family seat in Ballenstedt, he ran into a local grocer who became positively lyrical. 'Before Hitler, we had no pride,' the shopkeeper said. 'Now we believe in ourselves again. Work is good, pride is good, power is good.'

The man was soon in full flow. 'So what if I can't buy the newspaper I used to buy? I'll buy another. And as for getting the Jews out of Germany, I have nothing against that.'

Otto wrestled with the perennial dilemma: was it better to stand apart, his conscience unsullied, or to be on the inside, doing what he could from within? He was pulled in both directions; he could see the merits of both approaches. On the one hand, there was his mother, who was increasingly vocal in her loathing of the new self-styled Führer and who did not care who knew it. She once spent so long in heated conversation with a railway worker, lecturing him on the evils of *Mein Kampf*, that she missed her train. On the other, he was in touch with officials at the Foreign Ministry who had stayed on, men of conscience and often religious faith, whose moral opposition to Hitler was implacable but who believed they could soften, or even undermine, Nazi foreign policy if they were in the room — and who were equally clear that they would be wholly impotent outside it.

In time, that became Otto's view too. Which had the additional benefit of allowing him to accept some of the opportunities that were coming his way. He led a trade delegation to South America in 1934 and another to Asia the following year, when he had a meeting with Chiang Kai-shek among others. He took comfort from the fact that the work was designated as 'non-political', and both he and Hanna enjoyed being back in the diplomatic swing of parties and receptions. But there was no lightness in his heart.

Travel confirmed how unlike everywhere else Germany was becoming, what a global outlier Hitler was making of Otto's homeland. An outlier rather than a pariah: everywhere the Kieps would have to make polite conversation with foreigners full of praise for Hitler and the transformation he was effecting. The man was surely a marvel; the country's economic recovery nothing short of a miracle. The official representative of Germany might smile weakly, keeping his true feelings to himself. Those could be voiced only when the door was closed and there was no one to hear him but Hanna. The pair were alone with their fears for what the future might bring.

As the decade wore on, he did his best to tread that fine line, keeping faith with his conscience without straying into outright opposition, which promised only ostracism, isolation and worse. So when the paperwork for one trade mission required him to swear an oath of loyalty to Adolf Hitler — to refuse would be to resign — he told himself he was doing it not for his career, or to preserve his viability as a high-level civil servant, but rather for the sake of the German workers and their families whose livelihoods would be damaged if he abandoned the task at hand. Only they would be hurt by a grand gesture of defiance, he reasoned. Hitler could not care less.

Otto took the oath along with his assistant, telling his colleague, 'Adolf Hitler is a disaster for Germany. If he stays in power, he will carry us all to ruin. But he *is* in power, and we have to deal with him.' It was the timeless creed of the pragmatist: practical action was better than a futile, if principled, gesture. But Otto attached a caveat to the oath, at least privately. For him, an oath was a contract binding two parties. Hitler had duties too. 'If he betrays us,' Otto told his assistant, 'we won't owe him any allegiance.' That way, he hoped, he could swear fidelity to a man he regarded as indecent and still stay true to himself.

Occasionally there would be a crumb of encouragement, and he would seize it. He was glad to see that his brother's earlier enthusiasm for national socialism had begun to wane: Max had witnessed a Nuremberg rally and the spectacle — the flags, the uniformed men marching, the vast crowd singing and chanting the same words, over and over — terrified him, the sheer devotion to the leader most of all. 'Hitler is like a god to these people,' Max had said.

Otto found himself rereading the scriptures. He kept a copy of the New Testament at his bedside. The biblical prophecy, or warning, of a great evil arising in the world, cloaking itself in noble promises of a better tomorrow, suddenly seemed the stuff not of fairy tales and superstition, as his younger, sceptical self had come to regard much of the Protestant faith, but that day's headlines. Hitler was offering himself not as Germany's chancellor or even its leader, but as its saviour. You could, it increasingly seemed to Otto, be faithful and obedient to Hitler or you could be faithful and obedient to Christ; you could not be both.

That much was clear from the fate of his son, about which Otto learned only slowly and after much damage had been done. In 1937, when Albrecht was nearly eleven, Otto decided to do for the boy what his parents had done for him, packing him off to the monastery school at Ilfeld. Otto, who had boarded at the school when his family still lived in Scotland, associated it with some of the most joyful times of his life, remembering it with great gratitude. He would call it 'my real German homeland'. But in the four short years that had passed since the Nazis had taken power, Ilfeld had breathed deeply the spirit of national socialism. It had become the school of choice for the sons of the Nazi elite. Favoured pupils were those who not only performed well in their studies but who showed total devotion to the Führer. The strong were allowed to bully the weak; those who struggled with the compulsory eleven-mile night hikes, carrying thirty pounds on their backs through the dark, were punished and humiliated.

Albrecht tried to keep the details from his parents, but his strong faith marked him out for special torment. When the other boys discovered that he said his prayers at night, they too fell to their knees — not to praise God but to curse him, feigning shock that the Almighty did not strike them dead for their blasphemy. They stole Albrecht's Bible, returning it only to steal it again. They shunned him, when they were not mocking him without mercy. In the Nazi mini-state of Ilfeld, there was room for only one god and his name was Adolf Hitler.

When Otto and Hanna learned of all this, they made their decision swiftly. Otto wondered how to communicate it to the headmaster, seemingly a decent man and committed Christian who had nevertheless, like so many others, joined the Nazi party. What impact would withdrawal have on Albrecht's future prospects at other schools? And what would be the consequences for Otto himself of this small act of dissent, this rejection of the ethos of national socialism? But there was no alternative. Otto sent the letter and the head replied in such a way that the official record would contain no obvious trace of the Kieps' failure to comply with Germany's new expectations of its citizens. The note signed off, as all such correspondence did these days — 'Heil Hitler.'

Nineteen thirty-seven was also the year Otto Kiep finally confronted the pressure that had been building for years, not on his son but on him. Friends had been telling him since 1933, if he were to have any kind of career, any prospect of influence, there was one further step he would have to take. The arguments raged inside him as they always had. On the one hand, he had long ago accepted that if one wanted to exert influence, if one were to have any hope of advancing the greater good, that could only be done from the inside. On the other, this would be an act of surrender; he would be bending the knee to a great evil.

It could be put off no longer. He had to make up his mind, one way or the other. Otto Kiep would have to decide whether he would follow millions of others and join the Nazi party.

7
The Circle

Hanna and Lagi, 1938

THE MAN WHO had won Lagi Solf's heart was Hubertus von Ballestrem, a year older than her and a count. He was, like Maria von Maltzan, the scion of old Silesian nobility and shared his fellow aristocrat's low opinion of national socialism. He had despised it from the start, back when he was a student at the close of the 1920s. When he and Lagi came together shortly after meeting in Vienna in 1938, it redoubled for each of them their commitment to the cause of opposition to Hitler.

Hubert was a fixture in dissenting circles, but Lagi hardly needed her husband to draw her into that world. She already lived right at the centre of it. Her parents' home had long been a salon of political conversation, though in the era of the Third Reich that habit acquired a new seriousness, only intensifying after Wilhelm's death. The group would meet often, bringing together people of influence from the higher echelons of science, culture, government and diplomacy. In the latter category, Hanna took pride that, barring the representative of the Bolshevik rulers of the Soviet Union, every accredited envoy in Berlin – ambassadors, ministers and chargés d'affaires – was hosted at one time or another in the house on Alsenstrasse.

There, crucial connections were made. Well-informed, if rebellious, officials of the Foreign Ministry, the likes of Otto Kiep, might sit alongside US or European diplomats, seizing the chance to make clear to the foreign representatives that reports they might have been tempted to dismiss as mere horror stories – that, for example, Jews and critics of the regime were being dragged to concentration camps, where they were tortured or worse – were not only true, but just a fraction of the catastrophe then unfolding.

As the opposition to national socialism gradually took shape, those who either would become or were already its leading lights came in and out of the orbit of what would soon become known as the *Solf-Kreis*, the Solf Circle. It might be Carl Friedrich Goerdeler, mayor of Leipzig when Hitler took power and the man most frequently whispered of as a likely chancellor of Germany should the resistance ever succeed in ousting the Führer. Goerdeler had been a Solf regular even before the brownshirts celebrated their victory in January 1933. Indeed, it was under the Solf roof in that period that he had met the theologian and peace campaigner Friedrich Siegmund-Schultze; two men of different outlooks, united in their opposition to Hitler.

Or you could turn up one evening and see Dr Richard Kuenzer, a former Foreign Ministry official with close ties to what used to be the Catholic Centre Party and to Joseph Wirth, who for eighteen Weimar months had served as chancellor and who would, like Siegmund-Schultze, soon find himself exiled to Switzerland. While some at the Solf gatherings might content themselves with the relief of being surrounded by like-minded people, finding a haven where they could vent their disgust and despair, Kuenzer was a man of action. He was involved in preparations for what would become known as the Generals' Plot of September 1938, led by one Hans Oster, an army officer who would later serve as mentor to Otto Kiep.

What alarmed the September conspirators was the suspicion that Hitler was about to lead Germany into a war against Czechoslovakia over the Sudetenland, a war that Oster and the other military brass believed Germany was in no position to fight – or to win. If Hitler did as they feared, their plan would see a group of rebel soldiers storm into the Reich Chancellery, where they would either arrest or assassinate the Führer. Taking his place would be the grandson of the last Kaiser. The monarchy would be restored and Germany would avoid yet another humiliating defeat on the battlefield. The plan was aborted when, far from provoking war with Britain, Hitler's seizure of the Sudetenland prompted the acquiescence of Neville

Chamberlain: appeasement. At that moment, Hitler looked like a statesman who had both enlarged Germany's territory and averted war. The September plot was abandoned.

But Oster, Kuenzer and the others did not give up. They still believed Hitler's aggressive expansionism was doomed. To make that argument most effectively, they needed to be able to point to the certainty of a robust response from Britain. Chamberlain was not offering it, but the plotters could see one man who most emphatically was. Which is why Kuenzer flew to London not long after Munich to urge the British government to heed the warnings of Winston Churchill, the former Cabinet minister who had spent nearly a decade in the parliamentary wilderness, and who had been both vocal and early in insisting that Nazi Germany would have to be confronted. Kuenzer told those he met in London that Churchill needed to be back in Cabinet, the better to stand firm against the menace of Hitler. When it came to the Führer, argued Kuenzer, it was essential that the British not give in on anything.

Kuenzer took Hanna Solf into his confidence; they saw each other almost every day. At night, when it was easier to avoid detection, they would meet other dissidents. They sat regularly with Kurt von Hammerstein-Equord, who held a rank equivalent to that of a four-star general: he had served as commander of the army but immediately resigned in January 1933 in avowed opposition to Hitler. (When he died of cancer in 1943, his family refused an official funeral rather than see his coffin draped in a swastika.) Besides the general, Solf and Kuenzer met a cluster of senior figures in the Abwehr, German military intelligence.

One way or another, if you were a dissenter in the upper reaches of Berlin society, the chances were high that you would meet a kindred spirit in the drawing room of Hanna Solf. It might be Dr Herbert Mumm von Schwarzenstein, who had served in the German embassy in London and then in Tokyo, under Hanna's late husband, before he was expelled from the foreign service in 1935. He was dismissed because he was a homosexual, which put him on the wrong side of the Law for the Restoration of the Professional Civil Service, passed within a couple of months of the Nazis taking power and which banned Jews and others deemed undesirable from all public positions. Mumm von Schwarzenstein was a favourite at the Solf gatherings. He would team up with Nikolaus von Halem, a young industrialist and close friend of Lagi's husband, to perform 'Führer speeches' parodying Hitler's oratory and short, satirical verses sending up the leading lights of national socialism. In dissenting circles, the duo's reputation as entertainers, as bringers of forbidden laughter, spread. But the pair were not content to limit their opposition to the regime to drawing-room comedy turns. Instead, they were at the kinetic end of the spectrum of responses represented at Alsenstrasse 9: in time, they would become actively involved in efforts to assassinate the Führer.

It was at the Solf house that Kuenzer, who had a habit of arriving late, much to the irritation of his host, met Father Max Metzger, a Catholic priest whose experience as a chaplain in the Great War had made him a committed pacifist, one who grew ever more daring in his opposition to national socialism. Even though he had been arrested frequently by the Gestapo – held for three days as early as January 1934 and held again for a month when he was linked to a failed attempt on Hitler's life in November 1938 – Metzger refused to be cowed. Determined to move beyond whispers and coded messages, he decided to be direct. He wrote a letter, setting out why it was essential, morally and politically, for Adolf Hitler to step down. He then put the letter in an envelope and addressed it to . . . Adolf Hitler. It was only the intervention of his friends that stopped him from posting it. Not that he was entirely without an instinct for self-preservation: he backed away from Kuenzer when he feared the latter was about to draw him, and his church movement, into active conspiracy.

These, then, were the people of Alsenstrasse 9, this the tenor of their conversations. Several of those who came together in the Solf house were involved in direct plots to topple the regime, but when they were in Hanna Solf's drawing room they mostly traded nuggets of information, passing on morsels picked up via foreign radio or on the bush telegraph of gossip.

There was no defined political goal that united the shifting fellowship of the *Solf-Kreis*, no agreed programme. Instead, a common thread loosely tied them together. It consisted of a shared revulsion at the Nazi tyranny and particularly its persecution of those deemed racially inferior. That in turn prompted a desire to ease the pain of its victims and, in so doing, to follow what were, for some, the scruples of Christian belief and, for others, simple human decency.

Hosting such a group so often was risk enough for the Solfs, mother and daughter. But neither was prepared to leave it at that. They would soon make the move that exposed them to a far more immediate, far more intimate danger.

8

The Night of Broken Glass

Maria, 9 November 1938

Late at night on 9 November 1938, Countess Maria von Maltzan got in her car and drove around Berlin, surveying the wreckage left by an astonishing eruption of violence. She saw the shattered windows of Jewish shops and businesses, watching as SA men and others out of uniform, indistinguishable from regular Germans, ran in packs, chasing Jews. She saw synagogues burn to the ground, brownshirts tossing Torah scrolls, Jews' most sacred objects, into the blaze. She saw rabbis beaten. It was Kristallnacht, the 'night of broken glass' – a state-sponsored pogrom that would leave hundreds of synagogues destroyed, seven thousand Jewish-owned businesses damaged or ruined, and some thirty thousand Jewish men arrested and sent to concentration camps, to say nothing of the many, many Jews killed in the frenzy. In the quiet that followed, Maria helped a Jewish business owner she knew, proprietor of the upmarket Union Club clothing store, move his stock out of the shop where every window had been smashed. They stored what they could in the homes of friends.

Elisabeth, 10 November 1938

When news of the pogrom reached the Rural Education Home for Girls in Wieblingen, the headmistress, Elisabeth von Thadden, who until then had striven so hard to keep her outrage at the new regime discreet, at last found herself unequal to the task. Her defences had been breached. In the dining hall of her school, she let out a cry of pain, announcing that she was ashamed to be German.

Otto, 10 November 1938

Otto Kiep, the former consul in New York, had come to his own understanding with his conscience. A year earlier, in 1937, he had bowed to the pressure of friends, colleagues and family, and done what the times seemed to insist had to be done. Perhaps he viewed it the same way he had regarded the oath of loyalty he had earlier sworn to Adolf Hitler, as the necessary price one had to pay for a chance to advance the greater good. However he justified it, in 1937 Otto Kiep joined the Nazi party.

In his mind, he made the distinction between a formal act of fealty to the new order and the true allegiance he felt, which was to the old Germany, the country his parents had taught him to believe in. But increasingly that place was disappearing. A vanishing point came after Kristallnacht. Otto was appalled by the frenzy of violence and race hatred, but he was no less shocked by the sanction, the praise, it received in the press and on the radio stations controlled by the Nazis. You could not wave this aside as a riot led by a few hooligans. This amounted to an act of state policy and the state in question was the one he had served all his working life.

The November pogrom meant something else too. The way Otto read it, Hitler had lost all fear of international condemnation: he believed he could act with impunity. And who could blame him? Just a few weeks earlier, Otto and the rest of the Kiep family had huddled around the wireless, listening as word came of the pact agreed at Munich between Hitler and Neville Chamberlain. Most of the Kieps were delighted – there would be no repeat of the war that had ended just twenty years earlier – but Otto and his mother were downcast. They knew Hitler would see Chamberlain as weak – an 'old woman', in the words of his eighty-year-old mother – and that the Führer would conclude that he could do as he pleased. That would mean more acts of aggression, Hitler gobbling up more chunks of territory the way he had just snatched the Sudetenland, the part of Czechoslovakia that was home to some three million ethnic Germans. Britain had acquiesced in that land grab but, Otto concluded, it would not acquiesce for ever. Eventually Hitler would go too far. War was now inevitable and, Otto believed, imminent.

9

Someone Must Tell the Truth

Otto, December 1938

Now when he was offered a job – a posting in the US, where his duties would involve urging German-Americans to come back home to the fatherland – there was none of the previous agonising, still less any possibility of saying yes. It was easy to say no, even if Otto Kiep did string out the process to make it seem less obvious. Of course he could not urge Germans in New York or St Louis, even the 'racially pure' ones the Nazis were keenest to lure, to return to the country that existed now.

Instead, what work he could get took him to London, where he might meet up with an old friend who had once given him a guided tour of the slums of the East End or with the daughter of another, a Quaker now devoting herself to aiding Jewish refugees from his country. These felt like the people he wanted to be among. As for the former colleagues of his serving at the embassy at 9 Carlton House Terrace, he steered well clear. The conviction Nazis were obviously to be avoided, but these days he had less patience for those who knew exactly what Germany had become but who had concluded that they were powerless to make any kind of difference, that to speak out was futile and that, therefore, the best course was to keep on and pretend to believe in Hitler. He could not easily condemn those who had made that decision. At different moments, including when he had sworn that oath or joined the party, he had made it himself.

But as he became clearer in his own mind where he stood, he became more unabashed in giving vent to his views. On a visit home, at a dinner party at the home of his beloved younger sister

Ida, the conversation had turned to the coming war. Otto had called it as he saw it. Germany might direct its fire eastwards at first, he said, but within a couple of years it would look west and north, attacking France and Scandinavia. The foreign powers' response would be unrelenting; they would bomb every German city. 'We will be lucky if we have a roof over our heads,' he said.

At that, two of the other dinner guests, a couple, had got up from the table and asked for their coats. They told Ida they were appalled by her brother's lack of faith in Germany and its leader. Ida was shaken by the incident, later chiding Otto for what he'd said – not so much for the sentiment as for the indiscretion. It was risky to speak like that in front of people he hardly knew. But Otto would not be deterred.

'Ida,' he had said. 'The whole world is lying. Someone must tell the truth.'

The obvious path was to sit out the war abroad. In London, he had friends and contacts and complete fluency in the language, as well as a small flat south of Hyde Park and, later, a furnished floor of a house in Putney. All three of his children were now enrolled in English schools; they liked riding on Wimbledon Common and in Richmond Park. In Britain, he would be safe from the foreign bombardment that he was sure was set to rain down on German cities (though London would doubtless come under aerial attack from the Luftwaffe). Above all, he would be distant from the government that was leading his country into this new, darker place. He would not be complicit.

When German tanks rolled into Prague in March 1939, making a mockery of the piece of paper Chamberlain had so gratefully secured from Hitler and confirming Otto's prognosis of the imminence of war in Europe, he spoke about a London exile with a colleague at the embassy whom he knew to share his views, a man he could trust completely. Both knew it was a theoretical discussion. Hitler had to be removed from power. However that goal was to be achieved and whoever was going to do it, one thing was clear: it was not going to be done by expat Germans pacing around the mansion blocks of Kensington. If they cared for Germany's future, they would have to be in Germany.

They talked about where they could best hope to exercise even modest influence. In a country at war, and especially once initial German victories on the battlefield turned to defeats, as Otto was sure they would, the military would become central. Steadily, power would shift from the politicians to the generals. If he was to help end the current nightmare, he would have to be in the army.

And so, as the Wehrmacht marched into Poland on the first day of September that year, and at the age of fifty-three, Otto C. Kiep, who had fought with distinction in the Great War, was a soldier once more. He was more certain than ever that Germany was heading into the abyss; the invasion of Poland only made the future more ominous.

He wrestled with how much of what he knew, and foresaw, he should discuss with his young wife. But he could not bear to hide the truth, especially from her. He waited till the children were in bed and confessed his fear of what the Germans, his countrymen, would do in Poland, which was home to the largest concentration of Jews in Europe, well over three million people. He told Hanna, 'The shame of it will be remembered for a thousand years.'

10

The Detective

September 1939

LEO LANGE, THE failed law student shrewd enough to have embraced Nazism early, had moved to police work, joining the Kriminalpolizei or Kripo, the Criminal Police, and the Sicherheitsdienst or SD, the intelligence service of the SS, in 1938. But after the German invasion in September 1939, he was deployed to Poland and within a few weeks he would take on a pioneering role in the work that would come to define Nazism for ever.

Now aged thirty, he was initially attached to one of the Einsatzgruppen mobile death squads that followed the German army into Poland, charged with eliminating hostile or unwanted elements of Polish society. By November, he was deployed to the newly established Gestapo office in Poznań, where he was involved in the execution of Polish civilians convicted by German courts, many of them taken to a forest outside the city and shot.

He was also put in charge of the concentration camp in Fort VII of Poznań, a Gestapo prison that quickly became notorious as a site of horrifying torture. At that time Fort VII was engaged in experiments with new methods of killing, focused specifically on gas. A series of high-level meetings in Berlin had decided that Lange should try out cylinders of carbon monoxide, measuring its efficacy against a German alternative that had been invented less than two decades earlier, a cyanide-based pesticide marketed under the name Zyklon B. (In that early contest, carbon monoxide was deemed the winner.) The work had the backing, and close involvement, of those at the very pinnacle of power in the Third Reich. The head of the SS,

Heinrich Himmler, came to Fort VII to observe a gassing for himself in the run-up to Christmas 1939.

By January 1940, Lange had the privilege of heading a unit bearing his name: the Sonderkommando Lange, the Lange Special Detachment. He was given a team of some fifteen men drawn from assorted security services, together with an assistant, an SS officer, two non-commissioned officers and a black Mercedes that came with its own chauffeur. They were to take some of those early experimental findings into the field. Their initial subjects would be the disabled and the mentally ill, those deemed unworthy of life under the Nazi euthanasia programme. Such people were held to be both a drain on national resources – 'useless eaters', consuming resources but serving no purpose – and a threat to the German gene pool. It would be the task of Lange and his men to remove them, ensuring that the blood of the next generation would be strong and pure.

It was in that spirit that the Lange Detachment turned up at the Warthegau mental hospital at Kosten on 15 January, where a Dr Banse had been considerate enough to sort the patients into categories in advance. Those deemed to be the most useless, incurables and those with no family were then ushered into a specially designed van.

This vehicle looked benign enough, painted as it was in the livery of Kaiser's Kaffee Geschäft, Kaiser's Coffee Company. Except it was not selling coffee. Instead, it was an *Einsatzwagen*, custom-fitted with those cylinders of carbon monoxide. The driver would open the valve on the bottle and, through a rubber hose, pure gas would enter the van's sealed area, where perhaps forty passengers were crammed together. As the van drove away and gas filled the compartment inside, the screaming and groaning would begin. So too would the hammering and the knocking on the sides of the vehicle. But it would last only a few minutes and then all would be silent and still.

When Lange's men unlocked the doors, they would find a pile of corpses, dead from carbon monoxide poisoning, that had to be disposed of, a task that could take several hours. Once it was done, the Lange Detachment would return to the hospital with an empty van to be filled up with the next batch of victims.

They repeated that process over and over until, within a week, they had killed 534 Polish patients. Following a similar operation at the Dziekanka psychiatric hospital in Gniezno, east of Poznań, where they gassed more than a thousand people in two stages, on either side of the Christmas break, the Lange Detachment was demonstrating that it could deploy a new piece of technology: a gas chamber on wheels, a vehicle whose only destination was death.

The Lange Detachment would spend the spring of 1940 roaming the region of newly conquered Poland now renamed as Reichsgau Wartheland – a *Reichsgau* was a Nazi administrative subdivision – rounding up patients from hospitals and sanatoriums, or even directly from their homes, and packing them into the van with its bright promise of a cup of fresh coffee. The wife of one doctor in charge of a hospital emptied of 499 of its patients in the first week of April 1940, branded the group the 'psychopaths' club'.

Lange's team was soon hitting its stride. A senior SS commander in East Prussia was impressed enough to want to avail himself of Lange's services, even if that meant paying a charge. He 'rented' the Lange Detachment for nearly three weeks in May and June 1940, stationing it in the transit camp at Soldau. From there, and in short order, Lange's team gassed 1,559 German patients suffering from mental illnesses, as well as up to three hundred Poles with similar conditions. The process did not vary: Lange, by now promoted to the rank of SS-Obersturmführer, and his men would herd forty or so victims into the van, kill them en route, dump the bodies in the surrounding countryside and return to camp about three hours later. The agreed fee was ten Reichsmarks for each victim, though the SS commander never quite got around to paying the bill.

For a while, the Lange Detachment was told it could stand down. They were seen to have done an excellent job. The *Gauleiter*, or district governor, overseeing Lange's work presented him with a token of his appreciation, an inscribed amber box. Himmler himself decided to reward the team with a coveted prize: a holiday in a place of their choice. They chose to take a break in what was now the Nazi-occupied territory of the Netherlands. After all, they had earned it.

11

Time to Die

Maria, Winter 1940

THE NIGHT OF broken glass had left Maria von Maltzan with a redoubled motive to resist but she also now had greater means, in the form of a larger apartment. Soon, and throughout the coming years, it would become a refuge for those who were permanently on the run: above all, Germany's dwindling number of Jews.

There had once been just over half a million Jews in Germany, more than 160,000 of them in the capital. But those who had not fled after the Nazis took power in 1933 had been deported, the first wave despatched to a camp in newly occupied France in October 1940 and then, a year later, to mysterious destinations in the east. Now Jews were nowhere to be seen in the country, at least not officially. Those who stayed were known as U-boats, submarines, because they existed only below the surface — in the silence and the dark.

The Nazi hunt for hidden Jews had become part of daily life. It had intensified in 1935, with the passage of the Nuremberg laws, and intensified again after the November pogrom. Once Germany was at war a year later, it would become unrelenting.

Wartime made hiding harder and the risks graver. The deportations that began in 1940 were followed in September 1941 by the Police Regulation on the Marking of Jews, an edict that required every Jew over the age of six to wear a yellow badge in public, at all times. The instructions were very specific: the badge was to be in the form of a six-pointed star, the Star of David, the size of a human palm, edged in black on yellow fabric, and 'worn visibly, sewn securely onto the left breast of the garment'. Written in the middle, in black, would be the single word *Jude* — Jew.

THE GUESTS

Any remaining Jews were meant to live together in officially designated 'Jews' houses', those marked with a star. Their purpose seemed obvious: they would surely be nothing more than convenient collection points for deportation and were to be avoided at all costs. If a Jew in Germany were to stay alive, it was essential to remain submerged.

As word got around, a veritable fleet of submarines headed for the Maltzan apartment on Detmolder Strasse. It became a meeting place and a sanctuary. Traffic was constant. On any given night, there might be as many as twenty secret Jews finding shelter there.

The challenge came when there was an air raid, which from February 1942 happened nightly. Maria could hardly lead a troop of Jews into the official shelter in full sight of her neighbours, any one of whom might have denounced her by first light. Luckily, she discovered a side cellar which no one else seemed to be aware of. As soon as the siren sounded, she would lead her 'illegals' into that hideaway, instructing them to remain silent until she returned. She would then head to the main cellar, accompanied by her dogs. If she was spotted at that point by a neighbour, so much the better: they would have seen that she was alone. If someone asked why she was using the cellar rather than the designated shelter, she had an answer for that too: animals were prohibited and she was a good citizen who, naturally, always obeyed the rules.

Daytime presented its own problems for the secret Jews of Berlin. Not every submarine had a place to hide around the clock. In the hours of daylight, some had to break the surface. They might simply wander around the city, hoping that if they kept moving they would not be noticed − or stopped. They might stroll around the zoo or visit the park. At night, some would sleep in the woods or the doorways of shops. Or, if they were very lucky, under the roof of Countess Maria von Maltzan.

One was luckier than most. Just before the outbreak of war, Maria had been visiting a friend who taught private English lessons in her home. The woman's pupil that day was a man who had worked in business until his contract was suddenly terminated in the month of Kristallnacht. He was studying English now because he planned to get out of Germany and make his way to Britain. Everything was arranged; there was even an apartment in London, rented by relatives, waiting for him and his mother. But the move kept being postponed: he couldn't get a work permit or the required papers, and there was no question of his mother going without him. Like so many German Jews of her generation, she found it hard even to contemplate leaving. Berlin was the city she knew; Germany was the country she had always thought of as home.

And so, while so many others had escaped years earlier, Hans Hirschel, thirty-nine years old and a loyal son, was still in Berlin, living with his mother. Visiting him was a risk: pure-blood Aryans were not meant to enter a Jewish house. Most women would have stayed well away, for their own safety. But not Maria. She and Hans devised a protocol. They would fix an exact time and Maria would be there on the dot. Hans, stationed behind the front door, would open it at the appointed second, allowing his guest to slip inside. That way, there would be no lingering on the doorstep. She would be observable by eagle-eyed neighbours and would-be informants for the shortest time possible.

They quickly became close. She spent Christmas 1939 with the Hirschels, mother and son, smuggling into their home a large carp and a rabbit, which, given the increasing scarcity of food, was quite the festive feast. She talked of her plans with Hans, of how she wanted to fulfil the dream she had had since childhood and study veterinary medicine. Her mother had been dead several years now, so that obstacle was removed. Besides, it made practical sense: as a veterinary student, she should be able to resist the call-up to perform some other form of national service, one that might compel her to assist the Third Reich. Shortly after the November pogrom, she had come under pressure to join the Nazi party or at least an affiliated women's organisation. Her way out had been to join the German Red Cross. The experience had been infuriating: she had had to attend monthly squad meetings, where the women would march around singing songs of national socialism and the evening would end with a triple round of Sieg Heils, leading Maria to be scolded by her superiors for failing to deliver the cry as commanded. As a student vet, she should be exempt from such obligations.

For the next two years, Maria and Hans kept up a secret affair, she following her vocation, he keeping his head down as his mother held on, against the odds, to her home in Kaiserallee, the pair seizing stolen moments together whenever they could, including at Maria's place. They developed a cover story, should a visitor ever come to call. Hans would be Professor Schröder, a friend of Maria's who just happened to be in the house, the ruse aided, in Maria's view at least, by the fact that Hans did not look like the average German's idea of a Jew. Indeed, Professor Schröder could boast that he had fooled even those who might have expected to identify a Jew at a thousand paces, including a field marshal in Hitler's army.

For the rebel countess had serious Nazis in her family. The brother who had disinherited her, Carlos, remained a committed national socialist, right up until his death in combat in 1940. But he was outdone by Maria's brother-in-law, Walter von Reichenau, who had become Hitler's youngest field marshal and gave his name to an infamous order issued in October 1941, which instructed German soldiers to participate in the extermination of European Jewry. Specifically, the Reichenau Order commanded the German Sixth Army on the eastern front to be 'ruthless' in pursuit of 'the severe but just retribution that must be meted out to the subhuman species of Jewry'. It was in the zone of the Sixth Army, commanded by Reichenau, that tens if not hundreds of thousands of Jews had been murdered, shot into pits, by the beginning of 1942. The field marshal's only complaint about the Einsatzgruppen, who by the spring of the following year had murdered 1.25 million Jews and hundreds of thousands of Soviets, including prisoners of war, was that they were doing so much killing, and so quickly, that they were creating a shortage of ammunition. His proposed solution: an instruction that the SS executioners limit themselves to two bullets per Jew.

Reichenau made a point of looking up his sister-in-law whenever he was in Berlin, especially after the invasion of Poland. Though the two of them inhabited different worlds, and though he served the very regime she routinely defied, Maria would always say they had fun together. She liked his company. And so, inevitably, he met Professor Schröder, wholly unaware that he, the man who gave his name to the order compelling the Wehrmacht to participate in the extermination of the Jews, was in fact fraternising with a Jew.

TIME TO DIE

In February 1942, Hirschel's mother was served with an eviction notice on her apartment. As far as Maria was concerned, deportation was the obvious, inevitable next step, with the near-certain destination Theresienstadt, an already notorious concentration camp-cum-ghetto thirty miles north of Prague in the country that used to be Czechoslovakia. Hans's mother was set on staying in Berlin, albeit moving into a much smaller flat, and he felt it was his filial duty to remain at her side. Maria begged him not to do so, to open his eyes to reality.

'Hans, if you are taken to Theresienstadt, it will mean your death,' she said.

But it was not fear of death that finally succeeded in changing the Hirschels' minds, but rather the prospect of life. Maria had just discovered that she was pregnant with Hans's baby.

That was enough to break Frau Hirschel's stubbornness. Finally, she turned to her son, soon to turn forty-two, and said, 'You belong to your wife and child now.'

The plan was for Hans to move into Maria's apartment at Detmolder Strasse 11 as her ultimate secret tenant – a permanent one. But first, the countess had an ingenious idea.

It was time for Hirschel to die.

12

A Spy in Our Midst

Elisabeth, June 1940

FOR A WHILE, and a relatively long one at that, given the accelerated pace of change in the era of national socialism, Elisabeth von Thadden's peculiar blend of accommodation and resistance endured, surviving the 1939 evacuation of her school from Wieblingen to a rented hotel in Tutzing a month into the war. But it could only last so long. Eventually, the Nazis' patience ran out.

The prompt came at a school ceremony to celebrate the German victory over France in June 1940. Elisabeth marked the occasion by reading out a psalm. What she did not know was that one of her pupils took careful note of her choice of text, not because she was a particularly diligent student of the Bible, but because she was a spy.

The source of the trouble was that high-wire act Elisabeth had been performing between her principles and the pragmatic need to stay on civil terms with the new rulers of Germany. She had been meticulous in the effort, balancing every move she made. Even at the celebrations for her fiftieth birthday that same summer, as the girls performed scenes from *A Midsummer Night's Dream* in her honour, you would have found among her guests both a Jew and a Nazi. The Jew had been born Margot Kohn, though she was now a convert to Catholicism and the wife of Wilhelm Hausenstein, an eminent art critic banned from publishing since 1936, thanks to his refusal to remove the names of Jewish artists from his writings or to designate modern, usually Jewish, works as 'degenerate'. But also present was Baroness Martha Reichlin von Meldegg, who led the Nazi Women's Association in Tutzing.

It must have seemed a prudent act of local diplomacy, keeping one of the town's ardent national socialists on side. What Elisabeth did not realise was that the baroness's ardour extended to encouraging her thirteen-year-old daughter to act as a secret agent within the school, monitoring all that she saw and heard, and reporting any deviation from Nazi orthodoxy to her mother. Which, in turn, her mother then reported to the authorities as 'deficiencies of conviction'.

An official letter arrived soon afterwards. It had come to the attention of the regime that Fräulein von Thadden had read from the Old Testament at a ceremony devoted to the honour of the German people. She had sullied a national day with the taint of Jewish scripture.

Now began a war of correspondence, as the authorities confronted Elisabeth with an ever-expanding list of offences, including her decision to place the Jewish-born Margot Hausenstein in the seat next to her own at her fiftieth-birthday party, a titbit surely passed on by the sharp-eyed baroness, who had not been accorded the same honour.

The following winter a Gestapo inspector came to call, making two visits in February 1941. He discovered myriad deviations. The students did not issue the proper greeting of 'Heil Hitler!' Indeed, at that victory ceremony where a psalm of Hebraic origin had been uttered, not a word had been said about the Führer. The leader was literally missing: there was no portrait of him on display. (It had been left behind in Wieblingen.)

In English lessons at what the inspector called this 'Oxford for ladies', students were taught to sing, by heart, an anthem of the enemy: 'Rule, Britannia!', no less. (When the head was asked to justify this outrage, she explained that the melody was exceptionally beautiful.) As for the 'full Jew' Frau Hausenstein, the inspector confirmed that Elisabeth had not only maintained 'intensive contacts' with her but had the temerity to consider her only 'a half-Jew'. No less outrageous, this Hausenstein was a regular guest at the school and was received by the students with 'deep curtsies'.

As if to confirm the care Elisabeth had taken to stay on the tightrope between her conscience and the school's survival, the Gestapo examiner seemed to struggle to find much else he could pin on her in his fifteen-page report. He noted that, though students had knitted socks for soldiers in the winter of 1940, as the state had demanded, they had contrived to deliver fewer than had been required. Further, he complained that the head was 'extraordinarily bossy' and made the fairly astute observation that if Nazism was not 'openly' opposed at the school, it was, in effect, 'abolished' by the continued assertion of other values and sources of authority. In the Thadden school, it was clear that both the traditional ethos of the aristocracy and Christian belief still mattered, and that left little room for Adolf Hitler.

Overall, the indictment cast Elisabeth as conceited and arrogant, politically disloyal and insistent in her refusal to bend the knee before the state and the party. She had suspect relationships with fellow aristocrats and senior military officers, and it was clear that even official intervention would not shift her 'political attitude'. So long as the school existed with Elisabeth von Thadden as its director, Christianity, not national socialism, would be its organising principle. The girls it produced would be either indifferent to the German state, or injected for ever with the 'poison' of opposition.

By the end of the month, the decision had been made. Elisabeth's state permit was revoked and the institution to which she had devoted herself was closed down, on the grounds that it 'did not offer a sufficient guarantee of a national socialist education for young people'. In its place came a new, renamed 'secondary school for girls and German home school'. The pupils and most of the staff were allowed to stay on, but Elisabeth was out. To former students who sought to console her, she affected to be sanguine, even relieved. No longer would she have to disguise private dissent with public compliance: 'I don't have to burden my conscience with any more dishonesty.'

But for the second time in her fifty-one years, her life had lost its centre. As surely as running the family estate had supplied her with purpose and meaning when she was in her twenties, so the school had performed that function in the decade and a half since she had founded it. And now it was gone.

She did her best to keep busy, taking on some teaching in Tutzing, and she eventually got a job at the headquarters of the German Red Cross in the Berlin suburb of Babelsberg. It was not education, but it was close: she was tasked with organising the reading material that would be included in the parcels sent to German prisoners of war held as captives of the Allies. Meanwhile, her domestic arrangements brought a measure of stimulation, if not comfort.

She rented two small, sunless basement rooms at Carmerstrasse 12. The flat two flights up belonged to Anna von Gierke, one of those advocates for women's education who had so inspired the younger Elisabeth. Like several of the others, Gierke had been driven from her position because of her Jewish ancestry. Now she lived in retirement with her companion and former colleague, Isa Gruner.

That apartment was spacious, especially when the doors were opened out to the veranda, and the two women were welcoming hosts. So welcoming, in fact, that they had turned the place into an unofficial advice clinic, a refuge where Jews and others facing persecution could come for help. On Wednesday evenings, they would hold a salon, bringing together as many as eighty guests for a light supper and either a lecture or a session of Bible study. They might hear a talk from a dissenting cleric – Pastor Martin Niemöller was a regular, when he wasn't detained in a concentration camp – or from a scholar of astronomy or of the South Seas expounding on their latest research. Afterwards, the informal conversation would stretch on late into the night. And as these Christians of conscience talked, there would be a collection, the guests handing over food stamps for those persecuted souls who were in hiding.

Those evenings were both fascinating and useful, but Elisabeth was often distracted. She could not help herself: she still pined for what she knew best. So badly did she miss Wieblingen castle and her students that she looked forward to her trips back to Heidelberg, even if those were for board meetings where the only agenda item was the administrative winding-up of the now-defunct school. She could not let go of her dream. Sometimes she would meet up with a former teacher. 'You must come back,' Elisabeth would say, 'we're getting the school back.'

Perhaps her friends nodded politely. Perhaps they encouraged her. Maybe some believed that what she dreamed was true. However they responded, even the most pessimistic among them would have had no inkling that Elisabeth von Thadden's future was, in fact, slipping ever further from her grasp.

13
Trial Run

June 1941

AFTER AN INTENSE spell of killing, Leo Lange returned for a while to his duties in the Gestapo office in Poznań. But in June 1941, duty called once more and the unit that bore his name was reactivated. They returned to the Dziekanka facility in Gniezno that month, Lange and his men loading their gas van once a day, and kept at it through the summer. They murdered patients from a nursing home in Bojanowo, a home for the elderly in Stawiszyn and hospices in Łódź. They murdered patients at a Jewish hospital in that city's ghetto, and a group of Jewish men they picked up in Frankfurt an der Oder. They were tireless.

In August 1941, Lange would be paid a high compliment. Now rated as an expert in the field of killing by gas, his presence was requested by one of Himmler's most senior commanders, Erich von dem Bach-Zelewski, the man who had been the prime mover behind the construction of a new concentration camp in Silesia that would become known as Auschwitz-Birkenau. Colleagues speculated that the prompt for the suggested meeting was the ever-louder slew of complaints emanating from Einsatzgruppe B, one of the travelling death squads roaming Nazi-occupied territory and killing Jews. Shooting women and children was exacting too great a psychological toll on the killers. It was too direct. Perhaps Lange's piece of technology, which allowed murder at one remove, might offer an answer.

Accordingly, in September 1941, the focus of Lange's work shifted, thanks to a change in policy at the highest levels of the Nazi system. From now on, the Lange Detachment were to devote their ministrations not to the mentally ill but rather to those regarded by national socialism as the greatest threat to the racial purity of the fatherland. They were to engage in the mass killing of Jews.

Once again, it began with a test run. The subjects of the trial would be the six thousand or so Jews who had recently been herded into three small rural ghettos in Konin County, originally to make housing available for German families moving into the area. But now the decision had been made to liquidate those ghettos. The task would fall to the Lange Detachment.

They started with the Jews of Grodziec and Rzgów. The Jews of those ghettos were told they were to be resettled further east, to work as farm labourers. In Rzgów, they were ordered to assemble at the local fire station and to bring four Reichsmarks per person: they were told that that sum would cover the costs of the medical examination they would undergo to establish their suitability for work.

Once they arrived, they were instructed, politely, to hand over their bags and belongings: their luggage would travel separately, they were told, to be picked up at their destination. Next, they were loaded onto horse-drawn wagons driven by local Poles and taken, first, to the old synagogue in Konin and from there to the Niesłusz-Rudzica forest. There, in a period of twenty days that straddled the end of September and the start of October, they were murdered, their bodies dumped into three mass graves. The killings were done by Lange and the detachment that bore his name.

They used a combination of methods. On the first day, they seemed to operate like the other Einsatzgruppen working in Nazi-occupied territory, shooting the women, men and children of Konin with machine guns. But otherwise, and this was what the exercise was designed to test, they deployed the method the Lange Detachment had been perfecting: loading the Jews into the van previously reserved for the mentally defective and gassing them to death.

By now, they had a practised sequence. Ahead of the gassing, and in a forest clearing, the Jews were told to undress completely and leave their clothes in a pile. Then they would be herded into the van, which would set off. It must have taken a roundabout route through the forest, no doubt to give the carbon monoxide time to do its work, because it would come to a stop just a few yards away, at a series of pits dug in advance by a labour detail of Polish prisoners recruited by Lange. These same men would be the ones to remove the bodies from the van. From the way the naked bodies lay, a man and a woman entangled with perhaps a couple of children, they could see that whole families had been gassed together. As quickly as they could, the workers would throw the naked corpses into the pits, covering them with branches as a rudimentary and temporary form of camouflage. Less easy to hide was the ooze that soon leaked from the burial pits, a stinking liquid that smelled of chemicals.

The labourers' final job was to sort through the items left by the Jews when they were ordered to undress. At the end of one shift, the pile consisted not only of men's, women's and children's clothes, but also combs, soap, sponges, gingerbread and lemonade bottles. The clothing would be loaded into the gas van and later searched for valuables. In every area of their work, no matter when, where or how they did it, the SS were consistent in this pursuit of economic benefit. The aim was not only to murder Jews but to dispossess them too, to steal everything they had.

If Konin was a pilot scheme, it was deemed a success. So much so that, in November 1941, with Lange now elevated to the rank of SS-Hauptsturmführer, the Lange Detachment was invited to establish a camp of its own. No longer on the move or forced to improvise in a forest, this would be a fixed, stationary facility. It would be in a village called Chełmno, about thirty miles north-west of the city of Łódź, and it would be the first of its kind, not a concentration camp holding prisoners but a dedicated extermination centre, its sole function murder. And its commandant would be Leo Lange.

14

A Secret Funeral

Maria, January 1942

COUNTESS MARIA VON Maltzan sat her lover down and asked him to write a suicide note.

She had had an ingenious idea, one that turned on her realisation that in the Germany of the Third Reich, there was nothing more worthless than a dead Jew.

Hans Hirschel addressed the note to his mother, explaining that his life in Germany was over: it was no longer possible to live. He would drown himself in the Wannsee, the lake that was one of the city's prettiest spots. Berliners went there to swim, to mess around in boats, to picnic. Wannsee would be his final resting place. (He did not know that, during that same month of January 1942, Wannsee had also seen some of the Third Reich's highest-ranking officials gather to co-ordinate the implementation of what they called 'the final solution to the Jewish question'.) It was time, wrote Hans, to say farewell.

As planned, Frau Hirschel took the letter to the police, a distraught mother grieving for her beloved son. As predicted, the police did nothing – let alone mount a search for the body of a Jewish suicide – save for one critical thing. They recorded, in an official police document, that Hans Hirschel was dead.

The ink was scarcely dry on the paperwork when the ghost of the dead man moved into Detmolder Strasse 11. Not that he had the place to himself for long. In addition to the procession of overnight guests, the apartment was soon home to permanent residents besides Hans. There was the former chief chemist of a large nitrate factory and heir to a family fortune, Dr Max Botho Holländer, who entrusted all the jewellery and cash he had to his wife so that she might prepare an escape route out of the country for them both. Trouble was, she took the money and left her husband behind. Maria hid him for several months, along with one Günther Hirschel, who, despite the shared last name, was not a relative of Hans's but a former colleague.

Now there were three men in the house, who all had to be concealed and provided for by a pregnant woman with a single ration card.

The first requirement was an iron self-discipline. Sure, she could be slovenly herself — her table manners were atrocious, she was famous for them — but she understood that if the men in her charge were to stay alive, she and they would have to be in control of their every movement. When she was out during the day, officially tied up with studies that could keep her away from home for thirteen hours at a time, the apartment would have to be as quiet as a grave. If there was so much as a creak of a floorboard, one of the neighbours would hear it and a denunciation would follow.

Her instructions were, then, unwaveringly strict. In her absence, no one was to flush the toilet. No one was to warm the stove: the smoke of the exit pipe would be seen outside and give them away. No one was to talk above a whisper. No one was to turn on the lights. Above all, no one was to leave.

For Dr Holländer, those restrictions proved too much. Scalded by the disloyalty of his wife, he had fallen in love with one of the other crypto-Jews who had previously come to Detmolder Strasse, though this woman was American and armed with Aryan papers. Hans let Maria know that the couple were having daytime rendezvous, that Holländer was leaving the flat to go and see her. Maria gave him a stern warning, but it was no good. He kept at it. Eventually, she asked him to leave. Later she learned he had been caught by the Gestapo, and everyone knew what that meant. Maria was badly shaken, but she refused to feel guilty. She had done all she could.

There was so much to think about, so many dangers to guard against. Maria persuaded a local hairdresser, and fellow anti-Nazi, to teach her how to cut men's hair and beards. It was an essential precaution because a visit to the barber could prove fatal. Customers would sit for a long time, they would start talking: too many submarines had got caught that way. The hairdresser had been confident that Maria would pick up the requisite skills fairly quickly. After all, he said, 'You can already trim dogs.'

So much to think about, so many pretences to maintain. She had to keep up appearances even when that meant behaving like the model relative of one of the most senior figures in the Nazi military. Early in 1942, her brother-in-law, Field Marshal Walter von Reichenau, died following an improbable series of events. It began with a heart attack suffered after a cross-country run in freezing temperatures and ended with head injuries sustained when the medical evacuation plane Reichenau was on crashed. Naturally, he was buried with the full honours of the Third Reich, in a state funeral that the countess was obliged to attend. With her Jewish lover hiding at home, Maria did as protocol demanded, sitting among the leaders of national socialism as well as the top military brass. Hermann Göring was close by, offering words of condolence that struck Maria as horribly mawkish. She found him, and the other leading Nazis, disgusting.

All the while, she had to keep an eye on Hans's mother. Frau Hirschel – Luzie – had been used to seeing her son every day, but now that that was impossible Maria – to Hans she was always Maruska – felt obliged to make substitute daily visits of her own. Those drop-ins brought Maria closer to the woman who would become her baby's grandmother until the day, in the spring of May 1942, when she arrived at the apartment to find Luzie ashen-faced and distraught. She explained that she had been reported by an agent of the Gestapo for breaking the rules that now governed Jews. She had failed to display the yellow star sufficiently visibly: it had been partially covered by her fur boa.

Within a few days, the deportation notice had come. Heedless of the risk, which was grave, Hans emerged from hiding to go to his mother's flat to say a final goodbye. Maria looked on as the pair held each other in a long, silent embrace. When they talked, Luzie was preoccupied less with her imminent deportation to a place whose newly Germanised name was Theresienstadt, and more with her fervent hope that Hans, and the future grandchild, would survive.

THE GUESTS

Hans noticed she was wearing black, one of her most expensive dresses. Ready by the door were her suitcase and coat. Inside the coat's lining, sewn there by Maria, was some gold and jewellery, to be turned into cash or bribes.

After half an hour, Hans rose to leave: it was too dangerous to stay any longer. 'My life began so richly,' his mother said. 'The end was pretty bitter.' It did not escape her son that she used the past tense.

Once she was sure Hans had gone, she turned to Maria and asked if Hans would survive. Maria's reply amounted to a promise. 'If I survive, he will survive.'

'How will it end?'

Now it was their turn to hold each other until Maria too had to go.

She returned the next day, even though she knew it was hopeless. A neighbour confirmed it. Luzie Hirschel had gone with great dignity, she said. There had been no scene or struggle; the Gestapo had treated her with respect.

Then this same neighbour, who Maria knew to be married to a Wehrmacht officer, said, 'Hans is with you, isn't he? You can tell me, because I would never betray you. Is he all right?'

Maria's reply was instant. 'Hans is dead,' she said.

In the days and weeks afterwards, Hans would ask a version of the question Luzie had asked Maria: 'Do you think Mother will survive?' She would answer that it was impossible to know. But from all that she had picked up, whether from her late brother-in-law or her earlier reading of *Mein Kampf*, she assumed the very worst. So eventually would Hans.

The thought of it filled him with both grief and guilt. He knew that his mother had stayed in Germany four years earlier, rather than take up a chance to flee to England, largely because she did not want to leave her son, who had failed to get the papers that would have allowed them to leave together. Maria feared the emotion was building in Hans and would eventually explode. It finally did late one night.

Maria was returning home from a long day of work when she heard loud voices coming from the apartment. They were men's voices and they were singing, at full volume, in the very place that had to be silent. She rushed inside to find Hans and an actor friend, also a submarine Jew, belting out words in a strange, alien tongue. It was an insane risk and she demanded they hush. Eventually they did and Hans – the secular, avant-garde intellectual Hans – explained that they had been incanting one of Judaism's holiest prayers: *Shema Yisrael Adonai Eloheinu, Adoinai Echad* – 'Listen, O Israel, the Lord Is our God, the Lord Is One'.

Soon it was summer, and Hans and Maria could focus on the life that was to come. Maria had enlisted a Swedish friend, Eric Svensson, to play the public role of father-to-be. The pair had cooked up the story when Maria first became pregnant, a fiction that would work to their mutual benefit. She would have an Aryan name to give to the registry office; he would have a story that would help cover up his own violation of Nazi law. For Eric Svensson was a member of another category of banned persons: he was a homosexual.

He took to the part energetically. The faux couple would take evening walks together, Maria making a point of introducing him to shopkeepers she knew as her future husband. She wanted to lodge her alibi in the minds of others.

In September, a month early, she went into labour. A friend rushed her to a hospital run by nuns from the Order of St Vincent, where she would be in a state of agony for hour after hour, stretching into the next day. The baby eventually had to be pulled out with forceps, with Maria under ether. When the child emerged, she saw that she and Hans had a little boy, with ears to match his father's. He was taken away immediately and placed in an incubator.

The following night brought a round of bombing to Berlin so heavy that the hospital's power supply collapsed, leaving the incubators without electricity. The babies inside had no chance.

Maria had one request of the nuns: that they allow a secret visit by the child's real father. And so, in the early hours of the morning of 9 September 1942, when no one would be around to see him, Hans Hirschel was ushered into a ground-floor chapel at the hospital to spend a few minutes with the son he would never know. Later the body would be buried in a children's cemetery in Stahnsdorf, the funeral conducted by a pastor Maria knew and trusted. Because, of course, even that had to be secret.

15

The Walk to Freedom

Hanna and Lagi, 1940

THE SOLFS, MOTHER and daughter, were too well-known in Berlin society to go unnoticed. Early in the war, the younger woman was ordered to attend another interview with the Gestapo. This time, Lagi feared the worst. She phoned her mother and said that, if there was no sign of her after six hours, Hanna should get help.

The secret police were accusing her of serious crimes. They charged her with being a 'Jew slave'. She had been seen helping Jews. They had had reports that, when the air-raid sirens sounded, she tended to go to the Jewish section of the shelter in her apartment building. What did she have to say for herself?

She explained that the Jewish couple in her building, at that point still officially allowed to remain in Berlin, were friends of hers. Once again, she was released. Lagi concluded that she and her mother were being granted a special leniency thanks to the depth and breadth of their overseas contacts. Someone high up had concluded that, while diplomatic opinion might swallow the persecution of hundreds of thousands of Jews, the arrest of a couple of well-connected Aryan women risked a scandal.

But Lagi also knew that, whatever efforts she had made at discretion, people around her knew her secret. Her neighbours had clearly reported on her behaviour during the air raids; they were watching her. Some of those who had noticed what she was up to evidently approved, such as the butcher's wife who would regularly go beyond what the ration card allowed to give Lagi a larger piece of meat, along with a wink. But, just as clearly, others did not.

And yet that did not stop her, or her mother, courting ever greater jeopardy. That might mean helping Jews with food or money. It might mean assisting the persecuted in their flight out of the country, even, if necessary, escorting them personally to safety in England: Lagi did that for two of her closest friends, the eminent gynaecologist and writer Dr Ferdinand Mainzer and his wife, in the spring of 1939. But it could also mean taking the ultimate risk: hiding Jews in their own homes.

Lagi did it several times, concealing in her apartment the 'non-Aryan' writer Annie Kraus for six weeks, even though she had not so much as met her beforehand. Sometimes Lagi would offer a hiding place to those Jews who had taken advantage of the same loophole so ingeniously exploited by Maria von Maltzan and Hans Hirschel: Jews who were, officially at least, dead. In theory, no one was looking for them. But that did not stop her living in constant fear whenever she harboured a 'submarine'. It was terrible when she was out: what if someone came to the flat, what if they got in and looked around? And it was no less terrible when she was in: every time the doorbell rang, she would tremble. Obviously, remaining in hiding was only a short-term solution at best. Better for everyone would be to find a safe way out of the country. And, for a while, she and her mother thought they had discovered it.

Together they devised an elaborate, and secret, operation to spirit Jews out of Nazi Germany. They had hit upon the method thanks, initially, to a rumour. Among the *U-Boote*, the submarines, of Berlin, there was often excited talk of some new escape route, almost always illusory. But this one checked out. Once they were convinced it was sound, Hanna and Lagi set about using it to secure an exit for the Jews they had been helping and who were growing increasingly desperate – and there were many.

The plan hinged on a small farm close to the border in Baden, in southern Germany. This farm had two particular advantages. First, from there you had only to walk along a path, threading through a few fields, to come out in Switzerland. Second, the family who farmed the land were amenable, whether out of sympathy for the mission, the promise of payment or a combination of the two.

THE GUESTS

All the Solfs had to do was get the submarines out of Berlin. After that, the escapees would head south through the German countryside until they reached the farmhouse. Once there, the family would make sure no one was around, then hurry the fugitive Jews inside and give them something to eat and a bed for the night. Next morning, just before dawn, they would wake their secret guests and then, noiselessly and in the dark, guide them towards the path through the fields. After that, the Jews were on their own.

It was not far to walk, and if they made it, if the submarines were able to break the surface and emerge into the sunlight of free, neutral Switzerland, they had one last task: to make their way to a shop, buy a postcard depicting the Swiss countryside and send it – doubtless with an innocuous message, and no real names – to the Solf house, Alsenstrasse 9, Berlin. That would be the signal confirming that they had got through and were safe at last.

That was the system. But it was hardly failsafe. Not long before, there had been one Jewish couple, underground for months, who were lined up for the Baden escape route: the woman was hiding with the Solfs, her husband with friends. Hanna and Lagi had arranged a date with the farmer; everything was set. As the day approached, the couple made a grave error: they ate in a restaurant, where they were identified and grabbed by the Gestapo. Hanna and Lagi found out about it from a cousin of the would-be escapees, a cousin classified by national socialism as an Aryan. The news was bad. Not only had the couple been caught, they had talked. The Gestapo had asked them to produce their belongings, and when they could not, the police demanded to know where they were kept. The man and woman had told the truth: Alsenstrasse 9.

Lagi packed up the couple's suitcases and waited for the knock on the door that would announce the arrest of her mother and herself. But, strangely, no knock ever came.

After a judicious interval, the Solfs decided to have another try. Once more, Hanna made the arrangements, booking the next passage via that same route for another Jewish husband and wife she had been helping. Mother and daughter hoped that this time things would be different, that this time it would work.

And so they waited for the rattle of the letterbox, and the

postcard, that would mean they could exhale. There were two deliveries a day, even now, in wartime. They waited and waited. But no card ever came.

Eventually, Hanna and Lagi found out what had happened. The Jews who had survived in hiding so long, evading the long arm of the Gestapo, had been undone by their very attempt at freedom. Soon after they rose to the surface in Berlin, well before they could walk through those fields and step across the border separating Nazi Germany from neutral Switzerland, they had been arrested. They were interrogated and very probably tortured. Naturally, they had been unable to withstand the pain. They told their tormentors all they knew of the escape route. And when asked who had led them to it, they did not lie. The name they gave was Hanna Solf.

16

Cast Out

Arthur and Irmgard, 1940

STEADILY, THE SPACE the Zardens had once occupied shrank. Arthur, who used to be the most powerful figure in the German Ministry of Finance, and his wife, Edithe, heiress to one of the country's largest fortunes, receded from Berlin life, like rare birds pulling in their plumage. They socialised less. The last big party they hosted had been in March 1937 for Irmgard's confirmation – as a Christian – with no fewer than forty-four guests at a single table. At the reception, the Lutheran pastor who had presided over Irmgard's entry into the church caught sight of a Jesuit priest who was a known anti-Nazi and friend of Arthur's and promptly walked out.

That night had been billed as a new beginning, but in truth it marked the end of an era. After war broke out, the Zardens moved to a quieter part of Berlin and began a life of tacit seclusion. They dismissed the servants, save for a cook. At nine o'clock each evening, in a ritual that they would follow for several years, they would close the windows, draw the curtains and place a pillow on the telephone, to block any listening device that might be secreted within. Then the Zardens would huddle around the radio, the volume turned down to the lowest level above inaudibility, and wait for the words of the BBC announcer: *Hier ist London*. It was in these moments that they might learn for the first time that what the Nazis had called a 'regrouping' was in fact a 'retreat'.

One month followed another. Arthur would show his face at the odd gathering, encountering fellow dissenters. But, after the yellow star edict was issued, Edithe, the child of Jewish parents, stopped going out. It might have been fear; it might have been shame.

In February 1943, she fell ill. The doctor diagnosed flu and ordered her to stay in bed. The very next night, she was dead, aged just fifty-nine. Maybe there was a simple medical explanation as to why a woman who had only ever enjoyed good health would die so suddenly and so relatively young. But she would not have been the only Jew in Hitler's Germany to find that, shunned and despised by the country they loved, the will to live had drained away.

Arthur wanted to bury the urn containing his wife's ashes in the family plot in Hamburg, but the Nazi rules against racial mixing extended even to the dead. So the earthly remains of Edithe Orenstein were buried in the Jewish section of the cemetery. The Orensteins had done everything Germany had asked of them. Benno had played his part in building up the might of German industry, before investing a fortune in war bonds so that the nation could fight its enemies. His daughter had been the loyal wife to a devoted and faithful civil servant of the republic. His granddaughter had been confirmed in the Trinity Church in Berlin. But in the end, Edithe Orenstein was seen not as a German but a Jew, and cast out. Her family comforted themselves with the thought that, had she lived, she would have been deported and eventually murdered. That she was spared that fate was a kind of mercy.

All of this pressed on Arthur in the months of mourning that followed. The shock and grief barely faded. Once a man of stature, he was now often nervous and agitated. Irmgard went out to dinner one evening, only to find her return home delayed by what seemed an endless night of Allied bombing. When she finally made it back in the early morning, she was greeted by a sharp slap in the face from her father. He had been waiting all night, out of his mind with fear that, having lost his wife, he had now lost his daughter.

Visitors were infrequent; Arthur Zarden was not only yesterday's man, but potential trouble. Anyone of ambition would find it safer to steer clear. One of the few to come by was Carl Goerdeler, the former mayor of Leipzig often mentioned in dissenting circles as a possible chancellor when, at last, the post-Nazi era dawned. But Goerdeler's presence made Arthur anxious. The politician came armed with that damned address book of his, packed with names and annotations, some of them rendered in code: a contact called

Schwarz might exist in the book as Weiss, a fitting cipher for a topsy-turvy age when evil was cast as good and black had become white, but hardly impossible to crack.

As they talked, Zarden saw his guest scribbling in the book, adding his lightly encrypted notes. He was horrified.

'Goerdeler, put that book away,' he said. 'Never carry anything in writing.'

The one-time mayor should have followed that advice. Before long, Germany's small band of dissidents and rebels would have reason to regret that he did not.

17

Present at the Creation

8 December 1941

OPERATIONS AT SONDERKOMMANDO Lange's new, dedicated site began on 8 December 1941, the first victims Jews from the surrounding Warthegau region. They were brought to Chełmno by truck, deposited at the main site of the camp, a vacated country estate that now stood behind a high wooden fence. They called it the *Schlosslager*, named for the building that stood at its centre, somewhere between an old manor house and a castle.

Leo Lange and his men had worked out a routine. The Jews were unloaded, one truck at a time, in the courtyard. What greeted them was meant to be reassuring: the sight of several men in white coats, apparently doctors, overseeing a process that they explained was purely sanitary. The new arrivals were told that they would soon be sent to Germany, to work as labourers. Before that could happen, and solely for reasons of hygiene, each of them was to wash and have their clothes disinfected. They were guided into the building, unaware that those helping them were not physicians of any kind, but rather officers of the SS.

Inside, the Jews were taken to a back room, where they were told to undress and hand over any valuables. There to receive them was a Polish civilian employed by the Lange team for this exact purpose, under instructions to write out a receipt for each item. Soon the prisoners would be empty-handed and naked.

Next Lange's men would lead their shivering captives into the cellar, only to descend further still, steering them down a ramp that sloped into the back of what seemed to be another room, smaller this time, lit by a modest electric bulb. Except this was no room.

It was the airtight compartment of a truck, specially designed for this purpose.

From the outside, it looked like any other large, grey van, with no indication it had been customised. But inside there were clues: the way the rear doors did not simply close, but sealed hermetically; the absence of any seats; and the way the floor was replaced by wooden grating, the kind you might see in public baths, with straw matting placed on top. The sharp-eyed would have spotted something else: between the driver's cab and the loading area there were two peepholes.

Once the prisoners were all in, and the rear of the van was full, an SS man would step forward to close the doors. For the first few weeks, it was the same procedure as before: the carbon monoxide bottles, the valve, the rubber hose. It was, in fact, the same van, though now it no longer promised a cup of Kaiser's Kaffee. The sign had been painted over.

But as 1942 began, the Lange Detachment retired that vehicle from service, in favour of a pair of new, state-of-the-art trucks. At first glance, the differences might have seemed minor: under the wooden grating of the floor, for example, there were now two tubes, each about six inches thick, extending out from the front cab. And yet the change was anything but cosmetic.

The new vehicles' key advantage was that they no longer required bottled gas. In the preceding months, it had dawned on the SS leadership that, as far as that commodity was concerned, supply did not match demand. Killing the entire Jewish population of a town was a task on a different scale from disposing of a few hundred mental patients here and there. It would require vastly more gas. Fortunately, the best brains in Nazi engineering had hit on an answer, one that had been discovered by accident.

After driving home from a party heavily inebriated, Arthur Nebe, head of the Kripo, the Criminal Police, had made the near-fatal mistake of falling asleep in his garage while the car engine was still running. A close shave, but it gave him an idea. He mentioned it to colleagues and soon they were trying it out. The first trial saw five mental patients put in a sealed room, which was then filled via a hose with the exhaust fumes from both a truck and a car parked outside. It worked well; all five were killed.

It did not take long for the breakthrough technology to reach Chełmno. The new vans required the mechanic not to open a valve but to attach a tube to the vehicle's exhaust pipe and simply start the engine. The airtight area filled with carbon monoxide, just as it had always done, but where the earlier victims had been poisoned by the gas in its pure, bottled form, those crowded inside now choked to death from the smoke and fumes. The driver of the van, wearing his Death's Head SS uniform, would stay in his seat throughout, keeping the engine running. He could relax, knowing there was no need to replace any empty bottles and no risk of ever running out. So long as the engine had fuel, the gas vans would always be equipped. Lange and his men were now operating a smoothly efficient system.

Once the screams and the banging of fists against steel had fallen quiet and everyone inside was dead, confirmed by using a flashlight to look through the peepholes, the duty mechanic would detach the tube from the exhaust pipe. But he would not open the doors, not yet. Instead, an SS officer would drive the van, now weighed down with corpses, to the second Chełmno site, a clearing in the forest a couple of miles away. They called this place the *Waldlager*, the forest camp.

It was here that the doors would be opened at last, a job for eight men. They would have to brace themselves for the stench of gas, which could be overwhelming. Then they would take the bodies out and dump them into mass graves that had been dug in advance. If one of the bodies began to twitch or move, if one of the Jews had somehow survived, the SS had orders to finish the job with a bullet.

The handling of the corpses was hard, dirty work, each body bearing the marks of death by asphyxiation. Some would be blue, others wet with sweat and urine or else covered with faeces and menstrual blood. But Lange's unit had an ingenious solution. No detail of Polish workers this time. Instead, they would get Jews to do the job. A few Jewish male prisoners would be separated from an incoming transport and attached to a separate *Sonderkommando*, a special squad of some fifty or sixty men. That group would be stationed at the forest camp, where they would wait for the arrival of the trucks bearing the dead. Now it would be their job to remove the bodies – which might belong to a friend, a wife, a mother, a son – and put them in the ground.

They could not attempt anything like a burial. Instead, they had to dump the corpses, one on top of another, like rubbish on a heap. Often, that meant grabbing hold of them by the feet or hair. There was a division of labour: two Jews would stand at the edge of the ditch, hurling in the bodies; two more would stand in the grave, packing in the corpses as they landed, head to feet, face down. If there was a pocket of space, it would not go to waste: that was where they would squeeze in the body of a child. Usually the dead came in batches, three vanloads at a time, some two hundred corpses altogether. It was all done at top speed, watched over by the SS.

After five weeks, Chełmno had proved itself. In January 1942, it would be assigned its part in implementing 'the final solution to the Jewish question'. From now on, the mass shootings and ghetto liquidations were to be understood as parts of a much larger whole. The Nazi state was now bent not simply on killing Jews, but on a goal much more ambitious: the eradication of the entire Jewish people from the face of the earth. It could not be done haphazardly, but would require intense organisation and a method that could operate at scale. To that latter endeavour, Leo Lange had made a crucial contribution. In Chełmno, albeit using technology that could and would evolve further, he had shown how it might be done.

The key agency in the implementation of the Final Solution would be the Reichssicherheitshauptamt, or RSHA, the Reich Security Main Office, and one of its most senior officials, the man tasked with organising the mass deportation and killing of Europe's Jews, Adolf Eichmann, visited Chełmno to see Lange's work for himself (though he declined an offer from the driver of the gas van to look through the peephole to watch the death throes of the victims). Now Chełmno would be given a crucial and large-scale job: the murder of the Jews of the Łódź ghetto.

It was a huge undertaking, for jammed into Łódź were not only the Jews of that city and the surrounding area, but Jews who had been sent there from across Europe, whether the former Czechoslovakia, Austria, Luxembourg or even Germany itself. Still, the system Lange had established was more than equal to the task. By April 1942, some 44,000 Jews from the Łódź ghetto had been gassed in Chełmno. Murdered along with them were five thousand Roma, or Gypsies, who had been deported from Austria.

Naturally, such an enterprise threw up myriad logistical issues to resolve. Lange made several trips to Łódź, where he would discuss with the ghetto administrator, Hans Biebow, how best to process the piles of clothing and valuables stolen from the dead. Above all, Chełmno was fast becoming a victim of its own success. As a factory of death it was so efficient that it was soon producing too many of its core product: human corpses. The stench became unbearable: the reek of decomposing flesh filled the entire area, nearby villages included. Unfazed, the SS had a solution to that problem too. In the summer of 1942, they ordered that in future the bodies should be burned in makeshift, open-air 'ovens'. These would be fashioned out of surplus rail track, forming a kind of massive outdoor grill. Burning fresh bodies in this way, and digging up old ones for incineration, naturally fell to the Jewish slaves of the *Sonderkommando*, as did sorting the clothing of the victims and clearing the vans of the blood, vomit and faeces that caked them after each gassing. No SS man needed to fear that word of any of this would ever get out: at intervals, the members of the Jewish special squad would be killed, so that they could never tell of what they had seen. Replacing them was easy. There was a constant supply of new prisoners, selected from new transports.

Still, none of this was Leo Lange's worry, in the same way that he managed to avoid the summer stench issue entirely. By the end of March 1942, he had passed on the baton of command to a colleague – though not before he had spent five weeks training his successor in the most efficient way to run the camp – and been redeployed back to Berlin. He could leave the Polish countryside safe in the knowledge that he had delighted his superiors with a job well done. Chełmno would eventually be credited with the killing of at least 172,000 people, including many of the Jews of Berlin – every last man, woman and child a clear threat to the racial purity of the German nation. Lange had been present at the creation. He was thirty-two years old, handsome and armed with the résumé of a stellar servant of the Third Reich, ready for his next challenge.

Having taken on the mentally defective and the Jews, his target now would be those who might look like members of the Aryan master race, but who in fact constituted the gravest menace of all. He was to devote himself to finding and defeating the enemy within.

18

The Path of Resistance

Otto, 1940

CLASSIFIED AS ON active duty, Otto Kiep was assigned to the Oberkommando der Wehrmacht, or OKW, the armed forces high command. He would work in its Office of Counterintelligence, under a new boss: Admiral Wilhelm Canaris, head of German military intelligence, the Abwehr.

Like Otto, Canaris was an old-school German nationalist, a veteran of the Great War and holder of the Iron Cross. Just a few months younger than Otto, Canaris was likewise no narrow patriot, but a man of Europe and the wider world, fluent in six languages including English. But unlike Kiep, Canaris was a Nazi true believer. Or he had been, once.

He was captain of a battleship when Adolf Hitler became chancellor, and sufficiently thrilled by the development to lecture his crew on the merits of national socialism. He liked the new man's promise of a return to firm, authoritarian government, his pledge to reverse the humiliation of Versailles, his unbending opposition to communism. Canaris shed no tears for the Weimar Republic when it was swept aside. Why would he? While Otto was serving the republic, Canaris had been plotting to bring it down: he had taken part in the failed Kapp Putsch of 1920, aimed at toppling Germany's fledgling democracy and replacing it with the rule of a single autocrat. Adolf Hitler always unnerved Otto, but Canaris had liked the look of him: the nationalism, the antisemitism, the cod-Darwinian belief in a battle of the races, it all appealed. After all, Canaris too believed that what mattered was 'faith, race and nationhood', and that Germany suffered from a 'Jewish problem'. Indeed, he even devised a partial solution. In the mid-1930s, it was Canaris who proposed that German Jews be identified by the Star of David as citizens of an inferior category, with only the rights of foreign residents, at least five years before that innovation was first introduced by Reinhard Heydrich in Bohemia and Moravia, and then across the Nazi empire.

But by the time Otto came under his command, Canaris's early enthusiasm had long gone. A first cooling came during that autumn crisis of 1938, when the Führer seemed to be in a rush to trigger a European war. Canaris had wanted to see a strong Germany, capable of getting up off its knees after Versailles, but he dreaded another continental conflict: he had seen enough bloodshed in the last one. Yet Hitler was eyeing up Czechoslovakia, a move that would surely trigger an immediate declaration of hostilities from Britain. As things turned out, Britain under Chamberlain acquiesced, but Canaris could see that Hitler's appetite for war remained undiminished: he seemed to crave it.

When the admiral's fears were eventually realised and war broke out following Germany's invasion of Poland, his disenchantment deepened. He saw what Hitler's armies were doing, whether it was the torching of Warsaw or the massacres of Jews committed by the Einsatzgruppen, those mobile death squads of the SS who would murder some two million Jews, mostly with bullets, before the Nazi authorities decided that gas chambers were a more efficient method of mass murder. Canaris witnessed for himself two hundred Jews in the Polish town of Będzin being herded into a synagogue which was then set ablaze. The war was not yet a fortnight old when Canaris set out to voice his objections to the Führer directly, visiting Hitler's mobile headquarters – a train, come to rest in Silesia – on 12 September 1939. He did not get very far. Before long, Canaris concluded that Germany's future required the overthrow of Adolf Hitler.

At his side throughout was an even more trenchant opponent of national socialism. It was this man, Canaris's deputy, Colonel Hans Oster, who had pulled the requisite strings to secure the OKW job for his old friend O.C. Kiep. For his part, Oster had decided much earlier that Hitler had to go: he had been involved in that 1938 plot to use the Czechoslovakia crisis as a pretext for a military coup, in the name of averting an avoidable war. But the British prime minister had refused to play his assigned part. The plotters assumed Chamberlain would take up arms against Hitler; instead, he laid them down.

So this was the air Otto Kiep now breathed. At long last, he was surrounded by allies: fellow patriots, who had come to see, even if it had taken them a while, that national socialism was a blight on the true Germany. And these men were more than colleagues; they were friends. A keen horseman, Oster would always break his Sunday morning ride with a stop at the Kiep house. Every week, without fail, Hanna would send her daughter, Hildegard, to the front gate, carrying a goblet of beer for Oster to drink, which he would promptly down in one.

As 1939 turned into 1940, Otto lost one comrade and gained another. The loss was his mother, who had fallen ill and for several days refused to see a doctor. When one finally appeared, Frau Kiep immediately asked if he was a national socialist. In the Germany of the late 1930s, the best answer to that question was usually 'yes'. But when the doctor confirmed that he was indeed a Nazi, his patient turned her face to the wall and refused to be examined by him. Before long, she was dead.

Weeks later, Otto had a chance to add a new face to his shrinking circle. In his early thirties, Helmuth James von Moltke saw the world, and Germany, much as Otto did. They both had roots in, and affection for, Britain; both had studied law there. And both believed Nazism represented a disaster for Germany. Moltke was more radical than Otto: he was younger, a more ardent Protestant and a socialist. But what the men shared was an increasing preoccupation with the day after Hitler, the new beginning that would surely follow a thorough defeat in war. They debated how a new government would emerge. What would be its complexion? How would it protect freedom after years of dictatorship? What would be its relationship with the outside world?

Otto was not always sure of the answers Moltke gave to those questions; some were too strong for his conservative palate. But he liked him and the group of people that gathered around him, often at Kreisau, the Moltke family seat in Silesia. Among them was one Adam von Trott zu Solz, a man of remarkable lineage – one of his grandfathers had been an ambassador under Bismarck, while his American grandmother was the granddaughter of John Jay, the first chief justice of the US Supreme Court – who was not only a fellow Anglophile with a record of diplomatic work in the US and Asia, but who also shared Otto and Moltke's view of national socialism as a moral and spiritual disease. That such men were in his circle only commended Moltke further.

So, when a job opened up in the OKW's legal department in January 1940, Otto recommended his young friend. With Canaris and Oster at the top, and men like Otto and Moltke dotted through the upper echelons, an anti-Hitler faction was taking shape at the heart of the German military.

For Otto, there was value merely in the access he now had to the facts – his duties included reading *The Times* of London and the *New York Times* and listening to foreign radio broadcasts – and the chance to discuss them with people who did not refuse to hear them. That chance was rarer than outsiders might imagine. Clearly, there were those who supported the regime and would not hear a word against it. But less obvious were those who shared Otto's hostility to Hitler and yet refused to talk about it, even with those who, they knew, saw the situation as they did. Part of it was simple fear: opponents of the Reich tended to meet an unhappy fate. But part of it was self-protection of a different kind. Otto might be criticising the Führer, or setting out the troubles that lay ahead for Germany, only for friends to change the subject. It was not that they disagreed. It was that the current state of their country was just too painful to contemplate. It was easier to look away.

But Otto did not read the signs and quietly keep his views to himself. On the contrary, the more he knew from his work, the stronger the compulsion he felt to pass on that information to others. It drove him to distraction that what his friends knew of the world, and the war, was limited to what they read in the Nazi newspapers and what they heard on the Nazi radio. They were learning of one glorious military victory after another, the nations of Europe toppling like skittles, the Reich reigning supreme. Those military successes were real, but Otto could see Germany as the rest of the world saw it and the danger it represented.

Socially, he was spending more and more time with those embedded in various resistance networks, while at work he was surrounded by colleagues whose stance was, like his, toughening. In April 1940, Hans Oster had crossed the line from opposition to sabotage, into what the Nazis would not have hesitated to call treason. Oster knew the date of the planned German invasion of the Netherlands and promptly passed that information on to the Dutch. Perhaps if they were forewarned, they might mount a stronger defence, denying Hitler yet another sweeping conquest after the swift seizure of Denmark and Norway that month. Oster's gambit failed. The Netherlands fell in May, along with Belgium, Luxembourg and, the biggest prize, France.

Hitler was at the height of his powers; resistance must have seemed futile. Life in Berlin was good – Otto and Hanna would take their daughters to the opera and to concerts – and peaceful. And yet it was now that the small, unofficial resistance cell within the OKW stepped up its activities, Otto included.

He might act as an envoy for Oster, passing a nugget of especially sensitive information to a particular individual or, at Oster's behest, signing a document that would act as an alibi for a fellow rebel in the ranks. Sometimes it would mean warning this man or that woman of an imminent inspection so that they had a chance to get rid of any incriminating material. In all these efforts, Otto and Oster were following the example set by their commanding officer: Canaris was regularly risking his own position to keep potential suspects out of the clutches of the Gestapo.

Whatever his formal affiliations, Otto now saw himself and his allegiances differently. He avoided wearing his army uniform. In the previous war, it had been a point of pride to put it on; now it was stained with the symbols of Nazism. At his desk at the OKW, despite serving as a soldier in the army high command, he wore the suit of a civilian. His youngest daughter, the child everyone called Baby, liked him to dress up in his uniform, and for a special occasion – Baby's seventh birthday – he might put it on. But he felt only shame.

And still he kept speaking. While others might look over their shoulder or lower their voice to a whisper, Otto would offer his views freely, barely paying attention to whoever else was in the room. The habit became especially marked as Germany's fortunes began to turn. At a dinner in March 1942, attended by officials and at least one general, Otto offered a prognosis so 'deeply pessimistic' that one fellow guest made a note of it in his diary. (Luckily for Otto, that guest was aligned with the resistance.) Otto's sister, Ida, had already warned him to take more care, and now his wife, brothers, friends and even acquaintances were constantly pleading with him to be more cautious. They feared this solid, middle-aged diplomat, previously so practised in the arts of tact and restraint, was becoming reckless. Yet Otto did not see it that way at all. On the contrary, it was his patriotic duty to tell what he knew. Not because he believed that those who heard him would necessarily use the information he supplied, but simply so that they would know it. When the air was filled with propaganda, it mattered that the actual facts should still exist, that they should live in the minds of others, not his alone. 'We are surrounded by lies,' he would say. 'People must know there are still Germans who love the truth.' To be informed, to know the truth and to share it: in a republic of lies like Hitler's Germany, these were acts of resistance.

Despite the strictness of his upbringing in Scotland and at boarding school, he had always been a passionate man. When a woman caught his eye, he was not above filling her hotel room with sixty deep-red roses. His fervour for his wife, Hanna, was such that the pair were once caught making love in the bushes of the Tiergarten in Berlin. But now his ardour was for the truth.

By 1943, the course of the war had altered, as Otto always knew it would. The shift was visible in losses in the east and in North Africa and demonstrated most palpably by the bombs that started falling on German cities, sometimes night after night. In Hamburg in the late summer, a ten-day bombardment destroyed over a quarter of a million houses and killed some 37,000 people. By November, Allied air raids were striking the capital, intensively and several times a week, and they would continue for months.

A turning point had come in February 1943 with the defeat at Stalingrad. That left no room for doubt: the days of Nazi glory were past. Oster appeared at the Kiep front door one day alongside his wife. Now promoted to the rank of general, Oster was overcome. He could not speak. Eventually, Otto understood: the general's son had been at Stalingrad, ordered to lead an attack against the Red Army that he knew would be futile. The son had refused to send his men to their deaths, and had died alone instead. Oster was consumed with grief, but also rage. Hitler could not be allowed to hold power a day longer.

Before long, Oster was letting Otto in on a devastating secret. There was a plot to kill the Führer.

19

The Blonde Poison

Maria, 1943

BY JUNE 1943, the Nazis were boasting that Berlin was *Judenrein*, free of Jews, but most knew that was not entirely true. There were still a number of Jews clinging on, in hiding. Determined to root out the last few, the authorities created a new cadre of Jew-hunters – one that consisted entirely of other Jews.

They called it the Search Service and they housed it in a building on Grosse Hamburger Strasse, previously a home for the Jewish elderly and now an assembly camp, a holding centre for Jews awaiting deportation. The operation depended on a simple bargain. Become an informer and, in return, both you and your family would be granted leniency, deported only to Theresienstadt, a place that did double duty in disinformation – presented first in Nazi propaganda as a spa town, where older Jews might enjoy a safe retirement, and later as a showpiece concentration camp in an elaborate hoax laid on for the International Red Cross, whose visiting inspectors were shown a renovated barracks, newly planted gardens and staged cultural events to prove that rumours of Nazi brutality were grossly exaggerated. Considering the alternative was the death camp of Auschwitz, it seemed like a good deal. As an added incentive, those who agreed to join the Search Service were allocated their own private and relatively well-appointed rooms in the former retirement home. What's more, they were granted free movement, in the form of green permanent certificates of passage that allowed them to roam around the city unsupervised, leaving the camp whenever they chose. They did not even have to wear the yellow star.

For some of those who had spent years on the run, living in

constant fear, the offer proved irresistible. They put themselves at the service of Gestapo official Walter Dobberke, who ran the recruits from Grosse Hamburger Strasse, constantly looking for new ones from among the inmates. Eventually, Dobberke had at his command a Search Service of eighteen Jewish informers. Among the submarines of Berlin, they soon acquired a name: *Greifer*. Grabbers.

For Hans Hirschel and the others in hiding, the implications were as awful as they were obvious. From now on, they could trust no one. For Maria, the danger was almost as plain. If anyone who was aware of the unofficial safe haven on Detmolder Strasse had been turned, they might betray her in a heartbeat. Now she and Hans would have to be wary not only of officials and nosy neighbours, but also those they had seen as their natural comrades.

The threat took various forms. Most straightforward were the *Greifer* who acted like regular agents of the Gestapo, stopping suspected Jews in the street and demanding to see their papers. Those who failed to account for themselves would be pointed out to Gestapo officers nearby and bundled into a bogus furniture van, the grabber climbing in after them, before the van sped to the assembly camp.

Or they might operate more subtly. A *Greifer* might approach a Jew, engage them in conversation and then whisper an offer of food or a hiding place. If the Jew agreed, the *Greifer* would suggest a time and place to meet later. The grabber would be as good as their word, keeping the appointment – except now they came accompanied by the Gestapo.

Of course, most *Greifer* could be merciful, if the price was right. A Jew who had been discovered might just secure an exemption from deportation if they had enough food, tobacco or cash to put in the pockets of the Gestapo, with the *Greifer* taking a little extra on top. Tens of thousands of Reichsmarks were handed over that way.

Some *Greifer* found they had a talent for the work, a gift for winning the trust, even sympathy, of their intended targets. One particular *Greifer*, a woman, would stop a man on the street and plead with him to take her for lunch. She hadn't eaten for days, she'd say; she had no money. Once seated in the restaurant, she would make her confession: she was an underground Jew. If that drew from the man the expected admission that he too was a Jew in hiding, she would excuse herself a few minutes later to visit the ladies' room. The Gestapo, doubtless watching and waiting for the agreed signal, would arrive soon afterwards.

The woman who pulled off that particular trick was the most notorious of all the grabbers. Just twenty years old in 1943, she was strikingly beautiful and sharply intelligent, exploiting both assets ruthlessly. She was born Stella Goldschlag, and at eighteen became a teenage bride: Stella Kübler. The marriage did not last long. Indeed, ex-husband Manfred Kübler was her first victim: Stella betrayed him to the Gestapo when required to prove her readiness to join the Search Service. He was subsequently deported to Auschwitz.

She became a prolific denouncer of her fellow Jews, the star of Dobberke's team with the best stats of the entire unit: she led the Gestapo to over three hundred *U-Boote*, her favourite prey being former colleagues or classmates from school. Sometimes she worked alongside a fellow Jewish informer, her lover and future second husband, Rolf Isaaksohn. Among the submarines, they became known, with dread, as Herr and Frau Iskü, a compound of the first syllables of their last names: 'Is' for him, 'Kü' for her. But she had a name of her own, in fact she had two. To the secret Jews who feared her, she was the Blonde Poison. Even the Blonde Ghost.

Hans and Maria were right to be on their guard against the *Greifer*. One day in 1943 two strangers knocked on the door of the apartment on Detmolder Strasse. It was no less than Herr and Frau Iskü themselves, the It couple of Nazi collaboration, and they demanded to search the place from top to bottom. They had heard that Maria von Maltzan was hiding Jews – and they were determined to find them.

20

A Bomb on a Plane

Otto, March 1943

ON 13 MARCH 1943, Hitler would be travelling back from a series of meetings with the Wehrmacht general staff in the east. He would return to Berlin by plane, except he would never land in the capital. Because on board that aircraft would be a bomb, placed there by men loyal not to Nazism but to Germany. Adolf Hitler, founder of a Reich built to last a thousand years, would be dead before nightfall.

Otto Kiep did not endorse the plan, but nor did he condemn it. He was torn. He could hardly fault the underlying logic: he had long ago reached the conclusion that Hitler was leading the country to ruin and, more gravely, that he represented a new creed that was morally repugnant, an affront to Christianity itself. But Otto had been raised from boyhood to believe in order, not chaos; in institutions and the rule of law. Assassination was surely at odds with everything he held dear. What's more, he prided himself on being a systemic thinker, one who considered underlying causes rather than focusing solely on current circumstances or individual figures. Removing Hitler would address the most immediate aspect of Germany's crisis, but it would not alter the mindset of the German people, which surely explained much of the country's predicament.

If that was how the argument raged inside Otto Kiep, it scarcely mattered. The decision was not his to take. Instead, a group of senior officers, who styled themselves the Schwarze Kapelle, the 'Black Orchestra', had formed their plan and were set on executing it: they called it Operation Spark. All Otto had to do was wait for the afternoon phone call that would tell him the deed was done.

At that point, the army would seize control of Berlin, Munich and Vienna, overcoming any resistance from the SS, and establish a new government. Otto was to be its public voice: with a native speaker's English and experience in the United States, he would serve as press chief for the incoming administration.

The 13th was a Saturday. The hours dragged by. As Otto waited, the men of the Black Orchestra went into action. They had fashioned the bomb with the unwitting help of Germany's sworn enemy, using plastic explosives seized from captured British agents by the Abwehr. The detonator was ingenious, as thin and small as a pencil, and containing copper chloride which, once activated, would take around thirty minutes to eat silently through the wire that would set off the firing mechanism. Those thirty minutes were crucial, giving the would-be assassins time to get away. Best of all, this was a time bomb that did not reveal itself: no burning fuse, no ticking. The trick was to set off the detonator and get the device on the plane at just the right moment.

The conspirators cleared that first hurdle. They transported the device to the airfield in Smolensk as Hitler was wrapping up his visit to the headquarters of the Army Group Centre. It was disguised as a gift: a box containing two bottles of Cointreau, supposedly sent from one German officer to another in settlement of a bet. One of Hitler's men agreed to take it, comrade to comrade.

At the last minute, just as the Führer's retinue boarded the Focke-Wulf Fw 200 Condor designated for his exclusive use, one of the Black Orchestra's key players primed the device and handed it over. Now the bomb was on board, set to explode in thirty minutes. The doors closed, and the plane soared into the sky. Down below, the conspirators counted the seconds. In Berlin, Otto Kiep stared at the phone.

If all went to plan, the explosion would fill the sky near Minsk; it would be deemed an exceptionally lucky strike by the Soviet air force and the age of Hitler would be over. There was no reason for doubt. The detonator had been tested and tested again. It did its job every time.

Including now. The copper chloride worked its magic, gnawing through the wire. But down in the unheated hold, the key part of the explosive mechanism had become too cold. It did not fire; the bomb remained intact.

The flight reached its destination safely. Adolf Hitler stepped off the plane unharmed. Operation Spark had had everything – except the spark.

Whatever his earlier ambivalence, once Otto learned of the bomb's failure, he was consumed with disappointment. He had begun contemplating a different future, one in which Germany might end this accursed war and make a dignified peace with its European neighbours. But once the news of failure reached him, he found himself back in the same, ever-darkening present.

The whole episode had stretched his nerves to breaking point. Nearly a decade earlier, he had wrestled with insomnia. Now it returned, its grip tighter than before. He might lie in bed for hours, or he might get up in the early hours and pace. He might pick up a book, only to put it down again. He might eat. But he could get no rest. Instead, his mind ploughed over the same questions. Sometimes his wife would wake and see that he was missing, only to find him in his study. She would beg him to sleep, or at least to try.

'How can I sleep,' he would reply, 'when I am in pain over my country?'

There was so much to worry about: the state of the war, the fate of Germany, his own family. It wouldn't be long before his boy, Albrecht, would be of conscription age: he would have to wear the uniform Otto had come to despise. Meanwhile, nowhere felt safe. With the nightly bombing of Berlin getting heavier, he wanted to get his daughters out and into the countryside with his sister Ida. Except Ida had worries of her own.

She had asked Otto to have a word with her daughter, Irmgard. The girl was becoming ever more indiscreet in her opposition to the regime. She was cracking jokes that turned on the fading fortunes of the German war effort, jokes that would be instantly branded 'defeatist' if the authorities ever heard about them. She had stopped greeting people with the required 'Heil Hitler!', even when she knew the people in question were committed Nazis or, scarcely less risky, officials of the state. And, like her uncle Otto, Irmgard no longer cared who heard her opinion of the Third Reich: she was all but voicing her views openly. Ida was growing desperate that her daughter could go the way of those others who had been brave, or recklessly stupid, enough to speak out.

Otto knew all about that. He had friends who had been arrested for saying out loud what he and others said privately. Among them was the young pastor and theologian Dietrich Bonhoeffer, who, despite a long track record of outspoken criticism of the regime, had become a colleague of Otto's in the Abwehr, adding to the ranks of the anti-Nazi cell within German military intelligence, the group that provided a refuge, a kind of *innere Emigration*, for those who had become irredeemably alienated from their country. It was bold, if not extraordinary, that Otto's superiors had recruited Bonhoeffer, a man who had delivered a radio address lambasting Hitler just two days after he had become chancellor in 1933, warning Germany not to descend into an idolatrous cult of the Führer. Bonhoeffer had condemned the Nazi programme of involuntary euthanasia, which murdered the disabled and unwanted; denounced the persecution of the Jews; and become a leader of that dissident faction, the so-called Confessing Church, within German Protestantism which stood against the de facto Nazi takeover of their faith, insisting that the leader of Germany's Christians was not Adolf Hitler but Jesus Christ. He was banned from Berlin by the Gestapo, barred from having his words published and driven to preach underground. Despite all that, the rebels within the Abwehr had found a place for him, on the pretext that his contacts within international Christianity would be of use to Germany. But it had not been protection enough. In April 1943, Bonhoeffer was arrested and taken to Tegel prison.

That event was fresh in his mind when Otto sat with Ida's daughter. He knew that the risks of disobedience were greater than ever, that the first defeats to the enemy on the battlefield had only stiffened the Nazis' resolve to crack down on the enemy at home.

'I think you're being very foolish,' he told her. 'This is a time to take care.'

Irmgard swiftly pointed out her uncle's hypocrisy. 'You say things against them all the time.'

He explained that it was different for him. He was a man of

politics and, if he were to be silent now, he would have no right to speak later. He was thinking ahead, to the Germany that would exist once the Nazis had gone. If anything, he explained, he worried he had not said enough.

'When this is over, people will say to me, "If you were against them, why weren't you in a concentration camp? Why are you still alive? How did you escape, unless you too were a Nazi?"'

But she was not in that position. She did not have to think of that future. She needed only to think of this immediate moment, and survival. No joke, no refused Hitler salute, was worth risking that for.

'Didn't you say that a person had to speak the truth?' she asked.

He had said that, because he believed it. And before long it would cost him dearly.

21

Closing In

Hanna, Summer 1943

HANNA SOLF HAD been a widow for years now, and her daughter, though married, was living a similarly single life. She and Hubert had married in November 1940 but they had had barely a glimpse of domestic life together. In September 1939, he had been called up for military service, despatched almost immediately to Poland, before seeing action on both the western and eastern fronts and in Norway. Theirs would have to be a long-distance love. His presence was felt most concretely in her new title: as she could remind officials and police officers, she was a countess.

Of course, the Solfs did not lack for company. The circle that carried their name still met under their roof, though the solace it provided was weakening. The talk had grown especially dark when the 'stars' started to disappear from the streets. Even allowing for those who had gone underground, it was striking how few Jews were now visible in Berlin. In Alsenstrasse, and in whispers, the women and men of the Solf Circle traded what little information they had on where the deportees had been taken. It was mostly rumour, all of it chilling. They spoke and listened to each other in horror.

And no one needed to spell out the danger they themselves faced. They had seen what had happened to friends who had once been Solf regulars, and they had seen it early. In February 1942, Nikolaus von Halem and Herbert Mumm von Schwarzenstein, the duo whose knack for parodying Hitler's speechmaking would bring welcome comic relief to the Alsenstrasse deliberations, were arrested along with more than two hundred others in Berlin and Munich, after the Gestapo discovered a resistance network mainly comprised of left-wing intellectuals and communists. Still, the secret police never made the link between the two arrested men and the *Solf-Kreis*.

That was hardly the first flash of the warning light. Earlier came the case of Count Albrecht von Bernstorff, a nephew of the former German ambassador to Washington and himself a long-time diplomat, who had spent the decade before the Nazi seizure of power at the German embassy in London. The Nazis had recalled him from that post early in 1933: they had heard that he would receive British socialists and trade unionists who came to protest against the Nazi policy towards the Jews. Once back at the Foreign Ministry in Berlin, he had suffered a fate similar to that of Otto Kiep, being forced out following his early opposition to the new regime. Unmissable at six foot six inches tall, he hardly helped his cause by routinely greeting the vigorous 'Heil Hitler!' of the ministry doorman with a cold and equally pointed 'Good morning!'

He had tried to make a new life in banking, but still he would not fall in line. He used his job to help Jews in their efforts to transfer assets out of the country and, at one point, hid a Jewish family in his flat on Hildebrandstrasse. In May 1940, there came a knock on the door of the apartment: the Gestapo arrested him and sent him to the concentration camp at Dachau. He was given no reason for his detention, but it was clear that contacts with foreign diplomats and journalists, explicit criticism of national socialism and conspicuous support for Jews were deemed to be grounds enough.

Bernstorff was released a few months later. If he was supposed to have been taught a lesson, he refused to learn it. He had been a guest at Hanna Solf's table when the Nazi party first took power and now he renewed ties both with her group and the Kreisau Circle, the latter named for the country seat of Otto Kiep's younger friend and fellow lawyer, Helmuth von Moltke. As the months went by, Bernstorff became more active, not less, and more daring. In August 1941, he convened a roundtable discussion of like-minded men, afterwards noting in English: 'Good conversation: No. 1 must disappear.' It did not take a cryptographer to decode that 'No. 1' was Adolf Hitler.

Bernstorff kept in touch with the Solf Circle until the day in late July 1943 when he was arrested again. This time there would be no release.

If that sent a shudder through those used to speaking their mind at the home of Hanna Solf, it was not the first chill of the summer. A few weeks earlier, Max Metzger — the pacifist priest who had drafted a letter to Hitler urging him to step down, only for friends to stay his hand at the last moment — put pen to paper again. This time he composed a memorandum on his country's post-war, and post-Nazi, future.

Always an idealist, he imagined a new 'Nordland', his code name for Germany, which would be a confederation of 'free states' committed to peace, human rights and social justice, a nation ready to play its part in a new grouping of nations, a kind of 'United States of Europe'. These ideas, which would have read as distant fantasies in the Germany of 1943, were the subject of spirited discussion in both the Solf and Kreisau Circles. But Father Metzger would not wait for either of those groups to move collectively; he was used to acting alone. He wanted his document to reach the British, and thought his best route would be via the archbishop of Uppsala in Sweden, known for his network of international, ecumenical contacts. Luckily, Metzger was in touch with a well-connected Swedish woman, Dagmar Imgart, who offered to smuggle the document to the archbishop. Metzger told Imgart to meet him at the Pius Abbey in Berlin; he would hand her the paper which would, in effect, constitute a proposal for a lasting peace, to be implemented the day after the war was over. They met and he gave her his memorandum — which is when the secret police burst in and arrested them both. Though in her case the arrest was for show. For Dagmar Imgart was, and had long been, an agent — code name V140 Babs — of Gestapo Group IV B, the unit tasked with monitoring Christian sects.

Even then the priest hoped for the best. He went into his interrogation reluctant to believe he could face any serious punishment for the crime of seeking peace. Before long he had named two names: Count Bernstorff and Richard Kuenzer. Indeed, he signed a detailed statement that he doubtless thought would exonerate both of the men he had mentioned. He said he had been invited to the home of 'Mrs Governor Solf' to give a lecture on the Christian movement he had founded, aimed at nurturing closer ties between Catholics and Lutherans in the name of Christian unity, and though he had been told both Bernstorff and Kuenzer would be there, the former did not show up and the latter was more than an hour late. Metzger's efforts did no good. By the end of July, all three men – Metzger, Bernstorff and Kuenzer – all of them part of the Solf Circle, were in custody.

And yet, knowing the dangers as they did, aware that men had been spotted in front of the building taking down car registration numbers, the rest kept coming to those gatherings. Sometimes one or other might be looking for a word of advice. But often these evenings gave them nothing more concrete than the chance to speak freely, among others who saw the world, and their country, the way they did. In Hitler's Germany, that alone felt like something rare and precious. Something, indeed, that would soon not exist at all.

22

A Secret Mission

Paul, Summer 1943

PAUL RECKZEH WAS new to this, hardly practised in the wiles of secret work, but his mission was clear. He was to travel around Switzerland as a messenger of the German resistance, meeting those exiles who were potential comrades of the rebels back home. He would foster links, nurture connections, all in aid of a better Germany. To the naked eye, he might look like nothing more than a presentable young doctor from Berlin's Charité hospital with an admirable curriculum vitae: having trained under the eminent surgeon Ferdinand Sauerbruch, he had worked with children, volunteering to put in extra hours helping those ailing youngsters after he qualified. But he knew the truth: that he had been called to an even higher purpose.

His first serious house call would be at the Zurich home of the theologian and social reformer Friedrich Siegmund-Schultze. Now fifty-eight, Siegmund-Schultze had been exiled from Germany since 1933. Soon after the Nazis took power, he had lost his social work organisation, the Soziale Arbeitsgemeinschaft, the movement he had founded with his wife and which had so inspired the young Elisabeth von Thadden. No matter that more than two decades had been committed to alleviating the suffering of the poor, its offices were shut down. If that was inevitable, it was only partly because of Siegmund-Schultze's devotion to the meek of the earth.

He was also an activist for peace. On the eve of the First World War, in August 1914, he had co-founded an organisation devoted to friendship between the world's churches. He had stood on the platform of Cologne railway station with the English Quaker Henry

Hodgkin as the two men pledged to each other, 'We are one in Christ and can never be at war', a promise that led to the creation of a new body: the Fellowship of Reconciliation. Every instinct Siegmund-Schultze had was at odds with the aggressive, militaristic nationalism of Germany's new masters.

In case that was unclear, in the spring of 1933, when the new regime was only a few weeks old, Siegmund-Schultze helped establish an international aid committee for German Jewish refugees. It did not take long for the newly created Gestapo to arrest him on ninety-three charges of 'racial help'. His punishment was expulsion: he, his wife and their four children were forced to make a new life in neighbouring Switzerland.

But the secret police never took their eyes off him. He knew that and would warn his guests accordingly. Once he was visited by one of his closest cousins, Anne Rühle, a former model who was a lifelong friend of Elisabeth von Thadden's sister Anza. During the course of their time together, he led Anne to the front door, suddenly opened it, stepped conspicuously outside and pointed to two men lurking nearby, both of whom were hurriedly trying to conceal their presence.

'Be careful,' he said. 'There are always people like that. They're now reporting that you're here.'

The Gestapo were not wrong to be interested in Anne's visit. They had read enough of the letters between the cousins to know that Siegmund-Schultze was still in touch with plenty of people back in Germany. But, try as they might, comb through every piece of correspondence as they did, they could not find any contact that could meaningfully be described as political.

They wanted to search the place where Anne was staying in Zurich, but were thwarted on that score too: Switzerland was neutral territory and the Gestapo faced legal obstacles that no longer existed back home. Had they got inside, they would have found a secret radio transmitter in the basement. Starting in 1939, when the war was new, that piece of equipment had been used to put out the first, tentative feelers for peace. It had been used to trade messages priest to priest, between Berlin and Canterbury, in the hope that the men of God might avert the disaster brought by the men of war.

If there was political activity to be found, it was of this variety. To the extent that Siegmund-Schultze was agitating against the Hitler regime, he was doing it as a Christian. A year into the war, Elisabeth von Thadden had travelled to Zurich to see her old mentor. That was partly because she wanted to spend time with a man who had become something of a father figure to her, but also because she had agreed to act as a courier, conveying messages between Siegmund-Schultze and the then pastor of the Swedish Church in Berlin, who was keen to broker a connection between the exile and Archbishop Erling Eidem of Uppsala in Sweden, an opponent of Nazism who had planned to make an intervention with Hitler himself: the archbishop believed in his own ability to persuade the Führer to change course. (This was the same hopeful, if not naive, peace track that had been pursued at such great cost by Max Metzger. The world of Christian anti-Nazi dissidence was small; circles, and efforts, overlapped.) The Uppsala initiative would come to nothing. But it encouraged some of those involved, including Elisabeth, to believe that the only way forward was peace, and that it would only be achieved by people of good conscience working together, even if they were from enemy nations, separated by impregnable borders and deadly armies.

So the home of an activist cleric was Paul Reckzeh's destination. If he were to do his job, offering himself as a bridge between Siegmund-Schultze and the dissenters he had left behind in Germany, he would have to get past the suspicion any man would feel if his letters were routinely opened and his family home constantly surrounded by agents, as Siegmund-Schultze's was, and convince him that they could speak freely, without fear. It would not be easy.

The first tactical choice to make was his cover story. Obviously, Paul could not just come out with it, baldly announcing himself as an envoy of the German resistance. He had to be tentative, lest he walk into a trap. He had hinted at it in the several meetings he had already had in Zurich, but the initial pretext he gave tended to vary. To some, he said he was in Switzerland for the clean mountain air, to aid his recovery from tuberculosis. With others, he went for misdirection, drawing on his actual job in the Reich Health Office to claim that he played a small, indirect role in the Nazi project of racial purification. He would say that he was in Switzerland at the personal behest of the Reich Health Leader, Dr Leonardo Conti, the physician who had led the Aktion T4 euthanasia programme aimed at improving the quality of the German race by eliminating those deemed physically or mentally weak. In this telling, Paul's specific responsibility was to conduct blood tests in the remote, sheltered valleys where Rhaeto-Romance culture still survived, so that the Reich might more precisely establish the ethnic character of the people who lived there.

That was the story he told Siegmund-Schultze when he arrived at his door. The older man was worldly enough to know that many opponents of the regime were compelled to do their professional duty, even if that meant aiding an endeavour they despised. The theologian understood and offered to introduce Paul to a fellow physician, who just so happened to be doing research in the same, highly specialised area. Paul faltered, unsure how to answer. Surely a young researcher would jump at the chance to confer with a colleague working in a shared, and narrow, niche? But if he did, how long would he be able to keep up the bluff about his supposed area of expertise?

Siegmund-Schultze noticed the hesitation and thereafter was on his guard, passing on his scepticism to his family. This supposed emissary of the resistance, he warned them, might not be all he wanted to seem.

For Paul, embarked on his first mission, the timing was awful. He was at a dinner in a Zurich restaurant with a group of contacts when who should walk in but one of Siegmund-Schultze's daughters. The group were all friends of hers. Delightedly, they introduced her to their newest acquaintance, a visiting German doctor. She joined the table, waiting for her moment. As soon as Paul Reckzeh got up and left the room, she whispered to the group about her father's hunch. As he came back, she said, 'Be careful what you say.'

But at least one person around that table was too tipsy for discretion. And because nothing is funnier than disobeying a request that's just been made, Paul was still returning to his seat when a cheerfully lubricated voice called out to him: 'Listen, you might be an informer.' Paul laughed. If he had left it at that, it might well have seemed the natural reaction of a man shaking off an obviously false, and ridiculous, bit of banter. But Paul must have been nervous because he kept on laughing. Not a dismissive chuckle, but long, hard, loud laughter. Too long, too hard and too loud, it didn't seem natural. The young men and women around the table were staring at him. For the second time since he had arrived in Switzerland, he had made a stupid blunder, arousing suspicion in the very people whose trust he needed to win.

Maybe it was the drink, or the self-absorption of youth, but the moment did not last. After exchanging a few baffled looks, the group returned to their previous concerns, the conversations and flirtations of an evening out. Paul could disappear into his seat.

It was clear that the community of German exiles in Switzerland were wary: understandably so. They assumed anyone keen to make even a tentative initial contact might be working for the Gestapo, and who could blame them? Paul could not return to Berlin with nothing. He had to work harder. To overcome the unease he had encountered, he would have to take a different approach, one that was more . . . personal.

23

Go On, Shoot

Maria, 1943

CONFIDENCE, THAT WAS the thing. Absolute confidence. If she had learned anything from her previous, multiple encounters with the Gestapo, the trick was to convey unwavering self-belief.

So it was now, as the men of the Nazi secret police searched the apartment of Countess Maria von Maltzan, the notorious *Greifer* Rolf Isaaksohn inside the apartment, Stella Goldschlag, the Blonde Poison, lingering at the front door.

Maria was a young woman, only thirty-four years old, and armed men were crawling over every inch of her home, searching for the Jew or Jews they were sure had found refuge here. As it happens, there was a Jew in this very room, hidden and holding his breath – but still Maria would not allow herself to show even a hint of fear.

The Jew in question was her lover, Hans Hirschel, and they had long prepared for this moment. When he moved in, more than eighteen months earlier, he brought with him a sofa bed crafted from heavy mahogany, one whose base was large enough for a person to lie in. Once the cushions were on, you couldn't even see the opening. Maria added a series of hooks and eyelets, so that whoever was concealed within could lock the box from the inside. Once that was done, it was impossible to open from the outside.

Hans had raised the obvious objection: surely he would suffocate in there. So Maria had taken a hand drill and made several air holes, covering them from the inside with cloth in a shade of red to match the sofa. Each day, she would ensure there was a glass of water inside – and enough codeine to suppress the persistent cough that might give Hans away. The bed-box stood ready at all times, his hideaway in case of emergency.

Now the emergency was upon them and Hans was inside, doing his best to make no sound as the two Gestapo men turned the apartment upside down. He could hear them.

A warning had come a few hours earlier. The woman who served as concierge of the building had passed Maria a yellow index card that had been dropped in the hallway. Just five words, one of them not even really a word, but enough to constitute a death sentence.

At Maltzan's there are 'J'!

It was a denunciation of the kind that was not rare in the Berlin of that period, as one neighbour accused another of secretly sheltering Jews. Prying eyes were everywhere, on the lookout for any sign of an Aryan with a secret in the attic or basement. The accused would sometimes turn accuser, to divert suspicion and ingratiate themselves with the secret police. That, Hans and Maria felt sure, is what had happened here. The woman who wrote that note, apparently mislaid by an investigating Gestapo officer, had earlier had the finger of suspicion pointed at her.

So the knock on the door, when it came, was not a surprise. Maria opened up to find a woman, Goldschlag, and two men, one of whom was Isaaksohn, the Blonde Poison's lover. The men demanded to be let in. She stalled them just long enough for Hans to retreat to the bedroom and, without making a sound, clamber into the hollow under the mattress and lie flat. That was at half past two in the afternoon.

The Gestapo agents wasted no time, pulling out every drawer, tearing open every cupboard. Before long they found a row of suits, clearly belonging to a man. They confronted her with them.

Maria told the truth. That she had given birth to a baby boy the previous September and 'I can assure you, he was not born of the Holy Spirit.' Only then did she lie, naming the father not as Hans, but as Eric Svensson, the man who had posed as her lover.

The search of the apartment continued. Lying in the box, Hans could hear the sound of feet scurrying across the floorboards. Maria was throwing a ball for her two dogs. Audibly irritated, the Gestapo men asked her to stop, but she refused. This was the hour when the animals were used to their afternoon walk, she explained. They had to be exercised.

As three o'clock passed, then four, they kept up their fusillade of questions. 'We know that a Jewish girl used your apartment for two weeks,' they said. (Those prying eyes had missed nothing.)

'It's true that I employed a girl, but she wasn't Jewish,' Maria replied. 'The papers were absolutely in order.'

'No, they were fake,' said one of the Gestapo men. Maria asked how she, a mere veterinary student, could possibly know of such things. Indeed, she seemed shocked at the very idea.

By now, they were in the bedroom. Hans could hear the three voices as the formal interrogation began. The men told Maria to sit. She lowered herself onto the sofa bed.

'We know you are harbouring Jews,' they said.

'That's completely ridiculous,' replied Maria, with all the hauteur she could muster. Inches below her, Hans Hirschel lay motionless.

The countess was gesturing towards the portrait of her father, an aristocrat in dress uniform, that held pride of place in that room. 'You don't believe that I, as this man's daughter, am hiding Jews.'

Hans stayed rigid, listening to every word. Now came the moment he dreaded.

The Gestapo men insisted that Maria open up the two sofa beds that were in that room. Hans could hear as she opened the first easily, doubtless revealing the empty space within with a flourish that confirmed the agents were wasting their time.

They turned to the second. His one. He could feel movement, the effort to lift the lid.

'Sorry, it won't open,' Maria was saying. She explained that soon after she bought it, she had tried, but without success. It could not be done. The men were not persuaded. They were tugging at it, determined to prise the opening apart.

And now Maria took a gamble, one that required iron self-confidence. Hans heard the words she used but could let out no gasp as she made her suggestion to the Gestapo.

'Take out your gun and shoot through the couch.'

She seemed deadly serious. As if she were not setting a dare so much as offering a reasonable solution to the stand-off. 'If you don't believe me, all you have to do is take out your gun and shoot through the couch.'

How long did Hans lie there, waiting for the Nazis' response? How long did Maria's words hang in the air as he braced himself? It would have taken only a second for one of the men to pull out a pistol and call this imperious woman's bluff. If they did, how long would it take for Hans to die? A few seconds? A minute?

Was one of them even now training his weapon on the bed-box? The barrel would be just inches away.

And then Maria spoke again.

'However,' she said. She had one condition. If they went ahead and opened fire, 'I insist that you give me a credit note for new upholstery fabric, and that you pay the repair costs.' She was adamant that there was no room for 'a raggedy piece of furniture' in any home of hers. 'And I would like to have that in writing from you. In advance.'

It seemed that, after nearly a decade of dealing with the national socialist masters of the new Reich, and indeed with bureaucrats of every stripe, Maria had learned one thing: that such men feared straying beyond their authority. There would be an expenses form to fill in, a superior who would demand an explanation. Sure enough, the bullets remained in their chambers.

By six o'clock the Gestapo agents, including the Blonde Poison and her man, had finally left. They had spent the best part of four hours in the apartment on Detmolder Strasse and come away with nothing, save a promise that if the Jewish girl reappeared the countess would report her to the authorities immediately.

Only once Maria was sure the two men, and the blonde loitering outside, were gone and would not be coming back did she dare give the signal for Hans to unseal his tomb and emerge. He came out deathly white, his body clammy with sweat. He had believed those long hours might be his last. What saved him was the swagger, the ingrained self-belief, of the woman he called Maruska, a woman whose blood was so blue, she had grown up in an actual castle. These days she was a trainee vet living in an abandoned shop in Berlin, but she was of a class that had spent centuries ruling this land. Not even the Gestapo could intimidate her. For now, at least.

24

The Breakthrough

Paul, Summer 1943

FROM NOW ON, he would travel around Switzerland with his young wife, Inge. They would look up old family friends. His father was a professor of medicine; his parents had a serious address book. It was time to use it.

The couple took the Engadine bus from Chur to St Moritz. From there, Paul Reckzeh telephoned Bianca Segantini, an old friend of his mother's. She was the daughter of Giovanni Segantini, the Tyrol-born artist who had ranked among the most renowned European painters of the nineteenth century. He had become famous for his large-scale Alpine landscapes and had devoted a whole phase of his career to painting the Engadine. Now the region was home to his daughter. Paul wondered if he might come and introduce his bride to a woman who had always been such an important part of his mother's life. Bianca did not hesitate, urging the couple to come to lunch the very next day.

She lived in Sils Maria, or just plain Sils to those in the know, a small, picture-postcard village at the end of the valley where the Tyrol meets Italy. Tucked in between lakes and mountains, and nearly seven thousand feet above the sea, where the wisps of cloud seemed to be within touching distance, it felt like the top of Europe, maybe the top of the world.

Bianca welcomed them warmly. She had fond memories of Paul going back to the 1920s. The Reckzehs had spent many summers in the Engadine and, as a teenager, Paul had found his way to Bianca. He seemed to feel at home with her. He had been a somewhat lost young man, she thought, an only child very much in the shadow of a distinguished father. He seemed weighed down by the pressure to match the accomplishments of the great Professor Reckzeh, a gloom that was not lifted by his limited success as a student. So she had shown him kindness, listening to him and offering wisdom as he spoke of his teenage worries, including an unrequited crush he had developed on her niece. Was there also perhaps a hint of a young man's ardour in his feelings for Bianca, a charming woman with a famous name then in her early forties? At the very least, Paul seemed to draw self-confidence from her zest for life and her interest in him.

But long-distance friendships can be hard to preserve and the connection slowly weakened. The Reckzehs stopped spending holidays in Sils and Bianca lost touch with the family altogether. She had heard that the younger Reckzeh had studied medicine, but she had had no idea he was married. Which made the chance to catch up all the sweeter.

First, though, there was something to get straight. Bianca had little patience with social niceties. She preferred that, if they were to spend several hours together, everyone should be clear where they stood from the start. So she came right out with the question that would have been on the mind of anyone meeting a pair of Germans in the summer of 1943: Do you support the Nazi regime?

'On the contrary, Frau Segantini!' came the reply, almost in chorus and certainly indignant. It was a relief to be able to put one's cards on the table. Inge took the lead, confessing that her father had been briefly imprisoned — placed in 'protective custody', to use the euphemism of the era — because of his anti-Nazi views.

Now Bianca could breathe out, admitting that she had become a little paranoid, so great was her distrust of the national socialists. She had lost friendships over it; many. Did they know it had been four years since she had seen anyone from Germany? That's right, not since the start of the war.

She wanted to know *everything*. Given Inge's father's record, how on earth had they been allowed to leave Germany and enter Switzerland?

Paul explained that he suffered from tuberculosis of the hip and, because he was a doctor, he had been able to arrange treatment in

Switzerland. It was not easy to get by on the ten Reichsmarks he had been allowed to bring into the country, but they were managing. Besides, he was here in part to work. He was engaged in scientific research, focused on blood subgroups. It was the existence of these previously overlooked subgroups, he said, that helped explain why some transfusions failed. Switzerland was the ideal place to continue his investigations because it had all the facilities one needed. Besides, it had just the right people. You see, the aim was to conduct blood tests among the local population, which would reveal a history of past migration and that, he felt sure, would be relevant to his study. With that in mind, he had made contact with the chief physician at the hospital in Samedan. But there was also a lab in Bern he had his eye on. Ideally, he would like to stay in Switzerland and get out of Germany, where there was neither the equipment nor the people nor, frankly, the calm and peace of mind he needed to pursue his work.

Out it all came, and at some length. Much of the detail, to be honest, went over Bianca's head, but it was good to see Paul so animated, coming out of himself. For much of the afternoon he was quite taciturn, but not when there was a chance to discuss his work. It was impressive. Besides, there was no shortage of conversation thanks to Inge, who was a live wire, bursting with passion, especially when it came to decrying the state of Germany.

She poured out a torrent of complaints about life under Hitler, a litany that seemed to have been bottled up for months or even years and could only now be uncorked. The constant vigilance was more than a person could bear, the young woman explained, the fear that at every turn there was a hidden ear, eavesdropping on every conversation. To live in Berlin today, Inge explained, was to be in a permanent state of mistrust, waiting for the denunciation, whether made in earnest or out of malice, that could send you into God knows what abyss. 'In Germany, I can't even talk to my husband the way we are all talking now,' Inge said.

Ever direct, Bianca asked Paul if he was a party member. Grimly, he flipped back the lapel of his jacket to reveal the badge of the NSDAP. 'I had to become one in order to take my exams,' he said. He added that 'no one stopped me', castigating his parents in particular for failing to intervene. Admittedly, everyone knew that if you wanted to get on, even in medicine, it paid to be in the party. But now it was a source of great regret.

Bianca urged him not to be so hard on himself. Medicine was predicated on the love of one's fellow human beings. Whether he had a party card or not, that training would guide him. He would know that any measure at odds with the fundamental principles of humanity was wrong. He did not need to become involved with politics to know that. Being a doctor was enough.

But Inge was now looking at her husband with both astonishment and reproach. 'You never told me you were a Nazi,' she said. He faced her with sadness in his eyes, then made a gesture as if to wave the feeling away. To Bianca, he said, 'My wife wants a child, but I cannot take on the responsibility of fathering a child in this Germany.'

They mentioned a mutual friend, who had become a member of the SS. Bianca blamed the mother. 'Women play a sad and shameful role in Germany,' she sighed. Again, this was not a matter of politics or opposition but something far more fundamental. A woman's maternal instincts alone should be sufficient to tell right from wrong. It was the same for anybody, man or woman: basic humanity would show you what behaviour was acceptable and what was not.

Bianca was not finished. She added that religion had an invaluable role to play in such dark times. It could function as 'a stop, a guideline'. If people were unsure where the boundary between good and evil lay, religion would tell them. Religion would be the German people's way out of this nightmare, she was sure of it. And women would have a crucial role to play in that recovery. Much of the work would fall to them, and they 'must not shirk it', she said.

The trouble was, said Inge Reckzeh, there was no chance, even for someone like her, who clung to religion, to talk about it, not in today's Germany. It left her feeling both lonely and alone.

Was it her own mention of women or her reference to Christian faith that did it? Either way, at that moment Bianca found herself thinking of one of her most beloved friends, Elisabeth von Thadden. Elisabeth reserved her greatest passion for the church, for the humane treatment of others and for girls' education. If anyone could provide counsel and encouragement to this young woman who was in clear distress, it would be the former headmistress who had steered so many young women through crises of despondency. Given Inge longed for a conversation about religion, there was no one better suited. She did not need to think about it any longer. It was the obvious answer.

'Elisabeth von Thadden,' she said. 'Visit her and bring her greetings, a thousand greetings, from me!'

The Reckzehs were excited. A lifeline like this was exactly what they needed. Where, Paul asked, would they find Fräulein von Thadden?

At that, Bianca drew a blank. Absurd as it might seem, she did not know where Elisabeth was living; they had scarcely been in touch since Elisabeth had been forced out of the school. 'You'll be able to find the address in Berlin,' she said, aware that that was no help at all.

It was time to say goodbye. They stepped out into the garden for a while, in the July breeze. Inge took Bianca's hand and kissed it. She was brimming with gratitude for the gift Bianca had given her that afternoon, the gift of honest conversation.

Bianca closed the door, glad to see that the once-wayward young man had made such a good match, married now to a sweet young woman filled with a fierce compassion. Later, Bianca would even dream of her. 'If Hitler is killed, think of me!' Inge said, as if she might one day be the assassin who would end the current horror. Had Inge actually said those words when they met, or only in Bianca's dreams? Frau Segantini could not be sure.

Inge Reckzeh sent an effusive note of gratitude to Bianca Segantini that same evening, as soon as she and Paul reached St Moritz. Paul offered his thanks in a phone call, telling Bianca how grateful he was for the time they had spent together, for the way he and his wife had been able to relax in her company. But he had not forgotten his mission.

He was in Switzerland to forge links between German exiles there and dissidents in Germany, and Bianca had suggested one that seemed to have great potential. Now he wanted to cement the connection.

'You have allowed us to visit Fräulein von Thadden and bring your greetings,' he said. 'But because of the current atmosphere in Germany, the mistrust that everyone harbours of everyone else, Fräulein von Thadden would probably not receive us at all on a merely verbal recommendation. I would be very grateful if you could give me this recommendation in writing. But you would have to do it immediately, as we are leaving for Germany early in the morning.' While she was at it, might she write a similar letter of recommendation to the young Swiss diplomat in Berlin she had mentioned over lunch? He seemed a valuable person to know, someone who might introduce Paul to other people of good conscience.

Bianca scribbled a note to the Swiss official and another to Elisabeth – 'Take care of this young man!' – and sent both letters to Paul by express post.

He could not have been more grateful. Those letters meant everything. At last he had what he needed to do his work. In all the many meetings he had had in Switzerland, in every conversation with those German exiles, they had spoken of the need to build a better, brighter future for Germany. Now he would play his part.

25

An Invitation to Tea

Elisabeth, September 1943

BY SEPTEMBER 1943, Elisabeth von Thadden's presence in Berlin had become sporadic, and not only because the Wednesday Bible sessions had been banned since the end of the previous year. She had spent much of the summer on a Red Cross tour of soldiers' quarters in France. She thought she would be inspecting facilities, reporting on what was lacking. In reality, she was working as a nurse's assistant, a job for which the former mistress of the castle had no training or qualifications. She was told that if she was prepared to go through this internship as an auxiliary, she might later be handed the management of a soldiers' home in France. First, though, she would aid convalescing soldiers, initially on the French Channel coast and later in Meaux, outside Paris.

But when she was in Berlin she maintained what had become an annual commitment, hosting a 'Wieblingen tea' for her former pupils – her children, as she thought of them. Occasionally she saw relatives in the flat, but it was so tiny, fit really only for one person, that it was awkward. And that was before you reckoned with the challenge of catering, which was not easy on a single ration card. It nagged at Elisabeth that she was not able to reciprocate the invitations she had taken up in Berlin, including those meetings with like-minded others at the home of Hanna Solf.

But then came a chance to put that right. A few months earlier, Anna von Gierke had passed away, leaving Isa in that large apartment on her own. Isa mentioned that she was going away for a few days. In her absence, might Elisabeth like to make use of the living room?

Elisabeth took up the offer gratefully, setting a date to host a tea on the 10th of the month. That way she could both celebrate the fiftieth birthday of her younger sister Anza, and return the favour to those friends who had either welcomed her to their table or whom she had come to know on those Wednesday evenings.

It would be a delightful afternoon, a gathering of good friends and allied souls. The very idea lifted her spirits.

Arthur and Irmgard

Arthur Zarden was no longer one for parties. Once the top man at the German Ministry of Finance, he used to enjoy dancing with his wife at a ball or hosting dozens for dinner. But widowed and living with his daughter, Irmgard, these days he was wary of so much as a visit from a friend. He had been on edge when the former Leipzig mayor Carl Goerdeler came to call, and he was no less agitated when there was an unannounced visit from Hjalmar Schacht, the one-time head of the central bank credited with having found the cash that allowed Hitler to rearm Germany and so invade its neighbours. Now out in the cold, Schacht was looking to renew old acquaintances, including with those who had been similarly shunned. On the day he knocked on the door, the air-raid sirens sounded and so Arthur had to take his distinguished, and highly recognisable, guest to the basement. At that time, the Zardens had a wounded soldier, a convinced Nazi, billeted with them – and it was obvious that this man had identified Schacht. That too made Arthur nervous.

This was his mood when he received an invitation to tea from Elisabeth von Thadden. Still grieving for his wife, fearful and ridden with angst, he was hardly eager. But, perhaps swayed by the urgings of his daughter, a former pupil of Thadden's who remained attached to her, he said yes.

Otto

Otto Kiep was similarly uneasy. For months now, he had felt the net tightening. That much was plain after Bonhoeffer's arrest, but in the summer of 1943 it drew closer still. Otto's patron in the Abwehr, Hans Oster, was removed from active duty. No one needed to spell out why: he was suspected of membership of the resistance. It was surely only a matter of time before he would suffer the same fate as the dissenting cleric and all those others: he would be arrested and taken away.

Now the senior man needed his subordinate's help. Everyone knew the way the Gestapo operated: the midnight arrests, snatching suspects from their beds. Would it be possible for Oster and his wife to seek refuge in the Kiep family home, at least in the hours of darkness?

It would be an unmistakable act of defiance, as flagrant as the gesture Otto had made ten years earlier when he had toasted the most famous Jew in the world in a room full of Jews. There was no hesitation this time, no agonising. His son was away on a year-long programme with the Hitler Youth; his daughters were at their aunt's farm. Bombs permitting, the Osters could sleep in the children's wing of the Kiep house. And so they did, arriving after dinner and leaving before breakfast, in the hope of eluding the cold nocturnal grip of the secret police.

Bombing raids were becoming more frequent, and swanky neighbourhoods were not exempt. In early September, the Kiep house was hit. Given that whole streets were being flattened by Allied bombs, they got off pretty lightly: some cracked walls and broken windows. But it meant Otto had to change his plans. He had wanted to join Hanna and the two girls at Ida's farm up north, in the Harz mountains; it would be a relief to be out of Berlin, if only for a day. Instead, he would now have to stay in the city to oversee repairs. He had no plans to speak of, save for an invitation to a tea party on Carmerstrasse.

Later he would say that, had it not been for the air raid, he would never have gone, that he did not really want to go, that he viewed it as an obligation. But he was on his own and he knew the hostess, Elisabeth von Thadden, the headmistress whose school had been closed down because she had refused to bend to the demands of national socialism. And so, on Friday, 10 September 1943, Otto Kiep headed to Carmerstrasse for an afternoon tea in celebration of the fiftieth birthday of an acquaintance.

Maria

Countess Maria von Maltzan was a Solf Circle regular who would have seen plenty of familiar faces had she joined the others at Elisabeth von Thadden's table. She said yes initially and planned to go. Working relentlessly as she was, she welcomed a respite from her twin duties: it was a relief not to be ministering to animals that were sick or Jews who were in hiding. All the same, she stayed away from the September tea party. She had been privy to no special information; she just had a bad feeling at the last minute. She had got dressed and was ready to leave, Hans chivvying her along, urging her not to be late, when an inner voice warned her to steer clear, telling her it was too risky even to cancel by telephone. And this time, she listened.

26

Agent Robby

Summer 1943

PERHAPS THE GREATEST enthusiast for the party was a man who was not invited. By the late summer of 1943, Leo Lange had been back in Germany over a year. Following his success as the pioneer of the gas chamber – first introducing the mobile variety, then as the founding commandant of the first death camp – he was now working in the Reich Security Main Office, or RSHA, itself, as the deputy head of its IV E 3 section. In the language of national socialist bureaucracy, the Gestapo was Office IV of the RSHA, within which Group IV E dealt with overseas matters, with IV E 3 the section charged with the 'West', namely Switzerland, France and Belgium.

If the Gestapo's mission was to detect the first hints of a hostile opinion forming in the German population, and to prevent the holders of those opinions, dissidents actual or potential, from making contact with each other, then Lange's job was to stand between those rebels and any help from the outside. Officially, his work was branded as counterintelligence. The implication was that German exiles overseas desperate to see change in their homeland – for this was the group most likely to lend external assistance to would-be dissenters – were in fact agents of foreign espionage whose plans needed to be foiled. Specifically, Lange was to uncover and then sever connections between anti-Nazi networks operating in those three countries and what the bureaucracy referred to as domestic 'civil opposition': resistance activity inside Germany.

Such work required informers and agents. There were always rich pickings to be had among the curtain-twitching classes, the gossips, busybodies and nosy parkers who voluntarily acted as the eyes and ears of the state out of a sense of duty. No less fruitful for Lange and his colleagues were those who would not offer to betray their friends and neighbours, but who could nevertheless be coerced into it: those over whom the state had leverage. Anyone vulnerable to arrest fell into that category. It might be foreigners, dissenting clergy, prostitutes or homosexuals, to say nothing of common criminals.

If it were more than morsels of information the Gestapo were after, they liked to recruit from among young intellectuals, especially those whose career prospects had not looked bright until Adolf Hitler came along and who felt themselves elevated by the age of national socialism. Would-be scholars, filled with a blend of injured pride following the humiliation of Versailles and utopian idealism for an imagined future, were especially susceptible to the lure of Nazism, or so the talent-spotters of the SS and the Gestapo had found. The Gestapo had thousands of such people on their books, scattered throughout the country, including, by one count, forty-six young lawyers, eight philologists, five economists, two doctors and four theologians – three Catholic and one Protestant.

It was not obvious what had brought this particular agent-in-waiting to Lange earlier that summer. Was it wounded idealism, like those others? Or plain careerism, the desire to secure a better position within the Nazi state? Many had come to the secret police that way. Or maybe it was a simple human yearning for adventure? There was no shortage of those types either, people drawn to the excitement of life undercover, imagining that the lot of a secret agent was all glamour and thrills. Not that the question of motive mattered much. What counted with any potential recruit was that they be useful. And Lange had seen an immediate use for this one.

He had gone to talk to his superior, SS-Standartenführer Walter Huppenkothen, now head of the Gestapo's foreign intelligence service. They agreed the basic terms of engagement. Best to take things slowly: no immediate deployment in any positions of trust, no formal orders. Judge the quality of the information when it came in. Until then, watch and wait.

Lange had begun with a kind of test, presenting a list of names for the recruit to memorise. Lange explained that each one of those names belonged to a resident of Berlin suspected of activity that posed a danger to the state. But suspicion was not enough. The important thing was to find the evidence that might lead to a conviction.

Most of these suspects had contacts abroad, whether friends, relatives or politically dubious figures now living in exile. Lange wanted answers to the obvious questions. Who exactly were they in touch with? What were they saying to them? What might they be plotting?

The focus would be Switzerland, where several of these Berlin dissidents had contacts. One such name was Joseph Wirth, who had served as Reich chancellor in the 1920s and was now living in what Lange suspected was anything but quiet retirement across the Swiss border. Another was the reform-minded educationalist and cleric Friedrich Siegmund-Schultze. What hostile activity were these men involved in, and who was helping them? Lange wanted to know everything.

To find out, the new agent would have to win the trust of that Berlin circle of traitors. It would mean spending time with them, persuading them that they had found an ally in a shared cause. Only then would they reveal their secrets.

Lange handed his new agent travel documents, identity papers and then, doubtless with a flourish, he offered the blessing of a code name. His new recruit would be known as Agent Robby.

Robby had been thrilled. He would be doing something important for his country, something important for the war. Some might say he was drawn to the money he would be paid as a secret agent. Others might argue that his real motivation was the chance to dodge military service and especially combat duty at the front. Still others might think it was idealism that pulled Robby towards Lange, the lure of Adolf Hitler's promise of a national socialist paradise, a place unified and purified, indeed unified *because* purified, a land cleansed of disagreement.

All of those views had merit. But perhaps the key word, for Robby as much as for the other young, clever men who had so easily been turned into informers or agents of the Nazi state, was 'important'. Wasn't that what Lange was offering: the sense that one was engaged in work of national, even global significance, and the status that came with that feeling? Wasn't this the hard currency that Lange was putting on the table, the righteous satisfaction of involvement in a cause bigger than oneself and the flattering thought that your country needed you?

Of course, Robby was already a public servant, an employee of the Reich. But that was different. Yes, he was on the payroll of the Reich Health Office, but he had never been at the cutting edge of Germany's war against its enemies. That was about to change. Admittedly, he would still not be wearing his country's uniform. But he would be on the frontline.

And he had resolved to pay back the trust Lange had placed in him. He had been determined to execute this mission, using the contacts he had in Switzerland to burrow into that treacherous circle of aristocrats and eminences – the names on Lange's list – and expose them for what they were. In so doing, he would, he felt sure, earn his spurs and embark on a stellar career in espionage and counter-intelligence. Outwardly, he would still be the presentable young doctor from Berlin's Charité hospital, but he at least would know that he was so much more. He had completed the first stage of his mission with that trip across the Swiss border and the meetings he had secured, above all that long lunch in Sils with the painter's daughter. Now to finish the job.

His name was Dr Karl Otto Paul Reckzeh and he would make history.

27

An Unexpected Guest

Elisabeth, 9 September 1943

WHEN THE DOORBELL rang, it was almost welcome. The mood up until then had risked becoming maudlin, despite Elisabeth von Thadden's best efforts. It was the day before the big tea party and Elisabeth was hosting a separate, smaller gathering. The way things were going, she was glad of the interruption.

This was the annual 'Wieblingen tea' for her former pupils. But instead of playing her preferred role of elder and source of guidance, she was on the receiving end of moral support and something uncomfortably close to pity.

The young guests were expressing their incredulity that the woman they admired so much had been ousted from her own school. The sheer injustice of it.

They were gathered in the cramped basement flat at Carmerstrasse 12. The building had been hit by a bomb, severely enough for Elisabeth to have been given leave from the Red Cross but not so badly that she had to move out. Some of the furniture from the upper floors, intact if a little charred, had been moved down here and Elisabeth and her one-time charges were taking tea in a space that was narrow but which Elisabeth chose to see as cosy. The spread was modest: war cake, so called because of the defining role played by rationing in its composition, and some bread rolls spread with quark. If cake and soft white cheese were not to your taste, there was not much else on offer. Still, the young ladies seemed to like it.

Elisabeth persevered in seeing every half-empty glass as half-full. After she had explained the circumstances that had led to her removal from Wieblingen, the business with the Old Testament psalm, she sought to deflect her ex-pupils' sympathy. It was for the best, she insisted. She liked working for the Red Cross and, besides, it was a relief not to have to lie any more.

'Of course,' said one guest, no more solicitous than the rest. 'You're just too honest.'

'As my grandmother used to say,' Elisabeth replied, 'straight through has no corners.'

She was reassuring the girls that, really, they need not worry for her, when the doorbell rang. Elisabeth opened the door and saw a man she had never met before. Young, to her eyes at least, and presentable, he introduced himself with a flourish as Dr Paul Reckzeh. He explained that he had just come from Switzerland and that he had with him a letter from a close friend of Fräulein von Thadden's, which he handed to her.

There and then, in the half-darkness of the corridor, she scanned the letter. She barely needed to read the words – 'Thinking of all of you across the border' – because she instantly recognised the handwriting. The sight of it filled her with immediate and great joy. For this was a letter from Bianca Segantini.

There were few people Elisabeth cherished more than Bianca. They had met at the end of the twenties, when Elisabeth was walking tall as the head of her new girls' boarding school and Bianca was fleeing a failed marriage. They were so different, even physically: Elisabeth sturdy and strong, even stocky, her face wide; Bianca four years older, but petite to the point of frailty, her narrow face framed by a striking wave of hair. The two women clicked, their differences complementary. Where Elisabeth could be harsh, Bianca would be gentle; where Elisabeth was impatient, Bianca persevered. Where the headmistress focused on the big picture, the artist's daughter had an eye for detail. Where Elisabeth was all work ethic and self-discipline, Bianca was a dreamer, a poet who might spend long hours in her writing studio, with picture windows on all sides, 'but nothing finished', who, though she had edited a collection of her father's writings and letters, had had not a word of her own published. She lined the walls of her house with blue silk brocade, kept the mountains at bay with curtains of silk and chiffon, painted her ceilings and embroidered the rest. If Elisabeth was devoted to truth, Bianca worshipped at the altar of beauty.

They talked about society, the nature of existence and the troubles in Bianca's life especially. Before the war, the pair would spend time with each other often. They would meet in the summertime, when Elisabeth could at last be away from the school and her responsibilities. She liked to be in Switzerland: as a teenager, she had been at boarding school there. It was where she had perfected her French. They might take drives together, with Elisabeth at the wheel. She was not a safe driver, but Bianca did not object: she found it exciting.

It was in the summer of 1939 when, as Bianca put it, the relationship became *innig*, which can mean deep, tender or affectionate, and also intimate. Elisabeth was in Sils and they would see each other every day, sharing their rising anguish at what was to come. They noticed the exiled German families in the village, how they were always glued to the radio, desperate for news of the land, and the world, they had left behind. Bianca had good contacts, including an Italian gentleman of politics who visited and spoke with Elisabeth in particular; while they talked, Bianca would keep them sustained by baking waffles. The Italian predicted, accurately as it turned out, that Berlin and Moscow would soon sign a non-aggression pact, which was as sure a signal as there could be that aggression was about to follow.

In the last days of August, Elisabeth told Bianca she was leaving. The Germans who were staying at the Hotel Margna in Sils were all heading home and she was going to go with them; a young German man had offered to drive her car. She did not hide her grim assessment of what the future held for them and, unable to conceal her feelings from Bianca, she said goodbye. Her parting words were, 'From now on, we can do nothing but think of each other.'

A day or two later, Poland would come under attack from first Germany and then the Soviet Union, the two countries having sealed their pact a week earlier. Elisabeth was now returning to a country a war.

The pair remained in touch. Occasionally, Elisabeth made it across the border to Zurich and, once there, in a country where the post was not read by censors, she would write to Bianca. She took advantage of this small window of freedom to speak her mind, passing on her horror on reading a book by an ex-Nazi that purported to recount the author's conversations with Hitler. All of it appalled her, but its account of the Führer's views on education – 'General education is the most corrosive and dissolving poison' – and on the church – 'One is either a Christian or a German, one cannot be both' – was too much for Elisabeth to bear.

Elisabeth had read the book at speed, through the night, and Bianca was left in no doubt as to the mark it had left on her friend. What it said was right, Elisabeth wrote, and Germans knew it. From now on, Elisabeth von Thadden would be an implacable opponent of the Third Reich. That chimed with Bianca. Her loathing of national socialism was such that, though so often regarded as a delicate creature, she had volunteered for duty in the Swiss military: she worked as an assistant to the senior military men in the Engadine region. Even separated by so many miles, Bianca and Elisabeth were joined in spirit.

And so now, standing in the basement hallway at Carmerstrasse, with Bianca's message in her hand, Elisabeth had only to read the words 'Take care of this young man!' to want to usher him inside.

Bianca's note had mentioned another point of solidarity between herself and Elisabeth: their shared commitment to the Confessing Church. Several of the young women present had taken that same path and so now, to bridge the awkwardness that can intrude when a new guest arrives, Elisabeth introduced the church as a topic that might be of interest to everyone present, including the young doctor.

He took it up with enthusiasm, detailing the conversations he had had on his recent trip with leading Swiss pastors as well as several exiled German theologians. With concern, Paul asked after the welfare of Martin Niemöller and the thirty or so other pastors held in Dachau. How were they managing? 'A little better,' Elisabeth said, adding that every weekday evening there were prayers at St Anne's Church in Dahlem for the prisoners. You should come, she said, always glad to have the next generation represented. She explained that they used to read out the names of the detained, but that was no longer allowed and so they allowed the silence to do the work. The priest would pause, long enough for everyone to know what was not being said. Then he and the congregation would read responsively the words of Psalm 126: 'When the Lord redeemed the captives of Zion, we were like those who dream.'

One of Elisabeth's former pupils offered a word of caution to Reckzeh. If he were minded to attend the prisoner prayers, he should expect there to be agents of the Gestapo present. Back when Niemöller himself was in the pulpit, before his arrest, she had once sat next to two men in trench coats who wrote down everything they saw. 'I caught the glances they exchanged when Niemöller prayed at the end, "Lord, grant that even those who have come only to listen to us do not go away untouched by your word. Do not let them go away unblessed."'

At that, Reckzeh shot her a look she didn't like and, as she left, she mentioned it to Elisabeth. But Elisabeth was not fazed. She had that note from her dearest Bianca. And so she spoke freely to the young doctor, pouring out her heart to him in a conversation that ended up lasting some three hours. She spoke of her feelings and he of his, explaining his loneliness. He had made the mistake of being an admirer of national socialism a few years earlier, and for that he had been shunned by some of his old friends. But as the war had gone on, he had come to recognise the misfortune being visited on Germany by the Nazis and wanted to make common cause with those of a like mind.

After that, it felt wholly natural to make a spontaneous addition to the guest list for the tea party that she would host, in the larger apartment upstairs, the next day. Dr Reckzeh had already said how anxious he was to meet 'right thinking people who felt the way he did about the Nazis', so of course he accepted her invitation with enthusiasm. His eagerness touched Elisabeth. The young would be this country's salvation, she was sure of it.

28

Kindred Spirits

10 September 1943

To the naked eye, it was nothing more suspect than an afternoon birthday party, friends gathering for tea in a first-floor apartment on a wide, tree-lined street in Berlin on the second Friday in September 1943. No one hid the fact that they were gathering; there was no skulking behind upturned coat lapels or secret passwords at the door. Instead, they arrived in apparent good cheer, in ones and twos, ready to share a slice of cake and start the weekend early.

But this was not just a tea party. It was also a meeting of secret dissidents, individuals who had each fought their own private battle against Adolf Hitler, brought together at last under one roof and in one room.

Acting as host was Elisabeth van Thadden. Whatever her initial thoughts about national socialism, she had become immovable in her opposition to the regime, steady and unbending in defiance of a creed she believed was hostile to Christ, humanity and all that was good.

An early arrival was Arthur Zarden, once a prince of the German Ministry of Finance who knew as much about the running of the German economy as any man alive. His wife – born a Jew, a fact that had been enough to terminate his career – had died just seven months earlier and Zarden exuded a widower's gloom. Later, he would be joined by his daughter, Irmgard, who had what few others around the table could offer: the energy of youth.

Next came the summer bachelors, those men who had despatched their wives and children to the countryside while they stayed to attend to their duties and face the bombs then raining devastation on the capital. Hilger van Scherpenberg was fresh from a trip to Copenhagen. A member of the SPD, or Social Democratic Party, until it was banned in February 1933, he was now a civil servant, working in the trade policy department of the Foreign Ministry as head of the Scandinavian desk. If his words carried extra weight, that was partly because he was also the son-in-law of a former president of the Reichsbank, Hjalmar Schacht, the man without whom, or so it was said, Hitler would never have been able to start the war.

Alongside Scherpenberg was Otto Kiep, who enjoyed an even more elevated position, serving in the armed forces high command, liaising between his current colleagues in the Abwehr and his former colleagues in the Foreign Ministry, among others. Indeed, with the formal designation of envoy, he was the highest-ranked person present. That his career had not been destroyed was a marvel in itself: he was the man who a decade earlier had risked everything to honour Albert Einstein, then not only the world's most famous scientist, but also its best-known Jewish refugee from Nazism. Yet here he was, in a post that gave him privileged access to critical information, most crucially on the course of the war. When he spoke, the people assembling in the apartment at Carmerstrasse 12 listened.

Deference to seniority and family lineage ensured respect for Fanny von Kurowsky, the oldest guest at the table: in the 1870s, her father had been a member of Bismarck's Cabinet. In that body, her father would have been a colleague of Otto Kiep's uncle, head of the Reich Chancellery in that same period. In these circles, there were usually just one or two degrees of separation between one person and everyone else.

Almost all of the guests that afternoon carried either a name, or a fortune, associated with Germany's one-time elite. That was certainly true of the woman whose presence the others awaited before they felt proceedings could begin in earnest. Hanna Solf was one of the best-connected people in Berlin, in touch with top military officers, intellectuals, clerics and every diplomat of substance in the city, to say nothing of an even larger number scattered across the globe.

The official focus of the afternoon was Elisabeth's sister Anza, a mother of adult sons now living with relatives in Schönfliess near Berlin and paying her way by managing their household. It was Anza, alongside a childhood friend, former model Anne Rühle, who had brought the cakes and the cream: Anne had rested them on her lap in the car on the way over.

The women had set to work before the others arrived, arranging vases, filling tea bags, filtering coffee. Anne was now a social worker of sorts, as was Elisabeth, and the pair would speak often: heretical talk about the war that was clearly lost and the plans that would have to be made for the day after, whether for capable welfare workers or the supply of bread and bandages, the kind of talk that could land a person in deadly trouble.

Completing the group, and watching each of them closely, was a man unfamiliar to the others, a last-minute addition to the guest list. A young doctor by the name of Paul Reckzeh, well-dressed if a little full in the face, he was the son of a professor of medicine and working at one of the city's leading hospitals. He noted how the group relaxed in each other's company. Outside, there were Nazis demanding Hitler salutes and loyalty to the Führer. But here they were among friends, kindred spirits with whom they could speak freely and without fear. They were safe.

29

A Traitor to the Circle

Paul, 10 September 1943

HE HAD HAD so many close shaves, it was a minor miracle that he was even here. He could have been exposed much earlier; by rights, he *should* have been. It could all have come apart in that first meeting in Zurich with the theologian Siegmund-Schultze. The man had clearly suspected his story and Paul's response had been so hesitant. He must have looked guilty. And then at the restaurant, with Siegmund-Schultze's daughter and her friends: they had accused him of being an informer, to his face. They had rumbled him. But somehow the moment had passed.

The lunch with Bianca Segantini had ultimately proved a triumph, but that too had come perilously close to disaster: that moment when he had shown his party badge, and Inge's shock at the sight of it. His wife had confessed that she did not feel she could speak the truth, even to her husband, because of the 'hidden ear' that was all around. But Segantini had seemed charmed rather than wary. Even yesterday, at Elisabeth von Thadden's gathering for her ex-pupils, he had obviously bristled when that girl had started talking about Gestapo agents in the church. It was a stupid error on his part; he could so easily have blown his own cover, even at the very last moment. But the gods had smiled on him. And now here he was.

He had arrived early at Carmerstrasse 12, heading as directed to the apartment upstairs. It was so much brighter and more spacious than the underground broom cupboard where he had met Elisabeth twenty-four hours previously. Elisabeth was there along with two women introduced to him as her sister Anza and Anza's friend Anne.

As they prepared the room, Paul did his best to be polite and grateful. But he cut such an unlikely figure. A man in his thirties, not in the Wehrmacht even now, in the fourth year of the war: he was such a rarity.

The others arrived in quick succession. Lange had given him a list of names to memorise and now he was taking mental notes, ready for the briefing he would later give Lange. Here was the widowed Arthur Zarden, radiating glumness about the future. Next, the older lady, Fanny von Kurowsky. No sign yet of Hanna Solf, hostess of the salon of rebellion where so many resistance luminaries convened. But the arrival of not one but two high-ranking officials, Hilger van Scherpenberg and Otto Kiep, confirmed he had come to the right place. When she introduced him, Elisabeth told the story again: how yesterday had brought an unexpected joy when Dr Reckzeh had come to her door bearing a handwritten message from her cherished friend Bianca Segantini. At the mention of his name, the young doctor took an obliging bow.

Elisabeth went on to explain that Dr Reckzeh had come from Switzerland and would soon be going back. He was looking to make the right connections here in Berlin so that he could pass on the group's insights and analysis to friends and exiles across the border. By way of an example, she mentioned Siegmund-Schultze, but the name of the former chancellor Joseph Wirth also came up, possibly volunteered by Arthur Zarden. Reckzeh could not help but be pleased: he hardly needed to explain himself if Elisabeth von Thadden was prepared to do the job for him.

Soon they were sitting. 'Someone is missing still,' the doctor whispered to Anne Rühle, who was next to him. 'Isn't Frau Solf coming?'

He shouldn't worry, Anne told him. This wasn't a formal occasion where strict punctuality would be observed. Frau Solf and Fräulein von Thadden were old friends; they didn't need to stand on ceremony. Besides, perhaps Frau Solf had been stopped on the way.

Maybe he should have left it at that, but he was eager and could not contain himself. It was important for him to meet Frau Solf, he explained. He had heard her mentioned often. He paused. It was very good to be here, he said, among such a group. Bianca Segantini was a special person, he said, as if to underline his gratitude for the introduction that had brought him to this moment.

What about Anne herself, did she have friends or relatives in Switzerland by any chance?

Yes, she said. She had a cousin in Zurich; they had played together as children.

'Not Siegmund-Schultze? I know him!' As their hostess had indicated, he was a most excellent man, to be sure.

Lange's instructions had been clear: he wanted to know of ongoing contacts between dissenters in Berlin and anti-regime elements in Switzerland. He needed convictions; he had spelled that out. The Gestapo man had a bucketful of suspicions already. Confirmation of contact between troublemakers across the border, that's what Lange needed.

'And are you still in touch with him?' Perhaps Reckzeh tried to affect nonchalance as he said it.

'Occasionally. Of course. We are very fond of each other.'

Elisabeth chimed in to repeat what she had said the previous day, that she too was close to Siegmund-Schultze. That they had been friends for decades.

There was someone at the door. Reckzeh volunteered to open it. And there she was, the very Hanna Solf he had been so eager to meet. She was late partly because she had only been invited, in a telephone call from Elisabeth, once the gathering was under way, and partly because she had indeed made a stop en route, to visit her daughter, Lagi, then in hospital recovering from a firefighting injury. Hanna scanned the faces in the room, every one of them familiar to her, with the sole exception of the young man who had greeted her at the door. Elisabeth swiftly reassured her that Dr Reckzeh came unimpeachably recommended, and so Hanna took her place between Zarden and Kiep and listened as the conversation moved to the most recent development: Italy.

The news of the day was that the post-Mussolini government of Marshal Badoglio had been conducting secret talks with the Allies about an armistice. Hitler was about to lose an ally and gain an enemy. And all this after the fascist government in Italy had simply collapsed.

They talked through the implications, Reckzeh following the discussion eagerly, intervening less to express his own opinions than to draw out others'. Given the Badoglio negotiations, surely now there could be no doubt: a German victory was impossible. As for the toppling of Mussolini, was it too much to imagine the same could happen here?

There was consensus on the first point. The war was plainly doomed. The group listened especially closely to Otto Kiep, who knew more than most thanks to his access to the foreign press. He brought out an aerial photograph of Berlin that had appeared in the *New York Times*, with circles around each of the targets struck during a single night of RAF bombing. The war was 'already a lost cause for Germany', he said. The Allied attack on German cities was taking its toll: no one present needed to be persuaded of that, sitting as they were in a building that had itself been hit so recently. What's more, German forces on the eastern front were in a state of 'constant decline'. Otto spoke for almost everyone present when he declared, 'Unless a miracle happens, I see black for Germany.' That's what it would take to save the country: a miracle. 'That is quite clear.' Reckzeh echoed the sentiment, and committed each word to memory.

Scherpenberg chimed in with some stinging criticism of the military leadership and its failures. Earlier he had talked of the hatred the Gestapo had seeded in the territories it now occupied, citing Denmark especially. He too was heard with deference, given that Scandinavia was his area of professional responsibility. The government in Copenhagen had resigned, the German military command had declared a state of emergency, there were all kinds of 'antagonisms' to manage.

Reckzeh noted all of that too, but now Scherpenberg readied himself to leave. If the collection of verbatim statements from these dissenters was the first objective of the afternoon, the second was the gathering of documentary proof. The ideal was written evidence, in the suspects' own hand, demonstrating their collusion with foreign enemies of the state.

Reckzeh rose as Scherpenberg did, buttonholing him as he made for the door. 'I'll be going back to Switzerland soon. If you have acquaintances there . . .?' Reckzeh made his pitch, offering to act as a courier should there be a need to send messages to friends. He did not have to spell out why. Since the start of the war, all post sent abroad was censored, with any attempt to bypass the prying eye of the state, including by having a letter or message delivered by hand, illegal. But Reckzeh travelled to Switzerland often and would not be checked when crossing the border. Usefully, he also knew of a certain Pastor Müller who was operating an improvised communications centre near Lucerne.

Scherpenberg now examined Reckzeh properly, looking at him hard. 'Indeed I do have acquaintances, but what's it to you? I can use the post office, everything is legal.'

Reckzeh could have backed off then, but he wanted to deliver to Lange what the Gestapo man had demanded. 'The post office is checked,' he said.

'And so?' Scherpenberg let the silence hang, his gaze still on Reckzeh. Had he seen something in Paul's face that had given him away? Was the doctor about to be exposed?

Eventually, Scherpenberg headed for the door. Reckzeh had survived.

There were still rich pickings to be had at the tea table. He returned to discover they were now discussing what it would take to end this dreadful war. There was no appetite that anyone could discern for peace negotiations, either in the Allied capitals or in Berlin. Dr Goerdeler had attempted some kind of peace mission, but it had failed. Hitler was never going to do what had to be done. Which meant the war would keep going until the whole country lay in ruins. Only a coup d'état or revolution might stop it. Instead of cutting off such talk as scandalous, Otto was actively engaging with both those options, talking through the possibilities. Reckzeh only had to listen.

Fanny von Kurowsky was nodding enthusiastically, Hanna Solf seemed positively to glitter at such talk. Anza and Anne seemed excited by what they were hearing too, if more restrained. In the host's chair, Elisabeth listened with complete attention, a picture of calm. The only hint of unease appeared in the eyes of Arthur Zarden and his daughter, Irmgard, who had come to the house later than the others. The pair exchanged warning glances.

The first order of business, the group was saying, was to remove the SS and Gestapo. A shadow government would have to be standing by, ready to take over. As for Hitler, well, Frau Solf was clear on that point. 'When we get him, we'll put him against a wall.'

If Reckzeh felt the urge to punch the air, he hid it well. He had had to do so little, yet here he was, scooping the jackpot.

Then they were into a discussion of who would take the Führer's place. There was agreement that his seat would have to be filled immediately. That would require 'new men', capable of sitting down with Britain and the US to negotiate a peace accord, even, who knows, to form a new alliance to protect the west against Bolshevism. The risk was surely that, if the regime fell, Soviet-style communism would fill the vacuum. But who was fit for such a task?

Kurowsky made a case for Goerdeler, praising him as 'a capable man in the field of economics', giving Reckzeh the solidity of a name, even if agreement on her nomination was far from universal. Someone else mentioned Ludwig Beck, the military commander who had resigned as chief of the general staff in 1938 over Hitler's attack on Czechoslovakia. Now there was another name to add to the dossier growing thicker in Reckzeh's mind.

Zarden had lots to say on how a new government could be formed, but soon the conversation moved on to the relationship a post-Hitler Germany might have with the outside world. The country would be hated, but it would also be in desperate need of help. Elisabeth remembered the end of the last war, when she had brought destitute children from east Berlin to the family estate at Trieglaff so that she might nurse them back to health. They surely had to do all they could to prevent mothers and children from starving in the chaos that was bound to follow the defeat of the Hitler regime. In 1918, she recalled, Christians overseas had lent a vital hand.

Like the Quakers, Reckzeh chipped in helpfully.

Exactly, like the Quakers, agreed Elisabeth. Apparently Quakers were already hard at work in Switzerland, preparing aid shipments to send into Germany as soon as the war was over. Elisabeth noted the role Friedrich Siegmund-Schultze had played when such an effort had been required a quarter of a century earlier. Reckzeh saw his opening.

'You're related to him, aren't you?' he said to Anne, still at his side. 'Don't you want to . . .' He let the question hang in the air. She was not interested, but that did not inhibit the doctor. Before the afternoon was out, he had made the same offer to everyone present, volunteering to carry a note or card to Switzerland. He wanted the irrefutability of ink on paper.

Anne found a hiding place in the kitchen, helping Irmgard keep the tea and coffee flowing. Perhaps she had caught the younger woman's glance to her father because she said, 'I'd rather not give anything away, you never know what might happen.' She offered a similar word of warning to Anza.

But Anza's older sister was clearly free of any such misgivings. Elisabeth was listening rapt as her newfound friend confessed his fears for Germany's future, the pair of them bonded by their shared belief that once one knew what was right, one had no choice but to do it. She found his resolve, his willingness to step up, inspiring: at last, someone from the next generation with the courage to act!

When Paul Reckzeh made the same suggestion to her that he had to the others, offering to serve as a courier to fellow dissenters now in exile, she took him up on it. She dashed off a quick note to Siegmund-Schultze. It didn't say much, but that was hardly the point. The doctor was right: there was value simply in opening up a channel, in readiness for the duty of post-war renewal that would soon be upon them. She handed him her letter.

Otto Kiep was more wary. Hearing Reckzeh's offer, he shook his head, explaining that he had only one friend in Switzerland, a Herr Finkler, who was the brother-in-law of the former German economics minister Albert Neuhaus. What Otto did not add was that he just so happened to use Lucerne as a small 'communications centre' too: once a year he would make a trip to the city, visiting both his friend Finkler and a mailbox through which he could both send and receive messages.

Undeterred, Reckzeh offered to deliver Otto's calling card to Herr Finkler, as a courtesy. Eventually, Otto dug out his card and scribbled Finkler's address on the other side. 'Greet him from me, if it's convenient,' he said, and within a few minutes he was out of the door.

The Zardens said their goodbyes. As young Irmgard was leaving, she said something odd to Elisabeth in the hallway. Clearly referring to Reckzeh and his promise to act as messenger, she said, 'I won't send any mail.' Though the words were delivered quite emphatically, they were hard to hear. They might even have been 'I wouldn't send any mail'. Which, despite coming from a former pupil to her one-time head of school, sounded less like a warning than a reproach.

The doctor was getting ready to leave, along with Fanny von Kurowsky. Before he did, he said he had heard Frau Solf mention that she was anxious to get her late husband's archives to safety. Might he help by taking the papers to Switzerland? Hanna said no. But Reckzeh was nothing if not persistent. Might Frau Solf perhaps want a word passed to anyone? She had so many networks and contacts of her own, it was hardly . . . But now that he mentioned it, she did have in her bag some letters to acquaintances in Switzerland, including one to the Danish envoy in Bern. The content was hardly consequential, but she had been carrying them with her for several days: he could take those with him. She handed them over, stressing that if he had any trouble at the border, he should simply destroy them.

He put them in his pocket, together with the letter from Elisabeth, and bade the ladies farewell. He must have fought hard not to skip down the stairs and into the street. Together with the statements he had heard and committed to memory, what a haul he had made. *Unless a miracle happens, I see black for Germany . . . When we get him, we'll put him against a wall.* Was this proof that he was an unusually gifted secret agent? Or just that he had got very, very lucky? Either way, Lange would surely dance a jig in delight.

Back inside the flat, the atmosphere was one of exhausted satisfaction, as after any successful party, when the host and those closest to them can fall into their chairs and trade intimate observations of the event just passed. On 10 September 1943, that group consisted of Elisabeth, Anza, Anne and Hanna. They sat for a long while, munching sandwiches and talking through the afternoon. The mood was warm, even excited, fuelled by Hanna's confidence that change was coming and coming soon. She talked of an initiative she had caught wind of to end the war with the Soviet Union: the former

German ambassador to the USSR would be smuggled across Russian lines and onwards to Moscow before winter set in, to negotiate a separate peace. Who knew if it would come to anything? Whether it would or not, had it not been wonderfully freeing this afternoon to be among one's own? An increasingly rare treat. Informers were everywhere these days. Pretty soon, she sighed, everyone would turn out to be a spook.

But then Anne cast a cloud.

'I wouldn't have given him a letter,' she said, addressing both Elisabeth and Hanna and echoing Irmgard Zarden's parting words in the hallway.

Did she think the doctor was some kind of spy?

No, she wasn't saying that exactly. But you could never be sure, especially these days. And such communication, avoiding the censors, was illegal. 'If by some misfortune the letter falls into the wrong hands, you're in trouble.'

The afternoon had gone so well, but now Elisabeth could not calm herself. After her friends had gone, she went over it again and again. Anne was right: Reckzeh did not need to be working for the Gestapo for there to be a danger. He had a letter with her name on it in his pocket. What if he was stopped and searched? It could happen by accident. He might fall ill and collapse in the street; he could be run over. He would be in hospital, someone could be folding his clothes, and there they would be: her letter and those written by Hanna Solf. Damning evidence, in black and white.

She had to get those letters back.

PART II
After the Party

30

Secret Listeners

September 1943

JUST A TEN-MINUTE walk away from the apartment on Carmerstrasse, in a cluster of converted houses, they were listening. Not to the tea party itself: there was no bug in the room where Elisabeth von Thadden and friends gathered that Friday afternoon because there was no need. Paul Reckzeh was there to do that job. But they listened to almost everything else.

Since the mid-1930s, these buildings set back from the street on Schillerstrasse had served as the headquarters of the most secret, and most committedly Nazi, of the nine separate Third Reich intelligence agencies specialising in eavesdropping. It was blandly named the Forschungsamt, the Research Office. The name had appealed especially to its chief patron, Hermann Göring, because, as he once told the committed party comrade who dreamed it up, 'You indeed research the truth.'

It began in 1933 with half a dozen men working in an attic, but by the middle of the war it had six thousand employees, listening posts in fifteen German cities and agents in all the country's main post offices. It wanted to hear everything, foreign and domestic, its appetite insatiable. It tapped a thousand overseas telephone lines, while in Berlin alone its agents read nine thousand telegrams and telexes from abroad every day. If messages were encrypted, say, a diplomatic cable wired from Berlin to Belgrade, that posed little problem to the Research Office. Armed with decoding machines and a phalanx of specialists, its operatives would decipher three thousand telegrams from foreign diplomats in a month. Because the European cable system passed through both Berlin and Vienna, the office could cast its net widely. If you were a Bulgarian diplomat in London, a Turkish envoy in Moscow or a Japanese representative anywhere in western Europe, the chances were the Research Office was reading every word you wrote.

It was even more assiduous in monitoring its own citizens, gobbling up 34,000 telegrams and telexes from Germans daily. The heart of the operation was in the basement of the Berlin headquarters. There, surrounded by rows of teletype machines and runs of pneumatic tubing, staff would pore over intercepts of telephone calls, radio transmissions, telegrams, telexes and assorted encrypted messages which, thanks to a budget plump enough to pay for state-of-the-art technology, flowed in over hundreds of wires. The Research Office spied on the German people more effectively than any other German agency.

Initially, it confined itself to the monitoring of wireless radio signals, but it soon seized responsibility for telephone wiretapping in a bureaucratic land grab from the defence ministry. Units devoted to telephone intercepts were known as 'A' stations. ('B' was for wireless communication, 'C' for monitoring radio broadcasts, 'D' for teletype and telegraph intercepts and 'F' for censorship of mail. As for 'E', that letter seemed to go mysteriously unassigned.)

An 'A' station might be made up of several listening posts, which could handle up to twenty telephone lines each. At their disposal would be one or two interceptor switchboards that allowed the operators to cut in on any conversation at any time. Mechanically, the tapping was done at the main telephone exchange of the post office, then piped directly to the secret listeners who would be standing by, either at the post office itself or in a separate building. Each time a call passed through a tapped line, a bulb would light up. The designated monitor, known as a Z-man, would put on his headphones and make a stenographed record of what he heard. If the speakers talked too fast for him to keep up, he could preserve the call on a metal recording device. If they were speaking a language he did not understand, he might pass the headset over to a colleague who did.

Once the call was over, he would type up his notes into a Z report: white paper with a carbon copy and stamped in the middle, in red ink, with the words *Geheime Reichssache*: 'Reich Secret Matter'.

These, in line with the ethos of the Research Office, would stick fastidiously to the facts. No commentary or interpretation, and certainly no guesswork to fill in apparent blanks in the conversation. The goal was strict objectivity: just the words spoken, whether rendered in indirect speech or, if deemed of sufficient importance, direct quotation.

Those initial accounts were then sent via teletype machine to the report-sifting centre, Bureau III, tasked with separating wheat from chaff, before forwarding the former to one of the many branches of Bureau V for evaluation. If the tapped phone call took place out of office hours, at night or on a Sunday, it would be recorded for playback and analysis when staff were back at their desks the next morning.

Once an intercept was deemed to have value, the original Z report would be polished, to deal with any confusion about wording or over which speaker had said what, to produce an N message. A finished version that was for internal use would be transferred onto yellow paper. But if an N message was heading into the world beyond the hidden listeners of the Research Office, destined initially for whichever arm of the Nazi state had commissioned the eavesdropping in the first place, the final text would appear in purple on a distinct kind of light brown paper. In a regime whose path to power had been smoothed by the brownshirts, these documents were known as *braune Blätter*, or brownsheets. Others thought of them as 'brown birds' or even 'brown friends', perhaps a smirking reference to the fact that, for those whose words were preserved on these pieces of paper, they were anything but.

The brown birds flew first to Göring, who was said to read them all, even if that meant being confronted with a meticulous transcript of a vicious joke at his expense. Some brownsheets would then be circulated to the relevant agencies, delivered by courier in locked pouches, while others of even greater secrecy had a much narrower circulation, perhaps limited to fewer than half a dozen of the Third Reich's highest-ranking officials, including Adolf Hitler, who was said to be a particularly enthusiastic consumer of the Research Office's output, appreciating specifically its provision of bald facts, whether verbatim conversations or deciphered messages, unadorned by argument. Occasionally, the distribution list would be even shorter. A special courier service existed for this purpose, relying on bespoke despatch boxes for which only foreign minister Joachim von Ribbentrop, Göring and Hitler had the key. The messengers were under strict orders to travel with these boxes only in specially designated cars and never on trains. The documents could be read, but then had to be returned, with each sheet of paper accounted for. If the intended reader of a brownsheet was Hitler personally, it was to be produced on the Führer typewriter, a machine equipped with unusually large letters.

In September 1943, the Research Office received a new commission. The client was section IV E 3 of the Gestapo, in particular its deputy director, Leo Lange. Lange wanted telephone surveillance placed on a group of eminent Berliners who he had reason to believe were hostile to national socialism and were planning to make common cause with allies in Switzerland. His request was that a tap be placed on the phones of the following: Elisabeth von Thadden, her sister Anza Braune and her friends Anne Rühle and Isa Gruner; officials, current and former, Otto Kiep, Hilger van Scherpenberg and Arthur Zarden; socialites Hanna Solf and Fanny von Kurowsky; and known critics of the regime Carl Goerdeler, Friedrich Siegmund-Schultze and General Ludwig Beck.

At first, this would have seemed like a routine assignment for the eavesdroppers of Schillerstrasse, even if some of the names were those of especially prominent individuals. This, after all, was the agency that had intercepted the telephone calls of the Czechoslovak leadership in September 1938, allowing Hitler to conclude that Prague had given up all hope of holding onto the Sudetenland, knowledge that emboldened him to press Neville Chamberlain into the appeasement at Munich hailed by the British prime minister as 'peace in our time'. They were in the business of divining the true intentions and desires of nations, whether enemy or friend. By comparison, Lange's request would have carried the whiff of bread and butter: the basics. But it set in train a chain of events that would soon turn deadly.

31

A Mole at HQ

September 1943

NATURALLY, ELISABETH VON Thadden knew nothing of the massive, well-resourced intelligence operation just down the road from the place where she spent the early hours of 11 September 1943 so sleeplessly. She arose that morning with the words of her former pupil still ringing loudly in her ears: *I wouldn't send any mail.* That's what Irmgard Zarden had said, the sentiment echoed later by Anne Rühle. And now Elisabeth was resolved to undo whatever mistake she might have made. She set off for the apartment of Paul Reckzeh.

The young doctor was not home, but the old doctor was. It was Professor Reckzeh who came to the door. Pointedly, Elisabeth thought, he did not invite her in. Instead, she had to get straight to the crux of the matter, explaining that Paul had been a guest in her home the previous day. Reckzeh's father said he knew about that.

'I gave him a letter,' she said. 'I'd rather have it back.'

The older man's response came as an unexpected relief. 'My son has already burned the letter,' he said.

It was clear he did not want to provide any more details or linger in conversation, so Elisabeth replied simply, 'That's exactly what I wanted.'

This Professor Reckzeh lacked the fluent charm of his son. He was curt, if not conceited. Perhaps he feared the neighbours who might be watching this exchange – you never knew what might be reported as suspicious – but he could hardly see Elisabeth down the stairs and out of that building fast enough. She was not used to such rudeness.

Still, none of that mattered. For it was now clear that the younger

Paul Reckzeh had realised the risk of carrying such letters, which could so easily fall into the wrong hands. Evidently, he had thought better of his offer to act as a go-between linking Berlin dissidents to their potential allies in Switzerland and had done the right thing, destroying the evidence that could have brought them all such trouble. She could breathe easy.

Unless what had actually happened was that the father had found that letter, and perhaps the others too, realised what his son was up to and made a decision to stand in his way, destroying the prize haul his son had brought home. If it was Reckzeh Snr, not Jnr, who had burned her letter, that would be less reassuring. Either way, the immediate threat had receded.

Except what Elisabeth did not yet know is that, whatever the Reckzehs had done with the letters, Reckzeh junior had not disposed of the other evidence he had gathered: the words that he had heard and indeed encouraged the previous afternoon when he sat with those nine others and acted as agent provocateur, prompting and nudging several present to speak their minds. On the contrary, he had passed all of that on, in copious detail, to Herbert 'Leo' Lange.

Once he had heard it, the Gestapo man had made a calculation. Even if Reckzeh had already witnessed enough to damn Thadden and her friends, it was better to wait. Let the traitors of the tea party keep talking. Let them hang themselves with their own words. Let them inadvertently lead Lange and the Gestapo to other enemies of the Reich, to other conspirators against national socialism. Let Reckzeh travel to Switzerland, exploiting the connections and following up the leads that had been handed to him. The key was to sit back and, thanks to the secret eavesdroppers of the Research Office, listen.

So Lange did not order the arrest of all those who had participated in the treasonous gathering at Carmerstrasse. Instead, he applied to the Research Office for monitoring to begin of their telephones and those of at least three others they had named. Ultimately, this would be one for Bureau V, section 13: Internal Affairs Evaluation, where a staff of some eighty people kept a constant and suspicious eye on internal dissent, looking out for any individuals inside Germany who were, or might become, figures of opposition to the regime.

Lange would have had every confidence that his application would remain confidential. Unlike other agencies he could mention, the Research Office was known for its soundness: its founder was a conviction antisemite who had joined the Nazi party as early as 1920, and its number one client, said to value its work as very reliable, was the Führer himself. But the key fact that eluded Lange was that even inside one of the Third Reich's mightiest institutions of authoritarian control, there lurked dissent.

An official by the name of Hartmut Plaas sat inside the Research Office as a senior government counsellor. He did his job but he harboured a discreet sympathy for the German opposition and was connected to the loose group of resisters around Hans Oster, the deputy head of the Abwehr. When Plaas heard about the application for a wiretap against the tea-party group, he slipped the word to a like-minded friend, Captain Ludwig Gehre, who worked in the same foreign affairs and defence liaison office of the Wehrmacht high command, the OKW. This was no aberration. In fact, Plaas had made it his business to let the Abwehr know of any Gestapo surveillance requests that might be of interest, and he always did it in the same way, via the captain who, in turn, had long been in the habit of supplying his friends with well-timed warnings of unwelcome monitoring.

Once Gehre heard about this latest application, he passed the information to a colleague and ally in his office: Count Helmuth von Moltke, the young lawyer who had become a friend and intellectual sparring partner to Otto Kiep and who had formed a dissenting circle of his own, centred on his family estate at Kreisau. Moltke knew instantly that his chum was in danger. It was his duty to warn him.

He did it one morning during the third week of September, knocking on Otto's door and entering his office with a copy of Paul Reckzeh's Gestapo report on the tea party. Whatever discomfort Otto had felt that afternoon when Reckzeh offered to act as a messenger, there could now be no doubt. Reckzeh was a Gestapo spy who had given a full account of the event at Carmerstrasse. Worse, he had singled out Otto's contributions to the discussion as especially 'defeatist'. Otto and Moltke were both lawyers; neither needed to remind the other that defeatism amounted to treason, a crime punishable by death. Obviously the Gestapo would arrest everyone who had been present that day. The only question was when.

32

Sixth Sense

Elisabeth, Autumn 1943

BY A QUIRK of the diary, Otto was due to have lunch at the Cavalry Club the next day with Elisabeth von Thadden. There may have been a war on, but people of his station still went out for lunch and could still eat well. Despite everything, including the closure of many eateries as part of the 'Total War' austerity drive demanded by Joseph Goebbels following defeat at Stalingrad, restaurant life continued in wartime Berlin, even as the bombs fell. Irmgard Zarden had maintained her habit of dining at the place most considered the best in the city, Horcher, where the food was still superb and, better yet, one did not have to give up precious coupons from one's ration book. Even in 1943, young Fräulein Zarden could savour the pheasant à la presse with a fine Burgundy and imagine herself back in peacetime. Herr Horcher was able to keep up his pre-war standard of cuisine for one reason above all: despite their official demands for abstemiousness, high-ranking Nazis liked to eat there, Göring especially. Nevertheless, Horcher was a tactful host, carefully ensuring that his old customers did not have to rub shoulders with the Nazi big shots, keeping them apart by serving them in separate rooms.

Things were different now, of course, but not always in the ways one might expect. True, Berlin's restaurants were obliged to observe *Opfersonntag*, 'sacrifice Sunday', by serving a tasteless stew that was more of a soup. (The regulation dated from the early days of the Nazi regime when it was branded as *Eintopfsonntag*, or 'stew Sunday', requiring Germans to substitute their traditional weekend roast for a more frugal meal and to donate the savings, fifty pfennigs per person, as a sign of national solidarity.) True, too, that once-commonplace fish and seafood were now either strictly rationed or wholly unobtainable: the presence of mines in coastal waters and the Battle of the Atlantic meant the deep-sea fishing fleets had disappeared. But shellfish that thrived in shallow waters, such as lobster or oyster, were in plentiful supply right up to the middle of 1944: they were not even rationed. No less improbable, while decent beer had become scarce in Germany, French wine and Champagne, though rationed in France itself, flowed freely in the Reich. As a result, plenty of the aristocratic set, those counts and countesses who did not huddle in secret groups lamenting the state of the nation, found that much of their pre-war life remained pleasantly intact. They still enjoyed the same delicacies, still went to the opera, perhaps to see a touring production direct from Italy, still danced at fabulous embassy parties. It all carried on, even as the gas vans set on their way by Leo Lange were doing their work.

Even so, none of that made lunch at the Cavalry Club an enjoyable experience for Otto and Elisabeth. Otto began by telling her what Moltke had told him, then gave a summary of Reckzeh's report. Doing his best to approach the situation methodically, he had drawn up two lists: things that could be admitted and things that would have to be flatly denied. Following that rubric, they could accept that the gathering had taken place and that they had discussed the current situation, starting with the Allies' 'terror raids' on Berlin. Equally, they could say that Otto had passed around a photograph that had been published in the *New York Times*. It would be hard to regard that as a crime, given that that same image had since appeared in the official party newspaper to illustrate the wickedness of the Allied enemy. But what of Otto's prognosis of the course of the war, the one to which Reckzeh had attached the dread word 'defeatist'?

That was much more of a challenge. They would not deny the words had been spoken, but would stress that they were not delivered in a polemical way but rather in the manner of a dispassionate, objective analysis. They would suggest that Otto was speaking exactly as he would have done had he been addressing army officers or colleagues in the Foreign Ministry, offering nothing more than a detached, professional assessment.

Once they felt they had their story straight, they talked about how they should break the awful news to the others. Otto tried to put a positive gloss on matters. This day was always going to come, he told Elisabeth, but at least now they had advance warning. That gave them a chance to prepare, to fix on an account that might see them punished relatively lightly, facing prison rather than death. If that was a thin kind of reassurance, so was what he said next. 'The others may get away free. You and I are the ones they want.'

Maria

Even before Otto or Elisabeth had a chance to tell the rest of the group, some already had a nagging sense that they had been led into a trap. As they drove home from the tea party, Arthur Zarden had told his daughter why he had grown increasingly quiet during the discussion. 'I wish I had not gone,' he said, 'I have a bad feeling about this man.' Irmgard knew exactly what he meant. A young man in good health, obviously fit to serve but not in the army, free to travel to Switzerland, even though civilian travel abroad had effectively stopped in 1939? None of it made sense. It was not long before she noticed that the phone at her home began to emit telltale clicks whenever she made or received a call.

Even those who had not been there that Friday afternoon could tell something was awry in the days that followed. Countess Maria von Maltzan always believed she had a sixth sense for trouble. It was that same instinct that had told her to stay away from the tea party. But now her suspicions were aroused elsewhere.

She had long been involved in a group that helped Jews and others escape Germany for Switzerland by whatever means available. A particularly perilous route was the one taken by the 'black swimmers', volunteers who helped escapees across the stretch of Lake Constance known as the Untersee. In September 1943, Maria was told that one of the black swimmers had dropped out. Maria was known to be strong and courageous and accomplished in the water: might she step in? The work would be physically demanding and extremely dangerous. So of course she said yes.

She travelled to the meeting point on the lower lake. After dark, her contact led her to a particular spot and showed her a light on the Swiss side of the water by which she could orient herself. Next, she was introduced to the woman she was to take across, a Jew who, at sixty, was nearly twice Maria's age. The crossing would require both women to swim without rest for two hours straight.

They were given black swimsuits whose sleeves were long and necks were high: the less skin that was exposed, the harder it would be for the crews of the roaming patrol boats to spot them. As for the most crucial piece of equipment, Maria had brought that along herself. When the other two saw it, they were baffled.

The time had come to slip into the water. There could be no burst of energy, no wild splashing or thrashing. This would require steady, quiet strokes. As the minutes passed, the pair moving through the water, Maria could not help but be impressed. This woman was old by Maria's standards, but was drawing on deep reserves of stamina. Maybe she was just very fit. Or perhaps this is what determination to save one's own life, to be free of the constant threat of deportation, looked like. Maybe when you were fighting for survival, your body revealed previously hidden sources of strength.

At last, two hours later, they reached the shore. Exhausted, they had made it to Swiss soil. A man came to pick up the Jewish woman and usher her into her new life. Maria had time to take only a short break: if she was to reach the German side of the lake before first light, she would soon have to set off once more. She did and, somehow, she managed it: there and back, more than four hours of swimming, in a single night.

The following evening, she was back at that same spot. Her task now was to transport the woman's worldly goods, everything she could not live without, jammed into a single waterproof suitcase, attached to the inflated inner tubes of a car tyre. Maria's method was to keep the case in front of her as she swam, constantly nudging it ahead. It was so tiring but, once again, she reached the Swiss shore smoothly. A short break, and she was back in the water for the fourth and final leg. Except this time, there was a sound.

She listened and looked and there was no mistaking it: an engine. A police boat was approaching, accompanied by powerful searchlights that flashed on and off as they swept and scanned the surface of the lake. Now was the moment for Maria to deploy that piece of specialist equipment that had accompanied her on all four swims.

Equipment was perhaps too grand a word. It was a hollowed-out pumpkin, with two holes for eyes, attached to a long piece of string. Maria had read about it, and the trick it could play, when she was a girl, in a book of children's tales about Native Americans that she had never forgotten. She had dragged it along with her through all these long hours, ready for precisely this contingency.

She placed the pumpkin on her head and treaded water, waiting for the searchlight to catch sight of it. When it was finally fixed in its beam, Maria took several deep breaths and dived, getting as far away as she could. From below, and through the water, she could hear the sound of machine-gun fire shredding its target. Only when she could hold her breath no longer did she allow herself to rise back to the surface.

When she did, it was to see the patrol boat turn and head away, as if satisfied that the lake was now free of unwanted interlopers. The pumpkin head was no more, its blasted fragments scattered across the water. It had drawn hostile fire to itself so that she might live, just as in that childhood storybook.

Maria kept swimming until, utterly drained, she reached the German shore. Too tired to travel right away, she thought of her friend Lagi and Lagi's mother, Hanna, who had a family house nearby, in Partenkirchen. She called their number, only for the phone to be answered by a voice she had never heard before. It explained that the countess was out and asked Maria to call back in half an hour when she would be back. Maria's sixth sense struck again. Something was not right. She hung up without saying another word and resolved never to call that number again.

33
Be Warned

Autumn 1943

CONFIRMATION THAT THE group's darkest intuitions were right came as quickly as Otto and Elisabeth could pass word to their friends. Otto did little to sugar the pill: 'The conversations we had were absolutely lethal,' he told them.

One by one, they gasped as the facts were laid out and Reckzeh was named as a spy. Instantly, and naturally, each person thought of themselves, rewinding the mental recording they had made of that afternoon, trying to recall exactly what words had come out of their own mouths and hoping that the worst had been said by others.

For her part, Hanna Solf was livid. Her fury was directed at Elisabeth, who had been so cavalier with their security, allowing this fox to charm his way into their henhouse. It was Elisabeth's recklessness that had opened the door to Reckzeh. Hanna herself had given countless teas, convened hundreds of sensitive conversations: part of one's duties as host was to pick one's guests carefully. Elisabeth had vouched for this young man and the others had taken her word that he could be trusted.

If Hanna intended her rebuke to contain a tacit boast that nothing like this had ever occurred at the Solf salon, while Elisabeth had fallen at the first hurdle giving her debut party, she may have been on shaky ground. As it so happened, the Solf gatherings had acquired a reputation. Plenty of politicians and diplomats, even those wholly committed to the cause of opposing national socialism, avoided the Solf soirées, fearing they were too open. No one seemed to be paying sufficiently close attention to the question of admission. Carl Goerdeler always declined invitations from Frau Solf. He was not a

Otto Kiep, the seasoned diplomat who served as Germany's consul general in New York. With fluent English, and a young, attractive wife at his side, he proved a great success.

Otto's wife Hanna, with their son, Albrecht. Committed to home, family and nation, and willing to defend all three fiercely, she might have been a huntress from Teutonic myth.

Maria Helene Francoise Izabel von Maltzan, Baroness of Wartenberg and Penzlin, was young, but she had long kept her eyes and ears open.

The Maltzan family seat in Militsch, rural Silesia, where Maria was raised by English nannies and French governesses in a castle of domed halls and medieval galleries.

When tasked with restoring injured military horses to full health, Maria von Maltzan found ingenious ways to delay their return to frontline duty.

Maria's lover, Hans Hirschel. The couple developed a cover story, should a visitor ever come to call: Hans would be Professor Schröder, a friend who just happened to be in the house.

The countess and the tiger, 1950. If human beings had disappointed Maria, her animals never did.

Hanna and Wilhelm Solf in Samoa, where he was governor and already in his fifties when they married. It was a joint decision to make their home a salon for political conversation.

Lagi Solf, the beautiful countess who had been turning heads at Berlin parties since her late teens – and whose help for Jews in need made her some early enemies.

Irmgard Zarden. Once among Germany's richest young heiresses, she had been walked to school by a butler, travelled first class to Rome, Paris and New York and partied with debutantes in London.

Arthur Zarden, who for a while held one of the most powerful offices of the German government. In Berlin's ruling circles, he was admired for his 'cosmopolitan outlook'.

Alsenstrasse, the wide avenue in the select Berlin neighbourhood between the Reichstag and the headquarters of the German general staff that housed a dozen embassies and some of the city's grandest residences, including one apartment building that was home to both the Solf and Zarden families.

The daughter of landed aristocracy, Elisabeth von Thadden was initially quite well disposed towards national socialism.

Elisabeth and her pupils. She ran her school in Wieblingen like a family household, with herself as a maternal figure. Once a week, she would host a 'common evening' in her private living room.

Friedrich Siegmund-Schultze, the reforming cleric who would be exiled in Zurich. Elisabeth von Thadden admired his double commitment to the poor and to peace.

Hilger van Scherpenberg (*far left*), a Social Democrat long opposed to the Nazis, and fellow diplomat Count Albrecht von Bernstorff, unmissable at six foot six inches tall. Alongside them, then British Prime Minister Ramsay MacDonald and daughter Ishbel, at the German embassy in London in 1931.

Joseph Wirth, who had briefly served as German chancellor in the 1920s and was later exiled to Switzerland. The Gestapo believed he was at the centre of a plot to depose Adolf Hitler.

Father Max Josef Metzger. An idealist and pacifist, he once wrote a letter setting out why it was essential for Adolf Hitler to step down. He put the letter in an envelope and addressed it to ... Adolf Hitler.

Bianca Segantini. Friend and confidante of Elisabeth von Thadden. If Elisabeth was devoted to truth, Bianca worshipped at the altar of beauty.

Paul Reckzeh, the young doctor at Berlin's Charité hospital with an admirable curriculum vitae: he had worked with children, volunteering to put in extra hours after he qualified. He was to travel around Switzerland as a messenger of the German resistance.

Carmerstrasse, Berlin. On 10 September 1943, this would be the venue for a tea party. The hostess was certain it would be a delightful afternoon, a gathering of good friends and allied souls.

cautious man, his friends agreed on that – there was that little black book that had so unnerved Arthur Zarden – and yet even he concluded that the Solf salons were too risky.

Breaking the news to all involved meant more than informing those who had been in the room on 10 September. For Otto, perhaps the most painful conversation was the one he had to have with someone who had not been present that afternoon. He put it off as long as he could, waiting a day and a night after Moltke had appeared in his office with word of Reckzeh's betrayal. Only after he and Elisabeth von Thadden had lunched at the Cavalry Club, that evening after work, did he finally tell his wife, Hanna, what had happened.

He knew that he was warning her of not merely his own possible – even inevitable – fate, but of hers too. In the Germany of Adolf Hitler, there was no guarantee that the wives of those accused of political crimes would not suffer along with their husbands. When a man was arrested, there was a chance that his wife would be too. Their children might be picked up along with the parents. The aim was to send a message to every would-be resister or rebel in the land: come after the Reich and the Reich could come after you and your entire family.

Given how unguarded he could be in front of strangers, it would have surprised no one to know that, until that moment, Otto Kiep had been completely open with his wife. He would tell Hanna all that he knew about the plots and schemes against Hitler. The resistance cell in the upper reaches of the Abwehr was not some opaque, distant thing to her. On the contrary, the men at the top were people she knew well. Hans Oster, he of the weekly beer goblet by the front gate, was a family friend. She knew of the ideas her husband shared not only with Oster but Admiral Canaris; she knew of the role they envisaged for Carl Goerdeler and their hopes for General Beck. What Otto knew, she knew.

Just as he and Elisabeth had done at lunch, he and Hanna discussed as methodically as they could what could be admitted and what would have to be denied. They went through names of friends, acquaintances, colleagues, anybody who might be of interest to the Gestapo, which was everybody. It would be futile to feign an ignorance she did not have, to pretend she had not met people whom she had hosted or whose homes she had visited. No, it would be safer to admit knowing almost everyone on their notional list of names, but to insist her relationship with those figures was purely social. She would be the innocent and simple wife, whose pretty head was unfilled by the affairs of state that necessarily occupied her husband.

They went over it, Otto finding reassurance in the thought that Hanna had been a consummate diplomatic spouse, seasoned in navigating conversations with those whose intentions were unfriendly, skilled at saying only what was politically safe and saying it convincingly. If she could handle the chatter at a Washington garden party, she could handle an interrogation from the Gestapo. That, at least, is how Otto consoled himself.

But he also saw her face as he told her what Moltke had told him. He saw her reaction as they talked again about the tea party, about his damning verdict on Germany's prospects in the war and about Reckzeh, who had been noting every word for his masters in the secret police. He saw her shock; he saw her fear. And though she did not cry then, he pictured her later that night, alone with her tears. She would be frightened for her family. She would be frightened for him.

His openness with his wife came at a price, he could see that now. Other men might have kept their wives in the dark all these years. But he could not bottle up what he knew; he had felt it almost a duty to describe what he saw, rather than to keep it to himself. And so he had always spoken freely. But that habit had clearly cost him very dearly.

Worse, it had exposed his wife to grave danger, burdening her with forbidden knowledge. The least he could do now was to make that burden no heavier. Whatever he learned from this moment on, whatever information he picked up – names, places, plans – would have to remain his alone. He loved her but he could confide in her no more. He could confide in her no more because he loved her.

His duty did not end with his wife. He sought out his sister Ida, at a family gathering that same September to mark the day their mother was born. Otto told her he expected to be arrested. It was a kind of warning to her too, because if he was arrested, it would not be long before the Gestapo came to call on her.

Methodically, Ida set about rereading the letters Otto had sent her over the years, picking out any that included a word or line critical of Hitler and burning them. The pile left afterwards was small.

Elisabeth had to have hard conversations with her own sister Anza, who became seriously ill over the following months. Elisabeth also spoke to Anza's friend Anne Rühle, who resolved to live as normally as she could, even as she vowed to be more vigilant.

Harder was getting word to Otto Kiep's fellow diplomat Hilger van Scherpenberg. Elisabeth wanted to tell him herself, in person – obviously she could not speak over the telephone – but it proved impossible for him to get away from work. By now, Elisabeth had extended her vacation from the Red Cross and was staying at the Schloss Elmau at the southernmost end of the country. She wanted to be far away from Berlin, to clear her head. There was no question of running away: on the contrary, she was determined to do her duty.

From the castle in Elmau, she used what she hoped would be an untapped line to call Scherpenberg's wife, currently staying in Weilheim. The pair met at the railway station there and sat down together. Sure she was not being watched, Elisabeth felt at last that she could speak candidly. She told the younger woman everything.

'I can't sleep any more,' she said. Not that that was important. 'It doesn't matter what happens to me, it doesn't bother me.' But the reason she could not rest, the reason she could find no peace was that Inge's husband and Otto Kiep were fathers of children. If anything were to happen to those men, the children would be bereft. Elisabeth von Thadden was not a mother herself, but she had devoted much of her life to children. The thought of it was almost too much to bear.

What, she asked Inge, was she to do? She couldn't speak to Hilger, just as she could not communicate with Otto or anyone else. 'Everything is bugged, everything is seen.' She urged Inge to go to Berlin and talk to people who might be able to help. 'Go if you can, get advice for everyone.'

Inge van Scherpenberg listened quietly, taking it all in. Later, when she spoke to her husband, he offered her the reassurance that he at least had been careful. He had been on his guard, he explained, in part because Reckzeh had not been the only new face in the room that day. 'There were three people there I didn't know,' he told her; 'reason for me to be extremely cautious.'

For Elisabeth, with no family of her own and a sick sister, the nights grew more troubled. She was in grave danger, but what was much worse, so were several other people – and it was her fault.

Just when she thought the hole into which she had fallen could get no deeper, there came a message from the man she had hoped never to hear from again.

Paul Reckzeh wanted to see her.

34

Across the Border

Paul, September 1943

AFTER HIS TRIUMPH at Carmerstrasse and his debrief with his handler, Leo Lange, it was clear where Dr Reckzeh would have to go next. Thanks to the trusting nature of Elisabeth von Thadden, as well as Hanna Solf and, more unexpectedly, Otto Kiep, he was armed with enough leads to make a return trip to Switzerland. He headed there almost immediately.

This time there would be no need to use his wife as an unwitting prop, nor to raid his parents' Christmas card list for contacts. Instead, he had a meeting in Lucerne with the former chancellor Joseph Wirth and Wirth's ally, the writer and sometime politician Johann Jacob Kindt-Kiefer. They were both worth meeting, not least because, together with others exiled across the Swiss border, they were part of a working group called Democratic Germany, which was drafting a paper on how the country's future might unfold after the war. This was precisely the kind of treacherous behaviour Lange was trying to sniff out. After all, these were the very men who that summer had discussed along with Count Bernstorff the formation of a government-in-exile, one that might seek to broker a peace – a surrender, as Lange would see it – with the Allies. Bernstorff was now safely in custody, but these exiles were free and still plotting. And now they would speak of their plans to one of Lange's agents.

Wirth wanted to hear all Reckzeh could tell him about the tea party on Carmerstrasse, the shared analysis and competing views of those like-minded folk who were still in Berlin. But what he needed most was contact with Germans of the highest influence, those in or around the regime. He asked Reckzeh if he could connect him to one general in particular. If the good doctor were willing to act as an intermediary, then Wirth had a crucial question to put to the military man: would you agree to take part in the formation of a new government of Germany and, if so, under what conditions? He asked Reckzeh to take that message back to Berlin, along, of course, with warm greetings for Hanna Solf, Otto Kiep and Elisabeth von Thadden.

Reckzeh also secured himself a second audience with Friedrich Siegmund-Schultze, the social reformer and spiritual guide to Elisabeth von Thadden. That meeting did not go so well. Siegmund-Schultze had been suspicious of the doctor the first time they had met, but now he was sure. The apparently limitless supply of money, the repeatedly contradictory statements, the whole way Reckzeh conducted himself: Siegmund-Schultze was sufficiently certain that he had come face to face with an agent of the Gestapo that he notified both the Federal Aliens division of the Swiss police, which had oversight of foreigners, and the owner of the hotel where Reckzeh was staying. Next, he tried to warn Wirth, urging him to steer clear and say nothing. But it was too late.

No less futile were Siegmund-Schultze's efforts to tip off Elisabeth. He worked hard at it, tracking down a friend of the Thadden family, one Adrienne Gans zu Putlitz von Bülow, whom he knew to be holidaying in Switzerland. He urged her to act immediately, to interrupt her vacation and get word to Elisabeth and her friends. The woman did as she was told, putting her warning in writing. But, once again, it was too late.

Siegmund-Schultze also made his accusations directly. Looking the visiting doctor in the eye, he told him that he believed Reckzeh was an agent of the German secret police: 'I think it's vile that you're doing this,' he said. 'Stop.' And then, ever the educator and pastor, he added: 'You are making a mess of your life.'

Perhaps hastened on his way by the threat of a run-in with the Swiss police, Reckzeh cut short his mission and headed back to Germany. The meetings in Switzerland had only ever been means to an end, a way of flushing out dissenters not in Zurich, Lucerne or Bern but in Berlin, Munich and Hamburg. Now, thanks to those less suspicious than Siegmund-Schultze, he had several good leads. The calling cards he had gathered at the tea party had begotten new calling cards, one from a former chancellor no less, which he would use to burrow his way deeper into the treacherous movement against Adolf Hitler.

His first move was to renew contact with those who had proved so helpful, the men and women he had met that Friday afternoon on Carmerstrasse. If nothing else, it was what his cover story required. He had told the tea party that he was aiming to meet fellow rebels in Switzerland, to share information and tactics, and so it was natural that he would want to report back.

He managed to meet Elisabeth's sister Anza at Potsdamer Platz, greeting her as if they were the fondest of old friends, but he got nothing from her. He saw Hilger van Scherpenberg, who received him in his office in the Foreign Ministry with a great show of kindness. The pretext for the meeting was Reckzeh's declaration of a desire to work in the ministry and Scherpenberg promised to help. But when it came to anything that might count as information, the diplomat's answers were so superficial as to be devoid of any content.

Still, that was an improvement on the response Reckzeh got from the others.

He tried to see Hanna Solf, who sent apologies in a brief written note. When he turned up at the Solf front door, Lagi's husband, Count von Ballestrem, turned him away.

He called Otto Kiep repeatedly, purportedly to pass on greetings from Switzerland: Otto refused to take his calls and did not so much as reply to his letter, in which the doctor had asked for a meeting where he might seek some personal advice. Otto knew the risk he was taking, but he didn't care. To his wife he said: 'Let him realise that I know all about him.'

Arthur Zarden was more cautious. When, a few weeks after the party, Reckzeh telephoned to say he was keen to visit 'and continue the interesting conversation', he was at pains not to say a definitive no, lest that reveal what he knew. Instead, he agreed to a visit but ensured his daughter, Irmgard, was there too. The pair worked hard to keep the discussion general and as harmless as possible. Once again, Reckzeh offered to take letters to Switzerland, and Arthur was quick to say that anything he would want to write to his few friends across the border was too innocuous to trouble the censor.

It seemed almost every door was closed to Paul Reckzeh; those few that were ajar offered next to nothing. There was only one more left to try.

35

Double Bluff

Elisabeth, Autumn 1943

SHE HAD NOT returned to work but was still in Elmau when Reckzeh got in touch, announcing that he was now back and would like to call on her. Perhaps she found it harder than the others to blank someone so directly, because she did not give a straight no.

Instead, she began to panic. She called Inge van Scherpenberg, desperate for advice. It was topsy-turvy: the one-time headmistress turning to a woman no older than her former pupils for calm counsel.

'What should I do?' she asked, her heart thumping. 'Please come!'

Cannily, Inge said nothing on the phone. Instead, she made the journey by train and motor car to Elmau.

'Get sick,' she told Elisabeth. 'Avoid seeing him.' Make an excuse, do whatever it takes.

But what if he insisted? What if she couldn't get out of it?

'If there is no other way, then only meet him when you are with other people,' Inge said. Though just in case that gave Elisabeth any ideas, she swiftly added, 'But not with me.'

Elisabeth turned the problem over and over in her mind. She lay on the balcony, staring at the white mountains and soaking up the autumn colours. The leaves seemed to glow, but they gave her no comfort. She read the Bible, she talked to herself, but none of it helped. She was alone with her predicament.

Friends visited, but they brought either no advice or advice she could not use. Arthur Zarden came, his face etched with worry. An old pal made the trek to Elmau, offering to help spirit Elisabeth across the border to Switzerland. But that was not an option. For one thing, she had a brother in uniform, Reinold, serving then as the occupying district commander of the Belgian city of Leuven. He had already faced the interrogators several times over his membership of the Confessing Church. A sister on the run would only make his position more perilous. Besides, saving her own skin was not the point, not when she had endangered a whole group of people. If she fled, she would deepen the troubles of those left behind, among them the two fathers of young children, Otto Kiep and Hilger van Scherpenberg. It was not an option. 'It's not about me,' she said.

There were days when she wondered if, despite all she knew, she had got Paul Reckzeh wrong. Perhaps they all had. True, a letter had arrived from Adrienne Gans zu Putlitz von Bülow, saying she was breaking into her holiday to urge Elisabeth to avoid the young doctor, but could she really have misread Reckzeh so badly when she invited him into her home? Could Bianca Segantini have made a similarly gross misjudgement, to say nothing of the rest of the guests at the tea party, none of whom took exception to Dr Reckzeh while they drank coffee and ate cake together?

Even if the facts were as they appeared – chief among them, Otto's declaration that Reckzeh had filed a report to the Gestapo – maybe even then the situation was not irretrievable. During her career, Elisabeth had developed a deep faith in young people and especially in their capacity for change. Even those who had sinned gravely sometimes regretted the path they had taken and chose a better one. Maybe Paul Reckzeh could be persuaded to recant and repent.

She decided she would agree to his request after all. Whether to be sure of his true nature or to urge him to change course, she would meet him face to face.

That meant ignoring the first part of Inge van Scherpenberg's advice, but Elisabeth would at least follow the second: she would not meet Reckzeh alone. Acting in the combined roles of second and chaperone would be her friend Elisabeth Wirth, no relation to the exiled former chancellor, who had lived through these days of angst at her side, coming to see her after work, taking long walks with her. Now she agreed to host the meeting with Reckzeh in her rooms. As the two women readied themselves for his arrival, they set the table. The thought cannot have escaped Elisabeth von Thadden: here she was again, preparing yet another tea party.

If Reckzeh had a guilty conscience, he did not show it. On the contrary, he arrived as full of charm and energy as the first time they had met. Brimming with news from Switzerland and warm greetings from mutual friends, he was fluent and clever. There was nothing shifty in the way he put a pastry on his plate or stirred sugar into his tea, and Elisabeth was watching him closely.

He spoke as a fellow believer in the cause of a new, post-Nazi Germany. He was glad to report that he had seen former chancellor Wirth along with former minister Kindt-Kiefer and, good news, these men had a direct connection with the president of the United States, Mr Roosevelt. The link was Allen Dulles, who ran the Swiss bureau of the Office of Strategic Services, then the lead US intelligence agency (and forerunner of the CIA, which Dulles would go on to head). Reckzeh's information was that Roosevelt had pledged that, when the war was finally over, he would not let the people of Germany starve.

All this was offered as proof that the young doctor was getting things done, that he was advancing the cause of those who had taken tea together at Carmerstrasse. Of course, he was not content to rest on his laurels; there was too much more work to be done. He was particularly keen to be introduced to Generaloberst Franz Halder, the former chief of staff of the Oberkommando des Heeres, or OKH, the army high command, so that he could act as messenger, bringing word of Wirth's political plans, including his preparations for a new German government and constitution. It did not seem a fanciful request: though Halder had been close enough to the Führer to have been tasked with planning the invasions of both Poland in 1939 and the Soviet Union in 1941, and though his rank placed him just below the level of a field marshal, he and Hitler had fallen out badly over military strategy, culminating in Halder's removal from his post in September 1942. It made sense that Wirth would regard a once senior, now disaffected commander as a potential ally.

Reckzeh pressed the request several times; an introduction to the general would aid his work tremendously. Given Elisabeth's own connections, surely it would not be too difficult to arrange?

The two women decided to challenge the assumed premise of the conversation. Was it so obvious that the war was lost? Wasn't that unduly pessimistic? There was talk of Germany acquiring a new, powerful weapon; maybe that would lead to a breakthrough on the battlefield? Unless he knew otherwise, the front was still holding, wasn't it? No, they were not impressed by all these gloomy reports, which could well be exaggerated. Victory was still possible, surely?

All three remained in character, the two women playing the unwavering patriots, Reckzeh the disgruntled dissident. 'The war is lost,' he said, more adamant than ever. The question was what would come next. More specifically, and homing in on what he knew to be a particular area of concern to Elisabeth von Thadden, he wondered what would be required to ward off mass famine. 'What do you think we will need?' he asked, a picture of ingenuous concern. 'What do you estimate, madam? How many wagons?' He was talking about canned meat, flour, sugar.

Elisabeth insisted that she had given no thought to such things. 'The war is absolutely not lost,' she said, now clear in her own mind that Reckzeh was exactly who all the evidence said he was: an agent provocateur in the pay of the Gestapo.

'I could report you to the Gestapo,' Elisabeth said in mock-rebuke.

'Oh, that might not matter,' he said, in the same light register. 'I have friends in the SS too!' If only he were joking.

They kept it up as long as they could, the two Elisabeths exhorting the young man to be of better cheer, to welcome the fact that German U-boats were back in action in the Atlantic, that there had been encouraging developments in the war in Asia. He maintained his stance of stubborn pessimism.

Eventually, evening came. He suggested he stay the night in the Schloss Elmau, the castle where, as it so happened, Elisabeth Wirth was responsible for the allocation of rooms. With sadness, she told him there were no vacancies. They would walk him out.

They said their goodbyes at the edge of the forest, the leaves rustling in the night breeze. Only once Reckzeh was out of earshot did the two women speak. It was Elisabeth Wirth who broke the silence. 'Now do you think he is an informer?'

Elisabeth von Thadden gave her answer, stating definitively what she had surely known for so long, no matter how ardently she had wanted not to believe it. In a whisper, she said, 'Unquestionably.'

After that, all she could do was prepare for the car in the driveway, the knock on the door, that she believed was inevitable. She received friends, including young Inge van Scherpenberg, who visited her once more and who came armed with a *Stammbuch*, a kind of friendship book, asking Elisabeth to write something in it. Elisabeth was not sure that was wise. She was toxic now. Any association could only bring trouble. But Inge would not be refused.

And so in clear handwriting, Elisabeth inscribed these words: 'My time is but a passage through God's eternal today.'

Below that, she wrote out a few lines from the contemporary poet, the Austrian aristocrat Count Paul Thun-Hohenstein:

> So we all live and fall
> No one has a sure footing
> And I am only lost myself
> I know myself born into wonder
> And fall wherever I fall
> Into God's broad hand!

Finally, she scribbled 'Elmau' and the date: 24 October 1943.

Still, even if her faith demanded that Elisabeth now place herself in the hands of the Almighty, there was no rule that said she could not give the divine some help. Though she believed the men from the Gestapo could arrive at any moment, she would not wait passively for her fate.

36

Silk and Lace

Elisabeth, Autumn 1943

HER WORK RUNNING a school for the daughters of some of Germany's most prestigious families had given her an address book that had not entirely lost its value. At the very least she knew people who knew people. Among the latter, a woman who was one of a cluster of beauties who had become adornments to the Führer's circle, offsetting the gunmetal grey of the ruler's court with the silks and sparkle of wartime glamour. Some of them had been hanging around Hitler since the early days, back when he was barely known.

Most of these were married women. They were not lovers, past or present, of the leader's, nor were they confidantes. But they did have access. As such, they were sought after, if only for their ability to drop a word in the sovereign's ear at the right moment. There were officials in the Nazi state who relied on this channel as their sole means of drawing problems to the attention of the Führer. There was little evidence that it had ever effected a change in policy, but it could secure a favour or two.

Elisabeth had an acquaintance in common with one of the women of this gilded circle. She tried to make contact, failed and tried again. To her surprise, she received a summons to visit this woman – whom even Elisabeth's private journal was only allowed to identify as 'Frau H.' – in her suite at the Hotel Adlon, which stood directly opposite the Reich Chancellery. As the functionaries of all imperial households know, at court proximity is all.

Elisabeth was ushered into a world she thought had vanished years, if not centuries, earlier. While outside it was bomb craters and ration books, on the first floor of the Hotel Adlon it was

Hollywood meets Versailles. Frau H. was to be found in an enormous bed, at the centre of a vast suite, wearing a nightgown of such gossamer lightness, Elisabeth wondered if the woman within would float away.

There was chatter and small talk, and then a knock on the bedroom door as another friend, no less elegant, wafted in. Elisabeth hardly knew how to steer the conversation to clandestine meetings, Gestapo agents and her fear of imminent arrest. It would be like dropping a lead weight on a bowl of candyfloss. And then, as if to make the situation more awkward still, H. announced that it was time for her morning bath. Except that was not the cue for Elisabeth to leave, but rather to continue the conversation through the door.

They spoke of the old girls' school in Wieblingen as Elisabeth heard deep, cleansing breaths coming from the room next door. And suddenly H. appeared; tall, fragrant, gorgeous and quite naked. Elisabeth felt as if she were struggling for air.

What followed was an invitation to breakfast the next day. For the first time, she could glimpse a way out of the tunnel into which she had led her friends and herself. Even if this H. had won her place in the Reich's inner circle through her beauty, she was capable of using it to concrete effect. Elisabeth had seen that for herself, or rather heard about it, as H. had supplied friends with visas for Switzerland in forty-eight hours flat.

So she turned up the next day full of hope. She did her best to dress well and, as she entered the hotel, she only looked modestly out of place. She wanted to believe that her moment of redemption was at hand. It had been a Friday that had plunged her into this ordeal; perhaps this Friday would rescue her from it.

Her worry had been that it would prove impossible to wrench the conversation to the matter in hand. That concern only deepened when she saw that this was to be no solo encounter with H. Instead, there were other guests: more of Hitler's women, who arrived, one after another, each as perfectly scented as the last.

But Elisabeth's fears were not realised. She had the chance to explain her situation and the women discussed it. Not in any depth, but Elisabeth hoped that perhaps she had moved them to put in a word with the emperor. She had to believe they would; so much was at stake. And yet it would not do to show desperation. Such intensity would be a terrible social error, if nothing else. So Elisabeth did her best to chat and listen, and not behave like a woman whose life depended on it.

The encounter ended and the days passed. Did any of those women mention the case of Elisabeth von Thadden to Adolf Hitler? Did H.? If they did, nothing came of it. 'H. couldn't help,' Elisabeth told her journal. All the curls, silk and lace, like the starched towels, deep baths and rich, nurturing creams, had produced nothing more than fleeting beauty and a pleasant scent in the air.

Elisabeth was back in the basement flat in Carmerstrasse, which was still standing, though now surrounded by bombed-out ruins. Her best hope was to get out of Berlin, not as a fugitive whose very flight would be deemed admission of guilt, but in the course of her professional duties with the Red Cross. She waited for word of her transfer to France, to take up a post created in response to the recommendations she had made following her summer fact-finding tour. She was to be sent to Paris, as a staff officer tasked with the religious needs of soldiers now convalescing in residential homes in France.

The trouble was, although there was regular correspondence with Red Cross HQ and detailed conversations about reshuffling the Paris staff to make room for her new role, an actual start date refused to materialise. She was kept in limbo, waiting for confirmation. It made her wonder: had the Gestapo given a discreet order to block the move, to keep her in this state of uncertainty and unease?

Through it all, Elisabeth had not forgotten her duty, her obligation to mitigate the damage she had done by allowing Paul Reckzeh to join her friends at her table. She had got them into this hole; the least she could do was ensure it got no deeper.

That meant warning General Halder. She had not given Reckzeh the introduction he wanted, despite the insistence with which he sought it. At tea with Elisabeth Wirth, Reckzeh had pressed and pressed for help in meeting the former chief of staff, but the two women had deflected his every effort. Still, Halder was not difficult to track down. Eventually Reckzeh got his meeting.

As it turned out, the encounter was a disappointment to the young Gestapo agent. Halder expressed nothing that would count as an opinion, preferring to listen to what Reckzeh had to say. The most he offered was a statement that, of course, he would be available if it came to saving Germany from chaos, but that moment had not yet arrived.

In advance, Elisabeth had done what was required of her. Via a third party, she had told Halder to prepare for an approach from a man named Reckzeh, fresh from a visit to Switzerland. Indeed, together, she and Otto Kiep had been effective in tipping off all those who needed to be in the know. Thanks to their efforts, Reckzeh had run into a series of cold shoulders and brick walls. Those the doctor had wanted to meet were either away or indisposed. Those he did meet offered nothing but patriotic platitudes. Since his return to Germany, he had picked up almost nothing.

So, yes, Elisabeth, Otto and the others could congratulate themselves on a job well done. They had demonstrated admirable co-ordination and self-discipline. They had done precisely what the moment required of them. The trouble was, they had done it too well.

37
Himmler Decides

January 1944

LEO LANGE ASSESSED the evidence and the conclusion was obvious. He and his young operative had been betrayed. Or at least found out.

From his desk in the Gestapo's IV E 3 section, he had crafted a plan, which Agent Robby, though a novice, had executed with skill and efficiency. At his direction, Robby – real name Dr Paul Reckzeh – had found a way to infiltrate the Thadden tea party and used the connections he made there to burrow his way into anti-Hitler circles in Switzerland. Posing as a courier for the resistance, the doctor had returned to Germany equipped to flush out more, and more senior, figures plotting against the Third Reich. True, there had been a lucky break or two along the way – no one could have known how many traitors would attend a Friday afternoon birthday celebration or how unguardedly vocal they would be – but this had been canny espionage work, starting with his own decision to despatch the eager Reckzeh across the border. It had gone so well that a special commission would soon be established to carry out the multiple, extensive and complex investigations that flowed from Lange's initial findings. For what would be the second time in his career, Lange would give his name to a crucial Nazi operation: after the Sonderkommando Lange, there would now be the Sonderkommission Lange, or Lange Special Commission. Eventually it would be placed under the control of desk IV A1b – in which IV denoted Gestapo, A was for 'political opponents' and A1b the unit focused on 'reaction, opposition, pacifism, anti-Nazi activities, defeatism, etc.' – and be based at the Security Police School at Drögen, near Fürstenberg.

Except now their work had struck a major obstacle. Someone had given Reckzeh away.

There could be no other explanation. Wherever Reckzeh turned, he found the same response. Or rather non-response. Those he had met at the tea party had lost their previous garrulousness. They either refused to meet Reckzeh or, if they did, they would not say anything. The doctor got his meeting with General Halder but the general gave less than nothing away. On 10 September, Reckzeh had been greeted warmly; now he encountered only coldness. It was clear that the members of this traitors' circle were keeping their distance and that could only be because they had been warned.

The same pattern was evident from the material Lange was receiving from the Research Office. It was striking how little of it there was. The F stations were opening the letters of all those who had been at the tea party but had found next to nothing. As for telephone surveillance, the individuals who gathered on Carmerstrasse had made remarkably few calls since September, and this at a time when Germans in the cities used the phone often, if only for the sake of a quick word with friends and family, letting them know they had survived another night of bombing. The targeted had changed their behaviour, always a red flag to secret watchers and listeners. The eavesdroppers of the Research Office may even have detected a strange difference in the sound quality of the few phone calls the tea-party set did make: those who knew their lines were tapped were in the habit of putting a tea cosy over the receiver for every conversation they did not want overheard, which meant all but the most mundane.

For Lange, there could be no doubt. The group were taking precautions. Someone in their circle had discovered what Reckzeh was up to and told the rest to be on their guard.

A change of strategy would be required. It no longer made sense to watch and wait, hoping the 10 September group would inadvertently reveal more of themselves and their influential co-conspirators to the Gestapo. Lange had tried letting out more line in the hope of reeling in the bigger fish, but this crowd were wise to that now.

If the Lange Special Commission was to do its work and find

out more about the shadowy network of anti-Hitler rebels, it would have to switch its methods from indirect to direct.

Lange knew he could not make such a move alone. His targets now were not the usual brand of suspect. There were no communist lowlifes or down-at-heel socialist agitators in this group. These were people of standing, some in senior government positions, others bearing the fabled names of the German aristocracy. Counts and countesses, ambassadors and a revered diplomat's widow – no, there could be no sweeping of these men and women off the streets and into a Gestapo truck, even one disguised as a furniture van.

Lange would need the backing of a higher authority. So he submitted an application that duly worked its way up the Nazi bureaucracy until it had reached the man at the apex of the Nazi police state. In the end, it was Heinrich Himmler himself, Reichsführer-SS and also, since August 1943, minister of the interior, who authorised Lange's request. He accepted the view of his subordinate – no matter their stellar résumés and fancy titles, it was time these betrayers were placed under arrest.

38

Dawn Raids

January 1944

OTTO KIEP AT least had prepared for this moment. As 1943 drew to a close, he had told his sister Ida that he expected to be arrested in the first weeks of the new year. With that expectation, he had tried to savour what he feared might be his last Christmas as a free man. The family had gathered in Wedderstedt, taking in the Christmas Eve pageant at the village church before trudging home through the snow. They had put on evening dress, sung carols around the tree and exchanged gifts. He cherished the occasion.

But there were some difficult conversations. He warned Ida that when – not if – he was arrested, she too would get a visit from the Gestapo. They would want to search the room in the house she had long kept for his overnight visits. He had checked: there were just clothes in there, along with some old papers. He told her it would be fine for the secret police to turn the room upside down. 'There's nothing here that could hurt me,' he said.

One more task remained. His oldest son, Albrecht, was now of military age and due to return to naval service in the spring. Otto was as direct as always, telling the whole unvarnished truth: the tea party, Reckzeh, his own 'lethal' remarks, all of it. 'I could be arrested at any time,' he told his son, 'and I think it will not be long now.'

The boy was stunned by what he was hearing, but Otto had more to say. Risking your life in a just cause was hard enough, he said, but risking it an unjust one was too much to bear. Every German was now in that position, those in combat and those far from the front. All Albrecht should do now was devote himself to protecting his comrades in arms, those men who depended on him.

The young man was not ready to hear a lesson in moral instruction. He wanted to know what would happen to his father once he was arrested. Again, Otto offered no evasions or obfuscations. The former diplomat had no use for such tricks now. 'I will be sent to a prison or concentration camp, and then put on trial,' he said. 'And after that, who can say?'

Albrecht promised that, if he was overseas when it happened, he would get leave to come back to Germany and be at his father's side. Otto put his hand on his son's arm. 'Whatever happens to me, I want you to know that it is because I tried to speak the truth out of love for Germany.' Albrecht could find no reply.

The likelihood of Otto's arrest had been an open secret in Berlin opposition circles for weeks. One leading light of the resistance scribbled in his diary, 'I hear that various people are being harshly targeted, for example the certainly harmless but clear-sighted Kiep.' And yet, as it turned out, first they came for the others.

The Solfs, mother and daughter, had fled Berlin and were arrested on the morning of 12 January in the small Alpine village where Hanna's sister lived. The Zardens, father and daughter, were in the capital and arrested that same morning: he picked up at their home, she apprehended by SS men in leather coats who emerged from the bushes as she walked through the local park.

Over a few short hours, and across Germany, the SS and the Gestapo fanned out to capture their prey. They came for Anne Rühle at her place of work, using a colleague to interrupt a meeting to whisper to her that there was someone outside, 'a cousin from the front', who needed to see her. They bundled the oldest of the group, Fanny von Kurowsky, into a prison van without ceremony. Occasionally they ran into a delay that even they could not avoid. They had to wait for Elisabeth von Thadden's sister Anza, who had become seriously ill, to recover her strength before she could be taken anywhere. But as soon as she was deemed sufficiently fit, they did not hesitate: she too was taken into custody.

Elisabeth Wirth had not been at the tea party, but she had stood at Elisabeth von Thadden's side during that meeting with Reckzeh: that alone made her a person of sufficient interest to pull in. Except

Schloss Elmau, where she worked, doubled in these wartime years as an officers' recreation centre. Making an arrest there would cause a scene and break a taboo: the Gestapo intruding on Wehrmacht turf. So they summoned her for an interview in the nearby town of Mittenwald instead.

That left Elisabeth von Thadden, the only member of the group out of the country on that bleak January day. Throughout the autumn she had been kept in a state of suspended animation by the Red Cross, told to prepare for her new position in the staff bureau in Paris. But confirmation of the new job never came.

She could not hang around in Berlin. Her flat was still intact, albeit surrounded by rubble on all sides – 'an oasis in ruins', she called it when writing to relatives – but it did not feel wise to linger there. Instead, she kept moving, visiting and staying with family, including her youngest sister, Ehrengard, or Eta, in Göttingen. Eta scolded Elisabeth for her recklessness in allowing Reckzeh through the door, but she also offered consolation. Surely the fact that nothing had happened since the tea party, no knock had come on her door, offered the hope that whatever danger there had been had now passed. Eta's advice: lie low and stay busy.

So Elisabeth had occupied herself packing Christmas parcels for the front. At last, in December, the period she always thought of as Advent, she received instructions to head to France – not for the senior staff job in Paris, but to provide Christmas cover at the soldiers' home in Meaux, before a planned move to Cherbourg in January to manage the facility there. Still, Elisabeth would not succumb to disappointment. She would be away from Berlin, work was work and, besides, when it came to making a cosy Christmas for young people away from home, she was an expert. She had done it for legions of schoolgirls; she could do it for soldiers recovering from injury.

Except there was none of that. On whose orders, it was never clear, but Elisabeth was kept far away from the soldiers and their pastoral care; kept away, indeed, from conversation and friendly contact with any other human being. Christmas 1943 found Elisabeth von Thadden, once the mistress of a grand estate and the governing supremo of an elite boarding school, in the scullery behind the kitchen, the sleeves of her grey uniform rolled back and up to her elbows in dirty dishwater, washing pots, pans and plates for hours on end.

On the morning of 12 January 1944, with Christmas behind her, she was looking forward to her next move, that fresh start in Cherbourg. She sat eating breakfast in the dining room of the Meaux home, close to the industrial kitchen, her bags already packed in her room, preparing to set off for a meeting that day in the Paris suburbs to discuss plans with her superior.

And then they arrived: three SS men full of fake bonhomie and mocking jokes about the train ride she would now not need to make because she was being picked up by car instead. Watched by her colleagues, she was led to her quarters, which were searched in front of her, and then she was taken away.

With great despatch, the authorities had rounded up most of the Carmerstrasse suspects, no matter how far-flung they were. Besides Reckzeh, there had been nine people present at the tea party. Now seven were in custody. That left two men still free. But if they thought they could breathe easily, they were badly mistaken.

39

Free No More

Otto, January 1944

LEO LANGE HAD had his sights trained on Otto Kiep from the moment Agent Robby had briefed him on the treacherous conversation at Carmerstrasse. To Lange, Otto had been the loudest and most defeatist of that whole rotten group, uttering remarks that would be at the heart of any treason case Lange might prepare. As Otto himself later admitted, the words he had used that afternoon were 'lethal'. True, he was not the first to be arrested. But it was his destiny and there was no escaping it.

It came for him on Sunday, 16 January 1944, four days after the others had been rounded up. Otto was staying temporarily in a flat in Berlin's Dahlem neighbourhood, his fourth address in two months. Three times he had had to leave an apartment that had been destroyed or rendered uninhabitable by enemy bombs. Nevertheless, Otto considered himself lucky: his own house had not burned to the ground. True, it had been blown out inside and upwards by an Allied bomb, but he felt sure the house itself could be saved. All he needed was the installation of an emergency roof.

His new temporary address was opposite the home of his father-in-law, the banker Georg Friedrich Alves. That Sunday morning, the two men took a long walk together before making a plan to see each other later that afternoon.

When Otto didn't turn up, Georg crossed the road and asked Otto's long-time maid, Else Schwarz, where he might find his son-in-law. She told him that Otto had been arrested.

Before long, competing versions of what exactly had happened were in circulation. In one telling, the SS simply came to take Otto away, arresting him in his major's uniform in front of his seventeen-year-old son, Albrecht. The SS then forbade Else and Albrecht from leaving the flat, enforcing their edict by stationing two police officers, one man and one woman, in the apartment for the next ten days.

Another version allowed for no Sunday stroll with Georg, but instead had the three SS men pulling up in their car just before four o'clock in the morning. Albrecht was awake to see his father put on his uniform, Otto staying calm for the sake of his son. Otto gave the boy some instructions about the repair works to the house and then said goodbye.

From there, he was driven to SS headquarters, where an officer read him his discharge from the army. He was shown the document and asked to sign a statement that the text had been read to him in full. Then he was ordered to remove his uniform. Seeing no other option, he did what he was told. He was no longer an officer of the army. He would be prosecuted as a civilian, with no recourse to the military courts that still had a measure of distance from the Nazi state.

And there was a third version, in which Otto Kiep became the first Wehrmacht officer to be arrested by the Gestapo on army turf, a watershed moment in the enduring power struggle between the German military, long established and with its own traditions, and the Nazi apparatus built by Hitler. In this account, Otto was at work that day, at his office in what was officially a Wehrmacht compound. When the Gestapo men arrived, they were immediately challenged as to their authority to arrest an officer of the army. They were clearly irritated to be asked such a thing and gave the terse reply that they had come on orders of the RSHA.

That did not cut much ice with the men guarding the Wehrmacht compound. They directed the secret police to leave. Just as firmly, the Gestapo men refused. There followed a stand-off: between the army and the party machine; between traditional, conservative German nationalism and Nazism. Neither side was willing to move – and Otto Kiep was caught in the middle.

The Gestapo got on the phone to their superiors, who pushed the issue further up the chain of command until one of the most senior officials made contact with a counterpart in the office of the Führer. The issue came to no less than Field Marshal Wilhelm Keitel, head of the OKW, the high command of Nazi Germany's armed forces. He had been in that post since February 1938 but, for all the grandeur of his title, he had been installed to serve as a nodding dog to Hitler and he had played that role amply. He did whatever the Führer wanted him to do, submitting the Wehrmacht, which stood under his nominal command, to the will of the Nazi party and its leader.

Once the matter reached Keitel, there could be no doubting the outcome. Whatever restraint had kept the Gestapo's hands off the German army until now was swept aside. Keitel, who laboured under several nicknames, all of them synonyms for 'lackey', not only gave formal permission for the arrest of Otto Kiep, he personally telephoned the officer in command of the military compound and ordered him to comply with the request of Himmler's men from the RSHA. Otto was led away.

When Otto had first told his wife about Paul Reckzeh and the betrayal of the tea-party group, it had been part-confession, part-warning. Otto admitted that he had spoken that afternoon in forbidden terms, but he also prepared his wife for the consequences not just for him but for her. He was not wrong about that. On Monday, 17 January, the Gestapo came for Hanna Kiep.

She was not in Berlin but in Ballenstedt in the Harz mountains when the Gestapo arrived. Perhaps it was because, as Otto always thought, Hanna looked like the model German wife, blonde and blue-eyed, that the officer in charge was not harsh with her. It was evening and the secret police allowed her to put her daughters to bed first: Hildegard and young Hanna were poorly at the time. Indeed, Frau Kiep was given an extra dispensation. She was not taken away there and then, but rather allowed to spend the night in Ballenstedt and to take the first train to Berlin in the morning. Which she did. Even so, and despite all the courtesies, there was no mistaking her fate: she was now a prisoner of the Third Reich.

That left one more guest from 10 September. Hilger van Scherpenberg had gone to some lengths to avoid the fate that befell the others.

Once he knew the truth about Reckzeh, he had devised a plan, one that might save some of those who had been at the tea party even if it would not exactly help the rest. Unsolicited, he reported to his superiors at the Foreign Ministry that at a recent social occasion he had encountered a certain Dr Paul Reckzeh who had been offering to make illegal deliveries of post to Switzerland. Naturally, Scherpenberg had been scandalised by the proposal, which he had declined, and thought it his duty to alert his colleagues at once.

If it worked, the gambit would cast Scherpenberg and all those who had refused the doctor's offer to play postman as good, law-abiding citizens of the Reich — and all those who had handed notes or messages to Reckzeh as criminals. It might get Scherpenberg off the hook, but Otto Kiep, Hanna Solf and Elisabeth von Thadden would be right on it.

For a while it seemed to work. In January 1944, Scherpenberg was sufficiently safe in his post, overseeing trade with Scandinavia at the Foreign Ministry, to be sent on two official visits to Sweden. By the end of the month, his wife, Inge, who had been away from Berlin, returned to the city, partly out of fear for her husband's safety. But it was not arrest that worried her. It was the non-stop, nightly bombings.

She had had no letters from Hilger to confirm he was still alive, so she went to his place of work. There, in the stairwell of the Foreign Ministry, she saw pinned up a list of those who had been on air-raid duty during the previous night's bombardment. At last she could exhale. Her husband had been here, alive, just the previous evening.

She waited for him in his office, now certain he would appear soon enough. The minutes ticked past. She asked a colleague if he knew how long her husband might be. He did not — he was waiting for him too.

Inge called the Berlin flat, where the maid told her that Herr van Scherpenberg was currently 'out of town'. A secretary in the office knew a little more, explaining that he had only been in the ministry 'a short time': he had come and then gone.

Now Inge took herself to the personnel department. One of the men there, apparently summoning up the courage to pass on this information, told her that her husband had been away for two or three days. 'For questioning.'

So that was it. Her husband had not been killed by a bomb. Nor had he been in this office last night, despite the air-raid duty list that evidently showed those who should have been inside the ministry rather than those who actually were. Despite his best efforts to exonerate himself as someone who had resisted Reckzeh's invitation to break the law, he had been arrested.

'By the way,' said the man from personnel. 'Do you know what this is about?'

Instinct rather than strategy prompted Inge to tell the truth. 'Certainly. The Thadden–Kiep case.' The official looked at her blankly.

After that, Inge van Scherpenberg made it her business to tell whoever she could precisely what had happened. She held nothing back: the names of those involved, the fact that they had been rounded up in a series of arrests, all of it. In the process, she had torn through the veil of secrecy the Gestapo had taken such pains to weave. Anyone who knew of the case had either been arrested or ordered to remain silent. The maid in the flat, the secretary at the ministry, the personnel officer: all had received that instruction. But perhaps because she had been away, taking a few days' break in Vienna, Inge had been given no such order.

She tried to find out as much as she could, travelling through a snowstorm to Schönfliess to find Elisabeth's sister Anza, only to be told that the younger Fräulein von Thadden was also 'out of town' and had been so for just under a fortnight. The pattern was becoming unnervingly clear.

All the while, Inge was spreading the word, as far and as wide as it would go. She wanted to be sure that anybody who was anybody in Berlin would know of the Thadden–Kiep affair (a phrase that handily kept her husband off stage). There had been no calculated plan to circulate the news so assiduously, but had it been a strategy it would have been a sound one.

For one thing, Inge van Scherpenberg had made her own arrest less likely. It's not that Lange and his team did not regard her as a target: they most emphatically did. Lange had deployed three officers to pick her up, but they missed her twice. First they headed to Bavaria, knowing she was poised to leave Berlin for a hideaway there. Except she missed her train. Lange's men immediately headed back to Berlin, to arrest her there, unaware that as they sped towards the capital, she was driving in the opposite direction. They probably passed each other.

But as the story of the tea party travelled through the upper reaches of the Berlin bush telegraph, the value of her arrest diminished. Thanks to his network of secret listeners, Lange knew better than anyone that the word was now out. The whole purpose of detaining those in the know had been to keep the traitors' circle tight and sealed. But that effort had self-evidently failed. The seal was broken. There was now no point arresting Inge van Scherpenberg.

She had helped herself, but not only herself. In making the arrest of the tea-party set common knowledge, she had afforded all those rounded up a degree of protection. These were prominent people to start with, their names familiar in Berlin society. With their detention known, it became that much harder for the authorities to engineer their collective disappearance without trace. It could still happen; the men and women of that Carmerstrasse afternoon still might vanish, whether in a concentration camp or through a series of sudden, unexplained deaths. But if they did, their absence would, thanks to Frau van Scherpenberg and her admirable loquaciousness, certainly leave a mark.

And yet if that gave Inge a measure of reassurance, it could never be a guarantee of safety either for her husband or for his fellow accused. Proof of that came sooner than anyone would have expected – with the tea-party set's first death.

PART III

Prisoners

40

The Fall

Irmgard, January 1944

AFTER THE SS men had apprehended her in the park, Irmgard Zarden, the young heiress, was taken to Kurfürstendamm 140, the building on one of Berlin's wide avenues that had served as the staff headquarters of Heinrich Himmler in his capacity as Reich Commissioner for the Consolidation of German Ethnicity and that remained his office in Berlin. It also housed five Abwehr, or intelligence, units as well as section IV A 2 of the Gestapo, which specialised in counter-sabotage and, naturally, had holding cells for suspects. What no one told Irmgard Zarden was that her father, Arthur, former top mandarin at the Ministry of Finance, was there too.

She was formally arrested and then interrogated by the head of the Special Commission, Leo Lange himself. She was twenty-two, but had enough self-possession to ask some questions of her own. First, she wondered if Lange might telephone her office and explain that she would not be in that day. Second, she wanted to know where her father was and when she would be able to see him. She was anxious. Given how he had been in recent months and years – glum about his firing, his exclusion from Berlin life and, most recently, the death of his wife – no one could blame her for her concern.

But Lange was unmoved. This was a man who had organised the murder of thousands of civilians in the forests of Poland; he was unlikely to be swayed by a plea for compassion. He told the young woman nothing, focusing instead on his own line of inquiry. Who had said what to whom on that Friday afternoon in September?

Irmgard replied truthfully that she had missed most of it. She had come to the tea party late, not as a guest but simply to pick up her father and take him home.

But she had heard enough to get the gist, yes? She had heard enough to know that the talk that day had been defeatist and treacherous. She had been a witness to treason!

Irmgard denied it vehemently, even though Lange was not wrong. It carried on like that, back and forth, with Irmgard refusing to shift from her position that she had acted as a glorified chaperone for her father, that she had arrived after the event and had heard nothing of substance and certainly nothing that fitted Lange's description.

The hours passed until it was evening. She was told that she would not be going home but would stay here, in this room. There was no bed. Instead, she spent the night sitting on a chair. But she was not alone. Watching her throughout was a female Gestapo officer who kept her eyes fixed on her, sticking to her even when she went to the lavatory. Again and again, Irmgard asked about her father, but she was told nothing.

The next day, she was allowed, under escort, to return to the family home to pick up clothes and other essentials, a kindness not usually afforded by the Nazis to their captives. By then, the house had already been thoroughly searched, Lange's men rifling through any papers or documents they could find, looking for correspondence especially. Their big find was a postcard sent to Arthur Zarden by Joseph Wirth, the Weimar-era chancellor who had been living in exile in Switzerland since the Nazi takeover. Could this be the evidence Reckzeh had strained so hard to uncover, proving a link between the traitors of the tea party and a would-be challenger to Hitler across the border? Hardly. The postcard was dated 1930 or 1931, a relic from a country that no longer existed.

That did not stop the Gestapo seizing on it, claiming it linked a conspirator, Arthur Zarden, to a known enemy of the state, Wirth. Irmgard did her best to argue that that was nonsense, that her father and Wirth had had no contact for the last twelve years, but it was no good. The men in the leather coats took it, along with the letter of thanks Arthur had received from Hitler himself, a document that was itself now more than a decade old.

Soon Irmgard was moved, along with several other women from

the tea party. They would no longer be questioned in the Gestapo house near Kurfürstendamm, but taken somewhere outside the city and altogether more forbidding. They were transferred to one of the places they had talked about in whispers at their secret gatherings: Sachsenhausen, a concentration camp.

There, Irmgard and the others were herded into a wooden barracks, watched now by two Gestapo women who were as vigilant and unblinking as the first, monitoring them around the clock. These guards too remained at their sides even in the lavatory.

The move was presented not as a punishment but as a safety precaution, for the women's own sake. Berlin was under aerial bombardment; it was too risky to stay there. But Sachsenhausen was hardly out of harm's way. It was in Oranienburg, home to ammunition factories that were a daily Allied target. When the bombs fell, the barracks shook. The Gestapo's watchers were scared and demanded that Irmgard go into a shelter. But she refused, not least because she knew that she and the other women were deemed 'special prisoners' who could not be subjected to the usual physical pressure deployed so routinely by the Gestapo. That status was a function, in part, of the fact that, officially at least, these women had not yet been charged and were merely required to provide information. But it was also a nod to their class.

There was another motive for Irmgard's refusal to take refuge in the bomb shelter, instead being protected from the falling bombs only by the thin, flimsy wood of the barracks. She could see that the Gestapo women were terrified, and that gave her an undeniable pleasure.

Daybreak sometimes brought a journey back to Berlin for further interrogation. Lange kept at it, pressing and pressing for more details of the tea-party conversation. He wanted to know of treason and plot, but all Irmgard would give him was the same bland account of an afternoon of social chatter about nothing at all. That, she maintained, was all she had witnessed. And still she knew nothing of her father.

Until the day Lange came to see her at Sachsenhausen. It had been a week since her arrest and Irmgard braced herself for another round of interminable, futile questioning. But the detective did not look his usual self. He seemed unexpectedly rattled. It turned out he had news to give her.

Over the previous seven days, Arthur Zarden's fate had been similar to his daughter's. In that same Kurfürstendamm house, he had faced round-the-clock interrogation. But on 18 January, during a break in his captors' demands for information, he made a move they had not anticipated. He hurled himself out of a washroom window, landing on the street below. An ambulance had taken him to hospital, but he was dead before it arrived.

If Lange seemed distressed as he spoke, empathy was not likely to be the cause. He had lost a key witness and must have known he would be blamed, including by the dead man's daughter. Irmgard did indeed tear into him, accusing the detective of murdering her father and vowing that Arthur Zarden's death would be avenged, whether the war lasted another year or ten. To speak this way to a senior Nazi official was to take a mortal risk, but Lange tried only to calm her. He could not afford to have the death of another 'special prisoner' on his hands.

In Irmgard's shock and fury, there was something else too: an understanding that may well have eluded Lange. For the date her father had chosen for his death was not random: it was her mother's birthday. Later Irmgard would hear that her father had become especially dispirited that day, which for so long had been a cue for joy and celebration. To mark his beloved Edithe's birthday without her for the first time would always have been hard. To do it in a Gestapo detention cell was too much to bear.

Irmgard realised how determined he must have been. He was nearly fifty-nine, and not a fit or agile man. It would have taken all the strength he had to elude his guards, to stage what would have looked like a break for freedom.

Of course, at its simplest, his leap from the window was nothing of the sort: he would have known there was no chance he would survive. But he had staged an escape of a kind. For he understood the fate that awaited him as an accused traitor, and he had been determined to avoid it. In that, he had succeeded. Arthur Zarden was dead, but he was also free.

He had spent so much of the previous decade or more keeping

his head down, trying to play it safe. When he lost his job, he had ceased to be a man of standing. In truth, he had stopped being a man of much agency at all. But in that final moment, he had taken action.

The premise of his decision was that only agony lay in store for the men and women of the September tea party. In time, another member of that ill-starred group would reach the same desperate conclusion – and decide on the same course of action.

41

The First Round

Hanna, January 1944

WHEN THEY SEARCHED the two-room apartment in Upper Bavaria where Hanna Solf had been hiding out, the Gestapo officers may have humiliated the ambassador's widow, forbidding her to move and forcing her to dress in front of them, but they did not leave her clueless as to her fate. Instead, as they turned the place over, the man in charge, a Kommissar Strübing, explained that she was to be transferred to SS headquarters in Munich, and that all others present were to be taken too. That meant her daughter, Lagi, who had been staying next door, her sister, whose apartment this was, and the family's long-serving maid, Fräulein Richter. None of them would be able to tip off the Solfs' fellow conspirators because they would all be in the custody of the Gestapo. What's more, they would not be able to collude with each other: they would be transported to Brienner Strasse in Munich in three separate cars.

Once there, in a windowless room that seemed to have been stripped of all dignity, Hanna was plunged right away into an interrogation that did not let up for five hours. It filled the morning and stretched into the afternoon. They asked first about her wide network of friends – the Solf Circle – and then about the tea party.

The day was long and stretched into the next. But on the second evening, she was told that she was to be separated yet further from the other women. They would stay in Munich, but she would be moved to Berlin, to the Reich Security Main Office itself. As if she posed an urgent and mortal threat to the Reich, she was transferred by express train, guarded by no fewer than four Gestapo officers.

Despite what she had been told, her destination was not the

headquarters building in the capital or any other Gestapo premises there. Thanks to the nightly Allied bombing raids, those places were no longer deemed safe. She would be taken somewhere whose reputation was even more terrifying than Gestapo HQ. Driven by car, and still under guard, she was on her way to a concentration camp.

She was held in Sachsenhausen for three weeks, housed in barracks where she was watched over day and night: for her, too, the monitoring extended even to the lavatory. She did not know it yet, but in that same camp the host of the tea party, Elisabeth von Thadden, and the youngest guest, Irmgard Zarden, were also being held captive.

And yet, that spell in Sachsenhausen did not provide the glimpse of hell that those who had traded whispered talk of the concentration camps expected. There was food and it was perfectly acceptable. Hanna was taken back to Berlin for questioning, either at the RSHA at Prinz-Albrecht-Strasse 8, which housed those dreaded Gestapo headquarters, or at the Kurfürstendamm 140 building, where Lange and his team were based, but that happened only every few days and the journey was by car. The two women who guarded Hanna Solf were old police officers, people who had served in the before times. They behaved with decency, signalling to Hanna that they understood that the real criminals here were not her or her fellow tea-party suspects, but the people who had jailed them.

After three weeks, all that changed. Hanna and the others were to leave Sachsenhausen, despatched to somewhere far bleaker, a place that would become notorious.

Lagi

Throughout, Hanna was kept apart from her daughter. It had been quite deliberate, the separation enforced from the moment they were driven away from the house in Partenkirchen in different cars. Along with her aunt and the housekeeper, Countess Lagi Ballestrem-Solf was held in a Munich prison for two months straight, entirely cut off from the outside world. There was no one they could contact, no one who could sound the alarm about their arrest or disappearance. (That's exactly how the Gestapo wanted it: they had a civil servant and his wife stay in the house in Partenkirchen to collect the post and answer the phone, telling anyone who rang, 'The ladies are away.' Though, given that the entire neighbourhood knew that the Solfs, mother and daughter, had only just arrived, having fled a bombed-out apartment in Berlin, and that Lagi was too ill to have gone anywhere, that rote response to callers only made their absence more suspicious.) Lagi's husband, Count von Ballestrem, was fighting on the Russian front, as was her brother. Her mother was a prisoner, just like her, and her father was dead. She was alone.

Lagi's priority was getting her aunt Elisabeth and Martha Richter out. Whatever the case against Lagi and her mother, it was absurd to hold these two as prisoners. They had nothing to do with the *Solf-Kreis* or the tea party or any of it. Her aunt was not well; the housekeeper was old. It was cruel, as well as nonsensical, to detain them. Lagi pleaded for their release to whoever might listen, verbally and in writing, but she got nowhere.

Her captors were more interested in asking questions. In her first interrogation, she was approached more as a witness than a suspect: after all, Lagi had not been present at the tea party, having been thwarted by a firefighting injury. But that did not stop the Gestapo probing ever deeper into her past, including the years she had spent in Shanghai, where her refusal to bend the knee to national socialism had already attracted the attention of the secret police.

Now, in Munich, they wanted to know about a list of names they had found. They were especially intrigued because this was no straightforward list: it had been written in code.

Lagi knew instantly what they were talking about and she could not deny it. She had indeed worked out her own code for correspondence, so that she could write frankly about what she was seeing in Shanghai. She had code words for the Chinese, Japanese and, crucially, German diplomats and politicians she encountered, as well as encrypted terms for the institutions of the Third Reich: the propaganda office, the Gestapo and the SS.

If that had been the whole of it, she might have been able to dismiss it as a souvenir of a largely forgotten past; all this had happened a decade ago. But the list of names, once deciphered, included people who, in the eyes of Lange's team of investigators, were very much of the present, including Arthur Zarden and Otto Kiep. These were men who had been arrested at the same time, and for the same reason, as Lagi and her mother. The codebreakers of the Gestapo were convinced that they had found something of direct relevance to the here and now. From then on the young countess was no longer treated as a possible source of information. Now the Nazis regarded her as a criminal.

As a prisoner in that Munich jail, she knew exactly what that would mean. The treatment of the condemned was brutal. She saw the blue, swollen faces and hands of female Jehovah's Witnesses, hundreds of them passing through the Munich prison as they were transferred from one concentration camp to another. She saw inmates clearly hardened after years trapped inside the Nazi penal system, and she saw others who were newer to it, apparently astonished to find themselves incarcerated, such as the young women punished for becoming pregnant by prisoners of war held in this same jail, now prisoners themselves for sleeping with the enemy. Lagi soon learned that those women would give birth, only for their newborn babies to be taken from them. As if that were not punishment enough, the childless mothers would then be sent to a concentration camp.

Those who were believed to hold information that the Nazis wanted faced different torments. Every day Lagi would see men return from interrogation having clearly been beaten and tortured, sometimes covered in blood. Her neighbour in the next-door cell, a young man, returned from one session especially battered. He was, Lagi knew, increasingly terrified that he might crack and reveal the names of his friends. That night he strangled himself.

Eventually there came a rare act of mercy. An official came to tell Lagi that her aunt Elisabeth and Frau Richter were to be discharged, albeit under a barrage of severe threats and intimidation, warning them not to breathe a word to anyone. But there was to be no let-off for her.

On the contrary, she was to be despatched to Berlin. If her jailers thought that news would crush Lagi, they were wrong. She was pleased. Now, she thought, she would be nearer her mother.

She would make the journey on a train, an ordinary one, seated among regular, fare-paying passengers. Keeping an eye on her were two plainclothes Gestapo officers. Cheerfully unaware of their presence, the other passengers chatted about the nightly air raids and occasionally allowed themselves the odd moan about the Nazis who ruled them.

Eventually they pulled into the station at Berlin. It was only now that Lagi learned that her journey was not to end here, that she was to change trains. At which point one of her guards did the strangest thing. He handed Lagi her ticket, suitcase and purse, and said, as if they were companions on an excursion, 'In case we get into different cars, don't forget that you get out at Drögen.'

The shock paralysed her. She was in a packed public place: it would be easy to give her guards the slip and melt into the crowd. She had the means to escape, too: money, documents and her luggage. For two hours, as she waited for the appointed train to Drögen, she agonised over the dilemma her Gestapo escort had given her. Was this a trap? Or should she make a run for it?

What ultimately settled the question was a very simple calculation: she thought of what the Gestapo would do to her mother if she dared break away. So she stayed on the platform and got on the train as, she suspected, her captors always knew she would.

At the other end, a police car was waiting to pick her up. It was a gloomy evening, but clear enough to see the drab rows of barracks and the columns of prisoners in their unmistakable striped uniforms. The car pulled up by a low, narrow building that stood apart. She was taken inside. It was 15 March 1944 and Lagi Ballestrem-Solf was now a prisoner in one of the Third Reich's most infamous places.

Elisabeth

After she had been frogmarched from the Red Cross building in Nazi-occupied France, Elisabeth von Thadden had disappeared into

THE FIRST ROUND

the maze of the Gestapo penal system. She was taken first to a prison in the provincial French town of Fresnes, now under Nazi occupation. There she was interrogated for a full twenty-four hours without a break.

Next, she was transferred to Berlin, where, like Arthur Zarden, she was held in the Gestapo facility on Prinz-Albrecht-Strasse and questioned again, night after night. From there, like Hanna Solf, Irmgard Zarden and Elisabeth Wirth, she was taken to Sachsenhausen, where she too was held in a small room, watched around the clock by two guards, separated at all times from the others. She was forbidden from looking out of the window, but sometimes she couldn't help but catch a glimpse of the regular prisoners outside: they seemed grey.

The questioning did not let up. For that she would be taken to Berlin, sometimes by day, often at night. In the January chill, the cold was biting, not least because Elisabeth had been issued with no change of clothes. She remained in the nun-like habit of a Red Cross nurse, as if this were still the day of her arrest. She might be kept waiting for hours in a room as frigid as an icebox, only to be held later in another room that was suffocatingly overheated. Naturally, she got sick. And still no one in the world beyond even knew where she was.

For four weeks she was held in Sachsenhausen, her nights interrupted, her days endless. She was not allowed to break the monotony by jotting down thoughts on paper or even by sleeping; the guards were firm on that. There were those train journeys to Berlin for questioning: she, Hanna, Irmgard and Elisabeth Wirth always taken separately to prevent even a fleeting moment of human contact. They would travel by regular passenger train, each flanked by a pair of guards. The carriage was often so overcrowded that escape would have been possible, but the Gestapo barely gave it a thought: they knew their charges would not risk such a thing lest they bring a terrible reprisal down on the others. The captives' decency was their weakness.

In the case of Elisabeth von Thadden, the Nazis enjoyed a double indemnity. They knew she would do nothing that would imperil her friends, and nothing that could bring trouble to her brother. In

Fresnes, escape had crossed her mind: there seemed to be a way. But she had let that go for his sake.

Eventually, she found her way to the same place as all the others. It looked as bleak and terrifying to her as it did to them.

Otto

Like his fellow suspects, Otto Kiep was held first at the Gestapo building at Kurfürstendamm 140, where his inquisitors set to work on him immediately. They had a whole string of questions, but one was particularly urgent. Who had tipped him off? Who had warned him that the Gestapo were onto him and his fellow conspirators? It was obvious that someone had done that: Otto and the others had clammed up so suddenly, they had to have been told. Leo Lange wanted a name.

Otto refused. But the investigator was wily enough to suspect that a different tack might work. He sent in his superior, SS-Standartenführer Walter Huppenkothen, who addressed Otto not as a criminal but as a gentleman, one who had got caught up in an unfortunate episode that had been blown out of proportion and could surely be cleared up swiftly. As far as Huppenkothen was concerned, this tea-party business was trivial. He and his team simply needed Otto's help in clarifying the picture in Switzerland.

The danger seemed to be receding. Otto knew that he had next to no involvement in whatever the Swiss émigrés were up to, and this man's manner seemed entirely friendly. Finally, Huppenkothen gave his word of honour that nothing would happen to whichever individual it was who had warned Otto, the promise sealed with a handshake.

Reassured that there would soon be an amicable resolution of the whole affair, Otto named Helmuth von Moltke. That Otto had been deceived became clear almost instantly: on 19 January, Moltke was arrested.

Immediately the younger man faced the distinct brand of strong pressure favoured by Lange's men, one Otto came to think of as 'the breaking process'. He held out for as long as he could, but in

February he revealed the source of the information he had, in turn, passed to Otto and, via him, to the rest of the tea-party group. Moltke named the Abwehr officer Ludwig Gehre. On 2 March 1944, Gehre was arrested, though he managed to escape a few days later. Still, in the short time they had him in their grasp, the Gestapo got what they needed. Within twenty-four hours of his arrest, on 3 March, they had detained his source, Hartmut Plaas, the man who sat among the phone-tappers and eavesdroppers of the Research Office on Schillerstrasse as a senior government counsellor, the man who had made it his habit to pass on any information that might be useful to the group of dissenting officers within the Abwehr, the man who had heard about the application for a wiretap of a group of people that read like a roll-call of Berlin high society and wanted to ensure they knew they had been exposed. He too became a prisoner of the Reich.

By now, Lange had relocated his Special Commission, having decided that Kurfürstendamm 140 was no longer fit for his purposes. Thanks to the constant Allied air raids on Berlin, he could no longer guarantee the physical safety of his suspects there. Losing Arthur Zarden to suicide had been a misfortune; losing yet more valuable information through another premature death would look like carelessness. That meant moving his suspects to a new site, one that, as it happened, had its own cell block. Otto Kiep had been among the prisoners bundled into a police wagon and transferred in early February, travelling alongside his fellow guest at the tea party Hilger van Scherpenberg and several others, including Helmuth von Moltke. In a whispered moment during the journey, the two men spoke.

What had brought this pair, born a generation apart, together when they had met four years earlier was a shared set of principles, standards even. Patriots, men of the law, they believed there was a right way to behave and a wrong way. The right way included owning up to your actions and taking responsibility for them. And so Otto told the truth. He told Moltke that it was he, Otto, who had named him to the Gestapo.

Believing in the same code of honour, Moltke rewarded his friend's candour. He told Otto that he 'fully understood'.

Soon they were at their destination, the same place to which the rest of Lange's suspects had been relocated. They had arrived at a concentration camp whose name was already becoming a byword for cruelty. It was early 1944 and the men and women of the tea party were prisoners at Ravensbrück.

42

Ravensbrück

February 1944

IN THE ARCHIPELAGO of camps the Nazis had constructed across Germany and occupied Poland, Ravensbrück had a particular distinction. Since 1939, it served as the only main concentration camp whose chief purpose was the detention of women.

It had been built by men — five hundred male prisoners from Sachsenhausen, working as slaves — but its first inmates were women and so were all but the most senior of those in charge. Besides the male SS captain who served as camp commandant, flanked by a handful of male SS administrators, everyone else who wielded power in Ravensbrück was female.

Its population rose from hundreds at the start in 1939 to ten thousand three years later and more than fifty thousand three years after that. As Ravensbrück expanded, it became synonymous with women's imprisonment and enslavement, the place into which the Nazis herded those women they rejected: Jews, Roma, Jehovah's Witnesses, criminals, political prisoners and 'race-defilers', the latter referring to those Aryan women who had made the grave mistake of sleeping with non-Aryan men.

The women of Ravensbrück were despatched there from all points of the Nazi map: more than a third from conquered Poland, a fifth from the Soviet Union, another fifth from the combined Reich of Germany and Austria, with the rest drawn from Hungary, France, the former Czechoslovakia, Holland, Belgium and Yugoslavia. A small, adjacent camp for men was added in April 1941. By then Ravensbrück had developed a specialism and a reputation: it was where the SS trained the female guards it would deploy at the women's subcamps dotted around the concentration camp system. The reputation was for abominable mistreatment and brutality.

Prisoners were kept in barracks, where they slept on wooden slats stacked three tiers high, with just one washroom to be shared between hundreds of women. Food was scarce and the labour grinding, the women made to work, initially for SS-owned enterprises, doing their involuntary bit to advance Heinrich Himmler's ambition to make the SS an economic powerhouse. Before long, some of Germany's household names – the likes of Siemens & Halske – were enjoying the advantages of cost-free labour thanks to a steady supply of slaves. It was 'women's work', traditionally defined: sewing and weaving, done round the clock, on empty stomachs and on pain of death.

Tens of thousands of prisoners could not endure it, the hunger and disease killing them eventually, their bodies burnt in the crematorium whose chimney loomed over the camp. But other deaths were available in Ravensbrück too. At intervals, the SS would run a 'selection', weeding out those prisoners it regarded as too sick or weak to work. An inmate in that category, deemed unfit and unproductive, would be shot dead, her body incinerated with those who had dropped dead from illness, starvation or exhaustion.

Beginning in 1942, there was an alternative fate for those selected: they would be disposed of under a programme that used the same methods that had worked so well under Aktion T4, the 'euthanasia' programme that dealt with those with physical or learning disabilities. Initially, that might mean transfer to a dedicated killing centre several hours away. But eventually the process would be streamlined, with the construction by the SS of Ravensbrück's very own gas chamber. Once that was in place, there was no need to rely on costly and cumbersome transports: the ill, the elderly, the exhausted could be murdered within the bounds of the camp. For maximum efficiency and convenience, the gas chamber was in a hut next to the crematorium.

And yet, there were torments that may well have frightened the women of Ravensbrück even more than death – among them, becoming a 'rabbit', an involuntary subject of medical experimentation.

Just as some of Germany's leading corporations seized on the ready supply of labour offered by the concentration-camp system, so some of the Reich's most ambitious doctors could not resist the pool of human subjects the camps opened up. Since the summer of 1942, SS physicians had helped themselves to the unending line of live specimens on offer at Ravensbrück.

A particular focus of research was sterilisation. The Reich had long been keen to develop an efficient method of ensuring Jews and Roma people stopped reproducing. It was not enough to kill the undesirables; the ideal was to ensure the undesirables were never born. To that end, the doctors at Ravensbrück carried out sterilisation experiments on women and on children, too.

None of this was out of sight. On the contrary, Ravensbrück was built in an open, rather lovely spot, across the lake from the well-to-do village of Fürstenberg. The burghers of that place would need only to look across the water to see row after row of barracks, to see tens of thousands of inmates – to see the chimney.

This was the place where the accused traitors of the September tea party were now held. Except their lives were different from most in Ravensbrück. They were in a category of their own, kept apart from the rest of the camp. They were special prisoners, held in the 'cell block', known throughout Ravensbrück as 'the bunker'.

It consisted of seventy-eight cells in a solid, modern brick building, newly constructed in 1940, arranged like a regular prison – on two levels, with walkways, so that guards patrolling the upper level could easily look down on the locked doors below. Initially, the core population of the cell block was made up of women with mental illness. But soon, it became the place where the SS took inmates they deemed to have broken the camp's rules. That might mean an act of resistance, religious or political, whether an attempted escape, the smuggling of secret letters or a refusal to work. Indeed, the first prisoners kept there included a group of around four hundred Jehovah's Witnesses who had refused to carry out needlework shortly after the outbreak of war in 1939, because they believed their labour would be in aid of military ends. Just as easily, a spell in the bunker could be the result of the most minor infraction, the charge made arbitrarily. One inmate of the *Jugendschutzlager*, or 'juvenile protective custody camp', built next door to Ravensbrück for the incarceration of adolescent girls, was sent to the cell block for the crime of smoking a cigarette. In time, the block would hold political prisoners and those in pre-trial detention, women and men alike.

Once inside, there were degrees of further punishment, set out in detail in the Ravensbrück camp regulations, which specified who would be granted the privilege of a single electric light bulb and who compelled to sit in darkness, who allowed the luxury of a stool or wooden bunk and who held in an empty cell.

Officially, the 'special prisoners' were granted several valuable privileges that set them apart from the regular inmates of Ravensbrück. They might receive the same food rations as the SS men and women who held them captive, and many did not have to wear the striped uniforms of the concentration camp but were allowed to put on civilian clothes. They were not allocated a prisoner number but were rather addressed by their names. Most significantly, they would not be routinely deployed as slave labourers. Instead, many were allowed to read books and to receive parcels from the outside.

What's more, they were all in one place, a group of friends and acquaintances who had known each other for years or whose families had been connected down the generations. To the naked eye, it must have seemed as if the *beau monde* of Berlin high society had been relocated to the Nazi detention system, where they could provide support and solidarity for each other. But that impression would have been doubly misleading.

For one thing, most of the German elite were nowhere near Ravensbrück or its prison block: they had dutifully fallen in line, if not to their knees, in deference to the regime. For another, the dissidents and rebels who were held captive in Ravensbrück were scarcely able to comfort each other. On the contrary, they barely caught a glimpse of one another – and what they saw was more likely to crush their spirits than to raise them.

It was not easy, but through the narrow window in her cell, Lagi Ballestrem-Solf could see not only the chimney of the crematorium, but the small prison yard also. When her fellow inmates took their allotted quarter of an hour of exercise, she would glimpse them. Slowly she realised that they were almost all here: the circle of friends who had gathered so intently, so earnestly, in her parents' apartment through the long dark decade. One by one, she saw them: the faces she had known of fellow refusers, those who had not bowed to Hitler, those who had done what they could to hide, save or spirit Jews out of the country, those who had clung to the possibility of a different, better Germany, those who had held on to facts and truth. They all seemed to be here.

Some were hard to recognise. She watched one man, thin and deathly pale, struggle through his solitary fifteen minutes in the yard. Eventually the man spotted her; he took the risk of nodding in her direction. Only then could she identify him. It was Nikolaus von Halem, the young industrialist and chum of Lagi's husband who, back in the day, was one half of the duo that used to light up Berlin parties with their 'Führer speeches', parodying the great leader. He had always been larger than life, big, strong and funny. Now he was weak, the expression on his face oddly detached. The spark seemed to have vanished from him, as if he were a man finished with life. Lagi could hardly blame him. He and his sometime comedy partner, Mumm von Schwarzenstein, had been in Nazi custody since 1942, held not for their talent as providers of forbidden joy, but for conspiring to assassinate Hitler.

She saw the walking dead and learned of the long dead. In whispers she was told of the suicide of their old friend Arthur Zarden, a man whose intelligence and wide horizons – she thought of him as having a 'cosmopolitan outlook' – she had always liked.

So, though old friends were nearby, that did not translate into the warmth of renewed contact. Usually, they got no more than a brief sighting of one another, which lasted long enough only to confirm how much had changed. From her cell, Lagi's mother, Hanna, spotted a one-time *Solf-Kreis* regular, Albrecht von Bernstorff, being led by two guards. They seemed to be supporting him, as if he could not stay upright without them. He had once been a great devourer of good food and fine wine, a bon viveur. That man was gone. When he caught her eye, he still managed a smile but what Hanna could not forget was the look of pure suffering etched on his face. She would see him again, after a night interrogation. It was clear he had endured a terrible beating; his face was swollen and his eyes were bloodshot.

For this, of course, was the reason they were all here. Ravensbrück had not featured especially in the plans of the Special Commission that rounded up the men and women of the tea party. But once its head, Leo Lange, decided it was no longer viable to remain in Berlin under enemy bombardment, the choice had been easy. His new headquarters would be the Security Police School at Drögen, near Fürstenberg, that same pretty, affluent town that lay just across the water from, and within sight of, Ravensbrück.

Nor would he confine himself to the tea-party group alone. Lange had become convinced that the suspects he had picked up *before* 10 September – the likes of Bernstorff, Richard Kuenzer and the pacifist priest Max Metzger – had to be connected to the Carmerstrasse group because of their mutual ties to the *Solf-Kreis*. If there was a single plot to be exposed, he concluded, there needed to be a single commission to expose it. Now he would combine his various investigations and put all his suspects in one place.

The move out of Berlin meant he could hold them inside a concentration camp, in a cell block, part of which would now be under the direct control of Lange and his commission. Close by would be a facility ideally suited to Lange's driving purpose: to squeeze and press his captives until they had told him everything.

43

Threats and Menaces

Hanna, February 1944

AMONG THE FIRST to be transferred to Ravensbrück was Hanna Solf, who understood very swiftly that this was more than a change of location. From now on, the nights were regularly interrupted, guards entering the cell to make supposed checks on the inmates and the electric light — which, like the heating, was controlled from the outside — turned on every fifteen or thirty minutes. If it wasn't the light that kept her awake, it was the sound: the screams of strangers piercing the air.

The one constant was interrogation, almost always at night. To aggravate the sleep deprivation, the guards would come in each evening with a sleeping tablet, the taking of which was not optional — only to return an hour later to wake her up. They ordered her to get dressed, and in a great hurry. She would then be taken by car to the Security Police School at Drögen, some twelve miles away. Still groggy from the pill, she was to face a barrage of sustained and detailed questions. And the inquisitor would be none other than Leo Lange himself.

The session would last until dawn and beyond, usually ten hours, sometimes eight, sometimes fourteen and always without food, as Lange pressed her over and over again about the gathering at Carmerstrasse. He wanted to know exactly who had said what to whom, with a particular focus on Elisabeth von Thadden and Otto Kiep.

Sometimes the questions would be specific, pressing her on the letters Reckzeh had delivered on her behalf in Switzerland, though not delving too far into their content, which confirmed to her that both Reckzeh and the Gestapo had read them and seen that they were innocuous. Sometimes, Lange's inquiries were more general. What exactly was Frau Solf's attitude towards national socialism? Hanna made clear that she rejected it, spelling out her opposition on three grounds. First, the Nazis' curtailment of free expression. Second, their persecution of the Jews. Third, their intolerance of those Christians they deemed unacceptable.

Lange would make hairpin turns, shifting from insult one moment to encouragement the next, offering the purportedly friendly suggestion that she should make things easier for herself by testifying against the other suspects. Throughout she would be presented with wild distortions of something she might have said a minute or an hour earlier.

And of course, Lange deployed the interrogator's essential tools: threats and menaces. Sometimes these would be physical, Lange telling Hanna that an alternative existed to confinement in a room where the light came on every thirty minutes: she could be kept instead in permanent darkness. He told her that, if she did not co-operate, he could have her carrying rocks, doubtless in a labour gang drawn from the inmates of the main concentration camp. And there was the ultimate threat, the same one that hung over all these proceedings: namely, the death sentence.

That was only one of the ways Lange sought to prey on Hanna Solf's mind. Sometimes he would refer to her late husband, only to add: 'You will soon be able to shake hands with him.' Or he would threaten her sons and son-in-law, all in action as officers of the German army. Sometimes it would be thinly coded: 'If you are sentenced to death – because no state would put up with what you and your friends have committed – your sons can of course no longer be officers.' Other times, he would make the threat bald and clear: if you do not talk, we will arrest your sons. He would mention her youngest son in particular. There was no need to spell it out: the men would be stripped of whatever protection their rank afforded them and exposed to heaven knows what danger.

Round and round Lange went, all through the night, night after night. On one occasion, it only ended – at seven o'clock in the morning – when Hanna fainted. She was fifty-six years old, drugged and deprived of sleep. But Lange, a man who had directed mass killings just a couple of years earlier, could not make this woman budge.

In his frustration, he threw out the official policy on special prisoners' rations and put Hanna on a starvation diet, feeding her nothing but decaying turnips for weeks at a stretch. Indeed, he made that rancid vegetable, sometimes liquified into a soup, the standard diet of the Carmerstrasse group, knowing as he did how their stomachs would recoil from a fluid that reeked of mildew and rot, that tasted of putrefaction in a damp, dark cellar. When the food came, it would be pushed through a hatch, often delivered by one of the imprisoned Jehovah's Witnesses who acted as couriers and were barred from speaking to any of the special prisoners.

She was determined not to reveal anything that might harm her friends, determined too not to lose her temper or even show fear. It required every drop of strength she had and she did not have much. But somehow Hanna endured it, two months of it. Until the day she glimpsed something from her cell that should have been a comfort. Instead, it was a sight to break the heart.

Lagi

Like her mother, Lagi faced the torment of interrogation at the hands of Leo Lange. She was questioned less often, perhaps because she had not been present at the crucial tea party, but in the same fashion: the same alternating combination of wild threats and equally unlikely promises. She might be taken out of her cell at four o'clock in the afternoon, made to wait till 10 p.m., then questioned for six hours straight.

Lange's opening gambit was the same one he used with her mother. 'What is your attitude to national socialism?'

I'm opposed to it, Lagi replied. That had always been her style, ever since those first rounds of combat with the Gestapo in Shanghai. She would hold her head up high and tell the truth, without concessions. Unabashed, she spelled out to Lange her complete and total rejection of Nazism.

She knew the risk she was taking. She knew she and the others were accused of high treason, but Lange's zeal for information, his need for hard, concrete proof, told her that the Nazis wanted a sound legal basis for the action they planned to take. Punishing these rebels for their *views* was clearly not enough; Lange wanted to convict them for their *deeds*.

That meant he needed someone — anyone — to talk. Lange's desperation could drive him to fury. More than once, the investigator's anger grew so intense, Lagi felt sure he was about to hit her. The threat of physical violence was always present. At one point all the special prisoners were examined by SS doctors. The purpose: to determine whether their bodies could withstand torture.

But Lange's greatest threat was not to the body but to the soul. This was where he tested the young countess most. And he had at his disposal one particularly sharp instrument of torture.

From the start, Lagi had been determined to get the measure of Ravensbrück, to keep her eyes wide open, to see everything. Locked on her first day in a bare cell on the north side of the prison, she had focused immediately on the small, barred window high up in the wall. She listened carefully for any sounds from the corridor to be sure no guard was around who might catch a glimpse of what she was about to do. Then, with great effort, she grabbed hold of the high ledge and hauled herself up so that she could peek out. Now she saw the large open space of the camp square, like a parade ground. In time, she would witness the morning and evening roll-call as the inmates assembled after a day of slave labour.

The next day, she was taken to the prison yard for her daily exercise allowance: a fifteen-minute walk. She walked around the small patch of ground, taking in the cell building, sizing up the southern wall. And then she heard it. Her own name, called out not as a barked instruction or reprimand from one of her jailers, but in a wholly different voice, one as familiar to her as her own. It came from one of the prison cells.

Lagi strained not to make too sudden a movement. She had been a prisoner long enough to know that the guards across the yard, watching her intently, would be alert even to a gesture. Slowly then, she looked upwards. There, in another barred window, pressed against it, was the face of her mother.

THREATS AND MENACES

It took a conscious act of self-control for Lagi to hide her shock at what she could see. It was not only the sadness that was etched in Hanna Solf's features. It was what had happened to her. She was emaciated, a starved shadow of herself.

Lagi felt some relief to see her there, to know that the two of them were at least in the same place. And yet the melancholy on her mother's face suggested a different reaction, perhaps regret that her daughter had not somehow got away, that she too was ensnared in the Nazi net.

After that first glimpse, Lagi had been determined to make contact. Gradually she learned her way around the prison, discovering its weak points and hidden networks, aided not only by those special prisoners she had long known, but by some of the political prisoners, including from abroad, whom she had met for the first time behind bars. Before long, these old and new comrades were helping pass an occasional secret message to or from her mother. What Lagi learned through those fragments of contact enraged her. For she discovered that her mother's food rations had been slashed and that she was starving.

That knowledge pushed Lagi over the edge. She began a hunger strike, which after a few days brought a small result: not more food, but permission for some of Lagi's meagre ration to be given instead to her mother. But she knew it would not be enough.

The sorrow she felt for the ghost she had glimpsed at that window was Lagi's weakness, and Leo Lange knew it. During one especially intense round of questioning, the detective began to shout. Past caring, and consumed with rage, hunger and sadness for her shrunken, starving mother, Lagi shouted back. That incensed the inquisitor all the more. Lange now issued the ultimate threat: unless Lagi incriminated the other prisoners, Hanna would die.

That was the choice. Lagi could either testify against her friends or she could see her mother sentenced to death. Lange was clear; there could be no middle way. Finally, she gave her answer. Given those were her only options, she looked at Lange and said, 'I am sorry; then you have to execute my mother.'

44

Body and Soul

Otto, Winter 1944

IN RAVENSBRÜCK, OTTO Kiep's treatment grew more severe. He was now subject to what was known as 'aggravated interrogation', a sanitised way of saying beatings and torture. For one three-day stretch, his captors gave him the third degree: continuous questioning, day and night, without rest. He was tied up throughout, supposedly to prevent him from making an attempt on his own life.

As always, Lange liked to combine physical hardship with psychological suffering. That might mean threats designed to induce fear or mind games whose purpose was to unsettle. During one interrogation, his limbs restrained as usual, Otto had to sit on a stool, his back unsupported, a scorching hot Jupiter lamp trained on him. Throughout, a young man, elegantly kitted out in white tie and tails, as if fresh from the opera, smoked a fat cigar in his face as he fired off questions. But instead of burning Otto's flesh with the red-hot ash, the dapper inquisitor instructed his secretary to bring him coffee and French cognac, which he gave to the prisoner. Otto was bound and in pain, but was also lavished with luxuries from his previous life. None of it made any sense.

The questions were ceaseless; he might be interrogated for two or three long sessions in a single day, accompanied either by the threat or reality of violence if he did not say what they wanted to hear. Not so much about the tea party itself – after all, they had the report of an eyewitness about that – but about what Lange and his subordinates were certain was a wider plot. They wanted Otto to admit that he had been in contact with the now-exiled former chancellor Joseph Wirth, as the two of them, along with other enemies of the Reich, plotted the defeat of Germany, solely so they could seize power for themselves. That much the Lange Special Commission took as read. It was only the details they lacked.

And so they quizzed Otto, again and again. What exactly was Wirth planning? Who else, besides Otto of course, was he conspiring with? Who was Otto talking to among the Reich's Allied enemies? With which officials in London or Washington was he corresponding? And what was in it for him? What role did he expect to play in the government that he and Wirth imagined they were going to establish after they had got rid of the Führer?

Sometimes these questions would come with a snarl, sometimes with the gentle encouragement of a friend. Sometimes the grilling would go on until he felt himself nauseous with weariness, sometimes it would stop for no clear reason and he would be thanked, as if he were an expert testifying to a parliamentary committee.

He understood what a challenge this was, both to body and to soul. He would not neglect the former. Decades earlier he used to take runs around his school; now, and in that same spirit, he imposed an exercise regime on himself. He could not lift weights or take a morning jog as he used to. But even in his cell, he would begin every morning with fifteen or twenty minutes of exercise. For him, it was an act of defiance: he would refuse to let himself be ground down. He would not be destroyed.

As for his soul, he dug deep into the Christian faith that had been an intermittent companion throughout his life. He found comfort in knowing that not everything was up to him, that his fate was largely in the hands of God. But his greatest solace was the love he felt for his wife.

The rules on letter writing tended to shift: sometimes a total ban, sometimes a partial relaxation. A constant was a prohibition on writing to anyone about his own case or his treatment in Ravensbrück. He was allowed to write to his family, on the strict condition that he confine himself solely to personal matters and not refer to his current circumstances. Now he channelled all his energies into that task, mentally drafting and redrafting each letter to his wife before he put pen to paper.

Not long before his arrest, in the weeks leading up to Christmas, he and Hanna had read a novel to each other, aloud. It was *The Bridge of San Luis Rey* by Thornton Wilder. What lingered for them both was a passage towards the end, in which a character reflects on memory and death. 'Soon we shall die,' she thinks. It was in the nature of life to 'be loved for a while and forgotten. But the love will have been enough . . . There is a land of the living and a land of the dead and the bridge is love, the only survival, the only meaning.'

The words had rung out loud for both of them, and Otto wanted to return them both to that moment. He wrote a poem for his wife and he called it 'The Bridge of Love'.

What he did not know as he wrote those lines was that Hanna Kiep was right there. Not only in his heart, but in that very same cell block.

45

The Fallout

Winter 1944

IN THE TINY world of high-society dissent, few couples cut more of a dash than Erich and Elisabeth Vermehren. He was a young lawyer with both the academic prowess to have been awarded a Rhodes Scholarship to Oxford and enough of a record of anti-Nazi activism to ensure the German authorities barred him from taking it up. (Among his offences: his schoolboy failure to be an enthusiast for the Hitler Youth.) She had been born Countess Elisabeth von Plettenberg, was eight years older than her husband, and was renowned both as a beauty and as one of the bravest women of her time – a committed Catholic who had risked jail and worse by circulating anti-Nazi writings through the church, among them a banned text that slammed national socialism as a pagan creed. She had been born into one of the country's most distinguished Catholic families; he was a devout convert; together their ties to the Catholic underground were strong.

The start of the war had seen them retreat into a state of *innere Emigration*, so alienated from the society around them that they lived in psychological exile from Germany, even if they physically remained in the country. Like so many of their fellow dissenters, they had found a safe harbour in military intelligence, working for the Abwehr in Berlin. But they were keen to get out of Germany and enlisted the help of Erich's cousin in the Foreign Ministry, Adam von Trott zu Solz. Thanks to him, they secured a posting in Istanbul and the visas to get there.

Erich attended a course at the Abwehr training school, learning the basics of secret inks and codes, and then headed to Turkey, where in truth he was more of a secretary than a spy, filing the odd report on British shipping movements and not much else. He was alone for the first few months, because his wife was subject to a Gestapo ban forbidding her from leaving Germany. Getting her to Istanbul required yet more help from Trott zu Solz and a string of allies inside the Foreign Ministry and the German diplomatic corps, as Elisabeth crossed Europe while somehow evading the Gestapo, whether by secret passage on a diplomatic courier flight from Sofia or lying low on an overnight train while an intelligence officer of the SS slept in the compartment next door. But by the start of 1944, the couple were together in Turkey, the pressure and menace of Berlin far away.

Or so they thought. They had been together for not much more than a week or two when news came that a friend, indeed the man who had nominated Erich for the Rhodes Scholarship that never was, had been arrested. That friend was Otto Kiep.

The Vermehrens had barely had time to absorb the shock when Erich received a summons to return to Berlin. The timing, he felt sure, was not a coincidence. His name had somehow been connected to Otto's. Given that his hostility to the regime was so poorly hidden, it was obvious what would happen if he and Elisabeth went back: the minute their feet touched German soil, they would be arrested.

The only possible way out suggested itself immediately. It was an escape route open to the Vermehrens because of his position and because they were outside Nazi-held territory. They would defect to Britain.

As it happens, Vermehren had already had some contact with British intelligence's man in Istanbul, a figure who would become legendary in the field: Nicholas Elliott. He had greeted the German with the words: 'Erich Vermehren? You were coming up to Oxford, I believe?' By February, the British had spirited the couple out of Turkey and over to England.

Never mind the tedium of shipping logs that had constituted Erich's actual work, his defection was swiftly squeezed for maximum propaganda value. For the British press, the Vermehrens were glamorous German master spies, with Erich now recast as German intelligence's top man in Turkey. They had not only fled Istanbul in a dramatic escape via Cairo (true), but had brought the Abwehr codebooks with them and handed them over to the British (not true).

That was the story that reached Berlin and it drove Adolf Hitler into a state of rage, the flames of his fury eagerly fanned by Heinrich Himmler. It had long irritated the Reichsführer-SS that the army had its own intelligence service, boosting the Wehrmacht's ability to function as a rival centre of power, if not a shadow state beyond the reach of the Nazi party. The Vermehrens' defection presented an opening too good to ignore.

Himmler poured a stream of poison into Hitler's ear, telling him that they had long known that the Abwehr was useless, repeatedly failing to warn of crucial military developments, but recent events surely confirmed that the agency was infested with a defeatist intelligentsia at best, outright traitors at worst. Had not the Führer had to relieve Hans Oster, number two at the Abwehr, of all intelligence work just a couple of months earlier? And then in January, two other men of the Abwehr, Otto Kiep and Helmuth von Moltke, had been arrested. Now this man Vermehren. It was surely time to act.

Hitler summoned the head of the service, Admiral Canaris, to report to him on the situation on the Russian front. As Himmler looked on, Canaris started working through the bundle of reports he had brought with him, setting out his assessment. Having listened patiently for a while, Hitler suddenly leapt forward, overturned the table and grabbed the admiral by the lapels.

'Are you trying to tell me that I am going to lose this war?'

'Mein Führer, I have said nothing about losing the war. I have tried to explain the military situation on the Russian front.'

Hitler consulted with some of his chief lieutenants, Himmler among them, and on 18 February he signed a decree ordering 'the establishment of a unified German secret intelligence service'. In command would be Reichsführer-SS Heinrich Himmler. The Abwehr as was no longer existed, its functions carved up between the Gestapo and the SD, the intelligence service of the SS. From now on, the armed forces, which for so long had sustained their own apparatus separate from the Nazi structure, would have no intelligence service of their own. As for Canaris, he was not banished completely but shunted off into a non-job, the better to hide the circumstances of his departure. Friends urged him to leave the country with his wife and family, to head to General Franco's Spain for his own safety. But he would not go.

Otto Kiep had wanted to believe that what happened on 10 September was just a tea party, marked by some unwise chatter admittedly, but essentially just a social gathering of a few individuals whose impact could be contained. In fact, it had set in train a series of consequences affecting the highest reaches of the Nazi state – and which would soon come to overwhelm him.

46

The Bridge of Love

Otto, February 1944

OTTO KIEP KNEW nothing of what had happened to his wife. In fact, she had been arrested the day after her husband, allowed to tuck in her children and say goodnight before taking the train to Berlin the next morning. At Grunewald station she had been met by officers of the Lange Special Commission, who drove her immediately to Kurfürstendamm 140, where, as it so happened, Otto was already a prisoner. Not that the couple were allowed to know that. She was moved back and forth from Kurfürstendamm to the police cells at Alexanderplatz, before finally being transferred to Ravensbrück on 26 January 1944. Alongside her in jail was her husband's secretary, a sign that Otto was more than a mere person of interest to the Gestapo: he was central to their inquiries, because they assumed he was central to the conspiracy they were determined to expose. They wanted him and everyone close to him.

They held Hanna Kiep in Cell 28 at Ravensbrück and interviewed her at the training school at Drögen. There she too faced the same array of Gestapo tools and weapons: threats and withheld food, flattery and promises. Sometimes Lange would do the interrogation, sometimes it would be a kindlier colleague. One day the good cop, the next the bad cop; one day hope, the next despair. Lange was not above using Hanna's family, promising her distressed father early on that his daughter was 'in no way incriminated' and would be released imminently, only to transfer her to Ravensbrück forty-eight hours later. He kept this up for weeks and months, regularly reassuring Hanna that she was about to be freed. It was, like the deployment of the gentler interrogator or the permission to send and receive letters, or to take long walks in the garden nursery or to have an uninterrupted night's sleep or a portion of blood sausage for dinner, just another technique, designed to prompt Otto's wife into lowering her guard, so that she might trust her captors enough to give them information. And yet, despite all that effort, Hanna made not a single incriminating statement.

Instead, she maintained a facade of unblemished innocence. All she could tell the Gestapo was what she knew for certain: that her husband was a true patriot, as faithful to Germany as he was to her. When an inquisitor appeared to threaten her children, she would affect not to believe them: national socialism would never countenance such a thing. It was impossible that the NSDAP, the party the Kieps trusted wholly, would betray their own. After all, her children were not only loyal to their parents, they were faithful to the Hitler Youth.

She kept this up without faltering. It helped that she looked the part. She was the very embodiment of the Nazi ideal of womanhood: tall and blonde, her hair so long it fell below her waist. Committed to home, family and nation, and willing to defend all three fiercely, she might have been a huntress from Teutonic myth.

Hanna's plight remained unknown to Otto. He was still confined to his cell, cut off, as they all were, from his fellow accused. Until the day in late February when he saw her. He was being led off for yet another interrogation session and suddenly there she was: walking towards him, coming through the doorway with a prison guard at her side. For a second their eyes met. And yet, almost as fast, a survival instinct in each of them ensured they made no outward sign of recognition. Without a word needing to be said, both understood that if the guards saw that husband and wife now knew they were being held in the same prison, they would be separated immediately, with one transferred. All they could do was cherish that fleeting instant, that momentary glance. That night, alone in his cell, Otto wrote his wife a poem:

> I saw you. It was a dream
> Yet so clear, it was like reality

The dream would recur. Not long after that first glimpse, Otto was in the L-shaped prison yard, taking his allocated period of exercise, which came only two or three times a week. As always he was on his own, save for the guard who would watch him walk back and forth, like a tiger in a zoo, pacing his cage. At one point, as he got to the corner of the L, Otto looked upwards and there, in a third-floor window, was his beloved wife. Knowing the risks, he made a small movement of his hand, raising it just a little, so that she would know he had seen her.

His time in the yard was almost up. He glanced up twice more, savouring each sighting, and then it was over: he was led back inside.

After that, he doubtless counted the hours till his next trip outdoors. As soon as he was in the exercise yard, he looked up instantly and saw her. Except now she was pressing against the window a series of cards she had made, each one showing a single letter of the alphabet. As he walked, she held up one, then another. First a B, then an R, then a U, until she had spelled out a word: *Brücke*, or Bridge. It was the Bridge of Love.

They had already been exchanging letters, as if from afar, but now, aided by a handful of guards willing to act as couriers, they could send each other secret messages – sometimes hidden in, among other places, the lid of a Thermos flask – with the added immediacy of proximity. They might trade poems and words of love, but also practical talk of their children and the future. Somehow, Otto conveyed to her how his jailers were treating him and their very particular methods of interrogation, information that Hanna duly passed on to her father who, along with her son and housemaid, was allowed to visit her in Ravensbrück, a privilege surely granted by Lange in the hope that his eavesdropping agents might overhear a useful nugget or two.

By now, in the world outside the cell block and the concentration camp, winter had turned to spring. Hanna sent a card with a pressed forget-me-not to Otto's cell; he returned it, with a few handwritten words: 'To my dear wife – sent back with love,' doubtless because he had no other gift to give her.

In late May, the Kieps asked the prison authorities for permission to speak to each other about urgent matters relating to their family and their home, but the request was denied. They feared they might never speak to each other again. Then, without warning, they were granted a precious hour together.

It came during a weekend in mid-June, when the SS guards were absent and the regular prison staff were in charge. One of that group knew that Otto was due to be transferred to another facility the following day, so this might be the couple's last chance. And so, on the Sunday afternoon, that prison officer came unexpectedly to Otto's cell, unlocked the door and, with scarcely a word, led him to his wife, before leaving the two alone. There, in Hanna's cell, they had a precious sixty minutes together. Parting was rarely such sweet sorrow.

But there was an imbalance between them. For Otto knew far more than he was letting on.

47

The Scourge of Guilt

Elisabeth, Spring 1944

EVENTUALLY, ELISABETH VON Thadden found her way, as they all did, to the prisoner block at Ravensbrück. Like the others, she was kept apart from the rest of the group that had gathered in her sitting room on Carmerstrasse. Their captors did this meticulously, taking care to stagger the tea-party detainees' exercise times, so that when they paced around the yard for their few allotted minutes, they did so only with strangers.

Like the others, she was driven to the training college at Drögen, both for interrogation and for any visits from friends or family, the authorities shrewdly if cynically choosing to keep outsiders away from Ravensbrück itself. Such visits were a privilege to be granted just once a month. As for the other perks of being a special prisoner – permission to smoke, say, or do needlework – those were of small consolation to Elisabeth. They could hardly compensate for the cruelties of this place, including one Elisabeth found especially hard to bear: the sound of male political prisoners receiving a flogging.

When she was not in her cell, trying to block her ears, she was in the interrogation room. Elisabeth was a key target, deemed by Lange to sit, along with Otto Kiep, at the heart of the conspiracy he was determined to prove, the one that united Berlin high society with the German émigrés of Switzerland. If not every day, then every night, Lange went at her, prodding and probing, as he pushed her to confess what he wanted to be true: that she was the lead player in a tight, well-organised, cross-border plot to stage a coup d'état against Adolf Hitler.

Of course, Elisabeth denied it all. She could not confess, she insisted, because there was nothing to confess to. They were a group of friends and acquaintances, spending a Friday afternoon together, marking the fiftieth birthday of her younger sister. That was the long and short of it. Nothing had happened.

Lange dismissed that with contempt. He knew she was lying, he said. He knew because all the others had already confessed to everything.

That was bound to make her pause. She had been kept in such perfect isolation, she had no idea who else had been arrested, let alone what they might have given away as Lange pressed down on each of them. Did he really have in his grip her sister Anza? Were the Solfs his prisoners, both mother and daughter, the former doubtless still brimming with bitter anger at Elisabeth for her foolishness in allowing a perfect stranger into their ranks, a fury Hanna Solf had been unable to hide? What about the two men, Scherpenberg and Kiep, both fathers of young children, were they here too? Was everyone who had gathered on that stupid, needless afternoon here, all of them captives of Lange? The smug, triumphant look on the Gestapo man's face suggested the answer was yes. Save for one exception: she knew that Arthur Zarden had chosen to die rather than be at the mercy of Lange and his men a moment longer. He at least had slipped the Nazis' grip.

Had Lange set himself to devising the ideal instrument of torture for Elisabeth von Thadden, he could hardly have done better. More than the sleep deprivation, the hunger or even the solitary confinement – which, given her reliance on friendship, her need for social contact, stung especially sharply – it was guilt that was the most potent scourge. It tore through her as she contemplated all the damage she had done. To think those young ones would be deprived of a father because of her. It was unbearable.

Steadily, the guilt gnawed away and eventually broke down what had once been a defining trait of Elisabeth's, her defiance in the face of authority. This was the woman who had banished the Hitler salute from her school, who had admitted Jewish girls as pupils, who had taught the young women placed in her charge that, no matter what they might hear around them, they could ignore the newspapers and the radio and the banners hanging from every building:

the source of ultimate authority was not the Führer, but Jesus Christ. Yet now that granite resolve was crumbling.

Under Lange's bombardment, she gave ground. She accepted that the state had every right to defend itself against challenges from within as well as without, that it was duty bound to stand guard against those who wished it ill and to come down hard on its enemies. But the only such enemy she would point to was herself.

She claimed the only person Lange was looking for was right in front of him. It was she, and no one else, who had organised and led the proceedings that Paul Reckzeh had witnessed. It was she who planned the conversation he had heard and reported to his superiors as treachery. She and she alone who nudged her guests into talking politics, luring them into crossing lines they would never have crossed had she not enticed them to do so. She was a manipulator, even an enchantress, mesmerising good people into voicing thoughts they didn't even have. If he wanted to identify the culprit, he need search no further. The blame rested entirely with her.

It was a compelling story, well told. The trouble was, Leo Lange did not believe a word of it. Perhaps organising the deaths of thousands teaches a man a thing or two about human nature. Maybe seeing so many human beings in extremis, breathing their last, is an education in desperation. He was not old, barely into his mid-thirties, but Lange had already seen so much – and he could see right through Elisabeth von Thadden.

So he pressed for more than just a solo confession. He wanted her to give him the group. He wanted her to give up her friends.

He worked on her the way he continued to work on the Solfs and the others. The same turnip soup, with its taste of an unopened cellar, offering no nutrition to bodies already deprived of daylight and longing for vitamins. The same interrupted nights, either because the overhead bulb was flicked on at intervals or else a torch was flashed in the face, making it impossible to sleep. The same trick with sleeping tablets, the prisoners allowed to slip into chemically induced unconsciousness for just a few minutes before they were forced awake and sent for questioning, still in a state of blurry confusion. Often, and this would surely have been intolerable for

Elisabeth, the suspect would be barely clothed, in a state of permanent shame.

Convinced that she was the linchpin in the operation, Lange would often conduct the interrogation himself. But not always. That too was one of his weapons: changing the inquisitor, bringing in someone new who would insist on hearing the whole story again, in the same forensic but futile detail. Sometimes she would face a gentle questioner, sometimes a brute. The demeanour might vary, but not the determination to tread and retread the same old ground, pursuing the same irrelevant tangents, heading down the same dead ends.

After a marathon nocturnal session, the daytime brought little relief. Turning the screw, Lange had withdrawn the small privileges that made life just about bearable. Parcels from the outside world were held back; letters could not be received or, no less a punishment, written. The body was deprived of food and sleep. The soul was deprived of human connection.

Elisabeth von Thadden had been a woman of command, used to being in charge. She had headed her father's country estate while still a teenager. True, in recent months her confidence had drained somewhat; losing her school had sapped it. But she had a deep well to draw on, filled not only with experience but also faith. If anyone could endure the ordeal of captivity, privation and enforced isolation, surely it was Elisabeth von Thadden.

Of course, even she had her limits. She began to shut down, retreating ever further inwards into lethargy and inertia. For several weeks, she was mentally numb, the only expression in her eyes desperation. She was having a breakdown.

She was so completely alone. She was in solitary confinement most of the time. She was cut off from her friends, whose fate she knew so little of. When she did discover that this or that member of her circle was also a prisoner in that same Ravensbrück cell block, she did not clamour for contact but, on the contrary, avoided it. She feared deepening the pit into which, she was convinced, she had plunged them all. She had caused enough trouble: to exchange so much as a glance with a fellow inmate was bound only to make matters worse.

And yet, though she had broken, she did not crack. Paralysed in a state of sustained torpor she may have been, but still she did not give Lange what he wanted. She did not utter a word that would incriminate anyone but herself. She would bear the guilt alone.

Here too, however, she had her limits. She would not inflict on herself the ultimate punishment. It was not Elisabeth von Thadden who would follow the lead set by Arthur Zarden, concluding that suicide represented the only way out. Instead, that decision would be made by another one of the guests she had hosted that fateful September day.

48

The Hands of God

Otto, June 1944

ON 5 JUNE, Otto Kiep had lost his last shred of military protection: the Reich Military Court had formally agreed to hand his case over to the civilian judiciary, thereby putting an official seal on what had become a de facto reality on the day of his arrest. He would be judged not by the army, with its vestigial independence, but by the Volksgerichtshof, the People's Court, which was an arm of the Nazi party in all but name. A few days later Lange would make a point of handing the Kiep file, bulging with the transcripts of those endless hours of questioning, over to the Reich prosecutor in person. When the prosecutor skim-read the file, one detail leapt out. He noticed that no less than Heinrich Himmler had asked to be kept informed of the Kiep case, receiving regular reports on those repeated interrogations. If there had been any doubt about the importance of the tea-party case to the highest reaches of the Nazi state, it was dispelled now.

Before he let go of the paperwork, Lange wanted one last run at Otto himself. On 7 June, he told his prisoner that a 'death sentence was undoubtedly certain', that there was nothing more Otto could say that would either improve or damage his prospects. Lange no longer needed any more evidence or information: Otto had incriminated himself enough.

Otto replied that he had been deceived so often, he no longer believed a word Lange said. But it was all front. For Otto knew that, this time, Lange was telling the truth. For a year or so, the People's Court had been cracking down on *Wehrkraftzersetzer*, citizens deemed to have undermined the military strength of the country.

Since the summer of 1943, the court had been much less insistent on seeing proof of participation in a wider conspiracy of the kind Lange had been so desperate to pin on Otto. Statements criticising the regime were grounds enough for a death sentence. And those, Otto knew, the prosecution had in abundance, thanks to Paul Reckzeh and the first pages in that fat file of Lange's.

Otto's task now was to do as he had been trained, both as a lawyer and a diplomat. He needed to think through the facts, calmly, rationally and unsentimentally. The largest and most stubborn of those was that he was clearly going to be executed. What implications, he tried to ask himself, flowed from that?

The emotional ones were obvious. He had set about writing a private autobiography, a record for his children, so they might know him when he was gone. But he would need to do more. A treason conviction would not only lead to his execution; it would also trigger the state seizure of all his property, including his pension. Hanna would be a widow, his children would be fatherless and all of them would be left without an inheritance.

And what about the period between now and his eventual, inevitable appointment with the executioner? He could be tortured at any point, pressed and squeezed for even the tiniest morsel on others whom the regime would brand as 'defeatist' or worse. So far he had held firm, partly because he was trying to save his own life. But if that hope was extinguished, it was at least possible, maybe even likely, that he would crack. His own death certain, it would take godlike strength to withstand unending pain rather than simply sign whatever they wanted him to sign to make the agony stop. But if he did that, he would not be condemning himself to death, for he was already condemned. He would be condemning others.

The conclusion was clear. It would be better for his family and for those he regarded as his fellow patriots if he were not to wait for the preordained verdict of a Nazi court. Better to implement the unavoidable sentence himself, sooner rather than later. He would not do it here, so close to Hanna. But the imminence of the trial meant he would be moved from Ravensbrück before too long anyway, sent to another jail as a remand prisoner. He would make his move there and then.

He prepared himself, collecting what he would need: a razor and sleeping pills. He decided he would need to be physically strong for such an act, so he worked to stay as healthy as he could, continuing to exercise. He also wanted his wife to be left with no confusion, for her to understood that he had been driven not by despair but reason. He wrote a letter that was to be opened after his death, explaining that it was now clear that the Reich was embarked on a 'reign of terror' against those guilty of defeatism and rebellion.

'Therefore, dearest,' he wrote,

> I must go back on my word that I will persevere to the end . . . But this is the only way I can die for you, i.e., in your interest, and not <u>against</u> it, i.e., with the terrible effect of complete economic loss for you. I need not tell you how difficult the decision will be for me, dearest; but I cannot ask you, but must make it alone. I have already made it and would carry it out here if you were not here. For here I have all the means (blade and tablets) and do not know whether I shall still have them in the new place. But I cannot bring myself to have you face this experience here, after you have suffered, endured and helped here for so long and with such infinite bravery . . . If I do it, you know that I am doing it for you and that I can answer for it before God and you.

He hid the letter in the lid of the small suitcase that contained his belongings.

On Monday morning he and Hilger van Scherpenberg, the two serving diplomats at the September tea party, were transferred to the Brandenburg-Görden penitentiary. Otto could think only of the course of action he had set himself on, his resolve suddenly weakened by the insistent surfacing of hope. What if there was a last-minute, unexpected change in his situation? What if the regime made a shock announcement of a pardon for all political prisoners? What if the Allies mounted a surprise attack from the air, with American parachutists landing in and taking Berlin? What if Hitler were suddenly to die?

No, he told himself. Such a reprieve was impossible. His decision at Ravensbrück had been the right one: sensible, practical, realistic. Late in the evening of the next day, 13 June 1944, he sat down to write a final letter of farewell to his beloved bride and, as was their way, a poem. He called it 'My Ring, Your Ring'.

> Take back the ring, then, and continue to wear it
> For me, and think the ring were I:
> Always close to you and therefore happy, serene,
> Enclosing and protecting you for ever.

He took the wedding band from his finger and placed it, along with the poem, in an envelope. Then, he reached for the sleeping tablets and the razor blade that he had successfully smuggled in from the cell block at Ravensbrück. He swallowed the tablets, then cut into his wrists as deeply as he could. He was lying down and the night was dark. He had made his decision and was at peace with it. He had placed himself in the hands of God.

But God had other plans.

49

All But a Miracle

Maria, 1944

NOT THAT HE knew it, but Otto Kiep had slashed his wrists one week after the D-Day landings, as the Allies stormed the Normandy beaches and began to push the Nazis out of France. The course of the war was changing, but little or no word of it penetrated the thick walls of the cell block at Ravensbrück.

The odd crumb of information might make it through. The Polish prisoners picked up fragments, especially those who had contact with the concentration-camp guards. The inmates who served as the guards' hairdressers listened to the BBC and could be an occasional source. In early June, Irmgard Zarden had to see the prison dentist: it was one of the assistants, another Polish prisoner, who whispered to her the news of D-Day. But most of the tea-party group inside Ravensbrück remained sealed off from the outside world.

They therefore had no inkling that, among their fellow dissenters, a few leading figures had managed to stay out of the Gestapo's clutches and were still at large. Countess Maria von Maltzan, to name one, was still a free woman in 1944, able to continue her double life as a vet and volunteer for the resistance. Though even she came perilously close to giving herself away.

In the spring, she had made what she knew would be a farewell visit to the family estate in Militsch. Unlike her friends in Ravensbrück, she was able to listen to foreign radio broadcasts and she had heard enough to conclude both that the thousand-year Reich was living on borrowed time and that the Silesia of her childhood would soon be conquered by the Red Army. Once at Militsch, she toured the grounds, trying to catch hold of each precious memory for the last time, saying a particular goodbye to the walnut tree she had planted when she was seven years old and which now stood tall.

Army officers were billeted in the Maltzan castle, and Maria was compelled to dine with them. They discussed the political situation, a subject Maria approached with great caution. Mainly, though, she was keen to talk to her sister-in-law, who, as the widow of Maria's only brother, was now the keeper of the family purse. First, Maria urged her to move the family art treasures, which included the largest private collection of engravings in Europe, to safety. Second, she raised the matter of her share of the family inheritance, which she had never received. When her sister-in-law suggested that her allowance should be quite sufficient, Maria countered that, given the current state of the war, there was a strong risk that Militsch would be lost, and with it the source of her income.

The young widow seemed astonished that anyone could think such a thing, and refused to budge on either the money or the art. Now Maria dispensed with the caution she had maintained at dinner.

'For God's sake,' she said, 'do you think we're going to win this war?' The tanks were rolling towards Germany, she explained, and they 'won't stop rolling until they're in Berlin'.

Her sister-in-law was aghast and told her that what Maria had just said was 'extremely defeatist'.

Defeatist. Maria did not need to be told twice. A denunciation from her sister-in-law would lead to her arrest and worse. She made one last tour of her father's study, her mother's bedrooms, the gallery, the museum, the church belonging to the family estate and its tower, the library, the oval hall and the Renaissance room, the dining room, the 'marble house', the guest rooms, the stables, including the horse washroom and the harness room, and left Militsch for the last time. She knew she would not go back, not if that meant risking another exchange with her sister-in-law. She did not want to give the authorities an excuse to send her to Ravensbrück. Her friends might be there, but she had no plans to follow them — at least not on account of her words.

Actions were a different matter. She did not give up her efforts for the resistance. On the contrary, she intensified them. Sometimes that entailed acts of sabotage. As a vet, when tasked with restoring injured military horses and dogs to full health, she found ingenious ways to delay their return to frontline duty. She had no intention of helping the Nazi war effort in that or any other way. A pin inserted above a horse's hoof, just so, would render the animal temporarily lame. As for the dogs, it took only a quick jab of Maria's hypodermic needle just before the inspectors came to give an animal a disqualifying fever or, more spectacular, diarrhoea.

Briefly conscripted to the censor's office, working in an 'F' station along with plenty of other young women, she was required to read 'other people's letters', as she put it, and to report any hint of dissent. Instead, when she came across a sentence that might land the letter writer in trouble, she would quietly put the offending sheets in her pocket and head to the ladies' room. She did not flush them down the toilet: if nothing else, the prospect of a blockage made that too risky. Instead, and methodically, she tore each sheet into shreds – and ate them.

She continued to make Detmolder Strasse a home for those wanted by the Nazis, including a deserter who had refused to take part in a mass execution of French villagers and a journalist who had built a secret radio station, pumping out broadcasts aimed at stirring the German people to rise up. But now she was prepared to go even further.

Her way in was the church, just as it had been nearly a decade earlier when she would spend long nights typing up those fake radio listings for the rebel Jesuit, Father Muckermann. Now she worked with the Swedish Church in Berlin, on Landhausstrasse, which had turned its crypt into a refuge for those on the run, whether they were Jews or 'politicals'. It would hold them there until a chance arose to spirit the persecuted out of the country and to safety. All of this was in defiance not only of the Nazis but of the Swedish government, whose envoy in Berlin had warned the pastor in charge that, if trouble came, he would be on his own.

The key figure was a young man who struck Maria as an organisational genius. Erik Wesslén managed a constant flow of Jewish submarines into the church basement, even though a police station stood directly opposite. The constables pacing the street seemed to look the other way whenever Jews arrived. Maria couldn't say exactly how it worked, but it appeared Wesslén had contacts with the SS who were provided with enough coffee or cigarettes, schnapps or powdered milk, to turn a blind eye.

Of course, the Jews in the crypt could not stay there: they needed to be ushered first to a hiding place in the city and then across the border. It was Maria's involvement in that work that led her both to shoot and to be shot.

The former happened when she was leading a group of six elderly Jews through the sewers of Berlin. In the darkness and the stench, she steered them through the tunnels – until she felt another presence. They were being followed, she was sure of it. Even in the gloom, she spotted a turning off the tunnel, one that could function as a hiding place. Huddled in the dark, she and her group waited until, sure enough, their pursuer passed them.

But there was no certainty he would not return. Instinct made her raise her gun and, as accurate now as she had been the night she took Hitler's eyes out, she aimed for and struck the man's leg from behind. The sound, ricocheting off the subterranean walls, was deafening.

When she briefed Wesslén the next day, all Christian forgiveness deserted him.

'That was the stupidest thing you could have done,' he raged. By now, whoever she had hit would have reported what he had seen; thanks to her, the escape route through the sewers could never be used again. She should have shot to kill.

'I can't kill anyone,' Maria said.

The second encounter involving a gun came when she was chaperoning a Jewish couple from the crypt, though doing it in such a way that no one would guess they were together, when she was spotted by the Gestapo. The men called out and demanded she stop.

Instantly, she was filled with fear – not for herself, but for the pair behind. If they registered even a flicker of alarm, the Gestapo would see it and the game would be up: they would be arrested. There was only one thing for it. She would have to stage a diversion, distracting the Gestapo's attention. She made for a nearby wall and began to climb over it.

The Gestapo chased after Maria, one of them raising his weapon. As she ran, she heard the shot ring out.

The bullet came terrifyingly close to killing her. Afterwards, she would see just how close: it had grazed her temple. But she had got away.

When she got home, in the early hours, Hans saw the mark on her head and peppered her with questions. 'I can't tell you where I've been,' she said, 'and I won't tell you where I go sometimes in the future either. I know the Gestapo and their methods better than you do, and if, God forbid, you ever fall into their hands, you can't say anything you don't know. So don't make my life difficult and please don't ask any more questions.'

Hans accepted that, just as he accepted a fact he regarded as all but a miracle: that Maria had somehow, despite everything, remained out of the clutches of the Nazi authorities. How had she been able to evade them so often and so long, even as she harboured Jews and joined the resistance, wielding and using a weapon when necessary? Hans wondered if perhaps his lover's secret was that she was so absurdly busy, juggling multiple jobs and duties across the city, from morning till night, that the Gestapo were forced to conclude that she couldn't possibly have a side career in the anti-Nazi underground: there weren't enough hours in the day.

As it happened, Hans was half-right. Maria von Maltzan was able to maintain her underground activity thanks both to her fellow rebels, including those imprisoned in Ravensbrück, who never gave her up – and to a darker, more personal secret, one that she kept even from him.

50

Fate Has Intervened

Otto, June 1944

OTTO KIEP WAS determined to take his own life because he was certain that he faced execution. That conviction was based less on what his tormentor, Leo Lange, was telling him and more on the facts he could see in front of him: chief among them, the fate of Max Metzger.

Metzger was the idealistic, if rather naive priest who, in 1942, had drafted, though not sent, a letter politely asking Adolf Hitler to step down. His undoing had been the manifesto he had written a year later, setting out a hopeful vision of a post-war – and post-Hitler – Europe of peace and co-operation and, especially, his choice of courier. Metzger had entrusted the document to a woman he thought a fellow dissenter, but who was in fact an agent of the Gestapo section tasked with flushing out anti-Nazi elements within the church. He had been arrested immediately.

But in April 1944, when Otto and the others were in Ravensbrück, pacing their cells, word had come that the pacifist priest was dead. The man who had faced his Gestapo interrogators with no fear because, he believed, no one would punish a man for yearning for peace had been led to the guillotine at the Brandenburg-Görden prison and beheaded. His trial, six months earlier, on charges of high treason and favouring the enemy had lasted just seventy minutes. The judge, who had already completed three other cases that day, refused even to hear the defendant. 'Such a plague must be eradicated,' he said. Facing death, Metzger's parting words were: 'I have offered my life to God for the peace of the world and the unity of the churches.'

Perhaps their designation as 'special prisoners', set apart from the regular inmates of the concentration camp, had encouraged some of them to think as Metzger once had: that they surely could not face too grave a penalty for what they had done or merely said. If they had once clung to that delusion, the priest's execution tore it from their grasp.

Word of it reached the other prisoners, including Otto Kiep. Not that he needed more proof of the Nazi willingness to breach all bounds: he knew about the Gestapo's 'aggravated interrogations' first hand. Seeing the transformation of those he had known in Berlin high society, learning of the execution of Metzger, it all left no room for doubt: they were in the grip of a regime that would show no mercy to those deemed guilty of betrayal.

Otto understood that to his marrow. It was why he had swallowed sleeping tablets and slashed his wrists on just his second night in Brandenburg-Görden, a prison that had the advantage of not being Ravensbrück where, as he had explained in his farewell note to his wife, she would be too near: he could not put her through being in the vicinity of his suicide, after all she had endured. It was why he had surrendered himself to the mercy of God. Because he had no faith in the mercy of the men who ran his country.

That night, the Royal Air Force launched one of its regular air raids on Berlin. At around midnight, the British planes aimed their fire at Brandenburg-Görden. The guards dashed to the cells to move the inmates to the bomb shelters underneath. In the rush, one guard unlocked Otto's cell to see him bleeding and unconscious. He was taken to the infirmary, where doctors saved his life. The first he knew of it was several days later, when he woke up for the first time since putting a razor blade to his veins.

Slowly, he put together the details of his survival. He had been saved by the speed of the medical response, with an immediate operation and blood transfusion. The doctors told him that it helped that he was strong and physically fit: all that exercise, all those years of sport to keep himself in shape for his much younger bride, had made the difference. 'Now,' he wrote to Hanna, the success of this effort becomes the greatest enemy in the attempt to render you and the children a last decisive service by my death . . . I naturally find myself in a severely depressed mood, since all the problems which I had hoped to solve by this one deed are now laid bare to me.

He took some solace in the fact that his wife at least would be relieved – 'a grave disappointment for you has been avoided' – but, for him, the calculation that had led to an attempt at suicide still held good. He would soon be dead, and if his wife was to be a widow, better that she be a widow with her husband's pension. (As it turned out, Otto's assumption was mistaken: even if he had died by his own hand that night, the Gestapo would still have had the power to confiscate his assets. Suicide conferred no immunity from the long arm and grasping fingers of the Reich.)

Still, he had let God decide his destiny and the Almighty's decision had left no room for doubt. As Otto wrote to his wife, 'Only one thing is clear to me: that there can neither be, nor will there be, another attempt at the same solution; fate has once again intervened, as so often in recent months, and marked out the path for me: the cup of suffering must be drained to the last.'

A day or two after he wrote those words, the office of the chief Reich prosecutor at the People's Court issued charges against him, Elisabeth von Thadden, Hanna Solf, Hilger van Scherpenberg, Fanny von Kurowsky and Irmgard Zarden. It was the summer of 1944 and they would be tried as traitors to the Third Reich.

# PART IV
The Trial

51

The Court

1 July 1944

IT WAS A Saturday, the first day of July 1944. The weather was glorious, it was the weekend, and before long a crowd had gathered outside Bellevuestrasse 15. The building used to be the Wilhelms-Gymnasium, a grammar school, but now had an improvised courtroom on its ground floor. Thanks to the intense summer heat, the windows were wide open. People on the street, starved of first-rate entertainment, leaned through the windows to follow the proceedings within. Naturally, the court insisted this was a genuine legal proceeding, not a show trial. But it was a trial and it was a show.

By 8 a.m. the place was packed. There were between a hundred and 150 seats, and those were all taken in a stampede. Officially, the proceedings were open to the public but most of the seats seemed to have been reserved for invited guests: representatives of various officer training colleges and for students of a school of political leadership, with a large tranche set aside for the Gestapo. That latter group consisted chiefly of members of the Lange Special Commission, including Lange himself, there to see the results of their work and to pick up any remaining leads. Because there were always more dots to join.

Among the first to arrive were the relatives and friends of the accused. Elisabeth von Thadden had her sister Ehrengard and brother Reinold there, along with their spouses, a cousin and a couple of the cousin's friends who only just made it inside, finding a place by the door and squeezing in a pair of borrowed chairs. Otto Kiep's brothers were present too, along with his father-in-law and a nephew. Inge van Scherpenberg was there to watch her husband.

By now, there was little they could do for their loved ones. They had placed their fate in the hands of lawyers. Hanna Solf had done well, securing the services of the well-regarded Dr Rudolf Dix for her defence — though she had only met him, and briefly at that, the previous afternoon — while his brother, Dr Helmuth Dix, acted for Hilger van Scherpenberg. Otto's father-in-law, Georg Alves, had pulled some strings to hire as defence counsel Dr Alfons Sack, who enjoyed not only a high profile but good contacts in the office of the Reich prosecutor at the People's Court. That was no small thing given that only a limited pool of lawyers, those deemed politically reliable, were allowed to appear in the People's Court at all.

Elisabeth, an outsider in Berlin with fewer connections than the others, had no such luck. Her sister Ehrengard had tried to hire an established advocate, but he told her he considered the case hopeless: Elisabeth's best shot was to plead guilty and file a petition for clemency. When the indictment was issued, he was away on business, so the People's Court appointed a public defender to act for Elisabeth: Dr Wilhelm Kunz of Berlin. They met for the first time in court, on the day of the trial.

At nine o'clock, the defendants were led into the courtroom in twos, each pair bound together by a single set of handcuffs, which was not removed until they were in their places. Those who knew them were shocked by what they saw. Elisabeth was put in the first seat, to mark her status as the lead accused — the case was officially against 'Thadden and five others' — and her friends could not help but register how much older she looked than her sixty-two years. The others too, men and women who, until not long ago, would have been seen in well-cut suits and expensive dresses in Berlin's opera houses and on the terraces of its embassies, were now thin and haggard, drained and ground down.

Otto Kiep and Hilger van Scherpenberg were handcuffed to each other. It was clear that Otto was making a mighty effort: he had taken great care to dress properly and to stand tall, with the dignity of a soldier. But he was pale and could not hide his exhaustion. But what his father-in-law noticed above all was the poorly bandaged wounds on his wrists, just visible through the handcuffs.

The accused were not led into a dock, but rather, in this improvised courtroom, to a long table. Their seats were arranged in an order that appeared partly to reflect the gravity of the charges against them, with Elisabeth and Otto at one end, Irmgard Zarden at the other, and Hanna Solf, Hilger van Scherpenberg and Fanny von Kurowsky in between. Six of them seated together: other than the previous night, when they had been corralled into a single cell at Moabit remand prison, this was the first time they had been under the same roof since they took tea in Elisabeth's temporary living room the previous September.

It was not a complete reunion. Missing from the defendants' table was Elisabeth's younger sister Anza, whose birthday had brought the group together that autumn afternoon. Because she had been in and out of the kitchen that day, preoccupied mostly with keeping the cake coming and the teacups filled, she, along with her friend Anne Rühle, could not be proven to have taken part in the conversation that formed the crux of the trial. Neither faced any charges. All the same, both Anza and Anne would soon be in court: indeed, Anza was listed as a witness for the prosecution.

Other than Arthur Zarden, who had been dead nearly six months, that left one other guest: Paul Reckzeh.

Now the accused were assembled, the courtroom readied itself. The scheduled start time was 9 a.m. But there was a delay: one of the judges was missing. For nearly two hours they waited. But in that unplanned interlude came an opportunity for the defence lawyers to consult their clients and, more unexpected still, a chance for the handful of relatives present to approach and speak to the accused.

But then, at 10.45, the low murmur died away and the courtroom fell silent. Three judges entered, along with the court director and the chief prosecutor, but all eyes were on the fourth and chief judge, the president of the People's Court, Roland Freisler. Each man on the bench – a raised table, directly facing, and looking down on, the defendants – was clad in the robes of justice, adorned with the eagle and swastika of national socialism. But Freisler wore a robe of scarlet red: the colour of blood.

52

The Hanging Judge

1 July 1944

ROLAND FREISLER HAD come to this elevated position by an unlikely ideological route. He had fought for the Kaiser as a reserve officer in the First World War, only to be wounded and taken prisoner by the forces of Imperial Russia in October 1915. He did not waste his time as a prisoner of war, first learning Russian and then, following the Revolution in 1917, becoming a student of Marxism. It was only natural that, when the Bolsheviks took over the running of the prisoner-of-war camp, they made use of this inmate with communist sympathies, tasking him with organising food supplies. They even gave him the rank of 'commissar'.

Back in Germany by the summer of 1920, and having resumed the law studies the war had interrupted, Freisler soon made the move from red to brown. Perhaps he saw less a contradiction than an evolution in his move from socialism to national socialism; either way, he joined the Nazi party in 1925, an early enough recruit for his membership number to run to just four figures: he was party member 9,679. His legal qualifications swiftly made him useful – he could defend party members accused of political violence – and duly got him noticed, but the one-time commissar would struggle for years to shake off suspicions as to his ideological soundness. He did not help his cause by travelling to the Soviet Union in the late 1930s to witness for himself the show trials by which Joseph Stalin enacted his great purge.

Still, he clearly learned a lot from what he saw in Moscow and it hardly held him back. He rose to become state secretary in the Reich Ministry of Justice and, in that capacity, attended the Wannsee

Conference in January 1942, offering a legal dimension to the discussion of how best to eliminate the Jews of Europe. That same year, Freisler was elevated to the presidency of the People's Court, the body that Hitler had founded in 1934, chiefly out of frustration with the regular courts, which had an unfortunate habit of acquitting those the Führer wanted to see convicted. The focus of the new body would be political crimes, whether that was trading on the black market, treason or anything in between that might be construed as *Wehrkraftzersetzung*, the undermining of the nation's ability to defend itself. Freisler encapsulated the court's ethos in a simple motto, one that conveyed its novel approach to jurisprudence: 'Justice is whatever serves the Führer.' With striking frequency, what served the Führer was the death penalty: Freisler became known as 'the hanging judge'. Indeed, it was he who, some months earlier, had sent Max Metzger to his death.

Everything was set. At the right of the judges' table, the prosecution; at the left, the defence lawyers, placed in such a way that they could have no contact with their clients during the hearing. The proceedings began.

First came the reading of the indictment.

> In September 1943, the accused Thadden, Dr Kiep and Solf expressed the opinion to other persons at a tea party in Berlin, and partly on other occasions, that the present war was lost for Germany and that it was therefore time to look for suitable men for a new German government. In connection with this they attempted, through the mediation of German émigrés living abroad, to establish contact with enemy powers for the purpose of conducting peace talks and, with their help, to form a new German government.

In so doing, they had 'aided the war enemies of the Greater German Reich by undermining military morale and by preparing an act of high treason'. The remaining three co-defendants were accused of failing to report the offence they had witnessed.

At this point, in a regular court, it would have fallen to the prosecution to lay out its case. But this was not a regular court. They called it the People's Court, but everyone knew it was Freisler's domain. In this theatre, he was both impresario and star.

THE TRIAL

From the start, and all day, the lawyers hardly got a look in. It was all him. He would call a defendant forward and submit them to examination, asking all the questions, though he was rarely interested in, or even allowed, full answers. Instead, the accused were there to be goaded, berated and insulted by him, sometimes with an acid aside, sometimes at full volume. He had the transcripts of all the defendants' interrogation sessions to hand, as well as earlier statements each of them had made, and he would deploy the ammunition they contained to devastating effect. The result was rarely less than spellbinding; Freisler had become famous for it. Perhaps that was why that crowd outside were straining at the windows to listen.

On this day, he would keep it up for around twelve hours, save for only two short breaks, each lasting no more than fifteen minutes. His performance was sufficiently varied that he had no trouble holding the room. At one moment he might speak softly, full of fatherly understanding. The next, he was the penetrating inquisitor, homing in on a single fact with forensic precision, and then, just as suddenly, he would fill the court with bellowing rage. He could do it all, almost athletic in his rhetorical agility, his ability to leap between registers, from gentle cajoling to the temper tantrum of a child, screaming and shouting. As the show went on, he seemed to glisten and glitter, a virtuoso performer sparkling in the gaze of a mesmerised audience.

And now he was eyeing up his first victim.

53

In the Dock

1 July 1944

FIRST TO FACE him was Elisabeth von Thadden. She might have wrong-footed another interrogator for, plagued by self-reproach, she eschewed any form of defence. Instead, upright in a simple skirt and blouse, she tried to answer with full honesty, presenting in good faith an explanation of her beliefs and how they made opposition to the government unavoidable. She spoke in such earnest that one of Kiep's allies in court worried that Elisabeth was offering more of the truth than was strictly necessary, admitting things that could never have been proven against her.

Despite her candour, or perhaps because of it, Freisler was merciless. He went hard on Elisabeth's two defining allegiances: the Church and the nobility. Contempt for the former came easily to him – he was a devoted collector of the literature of atheism, assembling a personal library that ranged from the early Middle Ages to what was then contemporary fiction – while the latter made a deliciously tempting target.

He had to taunt it out of her, prodding and poking.

'Defendant, please, who should – if Germany is already so close to the abyss – save it? Well? No answer? Say it, say it! You had certain ideas, didn't you? Why don't you say it now? Who was going to save us? "The nobility," you said.'

Elisabeth carried within her all those forebears whose principles had been instilled into her from her earliest childhood, those families who, though privileged, believed they carried a heavy burden of responsibility to those with so much less, the ancestors who, she had been taught, were moved not by power or greed or the desire to humiliate their fellow man and grind the faces of the weak into the dust, but by a simple sense of duty. She thought of that inheritance and, under Freisler's relentless bombardment, said the words he had been determined to extract. 'The nobility, yes.'

The courtroom erupted into loud, braying laughter. The nobility and the church! That's who this woman wanted to 'save' Germany. The whole court, the 150 people inside, and no doubt all those eavesdropping through the windows, united in derision for this eccentric old teacher and her ancient, exhausted aristocracy. For gathered in that room was the new aristocracy, whose blood was not blue but Aryan pure. What need did this new nobility have of God? Were they not the priests of a new faith, as mighty as it was pitiless? The laughter was rolling through the room now, Freisler directing it with the satisfaction of a ringmaster who has led his crowd to an early explosion of delight. The lawyers had their heads down, scribbling on pages; the relatives of the accused did not know where to look. But in the centre of it all, standing before the men who would judge her, was Elisabeth von Thadden. She did not falter or recant or beg, but stayed exactly where she was.

Next it was the turn of the man the indictment cast as of equal guilt to Elisabeth. Freisler summoned Otto Kiep to stand before him.

Unlike Elisabeth, Otto had not the slightest intention of conceding an inch more ground than was absolutely necessary. He would admit what was true and nothing more. He would not be bullied by this man in his red cloak and golden party badge, awarded in 1933 only to those who had been among the first one hundred thousand to join the NSDAP and whose affiliation had been unbroken. He was resolved on that.

Wasn't it the case that Otto had made 'defeatist statements' about the state of the war at the tea party? Were not his exact words, 'Unless a miracle happens', the war would be lost?

Otto did not deny that. He had already admitted as much to his Gestapo interrogators, and he had made that admission because he knew that his words at Carmerstrasse had been reported by Paul Reckzeh. He would take responsibility for what he had said but, calmly and without losing his temper; he would argue that it

Horcher restaurant, Berlin. Despite everything, including an intense austerity drive, restaurant life continued in wartime Berlin.

The Hotel Adlon. While outside it was bomb craters and ration books, inside it was Hollywood meets Versailles.

The night of broken glass, November 1938: a state-sponsored pogrom that would leave hundreds of synagogues destroyed, seven thousand Jewish-owned businesses damaged or ruined, and some thirty thousand Jewish men arrested and sent to concentration camps.

The brownshirts of the SA, 1938. Their placards read: 'Germans fight back! Don't buy from the Jews!'

Berlin, 1941. The Police Regulation on the Marking of Jews required every Jew over the age of six to wear a yellow badge in public, at all times. Written in the middle, in black, would be the single word *Jude* – Jew.

German Jews outside a travel bureau, 1939. Others found it hard even to contemplate leaving. Berlin was the city they knew; Germany the only country they had ever thought of as home.

Stella Kübler and Rolf Isaaksohn (*right*), the It couple of Nazi collaboration, on Kurfürstendamm, 1940s. Stella was known as the Blonde Poison, for her skill at tricking her fellow Jews out of hiding and into the clutches of the Gestapo.

Herbert 'Leo' Lange. By the time he was thirty, he was in Nazi-occupied Poland heading a special unit bearing his name, devoted to the first, experimental killings with gas. His initial victims: the disabled and the mentally ill.

In the centre, Nazi propaganda chief, Joseph Goebbels. To the right, Admiral Wilhelm Canaris, who presided over a secret anti-Hitler cell inside the Abwehr, German military intelligence. Facing Canaris, the man who issued the arrest warrants of January 1944: Heinrich Himmler.

Hans Oster, Canaris's deputy at the Abwehr who believed Hitler's aggressive expansionism was doomed. A mentor of Otto Kiep's, he pulled strings to get his friend a job in the armed forces high command.

The Reich Security Main Office on Prinz-Albrecht-Strasse where several of the suspects were held in a Gestapo jail.

The entrance to Sachsenhausen. The slogan *Arbeit macht frei*, 'Work makes you free', was repeated elsewhere across the archipelago of Nazi concentration camps, most notoriously at Auschwitz.

Moabit remand prison, where the group spent a night corralled into a single cell, their first time under the same roof since they had taken tea together in September 1943.

The Wolf's Lair, July 1944. Adolf Hitler greets key advisers at his secret complex in the Prussian woods. On the far left, standing to attention, is Count Claus von Stauffenberg.

After the blast at the Wolf's Lair, Mussolini and Hitler inspect the damage, the German leader keen to be photographed very much alive.

Roland Freisler, president of the Volksgerichtshof. They called it the
People's Court, but everyone knew it was Freisler's domain.
In this theatre, he was both impresario and star.

Adam von Trott zu Solz appears before the People's Court. To add to
their humiliation, even the most distinguished figures were forced to wear old,
shabby clothing. The aim was to make Germans of standing look like criminal lowlifes.

The execution building at Plötzensee prison, an empty brick shed with a cold, hard floor, where the condemned were either beheaded by guillotine or else hanged on the butcher's hooks attached to the thick beam above the two arched windows.

Hanna Solf before the judges at Nuremberg, April 1947. There she could calmly explain her own actions and fulfil what she had always regarded as her highest duty: to show the world a different, better Germany.

IN THE DOCK

amounted to a relatively minor offence, if an offence at all. He had spent his entire life in the service of Germany; of course he was not a traitor.

Freisler confined his response to a cold stare of loathing: he was keen to move on to more fertile terrain. Why had Otto Kiep repeatedly travelled to Switzerland and how often had he spoken, once there, to the former Reich chancellor Joseph Wirth?

This line of questioning came as no surprise to Otto. He knew that the heart of the case advanced by the prosecution was an alleged plot involving well-placed dissidents in Berlin making political contact with German émigrés in Switzerland. In this scenario, he and Wirth were cast as central players. Before the trial, Otto's Gestapo interrogators had repeatedly put the same claim to him: that the former chancellor regarded Otto Kiep as the only one who could make peace with the British and the Americans. There was a logic to it: he had served with distinction in the US, had proved by his defiant attendance at that Einstein lunch that he was no Nazi and had been sufficiently effective in London that he had briefly become a late-night confidant of a British prime minister. (In 1924, while Otto was acting as an interpreter during international talks, the mild Scottish lilt that was a vestige of his Ayrshire childhood had caught the ear of Ramsay MacDonald, who invited him to spend several evenings in Downing Street, the pair chatting over a pipe and a glass of whisky.) And, of course, he spoke fluent, native English. The only problem was – it was not true.

He had denied it in the interrogation room and been rewarded for his honesty with the third degree: non-stop questioning for three days, tied up and with a constantly rotating cast of inquisitors. Now he denied it again. He had not spoken at all at the tea party about any possible contacts across the Swiss border: if that topic had been discussed it must have been after he left. Nor had he had any meetings with Wirth. In fact, throughout his visits to Switzerland, he had only seen the man once, and that was from a distance, while out walking along the promenade with a friend.

And who exactly was this friend, Freisler demanded to know.

Finkler, came Otto's answer.

A Jew! Freisler was appalled by the idea – and also, as it happens, factually wrong.

Otto explained that that he and Finkler had been friends for years, that they had known each other in London. He was a highly reputable individual: brother-in-law to a Weimar-era government minister, a German reserve officer and now attached to the German legation in Bern.

Back to the tea party. What about the discussion they had had about a new government for Germany? Otto said he could not recall it, stressing once again that he had left the gathering early; he had been there barely an hour.

But still he had pressed his calling card into the hands of the young doctor, Paul Reckzeh, urging this man to make contact with Finkler in Switzerland, hadn't he?

Not at all. Otto had only handed over his card at Reckzeh's request.

What about that aerial photograph from the *New York Times*, enemy propaganda designed to weaken the morale of the German nation, which he had so gleefully circulated that day? It had come into his possession as part of his official duties; it was classified information. He had no business taking a secret document to a party.

Back and forth they went, Freisler jabbing and striking at the defendant, Otto refusing to be cowed. He had filed a complaint about Dr Reckzeh to the Gestapo, hadn't he, blatantly trying to divert the focus away from himself and his treachery and onto this loyal young man instead. No, said Otto, that was inaccurate. He had merely informed his superior, the head of the OKW, of Reckzeh's reports to the Gestapo and he had done that long after the tea party, when Reckzeh travelled once again to Switzerland. It was not a complaint and it was not made to the Gestapo.

If Otto or any other witness happened to mention a well-known name, Freisler would pounce. Just because you are a traitor to your country, he would say, you must not assume that Envoy X or General Y is also a traitor. If a witness attempted a response, he would make a great show of tossing and turning in his chair. Often he would not ask a question or even make a specific assertion, but rather would allow himself a long, wide-ranging, high-decibel speech castigating the accused and the wider forces arrayed against the Reich, before returning to the defendant in front of him. His stamina was something to behold. His examination of Otto Kiep alone lasted three hours.

And he was not done yet.

54
'Anti-State Person'

1 July 1944

NEXT CAME HANNA Solf, whose home had served as a salon of dissent for so long. Or, as the indictment had it, who had met 'in her house with a circle of mostly anti-state persons'. If Elisabeth had been humble and full of self-reproach and Otto firm, Hanna was contemptuous. Small and wiry, she was nevertheless imperious, her manner and her tone combining to convey the highest disdain for Freisler and those he served.

The judge put to her the same charge he had put to the other two, that she had instructed Reckzeh to establish contact with Germans exiled in Switzerland, including Wirth, with a view to initiating peace negotiations with the Allied enemy. Hanna was having none of it. It was not true: she didn't know Wirth and had never spoken to him. What's more, there was no reason why it could ever be true. The very idea was absurd. She was an ambassador's widow, whose address book doubtless contained the name of every diplomat who had passed through Berlin since the last war: 'I did not need a Dr Reckzeh, unknown to me, in order to be able to contact any person abroad.'

Freisler moved on to Hanna's views. 'You called our treatment of the Jews "inhuman"?'

'Yes.'

'What was your husband's political ideology?'

'He was a humanitarian: he tried to be a good Christian, he served his country and helped his fellow men.'

'Then he was a liberal?' Freisler said, mockery in his voice.

'Yes, liberal in the Goethean sense', she replied, meaning a classical liberal, a believer in free trade and free cultural exchange as the best means of securing national well-being and international harmony. If she had wanted simultaneously to confirm the Nazi caricature of the educated German elite and to fuel Freisler's rage yet further, she could hardly have improved on her answer.

Later Freisler asked, 'What about the Quakers?'

'I believe they are the most unselfish and Christian people.'

'How can you, as an internationally educated person, say that? Don't you know that they are pacifists,' he said, insistent that the Quakers were little more than political activists posing as faithful Christians.

'I do not think so. Charity stands above all things and pacifism is, in my eyes, no crime. Love and faith in each other should be our goal. That is what we Germans have to learn again, and the churches fighting with us are going to help us.'

After that, the judge moved to those he cast as lesser players in descending order of presumed guilt. He summoned Hilger van Scherpenberg to approach the bench, the first of those accused of failure to report a crime. Scherpenberg had his lawyer, Helmuth Dix, to thank for that lighter charge, but first-class legal representation was not his only advantage. He also had a clear defence strategy, the same one he had pursued as soon as he understood that the young doctor at the tea party was, in fact, a Gestapo agent: incriminate others to save himself.

Scherpenberg testified that his fellow guests had indeed given a dismal verdict on the state of the war, one that crossed the line that separated mere grumbling from outright defeatism. Naturally, he himself had made no such statements. He confirmed the words Otto Kiep had admitted to uttering and added that he had immediately recognised their defeatist, demoralising character. So much so that he, Scherpenberg, had felt compelled to rebuke his fellow diplomat. There were some bitter smiles among the courtroom's spectators at that; the move was so transparent as to be bleakly amusing.

But it seemed to work. True, Freisler dug into the detail of Scherpenberg's political past, specifically his membership of the Social Democratic Party and its various affiliated youth movements. The accused dealt with that by explaining that, yes, he had indeed been drawn towards socialism, but that need had been amply met by national socialism (a line of reasoning that could have been designed to resonate with the one-time Soviet commissar). Freisler raised too the matter of Scherpenberg's father-in-law, Hjalmar Schacht, the former head of Germany's central bank who, while once applauded for funding the country's rearmament, had clashed with Hitler both publicly and privately and been steadily pushed out of the governing circle. And yet, despite those political and family ties, Scherpenberg received nothing like the grilling that had been applied to the first three.

That was truer still of Fanny von Kurowsky who, though just a few months older than Hanna Solf, was deemed by Freisler to be geriatric and, as such, not to be taken too seriously. Whether deliberately or not, Fanny played the role assigned to her to perfection, presenting herself as hard of hearing, somewhat confused and politically naive. She affected not to understand either the charge against her or the meaning of 'defeatism'. When asked about her suggestion of Carl Goerdeler as a future leader, she replied as if through a fog. 'Goerdeler, did I say? An acquaintance of mine, you know . . . There were so many clever people at tea, and they all said something, and I wanted to say something, and I said . . . Goerdeler.' When Freisler sought to get to the bottom of her ideological leanings, asking her which form of government she thought best for Germany, she declared dreamily that she would very much like to have the Kaiser back. After that, Freisler all but put the former grande dame of Berlin society out of his mind.

The last of the accused was the youngest, Irmgard Zarden, daughter of the late Arthur, charged with conspiracy to commit high treason by failure to report a crime. She had been told of the indictment in her cell at Ravensbrück, with Lange himself the messenger. As he left, he had turned to her and said, 'Chin up.' Her reply had been sharp: 'Easy for you to say.' Now she was all but undefended. Locked in a dark basement room in the hours before the proceedings began, she only met her lawyer minutes before the hearing got under way. He told her there was nothing he could do for her and that was that, though afterwards he did send a bill for eight hundred Reichsmarks. Even so, Irmgard had an ingenious answer to the central question posed by the prosecution, namely, why had she not reported what she had heard at Carmerstrasse directly to the authorities and, specifically, why had she not informed on her father, letting the Gestapo know what he had said at the party? Freisler put the question to her in the form of a shouted accusation.

'You are also guilty because you listened to these treasonable statements without reporting them!'

Calmly, Irmgard turned and pointed to the man in an SS uniform who had been sitting behind her throughout and said, 'Herr President, when I found out that Dr Reckzeh was a Gestapo stooge, I no longer considered a report necessary.'

It was bold, impudent even. But it caught the judge by surprise. For a moment, he was lost for words, reduced to clearing his throat and emitting several uncharacteristic ums and ahs. He finally conceded, 'This is an argument that one cannot dismiss out of hand.' He questioned the young woman for less than half an hour.

There were three other women left to examine, as witnesses rather than defendants. Elisabeth's sister Marie-Agnes Braune, known as Anza, was asked to step forward, to testify against the accused, including her sister. Anza was dressed all in black and, when asked a question, there was a long delay before her answer. She seemed to be in a state of shock. It was explained to the court that, the day before the trial, Frau Braune, who had already lost one son in combat, had received news that a second son – a naval officer who, months earlier, had gone from ministry to ministry demanding that his mother be released from Gestapo detention – had also been killed in action. It had happened the previous week.

One of the defence lawyers told Freisler about this 'heroic death' and, although the judge said that he could not take that into account, he made a show of sudden, conspicuous kindness. He had a chair brought for Anza, as if in recognition of her maternal sacrifice to the fatherland. His manner was now benign and patient, even if it was also cloying in its condescension. He did not keep the witness long, satisfied that, preoccupied with catering for her own birthday party and mainly confined to the kitchen, Anza had played no meaningful part in the treasonous business conducted that afternoon.

The questioning of Anne Rühle was similarly brief, before Freisler summoned Brigitte Zimmerman, who had worked as Otto Kiep's secretary. She was the first person called to testify who had not been present at the tea party. She confirmed that her former boss did indeed doubt Germany's chances of victory in the war but, in a bid to be helpful to Otto, she urged the court to bear in mind how overworked he had been.

Watching and listening ever since the noon recess, when he was brought into the courtroom, was the witness on whose word the whole case turned, the man in the SS uniform. Sharply dressed, his hair slick with pomade, he had been seated just behind Irmgard Zarden and just in front of Anza Braune, both of whom, like everyone else, had been constantly aware of his presence. During the breaks, when the defendants could eat the sandwiches, wrapped in paper, which had been placed under their chairs, Hanna Solf had noticed how amicably he chatted with Leo Lange, the two men getting up and down and walking over to each other.

Now, at last, the court called Dr Paul Reckzeh.

55

Star Witness

1 July 1944

SOME IN THE court thought they detected a diffidence, even a reluctance in the doctor. He seemed not to want to volunteer any information, only affirming what was put to him by the chief judge, whether about the first encounter he had had with Elisabeth von Thadden, when he had knocked on her door on 9 September, or about the tea party the following day. Had Otto Kiep told his fellow guests on the 10th that, barring a miracle, the war was lost? Yes. Was it the case that Dr Kiep and Fräulein von Thadden led the discussion, including when it moved to the question of a new government after Hitler? Yes. Had Kiep handed him a calling card and told him to meet a man named Finkler once he got to Switzerland? Yes.

To many of those watching, Freisler seemed to get increasingly irritated with his star witness, who was forcing the judge to draw every fact out of him. It was like pulling teeth and it lasted two solid hours. Was Reckzeh uncomfortable being the focus of so much public attention? Was he ever so slightly ashamed?

Others suspected that even to ask such questions was to misread what was, in fact, a legal formality. There was no extraction required because Reckzeh had already supplied all the key facts in his report to the Gestapo, submitted straight after the tea party. He needed to do no more than confirm details he had already provided, in full.

Besides, what Paul Reckzeh might have lacked in garrulousness, he made up for in compliance. Freisler did not simply lead the witness; he all but scripted his answers. From the outset, he advised Reckzeh to begin his responses 'I think I remember' or 'I believe', a lawyer's trick to ensure that even an inaccurate statement would not be a false one. The doctor did as he was told.

Freisler encouraged Reckzeh to dial up his hostility to Otto Kiep in particular, no doubt reasoning that the case against Elisabeth von Thadden needed little reinforcement given that she herself had barely disputed it. Again, Reckzeh gave the judge what he wanted, the shift noticeable to the spectators because until that point Reckzeh had scarcely mentioned Otto. By then, Freisler had succeeded in turning most of the room against Otto, so Reckzeh's change of tack went down well with most of those present. But not everyone. During one of the two short breaks, a Colonel von Steinberg, head of the personnel department of the SS and apparently offended by some aspect of Reckzeh's testimony or conduct, turned to him to declare loudly, 'You pig, you belong in the dock!'

Eventually it was the turn of the defence. In a regular court, in ordinary times, Otto's counsel would have been on his feet a dozen times already, objecting to Freisler's clear attempts to influence the witness. In the People's Court, where Freisler dominated proceedings so loudly and so completely, even lawyers who had made their reputations by being combative and disputatious became submissive and obedient.

Still, now that Freisler had finished his long examination of Reckzeh, the floor belonged to Dr Alfons Sack and the rest of the defence team.

The Kiep family, Otto's brothers and father-in-law, had every reason to be anxious. Sack had been consistently unavailable in the lead-up to the trial, which he had confidently insisted could not take place until the following week, disappearing at a critical moment to his villa in Heringsdorf or travelling out of town to appear in a different court on a different case. He had not so much as visited his client, a fact that Otto's father-in-law felt sure had added to the desperation that culminated in Otto's attempted suicide. For all his reputed brilliance, and even though he had happily pocketed a hefty bonus of ten thousand Reichsmarks for taking on the case, there was no way Sack could have mastered the materials to defend Otto Kiep properly.

Now the lawyer rose to his feet, positioning himself on the left side of the courtroom so that he could address both the judges and the public at the same time. Before long, his strategy became clear. His focus would be on character and credibility, building up Otto and taking down his accuser.

What kind of man was this Paul Reckzeh? His own father was ashamed of him, so much so that he had taken it upon himself to sabotage his son's efforts, burning those two letters the younger man had intended to take to Switzerland. Otto Kiep by contrast had a decades-long record of service to Germany, including as an envoy of the Reich.

And what, after all, was Otto accused of? Neither witness nor prosecutor had made a substantive case that he had incited high treason. That was surely because they knew such a charge could not be sustained. Instead, the gravest allegation they could make against him was 'defeatism', and on this point Otto had made an admirably candid admission. But that single aberration had to be set against all the good he had done for the Reich. Assessed that way, weighing one thing against the other, there could be no room left for the death penalty sought by the prosecuting counsel.

Rhetorically, Sack was an accomplished performer and, in any other proceeding, would have been making headway. But this was Roland Freisler's court: different rules applied. Here, Sack's very skill counted against him. From the start, it was clear that the judge was angered that anyone had dared draw attention away from him. Nor did he hide his irritation at Sack's effort to discredit Reckzeh, the very witness the president of the court had so assiduously nudged and prodded into delivering the goods and on whom the case relied. Still, Sack had not yet moved to his core argument, one that would again attack the accuser – and would turn on the generational contrast between him and the accused.

Otto Kiep was fifty-eight years old and had not been a member of the Nazi party until the Reich was firmly established. He was, Sack argued, of a generation that scarcely mattered to the party. The NSDAP had never tried to win them over, because it never expected them truly to understand the meaning of national socialism. Of course, when such people acted against the interests of the state, they should be punished, but any sanction had to take their age into account.

THE TRIAL

But Dr Reckzeh – that was a different story entirely. He was of the new generation, one that had come of age under the Reich. What excuse did he have for just sitting there, sipping tea and eating cake, as a group of old men and women spoke so foolishly? And not just sitting there, but *leading* these geriatrics into their foolishness, urging them to send word to contacts in Switzerland? If Paul Reckzeh had heard defeatist chatter that afternoon, it was his duty to slam his fist on the table and demand an end to it. Yet he had remained silent. Other than Fräulein Zarden, Dr Reckzeh was the sole representative of his generation in that room; he was the only member of the Nazi elite. Why had he not immediately declared his faith in victory and in Adolf Hitler?

Sack had spoken for twenty minutes, a performance that was brilliant enough to allay almost all the fears the Kiep family had had about their lawyer's preparedness before the trial. He had made a strong case, if not for acquittal, then at least for leniency.

What happened next amazed everyone who was watching.

56

The Verdict

1 July 1944

IN A FLURRY of activity, a messenger passed a note up to Freisler. Hanna's lawyer, Rudolf Dix, rose to his feet to request that his client's case be 'separated' from the others, handing a set of papers to the judge. Freisler looked through the documents and was visibly reluctant to acquiesce, but eventually he turned to the accused and said, 'Defendant Solf, you may leave the courtroom. You are heavily charged, but I have other inquiries to make about you.'

Initial confusion soon gave way to two competing explanations for what had just happened. One theory took Freisler's mention of 'other inquiries' at face value: the lawyer, Dix, himself believed that the prosecutors, working hand in glove with Freisler, had calculated that they would be better off tying Hanna to the wider Solf Circle, including those who had not been present at the tea party, charging her as part of a new and bigger haul of dissidents. Underpinning that calculation, Dix suspected, was a worry on the prosecutors' part that Hanna's role in the tea party did not by itself constitute sufficient grounds for a death sentence.

Others believed international diplomacy had worked its magic, drawing on a connection made decades earlier. In this version of events, envoys of neutral countries, headed by Sweden's man in Berlin, had persuaded the Japanese ambassador, Hiroshi Oshima, to raise Hanna Solf's case with the Führer himself. Oshima was said to have explained that Wilhelm Solf was still remembered fondly in Tokyo – not for nothing had Japanese naval attachés attended his memorial service in full dress uniform and bearing magnificent wreaths – and that a conviction of his widow, and perhaps at some point of his daughter, Lagi, too, would be taken as an act unfriendly to Germany's Japanese ally.

Either way, Freisler concluded that he would not be convicting Hanna Solf today. It was now 9 p.m., and both she and her lawyer left the court. That cleared the way for the nominal prosecutor, Dr Gerhard Görisch, to make his requests of the bench. In the case of Hilger van Scherpenberg, he announced that he was seeking a three-year prison sentence. For Elisabeth von Thadden and Otto Carl Kiep, he hoped for the ultimate sanction: a sentence of death.

It was time for Freisler and the rest of the panel to withdraw for a period of deliberation, or at least a show of it. The sharp-eyed in the crowd noticed that Reckzeh left the courtroom via the same door used a moment earlier by Freisler and his fellow judges, as if he were heading to the same private chambers. After a short while, Reckzeh returned to his chair near the other witnesses and was overheard saying to a man who had stayed seated throughout, 'That's that fixed.' He seemed pleased.

A few minutes later, the judges re-entered the courtroom. It was late now, around half past ten. Speaking 'in the name of the German people', Freisler delivered the verdict. It ran to nearly four thousand words.

He retold the story of the tea party, sticking with the account of it given by Elisabeth von Thadden in particular. He recalled how the man he called *Volksgenosse* Reckzeh, the people's comrade, had got himself invited thanks to a letter of introduction from 'an anti-fascist, and therefore anti-Nazi, writer', namely Bianca Segantini.

After the usual pleasantries, the main conversation had been started by Hilger van Scherpenberg, speaking about the state of emergency in Denmark. In so doing, he had offered information he could only have known because he worked in the Foreign Ministry. That, said Freisler, was 'an outrageous breach of official secrecy'.

But the judge was merely clearing his throat. The tea-party conversation had, he said, moved onto the matter of Italy's capitulation, which had prompted Otto Kiep to descend into rank defeatism. 'Just think,' Freisler said, 'a senior official in the Foreign Ministry, a major in the OKW, a party comrade, a man who has pledged allegiance to our Führer three times, a man who therefore has an increased responsibility, speaking in such a defeatist manner at an hour when it was particularly important to be a pillar of strength!!'

Freisler explained that Scherpenberg had felt 'uncomfortable' at this bleak assessment of his country's prospects but could hardly challenge Kiep, who outranked him. At least that's what Scherpenberg claimed and the judge was inclined to take his word for it, even if the diplomat had once been a member of the SPD and might 'still harbour remnants of Marxist sentiment today'. Nevertheless, Scherpenberg had 'witnessed a senior civil servant from his own ministry making seriously defeatist remarks at a tea party attended by complete strangers. He was of course aware that . . . Kiep was doing the propaganda work of our enemies of war. And yet he did not report this, not even to his superiors!' For this he would have to be punished.

Freisler moved to the next phase of the tea-party conversation, when the group discussed who might lead the future Germany. Fanny von Kurowsky had mentioned Goerdeler, but the court would not detain itself too long with her, given her 'obviously very narrow horizons, her unworldliness and her intellectual staleness', which might have been a hint at senility. As far as Freisler was concerned, the old dear was chipping in just to have something to say. He would accept the guidance of the chief prosecutor that she could not be deemed guilty, of either consciously taking part in a meeting hostile to the Reich or failing to report activities hostile to the Reich.

In his view, the ringleaders were obvious. It was Thadden, Kiep and Solf who were driving things that day. Thadden had pressed into Reckzeh's hand a letter to the Christian pacifist Siegmund-Schultze, in which she addressed the man as 'Dear friend' – imagine being so warm to an exile! – in the hope that he would use his 'American connections' to explore a settlement with Britain and the US. She and Kiep wanted Reckzeh to act as a liaison with émigré allies in Switzerland and to seek out Joseph Wirth especially, because the former chancellor could well be the best person to put out clandestine feelers for peace. The group were looking for new men who, in the event of a German defeat, would stand ready to negotiate with the western powers. They were planning for the day after, imagining a mercy mission of food aid led by the Quakers, 'apparently without realising how degrading such alms-taking would be for us as a proud people'. Meanwhile, Hanna Solf believed Denmark might be a potential channel, and had given Reckzeh a letter addressed to a Danish diplomat. The young doctor was to tell those he met across the Swiss border that he brought greetings 'from the circle'.

Freisler turned to the arguments advanced by the defence which, given that Hanna's case had been removed from the trial and Elisabeth had barely offered a defence at all, meant the speech of Dr Alfons Sack on behalf of Otto Kiep. The lawyer had clearly riled the judge, because Freisler went out of his way to criticise him, and did so at length. He accused Sack of having played the demagogue, which must have struck even the judge's admirers as a bit rich, in daring to wonder why Reckzeh himself had not challenged all the defeatist talk he had heard that afternoon. It was 'completely baseless and unjustified', Freisler thundered. 'It is sad that the defence was prepared to disparage a man of duty.' For his part, the judge had full faith in Reckzeh: 'We consider the witness to be entirely credible and would base the rest of the findings on his statements, and on them alone, even if they were not already proven by everything else.'

Part of that further proof, declared Freisler, was how the accused behaved after the tea party, behaviour that revealed a collective 'guilty conscience'. Kiep was tipped off that a mole had infiltrated their circle and had promptly 'warned the other people involved, and they warned each other'. When Reckzeh returned from Switzerland, 'they received him coldly and dismissively' because they knew they had been rumbled.

While in Switzerland, Reckzeh had learned all about their treasonous schemes. He had met Wirth, who was beavering away, armed with his US contacts. Why, the exiled ex-chancellor had all but appointed his future minister of the interior as well as his finance minister, who, wouldn't you know it, was related by marriage to a Jew. Wirth had spilled the beans to Reckzeh, mentioning Elisabeth von Thadden and Otto Kiep by name, even asking that the leaders of other such treacherous groups be told of his, Wirth's, efforts: the former chancellor would pass on their names to the Americans, so that the conquering enemy would spare those listed. But the perfidy did not end there, not by any means. This man Wirth had already decided 'that the future Reich would be without East Prussia'. That land had been promised to the Poles.

Surely the danger posed by these two, Thadden and Kiep – the sheer 'abysmal meanness' of their treachery – was now clear for all to see. 'That they attacked our spirit of vigorous defence with behaviour like this' was bad enough. 'But they were also serving our enemies', whether by their approaches to exiles across the border or, in Kiep's case, with defeatist musings on the war situation. They had damaged Germans' morale and were doubtless 'pleased' with their handiwork.

> As a result, the two of them have erased themselves for ever. They therefore must be punished with death. A different sentence would not be national socialist, if only because it would deprive our Reich of the necessary protection. It would be unjust, because it would treat Germans in elevated positions more leniently than those ordinary people who had to be sentenced to death for defeatism.

As if registering that he had taken evidence of good character into account, Freisler accepted that 'Fräulein von Thadden was in the service of the Red Cross for many years. But . . . she is also an enemy of national socialism through and through. She herself says that.'

His ruling was unambiguous.

> Otto Kiep, at the beginning of the fifth year of the war, made severely defeatist remarks about the war situation in a circle of fellow citizens, some of whom were complete strangers to him, and together with others sought to establish connections to our enemies and to locate men who would be suitable for entering into conversation with the enemy in the event of defeat. Fräulein von Thadden played a decisive role in this. Both of them have thereby attacked our capacity for muscular defence and aided our enemies in war. They are forever dishonoured and will be punished by death.

There were some loose ends to tie up. Scherpenberg had failed in his duty to report the defeatism he had heard, but at least he had objected and so, as Freisler put it, 'he gets off with two years in prison', minus the time he had already served behind bars. Fanny von Kurowsky and Irmgard Zarden were both acquitted.

But the core of the verdict lingered in the stifling air like a pall. Freisler had said it twice, so no one could think that they had misheard it the first time. It was nearly 11 p.m., and on a hot summer's night, after a trial that had lasted a single day, the hanging judge had condemned two people to death.

Everyone packed into the court that day would have assumed that this was as bad as it could get for those who had made the mistake of taking tea together on 10 September 1943. They did not know that, thanks to a deadly conspiracy far closer to the top of the Reich, their fate was about to become much graver still.

PART V
Punishment

57

Killing Hitler

July 1944

ON THAT SAME suffocatingly hot Saturday, 1 July 1944, an ardent German nationalist and decorated hero of the Afrika Korps received a promotion whose significance he could not have realised. He was named as chief of staff to the head of the Ersatzheer, the so-called Replacement Army, the body tasked with replenishing the ranks of the fighting divisions of the Germany army. The man with the new job held the rank of colonel and was an officer of impeccably noble lineage. His name was Count Claus von Stauffenberg.

At thirty-six years old, Stauffenberg cut an unmistakable figure. A year earlier, during the Tunisia campaign, his vehicle had been part of a column struck by the RAF bombers of the Desert Air Force: he had lost his left eye, his right hand and two fingers on his left. In his uniform and eyepatch, determined to remain on active service, he would have looked the very model of soldierly commitment.

And yet for all his conspicuous valour, Stauffenberg had been growing steadily more disenchanted. At least two years earlier, he had started voicing his outrage to his fellow officers at the Nazi treatment of the Jews. Long before that, an uncle had approached him about joining the resistance to the regime, while his brothers were in touch with the Kreisau Circle that had formed around Otto Kiep's friend Helmuth von Moltke. By the summer of 1944, his doubts had long hardened into resolve. He was determined to play his part in a military coup against Adolf Hitler.

By then, the burgeoning resistance cell within the Wehrmacht had made several attempts, including that effort in March 1943 to smuggle a bomb onto the Führer's plane whose failure had so disappointed Otto. Now, however, a much more serious plan was taking shape.

Once again, it would begin with Hitler's assassination. But that would set in train a far larger scheme. At its core was a protocol established for the scenario of a breakdown in the Nazi state, whether caused by a rebellion of the many millions of slave labourers from across occupied Europe now working in German factories or an outbreak of anarchy in one or several German cities bombed to destruction by the enemy. In that scenario, there was an emergency contingency plan that would see the Replacement Army take charge to quell any unrest and repel any challenge to the state. The plan was codenamed Operation Valkyrie and, with the right people in the key positions, it could be used as the mechanism for a swift installation of a new regime, one that would end both national socialism and the war, forming a government that could negotiate a peace with the western powers. Devoted to engineering just such a scenario, Stauffenberg was now in exactly the right place to do it.

That was literally true: his new post required him to attend the meetings the Führer regularly held with his military top brass. Stauffenberg had been in the job for only a fortnight when he attended one of those conferences with a bomb in his briefcase. He aborted that attempt because only Hitler was present: the conspirators wanted to kill both Hitler and his likeliest successor, Heinrich Himmler. The next day, Stauffenberg came ready to try again, and now the plotters had come to the pragmatic decision that removing Hitler alone would be enough. Except this effort had to be abandoned too: at the very moment Stauffenberg was about to strike, Hitler was called out of the room.

Fate seemed determined to stand in their way. What's more, there were whispers that the Gestapo had got wind of their plans and were closing in. If Stauffenberg and his comrades were to strike, they had to strike now. On 20 July, another meeting of the army leadership was scheduled. It would take place in the complex of bunkers, shelters and barracks hidden in the Masurian woods in East Prussia known as the Wolfsschanze: the Wolf's Lair.

Around eight o'clock on the morning of 20 July, Stauffenberg set off for the gathering, travelling by plane from Rangsdorf airfield. In his bags were two parcels of explosives, each with its own fuse. The meeting was due to take place in the afternoon in the specially reinforced underground bunker. Concrete, windowless and sealed by a heavy steel door, it was the ideal place for a bomb: the explosion would be contained, so that all its force, all the shrapnel, would be turned inwards. Everyone inside would be killed instantly.

But there was a change of plan. The 20th was yet another stiflingly hot day, thirty degrees Celsius, and so Hitler's aides moved the meeting to the briefing hut, a wooden cabin above ground, one with windows and fresher air. But those windows, as well as assorted items of wooden furniture, meant the impact of any blast would be diffused and diminished. The timing was altered too. To accommodate a visit from Mussolini later that day, they would start at 12.30 p.m. Stauffenberg would have to work quickly.

Explaining that the heat of the day meant he needed to change his shirt, which was drenched with sweat, he found his way to a lavatory along with his aide-de-camp and fellow conspirator, Lieutenant Werner von Haeften. Hurriedly, the pair pulled out the two blocks of plastic explosives, which were wrapped in brown paper, like hunks of cheese. Using pliers, they crushed the end of a pencil detonator into the first block, made up of 975 grams of Plastit W explosive, connecting it to two fuses, made in England. Even with Haeften's assistance, Stauffenberg could not move fast: he had the use of only one hand, or rather two fingers and a thumb. And then there was a knock on the door.

It was the sergeant-major, telling him that the meeting was about to begin. But only one bomb had been readied. Stauffenberg had to pass the second bomb – unprimed and useless – to his aide while frantically closing the briefcase that now contained just one kilogram of explosive.

Outside a group of officers were waiting. 'Stauffenberg, come along,' said one.

He walked into the briefing hut, joining the twenty officers who were already there and, at the centre, leaning over the heavy oak boardroom-style table, the Führer. A junior officer asked the men to clear a space for Stauffenberg close to Hitler; the colonel himself had requested that earlier, suggesting his injuries meant he needed to be near if he were to hear everything properly. Field Marshal Wilhelm Keitel introduced the young, war-wounded officer to the Führer.

As discreetly as he could, Stauffenberg placed his briefcase under the table, understanding that, since it packed only half the explosive punch he had hoped, it needed to be as close to its target as possible. The room hushed for General Adolf Heusinger to deliver his situation report on the eastern front. There was little Stauffenberg could do when a fellow colonel, Heinz Brandt, keen to get a better look at the map spread across the table, casually nudged the bag out of his way with his foot, in the process moving it behind the thick, wide table leg to Hitler's right. A moment or too later, as arranged, Stauffenberg excused himself, saying he needed to make a phone call.

The bomb went off at 12.42 p.m., announcing itself with a huge bang and a terrific leap of flame.

58

'The Führer Adolf Hitler Is Dead'

20 July 1944

A STENOGRAPHER WAS KILLED instantly; three others were injured so badly they would later die from their wounds, among them Colonel Brandt, who lost a leg. But Brandt's final act, that small, instinctive movement of his foot, pushing the deadly briefcase to one side, had a decisive impact. The table leg served to deflect the impact of the blast away from Hitler and almost everyone around him.

True, the explosion hurled one man through the window and sent several others flying through the door. And true, it created a massive cloud of smoke, filling the air with paper, wood and splinters, and making such a loud noise that the eardrums of all twenty-four people present, including the Führer, were perforated. Hitler's chief adjutant suffered burns to the face and Hitler's clothes caught fire, so that the Führer himself had to beat out the flames, leaving his black trousers and white long johns in singed tatters, a photograph of which would later be pressed into service as a choice propaganda image. Hitler would say to his valet as he was helped by two men back to his bunker, 'Linge, someone tried to kill me.' That was true, too, but the operative word was 'tried'. Stauffenberg and his bomb had got improbably close to removing the leader of the Third Reich, but they had not got close enough.

Not that Stauffenberg knew that straight away. On the contrary, when he saw the blast and heard people crying out for help, the colonel was sure Hitler was dead. How could he possibly have survived such devastation? The panic all around surely confirmed it.

He and his aide got into a staff car and talked their way through three checkpoints, before reaching the airfield and boarding the aeroplane that was waiting for them, ready to whisk them back to Berlin, where Stauffenberg would lead the next phase of the coup and topple the entire edifice of Nazi rule.

When he landed in the capital, he had Haeften call their co-conspirators, at that moment huddled together in the Bendlerblock, the headquarters of the army high command, for an update. It seemed the plan was on track. That would mean the initial Valkyrie orders had been sent by teleprinter to the key district commanders of the Replacement Army, including the first and most stunning message, on which everything that would follow was predicated. Drafted in advance, it read simply: 'The Führer Adolf Hitler is dead.'

Next would come the statement that an 'unscrupulous clique of party leaders' was seeking to exploit the situation and 'seize power for their own selfish ends', thereby stabbing those doing the fighting – the army – 'in the back'. To head off that danger, all executive power would now be transferred to the Wehrmacht.

Except, by the time Stauffenberg reached the Bendlerblock, the situation was not nearly so clear cut. There was confusion over the key fact: was Hitler dead or not? The generals could not agree. Stauffenberg was telling them that there could be no doubt: he had seen the bomb go off himself, as powerful as the explosion of a 15 cm shell. But Stauffenberg's superior, Friedrich Fromm, the commander in chief of the Replacement Army that was meant to lead Operation Valkyrie, had heard otherwise: he had spoken directly to Field Marshal Wilhelm Keitel who, from the Wolf's Lair, had told him that, while there had indeed been an attempt on the Führer's life, Hitler had 'merely been slightly injured'. He added that Hitler was 'now with the Duce', reassuring Fromm that their leader was well enough to be in talks with Mussolini. Stauffenberg said, and firmly believed, that Keitel was lying.

Amid the uncertainty, the most committed of the plotters strove to stick with the plan. They had the orders issued by teleprinter, stamped with the highest order of priority, albeit with that crucial first line announcing Hitler's death removed. Now it was official: they had proclaimed a state of emergency and seized power for the armed forces. That was the cue for military commanders aligned with the conspiracy to start arresting high-ranking Nazi officials across the German empire. The Wehrmacht general in charge of occupied France captured most of the SS leadership there, while in Vienna and Prague troops took control of Nazi party buildings and arrested the men of the SS. In Berlin, a battalion was despatched to surround the Ministry of Propaganda and arrest Joseph Goebbels.

All the while, loyalists to the Führer were telling anyone who would listen that he was still alive. Finally, Hitler himself got through by telephone to the young officer leading troops poised to seize Goebbels and his ministry. 'Do you recognise my voice?' Hitler asked. The major snapped to attention and was promptly placed in charge of all anti-coup troops in the capital until the arrival of Himmler. Before long, a radio broadcast had confirmed Hitler's survival and the conspirators holed up in the Bendlerblock had been overwhelmed by Hitler loyalists. Fromm, who had been held captive at gunpoint, was back in charge. Conscious that the lead plotter was a man under his direct command, and that therefore he would rapidly fall under suspicion himself, Fromm moved quickly to assert his fealty to the regime. That same evening, 20 July, he convened an ad hoc court martial and sentenced all of the conspirators to death. Stauffenberg, his aide and three others were executed by a hastily assembled firing squad in the courtyard of the Bendlerblock. Some weeks later, Stauffenberg's brother Berthold, who had helped draft the sequence of teleprinter messages that would announce the coup, was strangled at the Plötzensee prison in Berlin, his slow death filmed so that Hitler might watch it at his leisure.

59

A Name on a List

Otto, July 1944

OTTO KIEP SPENT 20 July 1944 far away from the action, in a prison cell. He had been moved at least once after Roland Freisler had sentenced him to death, delivering his judgement at full volume, but now he was in the prison at Brandenburg-Görden. He was visited there by his wife, Hanna, who had been released from Ravensbrück five days after the trial; now the pair could work together on seeking the only reprieve that seemed even faintly possible. Not a pardon or a quashing of the verdict that had condemned him, but a smaller mercy: they would plead for clemency.

Otto did his bit, setting down on paper the case for compassion, urging the authorities to look again at the course of his trial. He had acted on principle, refusing to incriminate his co-defendants, but now he could speak candidly. He aimed his fire especially at Hilger van Scherpenberg, who, he wrote, had testified against him 'most severely' and, more to the point, falsely. Scherpenberg had claimed that, at the tea party, he had challenged Otto's pessimistic estimation of Germany's war prospects, but that was untrue: on the contrary, Otto wrote, Scherpenberg had 'considerably surpassed me in his negative assessment of the situation'. So it had been a false account of events that had led the court to condemn Otto. For that reason among others, his sentence deserved to be reconsidered. He submitted his first formal request for clemency on 8 July, then filed an addendum three days later and added a second addendum a few days after that.

Meanwhile, his family were pulling every string and exploring every channel. His brother Johann wrote to Hitler directly: 'Our brother was remiss . . . But we believe and trust that you, my Führer, will exercise clemency after examining our reasons listed below.' They had friends deploy whatever prestige they had — whether as a countess, a retired artillery general or a director of forestry — to petition Hitler in the same way.

Hanna set herself the improbable task of winning over assorted Nazi politicians, with the finance and labour ministers particular targets. She even sought the support of the head of the Wehrmacht himself, Field Marshal Wilhelm Keitel, receiving a formal response to her letter on 19 July. The Kiep campaign was at full throttle when the events of the next day, Stauffenberg's briefcase under the table and all that followed, changed everything.

The bodies of the ringleaders were scarcely cold when the Gestapo, directed by Himmler but driven by an enraged Hitler, set about rounding up and raiding the homes and offices of anyone with even the most tenuous connection to the attempted coup. In the process, the secret police brought in a vast haul of hidden letters and diaries, laying bare not just the failed putsch of 20 July but the string of previous abortive efforts, going back to 1938. Before long, some seven thousand people had been arrested. Few denied their guilt or attempted to get away when they were picked up. They surely understood that any such effort was doomed.

Roland Freisler and his People's Court were inundated, meting out summary justice to the accused in their thousands. Freisler had cause for even more thundering fury and bellowed insults from the bench, as alleged conspirators came before him hour after hour. To add to their humiliation, even one-time officers of the most elevated rank were stripped of their uniforms and forced to wear old, shabby clothing, so that they would look less like decorated warriors for Germany and more like criminal lowlifes. The trials almost always ended the same way, in a guilty verdict and a sentence of death: some 4,980 supposed traitors were executed. Few would get the honour of a military killing, by firing squad. Hitler had issued specific instructions, directing that those convicted of treachery against him should be 'hanged like cattle'. The only clemency available was of the roughest kind, seized by those who decided to take their own lives rather than wait for trial or execution.

Among those who tried to escape was the man slated by the 20 July conspirators to be the next chancellor of Germany, the same man whose name had been floated by Fanny von Kurowsky at the tea party ten months earlier: the former mayor of Leipzig, Carl Goerdeler. He knew that his name appearing at the top of the plotters' list was a death sentence, so he swiftly moved to get out of Berlin. He succeeded, too, evading capture for three long weeks. But the Nazis were desperate to have him in custody, offering a reward of one million Reichsmarks to anyone who found him.

He was eventually arrested on 12 August, while visiting his parents' grave in Pomerania. Instantly, eight members of his family were sent to concentration camps, a punishment that had become more common after 20 July. The authorities were newly seized by the age-old *Sippenhaft* doctrine of blood guilt, by which an entire family could be punished, its name tainted for ever, for the actions of one individual. The measure sought to deter any German tempted to follow the plotters' lead with the fear that it would not be them alone who paid the price.

Now the former mayor's cavalier attitude to secrecy, including his habit of writing down names barely coded – the same habit that had so alarmed Arthur Zarden – would have grim consequences. For Goerdeler had set down on paper those who would serve in his administration once Hitler and the others were gone. Among them, designated as his future head of press and so returning to a post he had filled in the Weimar years, was Otto C. Kiep.

60

The Butcher's Hook

August 1944

GOERDELER'S LIST MERELY confirmed what the authorities already suspected. Within a week of the blast at the Wolf's Lair, Ernst Kaltenbrunner, the head of the Reich Security Main Office, who had been tasked by Hitler himself with investigating the attempted coup, had found that, under the conspirators' plans, 'The press was to be given a special position by being attached to the office of the Reich chancellor. In prospect was Kiep.' Of course, Kaltenbrunner explained, Kiep was currently facing the noose 'for undermining military morale and aiding the enemy', but the 'conspiratorial clique hoped that Kiep could perhaps be released from prison in time'.

Days later, Kaltenbrunner — mistakenly — identified Kiep as a member of the Wednesday Group, a rebel circle that included Goerdeler, among others. The authorities were now joining multiple dots to create a picture in which every dissenting group was connected and the failed putsch was the fruit of their collective, concerted labours. As the Gestapo put it, 'Some treason plots, which had been the subject of security police investigations in the past months, are now connected with the attack of 20 July 1944.' It cited the tea party, Otto Kiep and even Captain Gehre, the man who had warned Otto and his friends that their gathering on Carmerstrasse had been infiltrated and that they were under surveillance. 'The circles of persons run into each other,' the investigators concluded.

The view was hardening at the very top of the Nazi state that the events of 20 July had been the work of a vast, treacherous conspiracy that spread throughout the German establishment, combining a series of overlapping networks inside the army, the church and the civil service – with Otto Kiep as a crucial, connecting node. On 3 August, no less than Heinrich Himmler addressed SS *Gauleiter* in Posen in a speech whose chief purpose seemed to be to quiet any whisper of suspicion about his own allegiances. It was here that Himmler boasted, perhaps a little too loudly, of his heroic refusal to countenance an approach to the British and Americans aimed at forging a peace settlement between London, Washington and a post-Hitler Berlin, the latter headed, perhaps, by one Heinrich Himmler. The Reichsführer-SS insisted that he had only stopped short of killing the man who had made this outrageous proposal because the Führer had wisely counselled him to let the plot unfold, so that they might discover the true traitors in their midst.

Well, of course, Himmler explained to his most senior men, Hitler's tactic had worked. The Gestapo had steadily uncovered what they codenamed 'the Baroque conspiracy' against the Reich, so called, 'because it was so baroque'. Among those they had successfully exposed was 'a man from the Foreign Ministry who has already been sentenced to death, the envoy Herr Kiep. But he was also involved in this case. We were absolutely in the right circle.' In truth, what the Gestapo thought that they were uncovering *at the time* was nothing more than a troubling spread of defeatism. Now, though, they would claim that their discovery of the tea-party group proved that they were onto the conspiracy that would eventually explode into view with the blast at the Wolf's Lair.

That was the story they were telling. What they wanted was the proof, or at least the pretence of it.

A little over a fortnight after Stauffenberg's briefcase had ripped through the hut at the Wolfsschanze, Otto Kiep was transferred from Brandenburg-Görden to the Berlin-Plötzensee prison. The transfer paperwork came with a note written in large letters and underlined in red: 'Caution! Risk of suicide!!!' Five days later, he had a visitor.

SS-Obersturmführer Wilhelm Gogalla presented himself to Otto, though he was hardly making a social call. Instead, he had come to pick him up and take him to the Gestapo's in-house prison at Prinz-Albrecht-Strasse 8, a facility commanded by Gogalla. Otto was deemed of sufficient importance for the head of the prison to escort him personally. Once there, he would endure a kind of treatment he had never known before. Already sentenced to death, he would soon learn there was something worse.

The Gestapo were set on forcing him to admit that he had known of Goerdeler's plans to install a new government in place of the Nazi regime. But Otto swore he had never even met Goerdeler, at least as far as he could remember. He certainly didn't know him. He told his jailers that again and again, explaining that he had known nothing of this whole affair until now. The Gestapo refused to believe him.

At first, they relied on the familiar methods of interrogation. The questioning would go on all day and all night, officers working in shifts. They shone a bright light in his face and gave him nothing to eat. But dazed, exhausted and hungry as he was, Otto stuck to his story.

The Gestapo could not accept that. They were under pressure from the very top to prove the existence of a tightly organised conspiracy, one that was both wide and deep. Otto Kiep had been assigned a key role in that conspiracy, and it was the job of these officers to confirm it. They could not fail. So now they resorted to other methods.

They hung Otto up by his arms, stripped him of his shirt and proceeded to beat his naked back with sticks and whips. When Otto became unconscious, they would revive him by splashing him with cold water and the beatings would resume. Eventually, a thick-set SS man appeared, who proceeded to punch Otto in the face, hard and repeatedly. With his arms up and his hands tied, Otto could do nothing to defend himself: his head was a punchbag.

The blood poured out of both his nose and his mouth; he swallowed his dentures. The pain was so great that finally Otto declared that he was ready to testify, that he would say everything they wanted him to say.

They untied his hands, then presented him with a statement, in which he admitted to having met Goerdeler about twice a week, to having discussed the programme of the future government with him and to have known all about the preparations for the 20 July attempt on the life of the Führer. Otto barely cared what the document said as he signed it.

Throughout those August days, Hanna Kiep was searching for her husband. As he was dragged from one prison cell to another, she looked for him, whether in Plötzensee or in the jail on Lehrter Strasse. She was told he had been sent to Ravensbrück, but he wasn't there either. In the end, she found him at Prinz-Albrecht-Strasse 8, where she was allowed to bring him clean clothes and even some food. On 23 August, Leo Lange told her that Otto had been moved back to Plötzensee and two days later she was able to see him. The prison authorities allowed them a half-hour together, between 9 and 9.30 a.m. An officer remained present for each one of those thirty minutes.

Hanna was shocked by the sight of the man she loved. He was in a deplorable state. He explained to her that he had run out of strength, that he could hold out no longer. He told her about the confession, how he had signed whatever they put in front of him. He told her about the false teeth he had swallowed. And then he told her how he envied the actual plotters of 20 July, how he could not understand how they had been 'granted the privilege' of being executed only two hours after their sentence had been pronounced. He wished that it would finally be over.

As it happened, it was that very day that the Reich Ministry of Justice made the decision that Otto Kiep, in his desperation, longed for. The minister himself, Otto Thierack, received confirmation that Otto had now confessed to his crimes in full. Without delay, Thierack picked up the phone and ordered that he should be hanged within twenty-four hours.

Shortly before noon on 26 August, a bright clear day, he was led from his cell at Plötzensee and taken to a room where he was given a pen and paper and precisely half an hour to write a final letter. Efficient and professional to the last, he used the first ten minutes to make notes, planning the text, then wrote for twenty. He never so much as looked up at the clock on the wall. His timing was perfect: when the allotted thirty minutes were up, he had written what he wanted to say.

He was taken to the prison yard, where five other men were

readying themselves for the same fate. One of them was Adam von Trott zu Solz, the kindred spirit he had met in the Kreisau Circle that formed around Otto's old friend Helmuth von Moltke. He had found him sparkling company; the two men shared an admiration for England and a disdain for Nazism. Now it seemed that destiny had bound them together. Their eyes met, but they did not speak.

All six men were led across the yard to the place of execution, an empty brick building with a cold, hard floor. High across a back wall with two arched windows ran a thick beam. Dangling from it were a series of butcher's hooks. The executioners planned to be as good as Hitler's word and ensure that the guilty men were hanged like cattle.

Despite the beatings he had endured, Otto Kiep walked with a straight back that day. He held his head high, so that through the windows he could see the pristine blue of the sky. Once again, he was ready to place himself in the hands of God. And this time, there would be no reprieve.

61

Operation Swedish Furniture

Maria, August 1944

EVEN THEN, WHEN dissent was exacting its highest price, those who were free to resist kept at it. On 28 August 1944, just two days after the execution of Otto Kiep, Maria von Maltzan, the absurdly daring countess, would undertake her boldest mission yet.

It was the brainchild of Erik Wesslén, the indefatigable organiser who operated out of the Swedish Church in Berlin. That month, the Swedish envoy had decided that, with bombs falling almost nightly, it no longer made sense to be in the centre of Berlin: he relocated to rented premises outside the city. A decision was made to return some of the embassy furniture to Stockholm. For that purpose, the German national railway service, the Deutsche Reichsbahn, would offer the use of two sealed freight cars. Which gave Wesslén his idea.

The cars would be loaded up with beds, tables, chairs, wardrobes, all packed in crates. Then the sliding doors would be closed with a diplomatic seal, exactly as the rules demanded. The train would set off, as scheduled, late at night – but at an agreed spot outside the city, by a forest, the railway workers, encouraged by a bribe to the guard negotiated in advance, would briefly stop the train. Wesslén's team would be waiting.

Working quickly, they would remove the seal on one of the two cars, climb inside and throw out all the crates, furniture included. Next, they would shepherd into the wagon the group of the persecuted they had brought to this spot, along with enough metal plates to ensure that any overzealous inspector would see that the overall weight matched that of the original cargo, as logged in the paperwork. The twenty or so passengers would be given food and, just like Maria's lover, Hans, when he hid inside the mahogany bed, codeine to repress the cough that might give them away. The doors would then close, and the men carefully attach the copy of the diplomatic seal that Wesslén had prepared. After that, the wagon would not be opened again until it reached Sweden, where at last the submarines could emerge into the light.

Maria was to act as sherpa, bringing the Jews to the rendezvous point. She briefed the group, each one of them visibly terrified, on the dos and don'ts they would have to follow. They were to make no sound and leave no trail. That meant walking in the scrub at the edge of the forest, rather than on any stretches of sand where footprints would give them away. Of course, this ground would be covered with branches, but they were not to step on so much as a twig because that would make a noise – enough to betray them. So warned, they set out on the trek to freedom.

They had been walking a while when Maria spotted the first sign of danger: footprints in the same sandy path she had urged her charges to avoid. Or rather paw prints. The pattern told Maria that an SS troop had been here, accompanied by dogs. There was a labour camp near here: the SS were obviously patrolling the area.

Quietly she told the two young men acting as fellow sherpas to head back and report the danger to their comrades in the resistance. But to the Jews entrusted to her care she said nothing. They were scared enough already.

It was a shrewd call, for the countess succeeded in her mission. She got the group to the agreed place, where they were guided towards the train. In almost every other corner of Nazi-occupied Europe, to be a Jew loaded into a railway wagon was to take the first step on a journey towards death. In this one spot outside Berlin, the freight train meant life.

Now Maria had to make her way back, fully aware that she was heading directly into the crosshairs of the Nazi enemy. After all, this, she now knew, was terrain under SS patrol. Steeled for a threat that might appear at any moment, she began the return hike.

She made steady progress, covering half the distance without any sign of trouble. Had she struck lucky? Had the danger receded? And then she saw it.

A searchlight trained on the edge of the forest. Obviously she would have to stay well away from that beam. Except now she could see there was another light, trained on the opposite side. The searchlights were aimed very deliberately, as if marking out a large square. Whoever was operating them had a clear goal: to pen their prey into that square which would get ever narrower, until there was nowhere to hide. And she was the prey.

Maria had to think fast. She went deeper into the woods, away from the lights. She could see a small stream and, near it, a heap of animal manure. That gave her an idea.

She jumped over the stream, then walked to the dung pile, before retracing her steps back to the stream, taking care to walk in her own footprints. In fact, it was more of a run than a walk: the barking of the SS animals was getting louder and closer. Still, if what she knew about tracker dogs was right, they would lose her trail at the manure heap: the smell would overwhelm hers. She could then follow the route of the water, her animal pursuers left trailing and confused.

She knew that the stream eventually flowed into a larger body of water, one surrounded by trees. Some of the branches dipped and bent into the water, so if you concealed yourself among them and found the right perch, you might just find a hiding place where no search party, human or canine, would find you. You would be on neither land nor water, but suspended in between.

The countess spent the night like that, every muscle taut. She guessed that her trick with the manure had worked, and that the dogs had lost her scent, but it was clear that the search was continuing. The spotlights remained bright all night.

Morning came and the lights were turned off – but the patrols did not let up. Maria remained in the tree for what would feel like one of the longest days of her life. She could not move, she could not make a sound. All it would take was one servant of the SS, man or beast, to come near, or spot her from a distance, and she would be done for. If she tried to get away, by the time she was on solid ground, she would be surrounded.

The hours passed and night fell. The spotlights came back on, proof that the SS had not given up their hunt. In her perch among the leaves and birds, her limbs were aching and it was bitterly cold. But she could not surrender now. She would just have to wait it out.

She guessed it was around midnight when she heard the sound of an air-raid siren, coming from the city: bombs were falling on the north of Berlin. She watched and waited and then, at long last, the searchlights went out. The barking of dogs, the sound of the SS men, faded and disappeared. Finally, she gave herself permission to escape, lowering her body, stiff and sore, out of the tree.

She was close enough to the capital to see the glow of fire. The sight of the houses ablaze suggested a new plan.

Maria walked towards the flames, walking and walking until she could see a sight now familiar in Berlin: teams of people working to put out the fire, buckets of water passed hand to hand. She allowed herself to melt into the crowd, joining the volunteers in a collective effort that lasted the night.

When morning came, she looked no more ragged or rough than anyone else. Just to be on the safe side, she made sure to get written confirmation of her contribution to the firefighting effort from the air-raid warden on duty. Now she had official evidence of her good character – and an alibi for the night.

Somehow, despite the exhaustion and the hunger, she got back to the Swedish Church in Berlin, where she tapped on the window using the agreed pattern of knocks, a password in sound. The door opened and the pastor said, 'There's our veterinarian.' At which point Maria von Maltzan collapsed.

When she came around, her first thought was of Hans. He would be at home, desperate with worry. She needed to let him know that she was alive.

Only later did she learn that the mission that had taken her to the forest had been a complete success. Thanks to her, some twenty Jews, disguised as furniture in sealed railway cars bound for Scandinavia, had made it to safety.

And all the while the city glowed orange. At that tea party, which an inner voice had compelled Maria to steer well clear of, they had imagined this: Berlin burning, Germany heading towards disaster. It required even less imagination to picture it now. The Carmerstrasse defeatists had surely been right to predict defeat. It seemed inevitable that the Allies would conquer Germany eventually. The only question now was whether they would come in time to save those whom the Nazis had branded as traitors, fit only for death.

62

Death Row

Elisabeth, August 1944

ELISABETH VON THADDEN'S siblings, along with their spouses, assorted cousins and friends, had endured every moment of the day-long trial with her. They spoke to her before proceedings began and during the breaks, marvelling at her courage and, no less admirable, her composure and lucidity. She knew she faced the death sentence, but the little anxiety she voiced focused on the conditions in which she would be held as a prisoner convicted of a capital crime – or rather on one condition in particular. She dreaded the prospect of being shackled all day. She had seen death-row prisoners, their hands bound, and she feared she would not be able to bear it. Her brothers and sister promised they would see if there was any way that could be avoided.

Of course, there was not. They could only watch along with the rest of the court when Freisler condemned Elisabeth and Otto Kiep to death and as the pair had their hands tied behind their backs and were led away. They could do nothing as the dark prison van idled outside, and as Elisabeth and Otto, still unused to being manacled and therefore off balance, stumbled as they climbed in, eventually shoved inside by the guard.

Immediately, the Thadden family mounted the same operation undertaken by the Kieps: the quest for clemency. They too sought out university friends in the civil service or friendly generals of their acquaintance, anyone who might be of influence. They went to see the office of the public defender in Berlin, but came away with no more than hurried guidance on the correct procedure for filing a clemency petition.

Even so, every now and again providence showed her face, seemingly offering grounds for hope. Ehrengard, or Eta, and her husband had just left the public defender's building and were about to go into the S-Bahn railway station when a young man caught up with them. He introduced himself as a trainee lawyer in the office they had just left: come to think of it, they had glimpsed him across the room during their meeting. 'I followed you on purpose,' he said, explaining that he didn't want her to think that everyone involved with the People's Court was the same. 'There are others here too,' he said. 'We try to help where we can, we stick together, we've even tried to get through to the Führer.'

Hurriedly he gave her advice. Her sister's case was not a lost cause: they could make an argument that Elisabeth was not a young woman, that the war years had taken their toll, that sometimes periods of great strain can 'play tricks' on the mind. It sounded like an argument of, if not temporary insanity, then incapacity arising from senility. The Thadden family had seen how Freisler had waved away the charges against the conspicuously doddery Fanny von Kurowsky. Maybe this could work. The young man gave Eta the name of an official she should contact. She had so many questions she wanted to ask, and the name he had just given her had already slipped her mind, but as quickly as he had appeared, he vanished. He had melted back into the crowd of subway commuters, never to be seen again.

Still, sometimes desperation sharpens the memory and the official's name came back to her. They went to see him in the bombed-out ruin of the Ministry of Justice, where staircases went nowhere and long corridors were open to the skies. Eventually they found him at his desk – wearing an SS uniform. That put Eta on her guard. The conversation was cagey, as she tested out how frank she could be. But the trainee lawyer had been right: the official was sympathetic to her view that her sister deserved life imprisonment rather than the death penalty. Unstated throughout the exchange was the Thaddens' hope that life imprisonment would turn out to be nothing of the sort. It was the same hope shared by all those with loved ones on death row: that a stay of execution might keep the condemned alive just long enough to see the end of the war, the toppling of the Nazi regime and the freeing of all those jailed for defying Hitler.

Eta's efforts seemed to bear fruit. Freisler's sentence was not carried out immediately. Instead, Elisabeth was held on the women's death row in Barnimstrasse prison, itself cracked and scarred by enemy bombs, among thirty or forty other women waiting to be killed by the state. There she sat in her cell on the sixth floor, shackled for twenty-three hours out of every twenty-four, just as she had dreaded. She remained manacled even when the bombs fell: prisoners like her were deemed unworthy of the protection of the basement shelter.

The handcuffs irritated her body as well as her soul. Her wrists developed an itchy rash as the metal chafed and rubbed at her skin. With her hands bound, there were basic tasks she could not perform. In those weeks, she shared a cell with a shifting cast of criminals, regular convicts rather than fellow political prisoners. She would rely on these cellmates to do the jobs her own hands could not. But whether it was because she was with these women too briefly, or because they had been too hardened by the lives they had led, she was not able to make a connection with them. She simultaneously lacked privacy and was alone.

And yet she did not let any of that, or the death that lay in wait for her, break her spirit. On the contrary, the finality of her situation, the awareness it brought of the finitude of her time, seemed only to sharpen her determination to cherish every remaining minute. She kept reading, taking in a nineteenth-century memoir, Ernst Moritz Arndt's account of his travels accompanying a nobleman and Romantic German nationalist, heartened perhaps by the tale of someone who, by their fidelity to Christianity and the country's roots, helps rebuild a broken Germany.

She immersed herself in religious texts, closely annotating a pamphlet that invoked the story of Veronica, the woman who, on seeing Jesus stagger along the Via Dolorosa to Calvary, used her veil to wipe away the blood and sweat from his face. The pamphlet's author nodded to the contemporary resonance of such an act, suggesting that while today's men had set the world on 'the dark path of suffering', grace would come at 'the hands of women'. Soon there would be an awakening as if 'from a terrible dream', and it 'would be the great hour of the woman . . . the world has been waiting for it'.

Elisabeth read Paul's Epistle to the Romans, with its certainty that death could not come between a human being and God's love, and learned by heart Jesus' Sermon on the Mount. She memorised songs and poems, keeping her head full as she fought against the resignation, exhaustion and sense of defeat that consumed so many on death row. Nights were hardest, when sleep would not come and her mind was filled with images she could not shake. She knew what lay before her.

Even so, she and the rest of the condemned had to live with uncertainty: when exactly would the executioner come for them? Given the bombs that were falling on the Barnimstrasse prison, was it possible that the war would end before their death warrant had been served? Might they somehow outrun their fate?

Executions were always carried out on Fridays. The anticipation, and the dread, would build steadily from Wednesday onwards, hour by hour, until the unlocking of the cells at seven o'clock on Friday morning. Only then did it become clear who would live and who would die. After that, the long wait would begin again, because although death had not come this Friday, it might come the next.

That was how the summer weeks passed, July dissolving into August, finally giving way to September. Elisabeth's siblings were allowed to visit and they came away struck by how their sister seemed to be entering a calmer, more ethereal state, as if slowly slipping the bonds of earth. Her expression was kindly, but also somehow majestic. Her faith had, if anything, grown even stronger. Condemned and humiliated, facing a brutal death at the hands of those determined to cover her in shame, she felt she understood the story of Jesus more deeply than ever before. She felt closer to him.

On 6 September 1944, she saw Lisi, wife of her brother Reinold. They met in the visiting room, divided by a long table that stretched across the room and watched by a prison officer who did not leave. Lisi wore black, in recognition of the two sons she had already lost in battle and as an unwitting harbinger of the third who would soon be killed. They were allocated twenty minutes.

The two women had had their differences in the past, but now they spoke gently, of family mainly, Elisabeth taking care to ask about the boys who had been lost, the eldest of whom had been her godson. Lisi identified a kind of clarity in her sister-in-law, something you might even call rapture.

The twenty minutes became forty, the prison officer, usually so harsh, apparently unwilling to enforce the rules on this occasion. Finally, Lisi asked if she might shake the prisoner's hand. Silently, permission was granted. But there was no handshake. Instead, she embraced her sister-in-law, so gaunt and pale, and kissed her as a mother might kiss a child.

When she let go, she could see Elisabeth's eyes glistening with tears. Perhaps it was the shock of human warmth, of love, in this place of cold, hard stone and concrete.

Or perhaps it was the knowledge that Elisabeth had but did not share with her brother's wife.

63

The Murder Register

Elisabeth, September 1944

SINCE THE DAY after her trial, Elisabeth had spoken often with the prison chaplain, August Ohm. He would come and see her two or three times a week and, perhaps just as valuable, he devised a way around the rules that barred death-row inmates from attending services in the prison chapel, more than once smuggling her in. She trusted him.

Pastor Ohm would get early sight of the list of those who, come Friday, would be transferred to Plötzensee for execution. He knew before they did. On that first Wednesday in September, the day Lisi came, the pastor did not make his usual stop at Elisabeth's cell. That was the signal they had arranged, his way of telling her that he had glimpsed her fate and it was imminent.

On Friday morning, she and eleven other women were picked up from Barnimstrasse prison, loaded into a large police van and sent on the twenty-five-minute journey across Berlin to Plötzensee. There she was kept in one of several holding cells.

Ohm had got to Plötzensee early. He was a chaplain there too, and both the place and the staff were familiar to him. Except something was different this morning. When he walked through an entryway, he saw the barrels of as many as thirty guns aimed at him. Only later did he discover the reason for the extra security: several of those convicted of participation in the 20 July coup attempt had been brought here, to be executed that same day. That came as news to the priest because he had had no contact with the convicts of 20 July. They had been denied all pastoral care.

Their presence affected Elisabeth too. She was originally meant to be dealt with early. But now there was a long delay, the hours stretching into each other. Still, the day brought some small mercies. At last, her shackles were off; her hands, arms and wrists could move freely. How grateful she was for that.

And she was allowed a pen and paper. She wrote to her cousin Hans-Hasso von Veltheim, a scholar of India and of Eastern religion with a deeply spiritual cast of mind. The two had been in correspondence throughout these last weeks and she had drawn much comfort from it, taking to heart his advice that her suffering was not meaningless but was instead part of the forging of an inner strength.

'My dear Hans-Hasso,' she wrote,

> I am going from this spatial-temporal world to the . . . homeland of love! You, who have already travelled this path with me to the gates of eternity, may you receive a last special greeting of thanks and love! May God give you the strength to give strength and love to all of yours with the luminosity of the light of revelation until the hour strikes for you. Your Elisabeth.

She wrote too to 'My beloved siblings', signing off the same way: 'Your Elisabeth.'

Pastor Ohm was shuttling back and forth between the cells of the condemned, but he returned to Elisabeth several times and noticed how she never seemed in despair. She was without tears.

Finally, she dictated to him if not a last will and testament, then at least the facts that she had not been able to speak of before. She told him of her arrest in France nearly nine months earlier, about the all-night interrogations she had endured there and later in Berlin, how 'monstrous' her inquisitors had been and how 'terrible' Ravensbrück was. She told him there had been things that she could have said that might even have helped her, but that she did not say, lest she endanger her brother. She had been asked about the dissidents of the Confessing Church and much else, but: 'Not a single word escaped me that would have incriminated others.' For the record, she told her confessor, 'I had nothing to do with the assassination attempt of 20 July, I didn't know any of these people.'

All she had ever wanted to do was 'provide social help at the moment when it was needed'. When the day came – and 'It was clear that this moment had to come' – 'We wanted to be Good Samaritans, but nothing political.' There would be no reprieve for her, but she felt as if she had been spared all the same: 'Whoever believes in Jesus has eternal life.'

In one more modest act of compassion, the Plötzensee authorities allowed her not only to write letters but to read those that had come for her in the preceding days. There were three. She had read two of them but not yet got to the third when, shortly before five o'clock in the afternoon, she was told, 'Get ready.'

She pinned up her hair and put on a different dress and now, once again, her hands were bound. Pastor Ohm had made it his habit to accompany the condemned to the very end. But this time he was only allowed as far as the door of the execution room. After that, Elisabeth was on her own. He watched her walk towards her fate, without hesitation. Her tread was firm. She did not quake or tremble. She wanted no more delay.

Some of those deemed enemies by the Third Reich had faced a firing squad. Others had been hanged by a noose or on a butcher's hook. But on 8 September 1944, almost a year to the day since she had welcomed her friends for an afternoon of tea, cake and conversation, Elisabeth von Thadden placed her neck in a guillotine and waited for the blade that would, she believed, deliver her to Paradise and which, her rulers believed, would serve the cause of justice. In the ledger known as the 'murder register' of Plötzensee, she was entered as T 498, Business Number IV g 27/44 g Rs.

64

The Dead Centre

Hanna and Lagi, September 1944

ARTHUR ZARDEN WAS dead. Otto Kiep was dead. And Elisabeth von Thadden was dead. Hanna Solf was still alive, as was her daughter, Lagi. But their prospects looked bleak.

For one thing, although the chief judge of the People's Court had dismissed Hanna on that sweltering July evening, he had not set her free. Instead, she was simply transported to another prison while a new case against her could be prepared, one that would focus on her role as the convenor of what Roland Freisler had witheringly referred to as 'a political drawing room': the Solf Circle.

This investigation would stretch far beyond the small group that had taken tea with Elisabeth von Thadden. It would include anyone who had come to the Solf apartment on Altenstrasse to trade gossip and dissenting talk. For as long as the Gestapo were fixated on the tea party of 10 September 1943, Hanna's daughter, Lagi, had been able to rely on a rock-solid defence: she had not been there. Now that the Solf Circle was in their sights, she moved from the periphery of their gaze to the dead centre.

For a while, mother and daughter were back under the same roof in Ravensbrück. They were there in the prison block on 20 July, when Stauffenberg and the others made their ill-fated attempt on Hitler's life, and they felt the fresh fury of the Gestapo immediately. In the middle of the night, Hanna was taken to a dark basement cell at the north end of the building with a soiled sack of straw for a mattress. The Solf Circle regulars Count Albrecht von Bernstorff and Richard Kuenzer were nearby and given the same treatment.

As for Lagi, she was now the subject of a new, intensified round of interrogations that featured sudden, abrupt visits from the Gestapo, whose chief purpose seemed to be to test, or perhaps break, the morale of their prisoners. One officer asked her what she thought would have happened if the assassination had been successful. 'A great deal,' Lagi said. 'Above all, you would be in this cell and I would not.'

The prison block now became busier, its ranks increased by those arrested for their roles, real or imagined, on 20 July. Communication, whether among the prisoners or between them and the outside world, was all but cut off. Nevertheless, Lagi caught a glimpse of some of the new inmates. She recognised Hjalmar Schacht, former head of the central bank and father-in-law of the convicted tea-party guest, Hilger van Scherpenberg. She also spotted General Halder, the one-time chief of staff whom Reckzeh had been so keen to meet, and Johannes Popitz, the former finance minister: it was he who had, via an intermediary, tried to sound out Himmler about a possible peace approach to the British and Americans. Erwin Planck, son of the celebrated physicist and Nobel laureate Max Planck, was brought in, as was Ulrich von Hassell, a former ambassador to Italy. Wives and daughters of the accused were detained too, under the *Sippenhaft* doctrine of family liability, by which the actions of one individual would be paid for by their kin. A new, perhaps even richer portion of the cream of Berlin society was now behind bars in Ravensbrück.

Conditions became ever harsher. In mid-August, Lagi was put on starvation rations, fed only a diet of rancid soup known as the 'dog dish', depriving her of basic nutrition. That she survived was due in part to the fellow prisoners who might pass her a bit of bread, among them one Princess Elisabeth Ruspoli, the widow of an Italian diplomat.

Now Lagi, like her mother, was locked away in a damp cell in the basement, denied books, exercise and human contact for an uninterrupted two weeks. After 20 July, the older SS guards had been replaced by younger, even more brutal men who worked in teams of six, many of them Romanian, Hungarian or Russian. The prisoners called them the 'rats' and learned to dread their diligence, their habit of looking into each cell every twenty minutes, their constant intrusions through the night. In what should have been the hours of sleep, they would turn bright electric lights on and off, or burst in to a cell to fire off a fusillade of random questions, demanding to know the inmate's name, age, sex, religion and amount of savings. One night, Lagi was woken at 2 a.m. with the demand that she identify the units of the Nazi party to which she belonged. They never let up. If the guards were not barking out commands, they were running through the corridors, stamping their feet and ensuring everyone remained permanently on edge.

Presiding over it all, his domain expanded thanks to the wider scope granted him after 20 July, was Leo Lange. Now he had fresh victims to torment. The mighty had fallen and landed at his feet, their humiliation his to savour. He would come to inspect the prison block every Sunday, taking care to shout at each of his previously eminent charges in turn. In the cell directly below Lagi's was Johannes Popitz. She could hear Lange bellowing at him, 'Well, Minister, you old pig . . .'

But however bad the treatment got, Lagi was aware that she was one of the lucky ones in Ravensbrück. In late August, she and Princess Ruspoli were given a work assignment: they were taken to a larger cell, where they had to sort through some 77,000 paper bags, each one containing jewellery and a card signed by an inmate who had had to surrender their valuables on arrival. The names on the cards suggested the items had arrived from across Europe; there were rings and necklaces, earrings and bracelets cherished by women from Greece, Ukraine, Poland and beyond. Lagi and her friend were tasked with checking each bag, separating the precious gems from the junk, with the valuable items to be handed to the Gestapo officer who had given them the job. That man was then supposed to organise the goods' transfer to the Reichsbank, but it soon became clear that most of the hoard would, in fact, stay with him.

As she worked, Lagi thought of the women who had once worn these trinkets or treasures. She knew what had become of them because sometimes she would pull herself up to the window of her basement cell, looking up to ground level, where she would see the women of the concentration camp, standing for hours, forbidden to move, no doubt assembled for the morning or evening roll-call.

Nearby was the execution yard; in the evenings, she could hear the shots ringing out. And behind one wall of the cell block stood the crematorium and its chimney, pushing out smoke around the clock. As the months passed, as 1944 got older, she noticed the smoke getting thicker and heavier. She knew what, or rather whom, they were burning.

65

Indicted, Again

Hanna and Lagi, Autumn 1944

LAGI SOLF HAD little contact with her fellow prisoners, and therefore next to no information. She communicated with Count Bernstorff, who was held in the next-door cell, by knocking on the wall they shared, hoping to convey encouragement. She could exchange whispers with the chaplain, and they all hoped for morsels from Count Moltke, who had devised some secret channel to the outside. Otherwise, she knew almost nothing. While she was held in solitary confinement for that wretched fortnight, she heard that her mother had been moved from Ravensbrück. But no one told her where she had gone or when or why. All Lagi could do was worry.

And she was right to be frightened. Because events had made what was an already desperately bad hand even worse. When Hanna and Lagi were arrested at the house in Partenkirchen in January, the Gestapo had, naturally, searched the premises from top to bottom, confiscating every piece of paper they found. Among them was a letter that, at the time, had seemed of only modest significance. Now, after 20 July, it took on an entirely new meaning.

It was addressed to Hanna Solf and it was from Carl Goerdeler, the 20 July conspirators' choice of successor to Adolf Hitler. She was now deeply implicated in the attempted violent overthrow of the Third Reich.

Hanna was moved, spending three weeks in Moabit remand prison, where the guards routinely harassed and humiliated her, and then transferred to the jail in Cottbus, south of Berlin and halfway to Dresden. She was on the move constantly in those months, after the trial and the failed coup, transferred some nine times in all, but she would not forget Cottbus easily.

There she was woken each day at 3.45 a.m. and made to work till evening, sewing buttons on uniforms. The treatment was brutal, of the sick especially; the rest were subjected to constant insults. And death was never far away. Hanna watched as a contingent of three hundred French women were taken to Ravensbrück one day in November: they would be executed there. Hanna found it impossible to describe the depths of human misery she saw all around her. All talking between prisoners was strictly forbidden.

And yet, a silent camaraderie developed among the inmates, women and girls of all ages, classes and levels of education, and of several nationalities. Without the need, or freedom, to say it, they all knew that they had one thing in common: they were here, imprisoned, because they had insisted, in one form or another, that there were values higher than fidelity to the fatherland and its rulers. It might be the rule of law, it might be faith in God or Jesus, it might be simple humanity. Whatever it was, they refused to accept that there was no higher authority than Adolf Hitler; they refused to bow to the supremacy he claimed for himself.

Hanna was interrogated repeatedly. Now they wanted to know about that link to Goerdeler, and whether she had similar ties to any of the 20 July conspirators or to anyone else on the former mayor's list. In one all-night session, the Gestapo grilled her over her friendship with Father Metzger, the idealist who had inadvertently put his proposed peace plan in the hands of a Nazi agent. They were sure that every scheme and initiative, no matter how quixotic or eccentric, every dinner conversation and tea party, every scribbled note and hushed aside, was connected to the rest, in a single, vast, devilishly clever conspiracy. No matter how many times Hanna Solf told them they were mistaken, they put the same question again and again.

Eventually a fresh indictment arrived, with a trial date set for 13 December 1944. Hanna was named as the chief defendant, with five others charged on account of their frequent or intimate association with the Solf Circle. The former diplomats Richard Kuenzer and Albrecht von Bernstorff were named second and third, followed by the priest and philosopher Father Friedrich Erxleben. The sixth and last defendant was the writer and historian Dr Maximilian von Hagen. That left one name, in fifth place – that of Hanna's daughter, Lagi.

It accused all but Hagen of 'treasonous activities', alleging that at the Solf residence,

> in the years 1941–1943, in numerous conversations with each other and with others, they advocated the subversive idea that the Reich would lose the war, and, in accordance with their reactionary anti-state attitude, propagated the violent overthrow of the national socialist leadership and its replacement by a 'government' inclined to conclude a peace of submission.

In the process, they had become 'servants of our enemies in war'. Hagen was accused of knowing about this treachery and failing to report it.

The details were damning. Through her frequent invitations, Solf had created a forum where friends felt free to pass on and 'reaffirm their anti-state ideas'. But she was no mere facilitator of all this heretical, incendiary talk. On the contrary, she 'herself intervened in these discussions, taking a lively part in the debates and making cutting and crass remarks in support of her friends' plans to betray the Führer and overthrow the national socialist regime'. She had been in the room when her fellow defendant, Richard Kuenzer, had 'declared during a conversation with her eldest son that the Führer had to be shot down like a mad dog'. What's more, 'She did not oppose this view, but approved it.'

It was, ran the indictment, Hanna Solf who, in the spring of 1943, had convened in her own house a meeting between Kuenzer and the Catholic priest Max Metzger, the same Max Metzger who would eventually be convicted and sentenced to death for high treason. She knew of Metzger's subversive plan to topple the regime and, once again, she did not oppose it, but 'essentially agreed'.

But her crimes did not end there. When she wasn't busying herself with suggesting which men might serve in the new government, the widow Solf also dared speak out against the alleged suppression of free expression. And she 'sharply rejected the measures taken by the national socialist leadership against the Christian denominations'.

Perhaps most reprehensible of all, 'she took a particularly violent stand against the allegedly too harsh treatment of the Jews and, with tears in her eyes, regretted the fate of several Jewish women she knew'.

As for Lagi, she too was accused of being 'one of those defeatists who reject the national socialist state'. She too wanted a new government, one that would make peace with the western powers. She too had talked of a coup, and she too had been in the room when Kuenzer had made his 'mad dog' remark about the Führer. As if all that were not appalling enough, the young countess was there to hear 'the Jewish question in particular being discussed in an inflammatory manner and the worst atrocity fairy tales being spread'. Kuenzer was a serial offender in this regard, telling 'the most gruesome horror tales, especially about the alleged shootings of Jews'. Still, the prosecution had it on record that 'the women in particular stood out during these conversations' for the vehemence of their comments.

There was, however, one curious omission from the long list of accusations against the Solfs. For all their diligence, the state prosecutors had missed something that would have strengthened their case immeasurably. Unmentioned was the fact that the Solfs had not just wept for the Jews of their acquaintance, they had actively helped several Jews get out of the country and to safety. Hanna had been questioned about it, but when it came to drawing up the indictment, that most egregious offence against the Reich had somehow been overlooked.

By 1 December, mother and daughter were back under the same roof, held as remand prisoners in Moabit jail while they awaited trial. But it was a bitter kind of reunion. In Berlin, the bombs fell day and night and prisoners like Hanna and Lagi were deemed unworthy of the bomb shelter. They remained locked up on the second floor. They were kept apart, in cells where the temperature fell below freezing: the barred windows had no glass. Hygiene was impossible, the place was filthy. Food rations grew ever smaller and hunger soon took its toll, marking the two women differently. Lagi blew up, until she looked like a bloated rubber doll. Her mother became a living skeleton.

Hanna Solf was now fifty-seven years old. The starvation, cold and loneliness were becoming impossible to bear; there was no news of the war, just the knowledge that her sons were in combat and could be killed at any moment; the trial and certain death sentence were now just days away. Each morning demanded another shift of forced labour to be done, but she had no strength left.

The only comfort came from the prison chaplain, who brought words of consolation, the occasional note from mother to daughter and back again, and, no less important, whatever food he could smuggle in. No other visitors were allowed, save once, for Lagi – and yet, though she had yearned for it so ardently, that encounter marked perhaps the lowest moment of her captivity.

It came in December and the visitor was her husband. He was on a rare spell of leave from active duty on the Russian front and the pair were granted just fifteen minutes together. They sat, separated by a large table, while a female prison officer stood over them, constantly looking at her watch. They were both too stunned to know what to say; they scarcely said anything coherent. They both assumed they were saying goodbye. For all the physical hardships she had endured, Lagi suffered no greater pain than she did that day.

And then came the news that the trial had been postponed. It would not be on 13 December after all, but had been rescheduled for 19 January: apparently, the People's Court was overwhelmed with cases. That had to be good news, because time had become their greatest friend. The crumbs of information they had from the outside world suggested that the fronts were getting closer, whether it was the British and Americans advancing from the west or the Russians from the east. That was certainly the view from Detmolder Strasse in Berlin, where Maria von Maltzan, one of the few prominent members of the Solf Circle not behind bars, had begun hoarding food supplies and hiding anything of value, in preparation for a Red Army invasion. She concealed sausages and smoked bacon between the bathtub and the wall, and hid what cash she had in pots of lard. If food was scarce now, it was only going to get scarcer. Since the autumn German refugees had been streaming into the capital from the east, fleeing Russian forces as they swept into East Prussia and elsewhere.

It seemed conquest by the Russians, and liberation from the Nazis, was coming. For the likes of Hanna and Lagi Solf, a delay of even a few weeks might be the difference between life and death. Was it possible that, somehow and against the odds, they might survive?

66

An Exquisite Deliverance

Hanna and Lagi, December 1944

A SINGLE LAWYER WAS appointed to represent many of the political prisoners held on the most serious charges, a category that included the Solfs. Given the outcome of the 1 July trial, to say nothing of the proceedings at the People's Court after 20 July, where Freisler had been herding a steady column of German citizens towards the gallows, his chances of success were meagre. Prisoners from Moabit were being sentenced to death all the time, many of them held in the cell next to Hanna's: she could not forget the loud weeping and wailing of one young woman who had just been told she would be executed for her supposed crimes. Even so, the lawyer's visits helped keep despair at bay. Together with those hushed conversations with the chaplain and the occasional pieces of bread smuggled in by the prison doctor, they proved to be Hanna's great consolation.

There was no Christmas to speak of in Moabit. Outside it, Maria von Maltzan managed to put a meal on the table, and even get hold of some red wine, for herself and Hans, as they allowed themselves to hope that this might be his last winter in hiding. Encouragement came from the pirate radio station secretly operated by her friend Werner Keller, an official in the armaments ministry headed by Albert Speer. Ingeniously, Keller and a group of fellow anti-Nazis had engineered a tiny transmitter, concealed in a household iron, and used it to broadcast news from home and abroad from the vantage point of the resistance, in defiance of the Nazi control of all channels of information. They were on air only at certain times of the night and Keller had asked Maria to listen in, to tell him whether the group were getting the message right. She did that and, in whispers, passed on word of the station's existence, so that its audience began to grow.

As 1945 dawned, the trial loomed. But as 19 January approached, the defendants were informed of a second postponement. The new date would be 8 February. Was it possible that the Reich's enemies could break through by then? Was a combination of time and the Allied armies of London, Washington and Moscow about to rescue them from their appointment with death?

But January turned into February and the Third Reich was still in charge. The date on the calendar, 8 February, was getting closer and there was no word of a further postponement. It seemed that Hanna and Lagi would have to face their destiny after all. But then, five days before the trial was due to begin, fate took a hand. Or if not fate, then the fighter bombers of the United States Army Air Forces.

On Saturday, 3 February 1945, Lagi was locked in her cell, as usual, doing the forced labour of darning an apparently bottomless pile of military socks. Suddenly, the entire prison building at Moabit, which was huge and old, its walls thick and made of stone, shook to its foundations. The air was filled with thunder as one bomb after another fell from the sky in what was the largest American air assault on the capital of the war. It struck Lagi in that moment that the various court postponements had been meaningless, the months of waiting irrelevant: she and her mother had thought so much about the prospect of being sentenced to death in five days' time, only to be killed by the bombs of the Reich's enemies right then.

Lagi and Hanna remained stuck in their second-floor cells, denied the protection of the basement shelter, through what was said to be one of the most severe daytime air raids ever to hit Berlin. And yet they did not die.

The next day, a whispered rumour spread among the prisoners. At first, Lagi refused to believe it. It was too good, too perfect. But those delivering the news grew increasingly adamant that what they had heard was true. 'Freisler is dead!' they said. 'Freisler is dead!' An inmate emerging from the men's prison whispered to Hanna as he passed: 'No more People's Court!'

A version of the story circulated in which it was the judge's very zeal to send his fellow Germans to their deaths that proved his undoing. In this telling, Freisler continued working as the bombing began, preparing for the next day's docket of cases, refusing to go to the shelter while there was still Nazi justice to be done. When a bomb hit the court building, he was killed. Other versions added an extra detail to the story of his downfall: Freisler had eventually relented and was on his way to the shelter when he remembered that he had left a crucial file on his desk. He turned back to get it and was hit. In fact, it seems Freisler was underground when he was killed, struck by a falling beam in the basement of the court that he had turned into his own bloody domain.

It felt like an exquisite deliverance, but there was more. Not only had the air raid removed the man who was bent on being the Solf Circle's judge, jury and executioner, it had destroyed the case against them. Not legally perhaps, but physically. The blaze set off by the bombing consumed a large number of court records, including those relating to the prosecution of Hanna and her daughter. The authorities would have to reassemble the paperwork, thereby handing the Solfs yet more of what was, for those Germans accused of anti-Nazi crimes in the first half of 1945, the most precious commodity of all: time. The new trial date would be 27 April and, given that the court building in Berlin no longer existed, the case would be heard in Potsdam.

By the time April came around, that plan looked more notional than real. The system was beginning to crack. The word from outside, brought by new arrivals to the prison, was that the war could not possibly go on much longer. That assessment was borne out by the sound of artillery fire in Berlin and reports that Russian troops were already in the eastern and northern parts of the city. Some of the prison guards stopped coming to work, apparently fearful that if they were on the premises when the Red Army liberators arrived, they would be punished, and possibly killed, on the spot.

Each day, the jail got emptier as more inmates were let go: first the regular criminals and then those political prisoners held on relatively minor charges. Soon it wasn't just the inmates and some of their guards who were disappearing. By 20 April, all the judges and staff of the People's Court had fled.

PUNISHMENT

Suddenly, even the previously exhausted and resigned among Moabit's population of the accused became feverish, seized by a new and wild desire to live. For the first time in months or even years, they felt the possibility of a future. Lagi was no different. During her allotted exercise session – the rules still held – she noticed new signs of life. The trees in the drab prison yard were beginning to bud and turn green. She could hear birdsong. The cold was fading.

And yet freedom remained out of reach. For every guard who had discarded their uniform and walked away, there were those who became harder and more vigilant. The trial date was still there. On 23 April, four days before the hearing was due to begin, the head of the Moabit jail told Hanna that there was 'no question' of releasing either her or her daughter. Whether through hunger, in an air raid or at the hands of the increasingly jumpy prison guards, it seemed the Solfs were going to die here after all.

That was proving to be the fate of many of their friends and fellow dissidents. For Richard Kuenzer, the former diplomat and aged man of action who, a few years earlier, had been in the habit of speaking to Hanna almost daily, accompanying her at countless clandestine meetings, the struggle against Nazism had ended the previous night. He, along with fifteen other prisoners from the Lehrter Strasse jail, had faced a special unit of the Reich Security Main Office, who shot each man in the back of the neck.

On the 23rd, Count Albrecht von Bernstorff, the man who had been shipped out of the German embassy in London for meeting British critics of the Führer and who pointedly said 'Good morning' rather than 'Heil Hitler!' as he walked into the Foreign Ministry, was shot dead along with several others by a firing squad.

Herbert Mumm von Schwarzenstein, who used to amuse the guests at the Solf apartment as one half of a duo performing witty ditties satirising Hitler and his henchmen, was beheaded in Brandenburg-Görden on 20 April. (The other half of the act, Nikolaus von Halem, had been beheaded in the same place six months earlier.) Ludwig Gehre, the Abwehr officer who had helped warn Otto and the others that they were under Gestapo surveillance, had been sent to Flossenbürg, a concentration camp in a remote corner of Bavaria, where he was 'liquidated' on 9 April, along with the rest of the cell that had once nestled within German military intelligence, the group that had formed around Hans Oster and Admiral Wilhelm Canaris and which included Otto Kiep.

Canaris had been arrested three days after the failed putsch of 20 July, accused of being its 'spiritual instigator'. Hard evidence had proved elusive to his pursuers until his personal diary was discovered in April 1945 and shown to Hitler. That was enough to condemn him, and he was soon before an SS summary court along with Oster, Gehre and others – including, later that same day, the theologian Dietrich Bonhoeffer – where they were abused and humiliated, charged with and convicted of treason and sent to their deaths. They were executed together at around 6 a.m. the following day, 9 April. They were naked as they were led to the gallows, where they, like Kiep before them, were hanged on butcher's hooks. They said that Canaris took half an hour to die, that he had to be 'hanged twice'. The night before his death, Canaris had tapped on the wall a coded message to the prisoner in the next cell, his former counterpart in Danish intelligence. It declared that he was no traitor, for he had acted only out of 'duty to my country'.

The war against the Allies was nearly over, but the Reich's war on the German citizens it had branded as traitors would be fought to the very end. The Solfs, whose family had stood against the Nazi regime from the beginning, had every reason to believe they would be among its final victims.

And yet, only a few hours after the head of the Moabit jail had told Hanna Solf there was 'no question' of releasing either her or her daughter, an officer burst into Lagi's cell in a state of hysteria. She was shouting and Lagi could only just make out the words. 'Get ready for discharge,' she was saying. Get ready for discharge.

It turned out that the Solfs still had friends on the outside, people with enough clout and enough nous to work what was left of the system. One of them was a long-time opponent of national socialism, Dr Ernst Ludwig Heuss. He had secured the release of two men held next door to Moabit, in the Gestapo prison at Lehrter Strasse, both of them fellow defendants in the treason trial that still loomed over the two women: Hagen the historian and Erxleben the priest.

But he also persuaded the last magistrate left in Berlin to write discharge certificates for four family friends, all of them inmates of Moabit. Two were made out in the names of the widow and daughter of Fritz Elsas, a former mayor of Berlin who had been shot dead without facing trial three months earlier. Elsas's crime had been hiding Carl Goerdeler when the latter was on the run following the failed coup of 20 July; the *Sippenhaft* blood-guilt doctrine put his wife and child behind bars. The third certificate was for Lagi. And the final one was for her mother.

The whole scene was bewildering; no one knew what to believe, or who to trust. But the discharge was agreed and suddenly two mothers and two daughters were walking out of Moabit prison. Lagi was filled with relief, but also received a terrible shock. Her mother was barely there. On the night of her release, Hanna Solf weighed around ninety pounds, just over six and a half stone.

Within the hour, Joseph Goebbels got wind of the Solfs' freedom. Besides serving as propaganda minister, since the previous summer he had also gloried in the title of Reich Plenipotentiary for the Total War Effort, which placed him above the civil defence authorities for each province of the Nazi state. In that capacity he had agreed to release common criminals from jail, but had specifically excluded political prisoners on the grounds that they would 'cause unrest among the population'. Now he was furious to hear that two traitors, the Solfs, were on the loose. He demanded that this 'oversight' be reversed and the two women be returned to jail to face trial. But by then the artillery fire and aerial bombardment were so great that, in the chaos of fighting, bombs and shrapnel, the women could not be found. It was too late. They were out.

As they walked away, it would have taken a while for them to get their bearings. At one end of Lehrter Strasse, there was the men's prison where, for perhaps only an hour or two more, some of their friends and fellow dissenters were still held. At the other, what remained of the Lehrter Bahnhof, which had been one of the city's main railway stations. Now it was a ruin. Beyond that, over the River Spree, was Alsenstrasse, the place they once called home.

Behind bars for so long, the two women moved through a city that they barely recognised. Tens of thousands of bombs had fallen on Berlin. Half of all the houses were damaged, a third were uninhabitable. Street after street was just rubble, four thousand acres of it reduced to random piles of stone and brick. And it was empty: some 40 per cent of the population had fled.

Hanna and Lagi were gazing upon the devastation of the city they loved. They had been starved, and had not a pfennig between them. And yet here they were, walking in Berlin. Against all the odds, and after all they had endured, after they had grieved for so many of their friends, including three of their fellow guests at the September tea party, Hanna and Lagi Solf were alive and they were not in prison. For the first time in fifteen months, there was no one watching them, no walls surrounding them. They were free.

A few days later, and after twelve years, the Third Reich was no more. So many had waited for this moment. So many had longed for the chance to start anew, and it had finally come. And yet the ecstasy of that liberation was tempered by the agony of knowing that so many of those who had yearned for it, who had tried so hard to bring it about, were gone.

No less agonising was the knowledge that some of the guiltiest men still lived: among them, the man who had betrayed the supposed traitors of the tea party.

And he was not done yet.

PART VI

After the War

67

Into the Daylight

Maria, April 1945

ON THE EVENING of 19 April 1945, Countess Maria von Maltzan listened to a speech by Joseph Goebbels. She could hardly avoid it: it was broadcast from the loudspeakers that the Nazis had installed in every public place – in cafes and factories and on the city streets – back in the early days. The master propagandist sought to rally the German nation on the eve of the Führer's birthday, conceding that this was their darkest hour, that things did indeed 'stand on a knife's edge', that fate was putting them to the most severe test in their history, from which they would, nevertheless, emerge victorious. In fact, the Russians would surround Berlin five days later and when Goebbels spoke on the radio again, making what would be his last speech, Soviet artillery would be audible in the background.

Maria prepared for the invaders' arrival, boarding up the windows of the apartment and checking the building. She found two SS men setting up a machine-gun nest in the attic, readying themselves for the final battle. That would make them all a target and the countess was having none of it. Armed with a pistol, and accompanied by a couple of like-minded men, she crept upstairs and ambushed the would-be Nazi heroes. At gunpoint, she gave them a choice: die now or ditch the uniforms and try to survive the Russian invasion as civilians. They swiftly saw sense. Maria burned the uniforms on her kitchen stove and, before long, she was watching Russian tanks roll into Detmolder Strasse through the gaps between the boards covering the living-room window. Hitler killed himself on 30 April and what remained of the Berlin garrison surrendered on 2 May.

Maria looked on as the Russians wasted no time in taking what they wanted, whether rifling through apartments or raping women. She was pressed into service early as a vet, ministering to the Russians' horses in particular but, once again, she was careful to let Berlin's new masters know that she was not to be pushed around.

She had her arm deep in a horse's backside, cleaning out compacted manure, when a Red Army soldier walked behind her and pinched her bottom. Out came her hand, still filthy, which she used to slap the offender twice across the face. She soon confronted a more senior Russian officer, armed with a revolver, who warned he could shoot her on the spot for her impudence. She laughed in his face, warning him that if he did that, it would be the Red Army's horses who would suffer. The stand-off was resolved when the officer accepted her demand that, if she were to continue treating the Russians' animals, she would have to be given a senior rank in the Red Army, one that would protect her from further molestation. Which is how the countess became a major.

Only once he was sure that the Nazis really had been vanquished did Maria's secret lover, Hans Hirschel, dare emerge from hiding. There had been more than 160,000 Jews in Berlin before Hitler took power in 1933. They had enjoyed a position at the heart of society, eminent in science, the arts, industry and government. Now there were just 1,500 left. They began stepping out gingerly from basements or attics, tiptoeing over fallen masonry and rubble and into the daylight. The survivors tried to organise themselves, establishing a temporary office on Prinzregentstrasse, where they started to register the handful of Jews who had somehow clung to life. They wanted to help, including by ensuring food rations reached those most in need. But first they had to persuade German Jews that it was safe, rather than life-threatening, to have their name on an official list.

For many, the adjustment proved too much, Hans included. He suffered a complete collapse of his circulatory system, along with severe disorders of the stomach and intestines. Maria got him into a functioning hospital, one now run by the US army. Not for the first time, she saved him.

He recovered and, less than a month after the fall of the Reich, the Silesian countess and her Jewish boyfriend were in business together. She opened a veterinary clinic, and Hans did the paperwork. Word spread, until she had a roster full of clients from the occupying armies, whether British commanding officers or American generals. They all brought her their ailing pets.

The new authorities embarked on a process of denazification, promising to root out those who had played a part in the now-toppled regime. They sorted Germans into various categories, from the clearly guilty to those not incriminated at all. In a nod to the soap powder, confirmation of the latter was known as a *Persilschein*, a clean bill of health, and it soon became a highly prized commodity.

Faced with a conquered population, the occupiers needed guidance in separating the villains from the rest. The Russians had declared Maria a person of 'political integrity' and so she and Hans were in sudden and constant demand. It turned out that a surprisingly large number of people had never done anything wrong, indeed had opposed Hitler from the start, and now wanted Maria and Hans to vouch for them – far more people, in fact, than had ever hinted at such a position before. Maria soon found herself deployed as either a witness or assessor in denazification proceedings, judging whose record was clean and whose was not. The hearings were often poisonous, as neighbour denounced neighbour and gossip substituted for evidence. Maria found herself sceptical of those who claimed to be blameless and inclined to believe those who admitted that, yes, they had been in the Hitler Youth and had once supported the Nazis, but had changed as the years went on. That story at least fitted with what she had seen with her own eyes: a nation that had lined up to acclaim the Führer, with very few exceptions.

In 1947, Maria and Hans finally made their love, which for a decade had been a criminal act, official. They were married. But there was to be no simple happy ending. Though he had been restored to physical health, the damage of those years in hiding went deep. He struggled to return to a normality he had not known for years; he had been dependent on Maria so long, he could not quite break the habit. He could not help her as she expected from a husband; he could barely help himself. She worked as hard as ever and hoped he might at least attempt to return to his writing career, but he did not even try. He was lethargic, passive. He had survived; thanks to her, he had a fresh chance of life. But he seemed to have given up. He had lost almost all his relatives and she thought he wallowed in their deaths. 'We can't hold onto our dead,' she would tell him. 'We have to live now and build something from nothing.'

But if she could not understand what he had gone through, he barely knew what she had endured. For as long as she could, she had kept her darkest secret from him. But now it could be hidden no longer.

People, including Hans, had admired her phenomenal stamina, her ability to hold down a demanding, physical job by day and to find new sources of energy for resistance work by night. She had swum across lakes, run through tunnels and dodged bullets, only to return to Berlin at daybreak ready for her morning shift, apparently without need for either sleep or food. What her comrades in the underground and hidden lover in the apartment did not know was that those new sources of energy were not only drawn from inner reserves of character. They were also chemical. She had only been able to keep going, sometimes on her feet for twenty hours at a stretch, feeding several people with a single ration card, thanks to myriad stimulants accessible to her through her job, among them Pervitin, a methamphetamine deployed as an effective treatment for horses with lumbago and whose human use was so widespread in the Germany of the Third Reich that it became known as the *Volksdroge*, the people's drug. Maria was addicted.

She was convinced that the only way she could break the drugs' grip was by the kindness of cruelty. She needed a husband who would be merciless towards her, with the strength to deny her what she craved. Hans was too gentle, too tolerant, and by 1949, two years after they had married, they divorced.

But the addiction stayed with her, eventually sending her into a rehabilitation facility at Wittenau that adjoined a mental hospital and was run like a jail. She was dressed in prison stripes, subject to the whims of nurses who found a particular amusement in taunting the morphine addicts who, during withdrawal, would suffer extreme cold. The nurses would take their blankets away and watch them shiver.

Maria came off the drugs there, only to relapse later. After a second round in Wittenau, she attempted suicide, only to be saved by a friend who found her in the nick of time. Her veterinary practice fell apart, she was arrested and ended up back in Wittenau, locked up alongside some of the hardest psychiatric cases, people broken and in extreme distress. Most unbearable of all, for her at least, was the hospital's children's ward. She never forgot the misery she saw there.

When she emerged from that third spell, she was destitute. Born into one of the grandest estates in what was then the German empire, Countess Maria von Maltzan now had not a penny to her name. She applied for official recognition as a 'politically persecuted person', and therefore eligible for compensation, arguing that the strain of the efforts she had made for victims of Nazism had led her to contract diseases of both the gallbladder and the heart, but her application was rejected. An official ruling came in February 1953, noting that she had never been jailed and had endured no other deprivation of liberty. It concluded: 'It has not been proven that she suffered significant damage to her health, or experienced other serious damage as a result of her political activity.'

There was no family wealth to draw on. Thanks to the post-war redrawing of borders, the Maltzan seat of Militsch was now in a foreign land, part of communist-ruled Poland and out of reach. All she knew of it was what she had heard from an old servant who had sought her out two years after the war's end. He told her that when the Russians came, they marked their conquest of the castle by digging up the bodies of her parents and scattering the bones, an expression of Bolshevik contempt for the hated nobility.

She went to the welfare office and accepted what they could give her, but the humiliation of it stung. Better to work than to take charity. She got shifts as a cleaner and a shelf-stacker and eventually found a permanent job doing the night watch at a hospital. Slowly she rebuilt her life, eventually recovering her veterinary licence. She worked at a slaughterhouse, she worked at a circus, she worked as a travelling locum for cattle. If human beings had disappointed Maria, her animals never did.

She stayed in touch with Hans throughout those years. He had married again but when his wife died, it was to Maruska that he turned. They had lunch together, then a drink, and soon they were living together again. In 1972, the countess and the Jew she had hidden thirty years earlier married for the second time.

As an unambiguous victim of Nazism, Hans had found work as a lay judge at the office responsible for compensation payments to those who had suffered under the Reich. The job depressed him, because it forced him to see just how many of those who had inflicted great suffering on others had got away with it. He and Maria would talk about 'the great forgetting' they believed was now under way in their country. Every day they would hear that it was time to stop talking about the Nazis, that these things belonged in the past. To Hans and Maria, it made no sense: there was still so much to say. And so they would say it to each other.

Later, she would think of those as the best years they shared, living in harmony. But their time together now was brief. In September 1975, Hans Hirschel died. His heart, which had withstood so much, could cope no more. His wife, who had saved him so many times, could not save him again.

Maria von Maltzan lived out her remaining years in Kreuzberg, then one of the roughest parts of Berlin, among the Turkish *Gastarbeiter*, the guest-worker migrants, and the punks. She was one of the neighbourhood's characters, the old lady vet with a pet monkey called Texy, the ageing aristocrat who could talk to junkies as one of their own. Not many knew who she was or what she had done.

She died in 1997, aged eighty-eight. Ten years earlier, Yad Vashem, the Holocaust memorial centre and museum in Jerusalem, awarded her its highest honour, declaring her one of the Righteous among the Nations, estimating that she had been instrumental in the saving of at least sixty Jewish lives. It invited her to a ceremony, where she would plant a eucalyptus tree and receive a medal. But she was unhappy at the military action Israel had just taken in Lebanon and, besides, she was not one for ceremonies. As she put it to a visiting interviewer, 'such things I really don't care for.' She didn't go.

68

Bearing Witness

Hanna and Lagi, April 1945

THE DAY SHE was freed from Moabit remand jail, Hanna Solf weighed next to nothing and owned even less: she had no food, no clothes, no place to live. Later, she would calculate that in the year that followed the end of the war she received welfare payments amounting to a grand total of thirty-five marks. She and her daughter, Lagi, had their freedom but that was all. They were homeless and penniless.

When Hanna finally saw a doctor, it was not just her weight that was a concern. She also had a heart condition, a swelling of the liver, bronchiectasis, damaged tendons and inflammation of the right forearm. Fifteen months as a prisoner, much of it in solitary confinement and under the threat of execution, had, together with hunger and cold, left their mark.

She and Lagi found themselves dependent successively on the British and US authorities in Berlin, before eventually the Swiss and finally the Red Cross took them into their care. By July 1946, she was in Monte Verità, a mountain village in Switzerland overlooking Lake Maggiore, where she and her daughter had several months to rest and rebuild themselves. But after everything they had endured, that was easier said than done. 'It's like a paradise where we don't really belong,' Hanna wrote to a friend. 'The physical recovery is quick, of course; you're like a dry sponge that soaks up water quickly. But the mental recovery is very slow, especially when you hear a lot of sad things from home.'

Each week brought more proof that all she and the others had feared about the wickedness of the Third Reich was true. If anything, in their secret salons and tea parties, they had underestimated the scale and depth of the depravity. A glimpse of it emerged at Nuremberg, where twenty-two surviving members of the Nazi leadership were tried by the Allied powers for the crime of waging aggressive war, crimes against humanity and war crimes. It was a landmark legal event and, on 15 April 1947, Hanna Solf was called as a witness in one of several subsequent trials into specific aspects of the Nazi regime, asked to testify about the tea party, the Solf Circle, her interrogation and imprisonment.

It would not be the last time. She would be asked to tell her story over and over again, testifying in person or in written depositions to multiple proceedings and hearings. She would often go out of her way to mention those who had stepped out of line to help, the prison guards who had broken the rules to give her a crumb of extra bread or allow her a few precious moments with her daughter. She had committed their names to memory – Fräulein Mussgnug, Fräulein Schulz, Fräulein Giensky – those who had 'the kindness and moral courage' to treat their captives as human beings. Hanna was ready to describe the worst in her countrymen, which she had experienced first hand, including 'the power that the Germans like to display over the defenceless'. But she also wanted the world to know that some Germans had refused to become engulfed by 'the unimaginable terror that . . . assumed increasingly horrific forms' in the last years of the Reich. When one sees that defiance, she said, 'one cannot praise it enough'.

For a while, Hanna was taken in by one of her sons who had been living in England when the war broke out in 1939 and had stayed. But as soon as she had recovered her financial footing, she moved back to Germany. Not Berlin this time, but the small, lakeside town of Starnberg in the south. There she stayed, living in relative seclusion with her housekeeper, Martha Richter, the same loyal servant who had been arrested with her that January morning in 1944.

Hanna was fifty-seven years old when the war ended, and might have expected to have had two or three decades ahead of her. But she was dead by 1954; her body had endured so much. She was buried in a modest grave in Starnberg, one that was soon covered in ivy and weeds and lay all but forgotten for the best part of seventy years. In 2020, a retired doctor came across it and persuaded the local council to take charge.

For Hanna's daughter, Lagi, the end of the war did not bring an end to her troubles. She was as destitute as her mother and her health in no less parlous a state, but her greatest worry concerned her husband. He did not return to her once the guns fell silent, but remained a prisoner of war, held by the British, until the autumn of 1945. Once released, he had no more money than his wife and had to look for work. Eventually Count Hubertus von Ballestrem became a social worker and later a prison guard for a Catholic charity that helped young delinquents, most of them uprooted by the war. Lagi worked alongside him, the two of them now engaged in an endeavour mercifully free of politics.

The couple did not have much, but they still managed to lose a good portion of it, swindled by a notorious criminal named Harry Kübler, who disappeared with their money, only to resurface in prison in Potsdam, in the Soviet-run east of the country. Doubtless hoping to recover what was his, or at least learn what had happened to it, Ballestrem responded to a request from Kübler that he visit him. The count travelled to Potsdam in August 1949 – but he did not come back that day or the day after. Lagi petitioned first the Soviet military government and then, following the establishment of East Germany as a distinct country in October that year, the new German Democratic Republic. But they told her nothing. For nine months she had no idea where her husband was or what had become of him.

Eventually, she received a short letter from Hubert, explaining that he had been sentenced to ten years in a labour camp. It turned out that Kübler was not only a con man; he had also been involved in espionage and now the count was accused of knowing about those activities and failing to report them to the Soviet authorities. He was given no chance to defend himself or explain that the charges were completely baseless. Instead, he was held in Potsdam, then transferred to the former concentration camp at Sachsenhausen, where his mother-in-law, Hanna Solf, had once been held. Her jailers had been Nazis, his were communists, but it was the same place. In 1951, he was classified as a particularly dangerous prisoner and transferred to Brandenburg-Görden, where he spent three years in solitary confinement. There he suffered a fate that would have been all too familiar to his wife and her mother: endless interrogation, hunger, humiliation and cold.

Lagi did all she could to battle the judicial bureaucracy of the Germany next door and to draw attention to her husband's plight. In 1952, the GDR's justice minister told her Hubert's case had been examined and his innocence established. But that was not enough: his original conviction had been determined by a Soviet tribunal and the GDR did not have the power to overturn its decisions. For two more years, Hubert remained trapped in a legal limbo between two communist states, each one unmoved by the fact that he had been an anti-fascist when it counted.

He finally came home to Lagi in 1954. For him, the age of tyranny had lasted more than two decades. He found work fairly quickly, even if it was not quite what he would once have expected: the count acted as a representative for a boiler-making company in the new West German capital of Bonn, ensuring the firm's interests and concerns were known by the federal government. But the hope that he and his wife might now, at last, have a life together, and perhaps a family, was to prove a vain one.

Lagi had been relentless in her fight to free her husband, but she was drawing on reserves of strength that were no longer there. The many months as an inmate, at Ravensbrück and elsewhere, had wrecked her health and any chance of recovery was ruined by both the scarcity of nutritious food after 1945 and the strain of battling not one country but two to get her husband back. In December 1955, Lagi Ballestrem-Solf died, thirteen months after her mother and leaving no children of her own. Her best years had been taken from her, along with so much else. She was forty-seven years old.

As a prisoner in Ravensbrück, she had left a deep impression on those who witnessed her bravery and what one would later describe as her 'magnificent aggressiveness towards the Gestapo'. She had stood up even to Lange, refusing to be cowed by his threats: *I am sorry; then you have to execute my mother.*

But once free, that spirit seemed to fade. She did not testify to her experiences as frequently as her mother, nor did she draw much comfort from the knowledge that in the great moral struggle of her age she had been on the right side. Instead, she felt the menace had not been defeated, that it was still all too present. As she wrote:

> I do not want to think of the past because it has lost its meaning. The world has learned nothing from it – neither slaughterers nor victims nor onlookers. Our time is like a dance of death whose uncanny rhythm is understood by few. Everyone whirls confusedly without seeing the abyss.

It was a tragic end to a tragic tale, the two women taking their places alongside Arthur Zarden, Elisabeth von Thadden and Otto Kiep as victims of Paul Reckzeh. And yet that was not the whole story.

When Hanna Solf stood before the judges at Nuremberg in April 1947, less than three years had passed since she had been badgered and barracked by a German judge in a sweltering Berlin courtroom, barely able to finish a sentence without being yelled at. In Nuremberg, she could calmly explain her own actions, defend the honour of her late husband and fulfil what she had always regarded as her highest duty: to show the world a different, better Germany. It was this mission that had, in some ways, driven her to defy Hitler in the first place. She told the tribunal that her country had become 'dominated by a party whose ideology I could not accept, and whose actions had brought us all to a deep disaster, and brought dishonour on the name of the German people for decades'.

Later she would write to a fellow former prisoner of the Nazis who, like her, had been a member of a dissenting circle, explaining: 'My most important task was to educate people from day one and to . . . show that there are also true Germans.' When she had been beating down the doors of embassies and using all her contacts to get Jews out of the country and to safety, that too had been part of her motivation, to demonstrate that there was another Germany. As she put it to that same former member of the resistance, 'Oh, I can't tell you how we tried to save people and our homeland from all the shame and disgrace.' She would use a phrase of her husband's to explain that what she had been fighting for was 'the boundless fatherland of the German spirit', a place that was not measured in acres of conquered land but rather in compassion and solidarity with others.

Her goal had been to show the rest of the world that not every German was like the leader who took power in 1933. And, in her own way, she achieved it. Today a portrait of Hanna Solf hangs in the museum of the German resistance in Berlin. Improbably, and thanks in part to a deliverance that came from the sky, she survived to testify that another Germany was possible. She was living proof of it.

69
Through the Generations

LAGI BALLESTREM-SOLF'S WIDOWED husband would live for another forty years, devoting much of that time to campaigning work, in Germany and abroad, for people with leprosy, eventually heading one of the leading international organisations in the field. In the same period, his contemporary Hilger van Scherpenberg, the man who told the People's Court he had resisted the defeatist talk he had heard at the tea party, built a successful post-war career of his own or, more accurately, he returned to the one he had had previously. No sooner had the Nazi regime fallen than Scherpenberg was back in the civil service, taking up a post in the Bavarian Ministry of Economic Affairs in 1945, before moving to the equivalent job in the federal government and eventually, in 1953, returning to the same trade policy department of the Foreign Ministry where he had been working when he found himself at the wrong tea party at the wrong time. He ended his diplomatic career as the West German ambassador to the Holy See in 1964, dying five years later.

Irmgard Zarden, the youngster at the tea party, would eventually settle in the US but only after a series of adventures. In the last days of the Reich, she had been on the move, determined to get out of Berlin before the whole edifice came tumbling down and the Russians arrived. At one point, she saw Heinrich Himmler, dressed in a simple military coat, in a hotel restaurant. She thought he looked green, like a man who knew that his crimes would soon catch up with him: he would poison himself a few days later.

At the very end, she was in a country boarding house, where rumour rather than hard information was the currency. One day, the pages of *Mein Kampf* appeared as toilet paper: the landlady had heard that the war was over. But the next day, when she learned that the war had not yet ended after all, the pages were quietly removed. Finally, on 8 May, came confirmation of an armistice and this time *Mein Kampf* stayed in the toilet.

Irmgard reached Hamburg, then part of the British zone, and soon found work with the occupiers, serving as secretary to a Captain Bingham, who was charged with the denazification of industry in the city. He knew nothing of the subject and spoke no German, so it fell to Irmgard and another assistant to determine who had been a Nazi and who had not.

A brief trip back to what had been the family home in Berlin confirmed that there was nothing there for her anymore. Both her parents were dead and, while the house stood empty, refugees and bombing victims had moved in. She left after a week.

The Zarden name still meant something to at least one German official working under the Allies, and his advice, coupled with the stamina to wait in long lines for several days at a stretch and the charm of a one-time heiress, meant that by March 1947 she had an exit visa for Switzerland and on, eventually, to the New World. There she would become Irmgard Ruppel, a mother and grandmother, passing away in 2018 three years short of her hundredth birthday.

The families of the two people executed for their role in the tea party did their best to rebuild. Otto Kiep's widow, Hanna, followed in her late husband's footsteps, joining the diplomatic corps of the German Federal Republic in 1949. Within two years, she had been posted to a women's affairs role at the consulate general in New York, the very place where she and Otto had made such a splash attending the lunch for Albert Einstein two decades earlier. She was in the US through the 1950s and 1960s, putting down roots in the country that would endure. Her daughter and namesake would spend much of her life in Windham, Connecticut, married to a pastor and theologian who wrote a biography of the father-in-law he had never met, Otto Kiep. The younger Hanna Kiep was deeply involved in her local church and in founding and running a soup kitchen: having known need as a child, she wanted to do what she could for the poor and the homeless.

THROUGH THE GENERATIONS

The impact of Elisabeth von Thadden on her own family was less straightforward. Her father had had two sets of children, with Elisabeth the eldest of the five he had with his first wife. But he had six more with his second wife, and the eldest of those, a boy, was born in 1921, nearly thirty years after Elisabeth. When she was executed, he was twenty-three years old. His name was Adolf.

Adolf von Thadden had joined the Nazi party on the day war broke out, and he would see combat as a lieutenant in the Wehrmacht. In 1946, he entered politics for the Deutsche Reichspartei, the German Reich Party of the ultra-nationalist far right which by 1952 had made the shift to dog-whistle neo-Nazism. He spent much of the 1950s as both an elected member of the Bundestag and as a fixture in a social circle that included Edda Göring and Ilse Hess as well as the British fascist leader Oswald Mosley. Indeed, in 1962 Thadden and Mosley would launch what they hoped would become a pan-European fascist movement: the National European Party. Over the next decade, the assorted groupings of the German far right coalesced into the National Democratic Party of Germany and in 1967, Adolf von Thadden became its leader, advocating the return to Germany from Poland of Danzig, now Gdansk, along with a second Anschluss. In an unfortunate lapse during a TV interview, Thadden referred to his party not as national democrats but as national socialists.

He withdrew from frontline politics in the 1970s, and did not live long enough to see the reports that surfaced in 2002 claiming that he had acted as an intelligence agent of the British security service MI6, possibly since the 1950s. Speculation suggested that he had been recruited along with other European far rightists when western intelligence agencies were preoccupied by the rise of the radical left.

And yet, if one of Elisabeth's siblings had taken the path towards those who had destroyed her, others headed in the opposite direction. A nephew composed a chamber opera to commemorate his aunt's courage and he called it *Widerstehen*: Resistance. One scene consisted of a cacophonous montage of audio clips, chopped-up recordings of the rantings of Judge Roland Freisler, played in darkness.

And then there was Anza, the sister whose fiftieth birthday

Elisabeth von Thadden had wanted to celebrate on 10 September 1943. She lived until 1985. Called four decades earlier to testify against her sister at the People's Court, she remained unforgiving and implacable to the end on the subject of the man whose betrayal had sent Elisabeth to the guillotine. She told a niece that she considered Paul Reckzeh to be one of the 'desk killers' that were such a feature of the Nazi era, those who did not bring death to others 'out of conviction but out of self-interest', in Reckzeh's case probably nothing more profound than a desire to avoid military service at the front. In Anza's mind, there could be no doubt that Reckzeh knew precisely what fate would befall his victims once they had been hauled before Freisler. He knew where his actions would lead. Short of operating the guillotine himself, he could have done no more to condemn Elisabeth von Thadden to death.

What, then, became of the traitor to the traitors? What became of Paul Reckzeh?

PART VII
The Traitor

70

'The Defendant Is to Blame'

May 1945

DR PAUL RECKZEH had spent the final months of the war working as a medical examiner in a well-appointed military hospital in Berlin, but at the end of May 1945 he was arrested by the Main Administration for Counterintelligence of the People's Commissariat for Defence of the USSR, which was the long name for the body that would become renowned as 'SMERSH', a portmanteau coinage of Joseph Stalin himself which translated as 'Death to Spies'. The men from SMERSH proceeded to interrogate Reckzeh about his past service to the Gestapo. They asked him if he could name the people who had been arrested as a result of his reports to the secret police. 'I couldn't know that,' he said. 'I wasn't told anything about this by the Gestapo.' Eventually, he conceded that it was safe to 'assume' that everyone present at the Thadden tea party had been arrested.

But that was as close to making a confession of guilt as he would get. Instead, he sought to persuade his Russian captors that he was a good man unfairly maligned. In June, he wrote to the commandant of the camp where he was held in Frankfurt an der Oder, explaining that he was a specialist in internal diseases and that

> I was probably arrested on the basis of false information from people I did not know. My political credo is determined by my medical profession. My job has always been to heal both enemy and friend. As an example, I would like to point out that during the entire Nazi regime I provided work, medication and medical help to my acquaintances, some of whom were of Jewish descent, and generally tried to protect them in every way from the Nazi government.

351

Conscience, he claimed, had prompted him to desert the German army back in April. He had gone into hiding in Berlin, waiting for the Red Army to arrive, so that he could immediately volunteer his medical services to them, which he had done. Truth be told, he had been in hiding for years, compelled to conceal his true, anti-Nazi beliefs. Admittedly, he had joined the Nazi party in July 1933 – in fact, he had signed up on the first day of May – but that was only because he had been forced to do so in order to continue his studies at Berlin University. He had held no positions in the party, he wrote, adding for good measure a request that 'my application be examined as quickly as possible, especially in order to eliminate the suffering my family has had inflicted on them by the Nazi government'. He was presenting himself as someone who had not collaborated with Nazism but defied it, and whose family had paid a price for his principles.

His request was denied and he remained a prisoner awaiting trial, held in, among other places, the facility the Red Army had set up on the site of the former Nazi concentration camp at Buchenwald. In a camp at Jamlitz, he was used as a prison doctor, where he soon developed a reputation. Several times he took a beating from his fellow inmates, who accused him of stealing bread from his comrades and of only treating those among the sick who could afford to pay, again in bread.

Nearly five years went by. Nothing could happen until the Soviet military had passed administrative authority to the newly created GDR and a court system had been established for East Germany. Finally, in February 1950, Reckzeh was handed over to the new country's Ministry of the Interior; by June of that year he had been tried and convicted 'as an informer and denunciator'. The verdict declared:

> The defendant is to blame for the punishment of many anti-fascists through his activity as an agent . . . Through his position, he used his influence and his relationships with the Gestapo to bring about the suppression of political dissidents through coercion and threats. As an informer, he denounced anti-fascist people to the Gestapo if they verbally rebelled against the fascist tyranny and was therefore

fully responsible for initiating proceedings to the detriment of the political opponents of national socialism.

It further noted that 'His statements often led to the imposition of severe sentences', before concluding: 'The defendant is therefore guilty of aiding and abetting crimes against humanity.' On 3 June 1950, he was sentenced to fifteen years in prison by the regional court in Waldheim.

But if justice seemed to have been done, it would not hold for long. Less than two years into his sentence, Reckzeh received a pardon from the president of the GDR, on the recommendation of the Commission for Early Release. It was a puzzle that, to some at least, would only begin to make sense decades later.

71

'A Congenital Psychopathy'

1952

O NCE FREED, PAUL Reckzeh returned to the man whose shadow Bianca Segantini had believed he longed to escape: he went to work for his father's medical practice in West Berlin. Inge, who had been at his side for the pivotal lunch with Bianca in Switzerland in the late summer of 1943, was no longer his wife: the couple were legally confirmed as divorced in July 1951, while he was serving that spell in prison. But he would be back with his family, including Ingeborg, the daughter he and Inge had had together, born a year after the tea party in September 1944.

Even so, his past did not stay past for long. Hearing that he was now in West Germany, Hanna Solf joined with some of the surviving guests at the Carmerstrasse gathering, as well as the relatives of those who had not survived, to demand Paul Reckzeh's arrest. The judicial authorities of the federal republic suddenly found themselves torn. On the one hand, they did not consider the GDR legal process that had already convicted Reckzeh to be legitimate, so they issued an arrest warrant. On the other, it was a principle of the law − double jeopardy − that no one could be tried for the same crime twice. So, having issued the arrest warrant, the authorities promptly suspended it in October 1952, pending an investigation into how best to deal with the Waldheim verdict. When it came to the case of the treacherous doctor and those like him, the law was in two minds.

In 1954, the West German courts decided that all the Waldheim convictions were invalid in principle. Nevertheless, in practice, there was not yet enough evidence for the authorities to lift the specific block on Paul Reckzeh's arrest warrant. So they began to gather it.

They took statements from witnesses, including yet another full account from Hanna Solf to match one she had given two years earlier. Once again she recalled the events of the tea party, how Reckzeh was 'completely unknown' to her until that day, and how, before the People's Court, he had falsely claimed that she had instructed him to contact the exiled German chancellor, Joseph Wirth, when nothing of the sort had happened. That much was familiar, but new facts emerged too.

A former medical colleague told how he had been arrested in January 1944 and remained in custody till March for a supposed 'connection to Jews in Switzerland'. He had no doubt who was behind it: 'For me, it is clear that Dr Reckzeh handed me over to the Gestapo.' A retired police constable recalled how, during the war, he had had to visit the address of the then SS doctor Paul Reckzeh several times following the terrified complaints of his landlady, a Frau Weber, who said that the young doctor had 'tyrannised' her. The policeman testified that Reckzeh had told him 'he would kill the highly strung woman if she was not picked up by the Gestapo' first. Frau Weber was eventually arrested and handed over to the secret police, the implication clear that Reckzeh had used his position to denounce and condemn a woman who had become an irritant to him.

Most dramatically, this new legal process heard from a witness who had remained silent until now, someone uniquely placed to shed fresh and revealing light on the case. Called as a witness in June 1954 was one Professor Paul Reckzeh – not the young physician who had betrayed his fellow guests at the tea party, but his father.

Reckzeh Snr acknowledged that he had been advised of his right to refuse to testify, but explained that he wanted to be heard. The examining judge had asked about his son's physical and mental development and that is what he was ready to address.

He said that the boy had a history of pancreatic tuberculosis. The illness that had driven him to seek treatment in the Swiss mountains in 1943 was in fact a relapse. But that was far from the younger Reckzeh's only malady. 'Mentally and psychologically, he suffered from an inferiority complex from an early age, perhaps due to his father's strict upbringing,' Professor Reckzeh said, speaking of himself with professional detachment. 'In addition,' he went on, 'there was a congenital psychopathy, probably on an inherited basis, since some forebears had ended their lives by suicide. As a result of this psychopathy, a strong servility was conspicuous from childhood.'

He said he had noticed the tendency in his son early. It was first manifested in his behaviour with other children, and persisted into adolescence. He was obedient at home and capable as a student, if 'not always diligent and easily distracted', but he was 'extremely nervous'. One of his teachers had described him as 'an absolute bundle of nerves'. That psychological stress manifested itself in convulsions, especially when there were high expectations of young Paul Reckzeh, but it had also happened during the summer holidays, 'after exposure to strong sunlight'.

The condition did not fade with adulthood. On the contrary, the now retired physician revealed that three times his son had

> threatened to commit suicide, once when we parents did not give him permission to marry an actress, once in the last weeks of the war, when he suffered from constant fear, once because of military difficulties. During this mental depression, he threatened to shoot himself with his service pistol in two cases, and to poison himself with a narcotic in the third.

If the court suspected that the father was trying to diminish the son's responsibility for his actions, casting him as the victim of mental illness, a 'congenital psychopathy' no less, for which he should not be punished, that suspicion would have only grown with what Professor Reckzeh said next. Having first shifted the blame onto his son's genes, he now sought to shift it further away still – onto the younger man's wife.

The boy was in thrall to Inge, locked in 'an extraordinarily strong and fatal bondage' to her, even though she was slovenly and 'neglected her housewifely duties', his father said. It was she who had 'encouraged him to go to Switzerland', and such was her power over him, he could hardly refuse. It all got worse when their child was born, because Inge fell into a psychosis of her own. 'She completely rejected the child.' Indeed, the doctors advised that she be placed in an institution, because she had expressed the intention to kill both herself and her daughter. The Reckzehs tried committing her, but she ended up at home with them 'for weeks', where the talk of suicide and 'the desire to "get rid of" the child' did not let up.

This, the father, explained was the context for the couple's divorce. Inge had been talking about it before her breakdown, but there was a brief hope that she might drop the idea once the war was over. Odd as it may seem, his son had been able to come home in June 1945, even though he had been arrested by the Russians a month earlier: it seems the Red Army were using him as a doctor and were prepared to escort him back to his parental home so that he could pick up some much-needed medicines. The couple were able to spend the night together and seemed reconciled. The son reassured his father that there would be no divorce. But he was wrong. Inge's mind was made up. Her husband pleaded for her to reconsider, 'if only because of the child, which is our flesh and blood', but she would not bend. The marriage was dissolved, 'by mutual consent' in law if not in fact.

The retired doctor had offered the court the profile of a weak, mentally unwell man bound to a demanding, unstable woman, but he had one more piece of exculpatory evidence to offer.

'In the autumn of 1943,' he said, 'I learned that my son . . . wanted to travel to Switzerland again.' Reckzeh Jnr had visited earlier that summer and his father worried that another such absence would put his son's job in jeopardy. And so, without telling his son that he was doing it, the father went to see Leo Lange in the Reich Security Main Office. 'I told Detective Counsellor Lange of my fears and asked him not to help my son travel to Switzerland again.'

With that statement, Reckzeh Snr had admitted that he had known his son was working for the Gestapo. But next came the attempt to deny the younger man's culpability. Lange, he said, had been unfriendly throughout the conversation; still the tone turned much darker once he heard Reckzeh Snr's request. The Gestapo officer said, 'If your son does not carry out an order that we give him in the interests of the state, it will cost him his head.'

The professor asked if he could pass on this information to his wife, but Lange was clear: if he breathed a word to anyone, he would find himself arrested. The old doctor told the court that he came away from that meeting convinced that the younger Reckzeh was now completely under the control of Lange. The 'strong servility' he had diagnosed in his son as a child seemed to have manifested itself yet again, directed this time not at friends or his wife but at a senior officer of the Gestapo.

So this was why Dr Reckzeh did not deserve to be punished for his betrayal of the tea-party group. In his father's telling, he was a weak, mentally ill man compelled to do the bidding of the Gestapo on pain of death. He could not be blamed because he was himself a victim.

Whether a court would have found any of that believable, or merely an attempt by a father to get his son out of a deep hole, could not yet be tested because of the legal limbo in which the Reckzeh case was still suspended. For now, the West German courts chose to inflict what modest punishment they could within the law: they stripped Reckzeh of his doctor's licence.

It would take until 19 March 1955 for the authorities finally to decide they had enough to go to trial, and so the order that had protected Reckzeh was lifted. From that day on, he was vulnerable; he could be picked up at any time. Reckzeh was not meant to know that decision had been taken but someone clearly tipped him off. On 24 March, he fled from one side of Berlin to the other, taking refuge in the east before the police in West Berlin had a chance to knock on his door. He immediately sought asylum, which was granted: the last thing an East German court wanted to do was comply with a verdict of the west. In that same spirit, when a request arrived from West Germany seeking Reckzeh's extradition, it was rejected.

Barred from practising medicine in the west, on the eastern side of the divide he remained Dr Reckzeh. His ID card showed his body had taken a battering in the preceding years – 'leg damage, liver damage on both sides, lung damage, heart damage' – but none of that prevented his appointment to a senior physician's post in the Perleberg district hospital.

It was curious, the speed and warmth with which he was embraced by a state that had, just a few years earlier, convicted him of complicity in crimes against humanity. No less curious was the way he had received a pardon just two years into his sentence for those crimes. Was it just the well-documented pleasure Cold War adversaries took in winning a defector over from the other side? Or was there a darker explanation?

72

'Such Dirty Things'

1955

THE EXPLANATION MAY not have been that complicated, even if it would remain hidden for many decades. Soon after his arrival in the east, Paul Reckzeh caught the eye of the Ministerium für Staatssicherheit, the Ministry for State Security. It was the body that liked to think of itself as the 'shield and sword' of the ruling communist party and it was more commonly known as the Stasi.

In a 1955 memo discussing Reckzeh, the order was given. 'Prepare him as a GI and get him to sign up.' GI stood for *Geheimer Informator*. They wanted to recruit him as a secret informer.

The Stasi bided their time, making their first approach late the following year through an agent in the Perleberg district office. Reckzeh was open to the conversation and quite forthcoming, seeming to speak with great candour. He admitted he had been a 'very active Nazi', and that he had worked for the Gestapo, though of course he regretted all that now. Indeed, he suggested it was his remorse for the past that now compelled him to refuse to become a formal source for the Stasi. As his would-be recruiter recorded it, Reckzeh insisted 'he will never again indulge in such dirty things as he did before 1945'.

But for all the protestations that he was now a changed man, and for all his father's earlier insistence that he had worked for the Gestapo under deadly pressure, Reckzeh agreed to have further 'discussions'. It's easy to see why the Stasi were keen to keep talking. In those clandestine conversations, Reckzeh was a natural. Adamant though he was that his informing days were behind him, he left his handler in no doubt: 'He always has his ears open so that he hears everything.' Even in that first meeting, Reckzeh had willingly reported on his superiors and colleagues, singling out for criticism the director of the clinic, who he suggested should be regarded as suspect. (The Stasi agent concluded that Reckzeh aspired to the more senior man's job.) In a subsequent conversation, Reckzeh spoke more freely still. A formal recruit he may not have been, but the doctor was happy to provide the Stasi with exactly what they needed. He named one colleague who had 'connections in the West', adding for good measure, 'These kinds of people, who are always speaking well of the West, should be examined more closely.'

When Reckzeh transferred to a clinic in Wildau in 1958, the Stasi had another crack. They were satisfied that this ambitious man in his mid-forties had become a committed citizen of the socialist republic, not least because a return to West Berlin was now barred to him, with that warrant for his arrest still outstanding. What's more, the Stasi men noted, he said all the right things, voicing 'healthy views that serve our cause' with a political awareness absent among most of his profession. To take one practical example, Dr Reckzeh was not a soft touch for patients who sought a sick note 'for every little thing'. On the contrary, he would 'represent the interests of our state' by explaining matters to the reluctant worker and 'convincing him of what is right through education'. Paul Reckzeh had been a good Nazi, and now he was a good communist.

But it was not to last. By 1963, the Ministry for State Security was revising its view of its previously admired source.

> The political attitude of Dr Reckzeh, Paul, towards the socialist development in the GDR is negative . . . outwardly he appears to have a very positive manner towards comrades and progressive people and repeatedly shows what a conscious citizen he is. In reality, however, he orients himself towards the West in all matters.

But the problem was not solely ideological. 'R. does not have a good reputation among the doctors in the polyclinic. He is seen as a careerist with a strong tendency to dishonesty.' Once the Stasi had confirmed Reckzeh's determination to be appointed chief physician at the hospital, they decided to break off contact altogether: he may have been willing to inform on his colleagues, but his motives were all wrong. Besides, they noted, as if discovering it for the first time, 'R. was a notorious Gestapo spy, and many upstanding communists paid the price for his work. Even today he has not yet drawn any conclusions from his punishment and is playing a political double game.'

At last, it seemed, Paul Reckzeh's deeds were about to catch up with him. In 1964, the Committee of Anti-Fascist Resistance Fighters in the GDR launched an investigation of its own into the doctor. Once it was complete, the committee submitted an application for Dr Reckzeh to be struck off, his licence to practise medicine revoked. The application was rejected, but it was a sign of things to come.

In 1966, there came an order from on high that Reckzeh 'should receive no further opportunities for advancement in his medical career'. The edict seemed to be linked to a tip-off the Stasi had received from their counterparts in Czechoslovakia, reporting that while at a cardiology conference in Prague, Reckzeh had looked into the possibility of getting hold of a Swiss or Austrian passport. Perhaps sensing his new vulnerability, it seemed the man who had defected from west to east was hoping to defect back the other way. True or not, his professional progress in the socialist republic was now officially blocked.

The walls seemed to be closing in. That same year, a letter from a US-based historian reached the GDR bureaucracy asking after the whereabouts of a former Gestapo spy by the name of Dr Reckzeh. Officials recorded their decision 'Not to provide an answer for political-operational reasons', but it added to the sense that Reckzeh had become a headache that needed to be addressed. In 1967, the GDR decided to see for itself the files from Roland Freisler's People's Court and from the Soviet authorities that had imprisoned Reckzeh; by October a 'plan of action' had been settled on, one aimed at 'compiling evidence to expose the incriminated person Dr Reckzeh, Paul'. Eighteen months later, the Stasi would note that

> the recorded person Dr Reckzeh . . . is listed in the West German book of arrest warrants for the month of January 1969 for murder . . . We request that you take note and, if necessary, take action in accordance with the Comrade Minister's Order 23/67.

'SUCH DIRTY THINGS'

By 1971, Reckzeh was under intensive Stasi surveillance. Now, in a reversal of the fate he had inflicted on the tea-party group nearly a quarter century earlier, his telephone was tapped and his post opened.

And yet, though he was in their sights for a decade or more, the East German authorities never did move in on the Nazi spy in their midst. Was that because they were persuaded by the argument Reckzeh made to his Stasi not-quite-handlers, that the net tightening around him was the handiwork of senior figures in West Germany, convinced he had wronged them decades earlier? The two men he had in mind were Reinold von Thadden, then president of the German Evangelical Church Congress, since, as the Stasi officers put it, 'his sister was executed based on Dr R's message to the Gestapo', and Hilger van Scherpenberg, once a tea-party guest but then West Germany's ambassador to the Vatican, who would likewise 'ensure that Dr R is held accountable'.

Or was there a murkier explanation, one that stretched back to the immediate aftermath of the war? After all, Reckzeh had enjoyed a remarkably long run of luck. Plenty of the active Nazis tried in the earliest days of the GDR had been sentenced to death, but Reckzeh's punishment was only fifteen years in jail. Of that, he had served a mere twenty-seven months thanks to the mercy of a pardon. The veterans of the war against fascism had tried to strip him of his doctor's licence, but they had failed: the authorities had sided with Reckzeh. In Prague he had tried to obtain the exit papers needed to make an illegal break for the west and yet, though 'passport and foreign exchange offences' were punished severely in East Germany, he was left untouched. Even the edict that his medical career be frozen was not enforced: he continued to be promoted. What's more, he lived a life of privilege by the standards of the GDR. The state security agents who monitored him could never explain why this mid-ranking, small-town doctor always drove an imported western car, a luxury that required the permission of the responsible ministry and was granted to few.

As they investigated him, the Stasi began to work up a theory as to why a one-time Nazi like Reckzeh had repeatedly escaped the consequences of his behaviour. In internal correspondence, they wondered again about that early release from jail in 1952. Some speculated that a historic favour had been returned, that Reckzeh's father had once treated V. I. Lenin himself when the future Bolshevik leader was in Germany. But a less sentimental transaction occurred to the Stasi officials as more likely. 'What were the reasons for Reckzeh's release?' asked one Stasi memo. 'After his release, did he work in any way for the Soviet friends?' After all, given that 'Dr Reckzeh travels to socialist countries and meets with Western citizens there, there is a possibility that the Soviet friends are working with him'. That delicate formulation, 'Soviet friends', was how the Stasi referred to their opposite numbers in Moscow: the KGB.

So maybe that was why Paul Reckzeh had kept getting away with it, and why he had refused to be signed up as an official agent of the Stasi. Not because he had genuinely put the 'dirty things' of his Gestapo past behind him, but rather because he had found an even more powerful master to serve, one that would protect him for decades.

If that was the case, then surely the fall of that master, the collapse of the Soviet Union along with the dissolution of the GDR, the KGB and the Stasi, would finally expose him to justice. That was certainly the hope of those who still remembered what Paul Reckzeh had done more than forty-five years earlier. Only one of his direct victims was still alive in the 1990s. She had been the youngest guest at the tea party of 1943 and had made a new life in America. But she had forgotten nothing.

73

'Can You Sleep?'

1990

IN LATE SEPTEMBER 1990, the reunification of Germany was days away and Irmgard Zarden, now Irmgard Ruppel of New York, made a journey back to the old country, hoping that justice might, at last, be done. If there had been a way of holding Herbert 'Leo' Lange to account, he could well have been her prime target. But Lange had melted away with the rest of the Third Reich. By the spring of 1945, all trace of the Special Commission that had once borne his name had vanished and so had he. It was said that he had left Berlin around Christmas 1944, fearing Allied bombs. A superior added that Lange had joined a security police battalion based in Fürstenberg near Ravensbrück in the war's final months, returning close to the place where he had inflicted such torment on the tea-party group. Others claimed he had been killed defending a building in Posen, soon to revert to its Polish name of Poznán, or fighting the Red Army in Bernau, just a few miles north-east of Berlin. After the war, Hanna Solf was sure she spotted him: Lange immediately fled. Later, he was reported to have resurfaced in the east, having made the ideological journey from right to left: now he was working for the state security service of the GDR, the Stasi. Indeed, by 1949 the West Berlin papers had Lange back to doing what he did best, claiming he now served the GDR as the 'chief of a special interrogation office'.

A decade later, however, and Lange's career seemed to have stalled: a CIA report identified him as a police commissioner in East Berlin 'in charge of motor vehicles'. Less than two decades earlier, he had been despatching gas vans around Poland tasked with the cutting-edge work of murdering Jews and those deemed mentally defective in their thousands, placing him at the forefront of the creation of a new master race. Now he was handing out parking tickets.

But thirty years on, there was no sign of him. If Irmgard were to have even a measure of justice for the death of her father and her own imprisonment, she would have to look elsewhere. For that reason, there was one particular trip she had to make.

With a friend, who also happened to be a lawyer, she drove to Zeuthen, south-east of Berlin. She knew what she was looking for and she found it, a beautiful property on the lake, with a large garden and a double garage, the house set well back. Parked outside was a Mercedes-Benz, a car beyond the reach of almost every other citizen of the GDR. Irmgard had wanted to know how Lange's informant, Dr Paul Reckzeh, lived and now she knew. Her father had thrown himself from a window because of this man, but for Reckzeh himself, now seventy-seven years old, things had worked out pretty well.

On 2 October 1990, Irmgard did two things. First, she channelled her rage into two postcards, written in a furious, bellowing string of capital letters, which she posted to the house on the lake. The first read:

HERR RECKZEH!
YOUR CRIME AS A GESTAPO INFORMER WAS AIDING AND ABETTING MURDER. THROUGH YOUR DENUNCIATIONS, MY FATHER TOOK HIS OWN LIFE IN PRISON IN 1944, AND ELISABETH V. THADDEN AND OTTO KIEP WERE EXECUTED BY THE GUILLOTINE. ARE YOU ASHAMED?
IRMGARD ZARDEN

She had drawn a box around the words *Gestapospitzel*, Gestapo informer, and *Mord*, murder, for extra emphasis. As for the second postcard, it showed an image from the Ravensbrück Memorial Centre. Irmgard had drawn an arrow pointing to a window on the second floor of the cell block. The message read:

HERR RECKZEH!
CAN YOU SLEEP AFTER YOU, AS A GESTAPO SNITCH, BROUGHT MY FATHER TO HIS DEATH AND ME TO THE CELL OVERLEAF?
IRMGARD ZARDEN

The other thing Irmgard did on 2 October 1990, which would be the last full day of the GDR's existence before German reunification, was to apply for a reopening of the case against Paul Reckzeh on charges of aiding and abetting murder. Slowly, her petition worked its way through the newly unified system, passed from one court to the next, until, in 1993, she was notified that there would be no resumption of proceedings after all. In a case such as this, where the crime was more akin to manslaughter than murder, the statute of limitations had run out at least eight years earlier. A Berlin court had decided that the file on Paul Reckzeh, catalogued as StA Berlin 3 P (K) Js 68/62, should be closed. Irmgard wrote to the German president and he wrote back expressing great sympathy, but there was nothing he could do: the law was the law.

At one point, Irmgard's lawyer was told that the whole question was academic since Reckzeh had died in 1993. But that, like so much else in the life of Paul Reckzeh, turned out to be a lie. In fact, he had moved west once more and was living quietly in Hamburg. There he would remain until his death in 1996, aged eighty-two.

It had been a life of deception and betrayal, in which he had served each of the twin gods of twentieth-century totalitarianism, fascism and Bolshevism, in succession. And yet, that was not the sum total of his life's work. It seems Paul Reckzeh had had one more great betrayal in him – and its victim was much closer to home.

74

Betrayal

In the early 1950s, Paul Reckzeh had found himself young-ish, entering his forties; free, in that he was no longer a captive of either the GDR or the Soviet Union; and single, now that his marriage had ended in divorce. He was a doctor in West Berlin, ready to start on the next chapter of his life.

Someone had the idea of organising a reunion of those who had been imprisoned in the east and Reckzeh went along. There he met a woman in her late twenties, Ruth Hensel, who had been captured almost at random by the invading Russians in 1945 and held prisoner for two years. She was training as a nurse; she fell for the doctor and soon they were married. When, fearing a new trial, he fled to the GDR in 1955, she went with him. Soon they would have a daughter, Barbara, and a son, Paul-Günther.

Reckzeh family holidays tended to be in other parts of the communist bloc, with Hungary a favoured destination. During one vacation in Lake Balaton in the summer of 1973, seventeen-year-old Barbara met a boy a year older than her. His name was Michael Böttcher and they fell for each other instantly. She had, he said, 'such beautiful, big eyes'. But their stars were crossed. She was from the east, and he was from the west. At the end of the summer they had shared together, she had to return with her parents to East Berlin and he would fly back to Hamburg. They would be separated, an iron curtain keeping them apart.

They pined for each other. She sent him 532 letters, including one that issued a simple plea from the heart: 'I love you, please come!' He could bear it no longer and, since travel from west to east was not prohibited, Michael got a GDR visa and found himself standing outside Schillerstrasse 19 in Zeuthen, the Reckzeh family home. He had heard all about the drab, austere Germany on the other side of the border, with its rabbit-hutch apartment blocks. This was not that.

Young as he was, Michael knew enough about the GDR to know that retired doctors did not live in detached, lakefront houses with a Mercedes parked outside and art on the wall. (Among the works displayed was a print of the 1886 painting *Ave Maria a trasbordo* by Giovanni Segantini, the same Segantini whose daughter, Bianca, had smoothed Reckzeh's path to the tea party of September 1943. It was there in Zeuthen, as a permanent reminder.) This man was clearly some kind of high-ranking official. Still, none of that mattered. He and Barbara were together, they loved each other and within a year they were engaged to be married.

Except being together was not quite enough, for Michael at least. He was determined that he and his bride should make their future in the west. He explained this to his prospective father-in-law, setting out his hope of returning to the federal republic with Barbara, officially, if he could. But if that was not possible, he would find another way. The doctor and his wife would be able to visit their daughter in the west often; they were now pensioners, allowed by law to travel back and forth across the border. There was really nothing for the Reckzehs to fear.

Now, Paul Reckzeh's colleagues had regarded him as untrustworthy from the start. His wife's friends found him creepy and pompous, whether because of his tendency to pepper any conversation with Latin tags or his constant bragging. His own relatives believed he exploited his position as a doctor for personal gain: he would trade medical consultations not for money, which had no real value in East Germany, but for extra supplies, often basic household items including light bulbs and toilet paper. All those years earlier, Bianca Segantini had diagnosed in him 'Moral weakness, laziness, addiction to material advantages and a desire for recognition'. Those closest to Ruth feared her husband exerted a controlling hold on her so complete, it literally crippled her: she was left severely disabled by neck and spine problems because she would not submit to surgery, against which he had an implacable prejudice. But now young Michael saw something else in Paul Reckzeh: an unbiddable anger.

He began shouting at his daughter's fiancé, dismissing any idea that he might allow Barbara to live in the west. 'Absolutely out of the question. Or do you think I'm here voluntarily?'

At the time, Michael did not understand what Reckzeh meant. But he would not have to wait long to find out.

The young lovers had worked out an escape route. In those years, organisers from the west could be hired to help those in the east looking to get out and Michael enlisted a couple to extract Barbara: Christiane Dirrigi, a nurse from West Berlin and her boyfriend, Leopold Spindler, or Poldi. The method was well rehearsed. Christiane would travel from West to East Berlin, a journey allowed to citizens of the federal republic, where she would pick up Barbara. The two would then drive out of the city and onto the motorway network heading for the rest stop at Michendorf, whose singular advantage was that it served the link road that connected the enclave of West Berlin with the rest of West Germany. Regular GDR traffic ran through Michendorf too, which made it a rare meeting place of the two Germanies. On a warm day, you might see citizens of the GDR and FRG sharing an outdoor table together, sipping coffee before getting back behind the wheel.

The place was closely watched by the Stasi, naturally, but if you choreographed it right, it was possible to slip into a vehicle that bore the plates of the federal republic and was allowed to cross from east to west. Poldi would be waiting at Michendorf and, as seamlessly as they could, Barbara would transfer from Christiane's car to his green Opel Admiral: she would curl up and hide in the boot as he drove west. So long as she could sit tight until they had gone through the Helmstedt border crossing, Barbara could eventually unfold herself from her hiding place, safe in the knowledge that she had left the GDR behind – and that she and Michael could live happily ever after.

At the appointed hour, 9 p.m., on the appointed day, Saturday, 12 August 1978, Michael Böttcher stood and waited on the western side of the Helmstedt crossing. For those on the other side of the divide, it was known as the Marienborn crossing, but for the Allies who drew the map, divided the defeated enemy into two and set up this whole system, this was Checkpoint Alpha, a nod to its status as the principal land crossing. (Checkpoint Bravo was the Allied name for their side of the crossing for entry into West Berlin, while the Allied entry into and exit from East Berlin was, famously, Checkpoint Charlie.)

Michael was nervous, chain-smoking. He wanted to see that Opel Admiral, carrying his bride towards him. But the minutes ticked by, the cars kept coming through the gate, one after another, and none of them contained Barbara. Nine p.m. became 10 and 10 became 11. At 11.30, he gave up. He did not know when or at what stage their plan had failed, but he understood: there was to be no escape.

What he did not yet know was that Christiane had picked up Barbara at the agreed meeting place in East Berlin and they had driven together to the Michendorf rest stop, exactly as planned. Half an hour later, Poldi arrived and began walking towards them, as planned. But, as Christiane would later explain in a phone call to Michael in Hamburg, 'When Leopold appeared, he walked past us as if he didn't know us.' He blanked them. Christiane realised instantly what that meant. 'Poldi was signalling to us, "We are being watched."'

Leopold bought some cigarettes, got back in his car and kept driving. When he reached Marienborn, the town on the East German side of the border facing Helmstedt, he was arrested. Meanwhile, Christiane and Barbara drove back to East Berlin and parted there. Christiane returned to West Berlin, but when she crossed back into the east for another meet-up the next day, she too was arrested. Now both of the helpers were held by the GDR, each facing five years in prison.

Initially, it seemed that Michael, an out-of-towner, had blundered by hiring an escape agency that streetwise West Berliners had long suspected was infiltrated by the Stasi. But a more sinister explanation suggested itself, one that would be swiftly confirmed.

Thwarted at that first attempt, Barbara tried to hatch an escape plan of her own. She headed to East Berlin's Schönefeld airport, her destination the land where her romance with Michael had begun: Hungary. But she got no further than the terminal building in Berlin: the Stasi had got there first and promptly arrested her. And yet no one had known about that flight, certainly no Stasi-infiltrated escape agency. No one knew, except for Barbara herself, her mother and her father: Dr Paul Reckzeh.

In Hamburg, Michael had done some digging. He now learned of the past of his father-in-law-to-be, how he had been a member of the Nazi party and a Gestapo agent, how he was still wanted in West Germany for his role in sending at least two people to their deaths. Now that outburst of Reckzeh's made sense. *Do you think I'm here voluntarily?* Of course. If his daughter moved to West Berlin, he could not visit her: he could not so much as set foot in the west without facing the risk of arrest and trial as a Gestapo spy with blood on his hands.

Michael sat alone in his apartment in Hamburg, reading and rereading those 532 letters from the woman he loved, clinging especially to the one that read, 'Put your hand where you feel your heart. It's mine.' He was convinced that their love had been undone by his bride's own father. He believed Reckzeh had informed on his daughter. As Michael Böttcher told a German journalist less than a month after he had stood in the dark at the Helmstedt border crossing, waiting for a woman who never came, 'I am firmly convinced that Reckzeh betrayed Barbara's escape plans to the Stasi.'

Others whose view was less coloured by personal pain, and who were expert in the ways of the GDR's Ministry for State Security, would later look at the case only to come to the same view. Paul Reckzeh betrayed his own daughter.

In the end, Barbara Reckzeh was sentenced to two years in prison. She served one year in Bautzen, one of the most notorious of the GDR jails and known as the 'Yellow Misery' for its distinctive yellow exterior, before being released and eventually settling in the west. After reunification, her father made the same journey, living out his final years in Hamburg safe in the knowledge that he was a wanted man no longer. There would be no knock on the door, no dawn arrest, for Paul Reckzeh. Instead, he would die a peaceful, old-man's death on the last day of March 1996, his remains buried in the anonymous field of urns in the Ohlsdorf main cemetery. Like so many Nazis who had spilled the blood of innocents, he was allowed what his victims were denied: a life.

In Germany today, there are still Reckzehs, who wrestle with the legacy of the name they carry. Some of them only learned the story when they were adults, in one case when a boss put a newspaper article on their desk. The truth had been hidden for so long, brushed under a carpet where no one would have to look at it. When it surfaced, they found themselves alternating between shock and shame. They realised that too many in their family, along with so many in their country, 'knew, but didn't want to know'.

But there are also Kieps and Thaddens and Maltzans in today's Germany and in today's world, who look back at their forebears with pride. Because when their country was in the grip of a terrible darkness, those men and women risked everything to break ranks and say no. They could have kept their heads down and stayed safe, seeing out the war with their lives and their families intact. Instead, they took action they did not need to take, helped people they could have brushed off, told truths they could so easily have ignored. They did what needed to be done, even though they had no need to do it. By that choice, they set an example that lives on, down the generations. When the moment came, they dared to be traitors – not to their country, but to tyranny.

Acknowledgements

THIS BOOK TOOK me into an unfamiliar past via an unfamiliar language. I was helped into the latter by the translation skills of several people, but especially Austin Davis and Rachel Preece. Sol Abrahams did translation of a different kind, ingeniously turning long-forgotten, sometimes dog-eared pages into a form that could be read digitally. Searching through archives became a collective effort, aided among others by Birgit Dencker and Gerald Wellershoff.

Thanks are due too to Dr Martin Luchterhandt of the Landesarchiv Berlin; Christian Carlsen and Torsten Zarwel, both of the Bundesarchiv, not least for helping excavate material from the former Stasi archives; Henry Leide of those same Stasi archives, who shared his research into Paul Reckzeh's life as a Stasi informant; Claudia Schelling and Dr Esther-Julia Howell of the Institut für Zeitgeschichte in Munich; Stephanie Thomas, archivist at the Elisabeth-von-Thadden-Schule in Heidelberg; Dr Katharina von Ruckteschell-Katte of the Goethe Institute in London; Professor Christina von Hodenberg, Christiane Swinbank and Jolanta Gambus of the German Historical Institute in London; Professor Peter Hempenstall of the University of Canterbury, New Zealand; Professor Paula Tanaka Mochida of the University of Hawaii, who supplied some useful information on the diplomatic career of Wilhelm Solf; Dr Bjoern Weigel, who did the same on the 1933 membership records of the Nazi party; Andrew Wallis who shared his findings on the early life of Herbert Lange in Stralsund; the novelist Esther Dischereit; and Melanie Frey, who does so much to ensure the story of 20 July 1944 is not forgotten.

I am additionally grateful to Jeff Boehm, grandson of Erich Boehm whose post-war interview with Lagi Solf proved indispen-

ACKNOWLEDGEMENTS

sable; Irmela von der Lühe, the cousin of Elisabeth von Thadden's biographer Irmgard von der Lühe, who shared the remarks she had made about Elisabeth at a commemorative event at Ravensbrück; Irmgard von der Lühe's children, Hilde von Massow and Hans-Werner von Massow; Linden and Jeff Gross, who made available to me the remarkable interviews with Maria von Maltzan and Hans Hirschel conducted by their late father, Leonard Gross, and held in his archive; Katrin Himmler, the great-niece of Heinrich Himmler; and Margareta Marmgren of Stockholm, who shared correspondence that ran from the 1930s to the 1960s between her father, Bertil, and Inge Graef, later Inge Reckzeh. Their letters provided an additional, painful perspective on the lives of those touched, often for the worse, by Paul Reckzeh.

Though no book wholly devoted to these events has been written until now, several scholars have tackled central aspects of this story. Many of them are cited in the bibliography and endnotes, but two should be singled out. Johannes Tuchel is the leading contemporary historian of German resistance and is entrusted with its memory as Director of the German Resistance Memorial Center in Berlin. There, in the very Bendlerblock where the 20 July plot came to its bloody end, he welcomed me one September afternoon as I was embarking on this voyage. After that, he patiently received my questions and answered them with great care. The hours I spent with Professor Gerhard Ringshausen, a noted expert on Christian opposition to the Reich in particular, were no less valuable, and his willingness to share the fruits of his own extensive research into this episode was the very model of academic generosity.

As I noted early in this book, there are no survivors of the 1943 events, but there are several descendants or others with family ties to this story who were unfailingly generous. Dagmar Aßman, whose godmother was married to Paul Reckzeh, and Marianne Wellershoff, a niece of Elisabeth von Thadden, deserve special mention for the time and energy they gave so warmly. I also owe thanks to a great-niece, herself named Elisabeth von Thadden, whose remarks to the girls of the Elisabeth-von-Thadden-Schule deepened my understanding of the school's founder, and to Elisabeth's nephew, Christopher Fox. I spoke, too, to Nikolaus Rauch, a grandson of

ACKNOWLEDGEMENTS

Otto Kiep; to Eugen Solf about his grandmother Hanna and aunt Lagi and to Count Mortimer von Maltzan about his aunt Maria. I am also grateful to Philip Ruppel, son of Irmgard Zarden Ruppel, for sharing photographs of his mother and providing some key information about her, as well as to Bruce and Hanna Clements, son-in-law and granddaughter of Otto Kiep, and to Gioconda and Muni Leykauf, daughter and granddaughter of Bianca Segantini. I much enjoyed my conversation with Bill von Bredow, whose indomitable mother, Hannah von Bredow, was part of the Solf Circle. I am also indebted to Carola and Laura Reckzeh, for their candour and willingness to confront a difficult past.

Further thanks go to Helene von Bismarck, not only for her insights but also for her willingness to contact several relatives and acquaintances, encouraging them to speak to me. I am particularly grateful to Helene's mother, Claudia von Arnim, née von Maltzan, for her recollections of her distant cousin Maria.

There are several others who I have thanked before and who it gives me great pleasure to thank again. At John Murray, Joe Zigmond was patient and encouraging in equal measure, and always astute in his judgements. Caroline Westmore is the exemplar of precision and rigour to which every writer should aspire, supported by the vigilant Robert Shore and Tim Ryder, and the indefatigable Juliet Brightmore. At the helm was Jocasta Hamilton in London and Sara Nelson of HarperCollins in New York, each with a ready supply of energy and enthusiasm for this book.

The team at Curtis Brown have been consummate allies once again, whether it's the smart advice of Natalie Beckett and Viola Hayden or the unstinting efforts of Kate Cooper and Samuel Loader to spread this story far and wide. As for Jonny Geller, I have been his client for thirty years, but his friend for much longer and I consider myself very lucky on both counts. There is a reason he is the best agent in the business, and much of it comes down to a combination of wisdom and loyalty that is rare indeed. I cherish it.

Jonathan Cummings and I have worked together on twelve books now, but on this one his contribution was truly indispensable, from the very start. His ability to track down facts, documents or people that would be beyond the reach of mere mortals fills me with awe

ACKNOWLEDGEMENTS

every time. If this book is about friends working together in pursuit of a shared goal, I hope he and I can keep doing that for many years to come.

Finally, a word for my wife, Sarah, and our sons, Jacob and Sam. There are times when the world seems to be darkening, the clock turning back. But they provide constant light and love. I could not be more thankful.

Jonathan Freedland
London, July 2025

Picture Credits

Inset pages 1–16

akg-images: 13 below. Alamy Stock Photo: 1 above/Alpha Stock, 10 below/Shawshots, 13 above/CBW, 15 below/Album, 16 below/PJF Military Collection. Bridgeman Images: 11 centre/SZ Photo/Scheri. Federal Archives, Berlin: 8 above right, 12 above right. Courtesy of German Resistance Memorial Center Foundation, Berlin: 16 above. Hulton-Deutsch Collection via Getty Images: 14 below. Photographer unknown: 2 below, 4 above, 5 below, 6 below, 11 below. Pictures From History/Universal Images Group via Getty Images: 10 above. Paul Popper/Popperfoto via Getty Images: 13 centre. Private collection/reproduction courtesy of Silent Heroes Memorial Center, German Resistance Memorial Center Foundation, Berlin: 2 above, 3 below left and right. Courtesy of Philip Ruppel: 4 below left. Süddeutsche Zeitung Photo/Alamy Stock Photo: 9 above, 11 above, 12 centre left, 15 above. Courtesy of Elisabeth von Thadden School, Wieblingen, Germany: 6 above left and centre. ullstein bild via Getty Images: 1 below, 3 above, 4 below right/photo by Frieda Riess, 5 above, 7 above/photo by bpk/Salomon, 7 centre right, 7 below left/photo by Rydde, 8 above left/photo by Lili Baruch, 8 below/photo by Schnellbacher, 9 below, 12 below left/photo by Tita Binz, 14 above.

Every reasonable effort has been made to trace copyright holders, but if there are any errors or omissions, John Murray (Publishers) will be pleased to insert the appropriate acknowledgement in any subsequent printings or editions.

Notes

Author's Note

xiv **one Allied investigator**: Boehm, *We Survived*, p. viii. According to Boehm, a Gestapo report compiled in April 1939 estimated that, in the six years after Hitler came to power in January 1933, Germans charged with political crimes included nearly 163,000 held in concentration camps, with another 140,000 either sentenced or awaiting trial. In 1936, when the Nazis aimed to use the Olympic Games in Berlin to showcase supposed Aryan supremacy, some 12,000 Germans were arrested for making illegal 'propaganda', with another 17,000 tried for sedition. In the single month of May 1938, 1,639 Germans were executed for political offences. Boehm suggests that those arrested for concrete anti-Nazi acts made up some 800,000 of the three million punished for dissent and, of those, only 300,000 were thought to have survived the war. It would mean some half a million Germans paid for their defiance of Hitler with their lives.

Prologue

3 **seven Gestapo officers**: Boehm, *We Survived*, p. 135.
4 **a chambermaid and nanny**: Warkocz, 'Die vergessene Widerstandskämpferin'.
4 **'You'll be picked up by car!'**: Irmgard von der Lühe, *Eine Frau*, p. 98.
5 **the Gestapo, the Secret State Police**: By the time war broke out, the Gestapo, the Geheime Staatspolizei, was under the command of the Reichssicherheitshauptamt, or RSHA, the Reich Security Main Office, itself subordinate to Heinrich Himmler's SS. The Gestapo's senior officials were often members of the SS, but most regular Gestapo

officers were not. While the Gestapo's chief mission was political policing, crushing dissent and enforcing obedience to the regime, it achieved its greatest notoriety through its role in the Nazi extermination of six million Jews.

5 **size of a decent flat**: Ruppel, *Memories*, p. 13.
6 **last great 'season'**: Ibid., p. 52.
6 **by Heinrich Himmler himself**: Tuchel, 'Zur vergessenen Vorgeschichte des 20. Juli 1944', p. 1.

Chapter 1: The End of Germany

11 **the last foreign minister**: Wheeler-Bennett, *Nemesis of Power*, p. 593.
11 **to President Woodrow Wilson**: Solf, Nuremberg Military Tribunal (hereafter referred to as NMT) 3 Justice Case testimony, 16 April 1947, p. 2145.
12 **prerequisite of a free country**: Warkocz, 'Die vergessene Widerstandskämpferin'.
12 **nannies and French governesses**: Maltzan, *Schlage die Trommel*, p. 10.
13 **grammatical errors**: Ibid., p. 74.
13 **covered the seat with kisses**: Ibid., p. 73.
14 **'look after your people'**: Ibid., p. 33.
14 **holding him by the legs**: Ibid., p. 22.
14 **more beautiful**: Block and Drucker, *Rescuers*, p. 154.
14 **'if a doctor'**: Maltzan, 'Irgendwie Pack Ich Es Immer!'
14 **defied her mother's authority**: Block and Drucker, *Rescuers*, p. 154.
15 **house dressmakers**: Ruppel, *Memories*, p. 22.
16 **campaign tour through Mecklenburg**: Ibid., p. 26.
17 **Zarden's wife was a Jew**: Solf, NMT 3 Justice Case testimony, 16 April 1947, p. 2147.
17 **no desire to serve**: Bundesfinanzakademie, *Arthur Zarden*, p. 28a.
17 **an involuntary exit**: According to his daughter Irmgard, Arthur Zarden 'loved his work . . . and it was tragic for him to be involuntarily retired at a comparatively young age.' Ruppel, *Memories*, p. 30.
17 **custom dictated**: Hank, 'Das abrupte Ende einer Karriere'. What was said at that meeting between Zarden and Hitler, and even whether the encounter happened, would become a matter of dispute between Zarden's daughter, Irmgard, and his former boss at the Ministry of Finance. The post-war memoirs of the latter, Count Johann Ludwig 'Lutz' Schwerin von Krosigk, claim that Zarden worked hard to secure

an audience with the new chancellor and that, when the two men met, Zarden 'managed to get Hitler to offer him another position commensurate with his rank, and he had this confirmed in writing.' Irmgard Zarden wholly rejected this allegation, writing in 1985, when the German Ministry of Finance honoured Arthur Zarden in a commemorative exhibition, that her father regarded the Nazi regime as 'criminal' from the start, that he had no intention of serving it in any capacity and that it was 'especially grotesque' to claim that he had attempted to secure a different job in the meeting with Hitler. 'It dishonours my father's memory when claims are made that he sought continued employment under Hitler in the Third Reich,' she wrote, noting that while her father had paid the gravest price for his opposition to Nazism, Schwerin 'served the regime with such enthusiasm' that he was convicted of war crimes at Nuremberg in 1949. See Schwerin von Krosigk, 'Persönliche Erinnerungen', IfZ, ZSA 20/12, vol. II, p. 139; Bundesfinanzakademie, *Arthur Zarden*, p. 28a. Correspondence with Philip Ruppel, 8 July 2025.

18 **The Führer sent a letter**: Ruppel, *Memories*, p. 84.
18 **quite well disposed towards national socialism**: Irmela von der Lühe, 'Das altadlige Fräulein aus dem Osten', p. 6. 'Das altadlige Fräulein aus dem Osten' is the title of a speech given on 13 September 2014 at the opening of an exhibition about Elisabeth von Thadden at Ravensbrück, marking the seventieth anniversary of her execution on 8 September 1944.
18 **district administrator**: Meyer, *Elisabeth von Thadden*, p. 473.
18 **organisational, economic and social centre**: Irmela von der Lühe, 'Das altadlige Fräulein aus dem Osten', p. 3.
18 **the social needs of the villagers**: Meyer, *Elisabeth von Thadden*, p. 474.
18 **duty, reliability and selflessness**: Irmela von der Lühe, 'Das altadlige Fräulein aus dem Osten', p. 3.
19 **harvest festival sermon**: Meyer, *Elisabeth von Thadden*, p. 474.
19 **'not too rambling'**: Ibid.
19 **peasants on their estates**: Huch, *In einem Gedenkbuch zu Sammeln*, p. 128.
19 **'Where is a woman with spirit to begin?'**: Irmgard von der Lühe, *Eine Frau*, p. 11.
19 **gifts and achievements**: Ibid., p. 21.
19 **a deeply Christian one**: Irmela von der Lühe, 'Das altadlige Fräulein aus dem Osten', p. 5.
20 **Rudolf Steiner speak**: Meyer, *Elisabeth von Thadden*, p. 475.

20 **She was against co-education**: Ibid., p. 476.
20 **'loyalty to duty, order and cleanliness'**: Ibid., p. 477.
20 **tall, strong and stately**: Huch, *In einem Gedenkbuch zu Sammeln*, p. 128.
20 **the girls did handicrafts**: Meyer, *Elisabeth von Thadden*, p. 477.
21 **colours and fabrics**: Ibid., p. 478.
21 **a tour of Venice**: Ruppel, *Memories*, p. 48.
21 **the girls dressed as water spirits**: Ibid., p. 478.
21 **numbered nearly a hundred**: Ibid., p. 481.
21 **provoke anger or prompt laughter**: Huch, *In einem Gedenkbuch zu Sammeln*, p. 129.
21 **bright straw hat and sleek sunglasses**: Thadden, 'Elisabeth von Thadden: Damals – dann . . . und morgen', 7 November 2014, p. 1.
21 **no money to speak of**: Author interview with Marianne Wellershoff, 12 September 2023.
21 **'fully conscious members'**: Meyer, *Elisabeth von Thadden*, p. 480.
22 **country houses of the New York elite**: Kiep, *Mein Lebensweg*, pp. 125–6.
22 **55 East 77th Street**: Ibid., p. 122.
22 **'with blood, if necessary'**: Clements, *From Ice Set Free*, p. 150.
23 **the Nazi seizure of power**: Barnes and Barnes, *Nazis in Pre-War London*, p. 85.
24 **money came from her father**: Wellershoff, *Von Ort zu Ort*, p. 17.
25 **jobbing labourer**: Wallis 'Herbert Lange', p. 87.
25 **'timeless values'**: Ibid.

Chapter 2: The Diplomat

26 **twenty thousand different German-American clubs**: Kiep, *Mein Lebensweg*, p. 125.
26 **an entirely new meaning**: Clements, *From Ice Set Free*, p. 155.
27 **students at Columbia University**: Ibid., p. 156.
27 **to attack and kill Einstein**: Kiep, *Mein Lebensweg*, p. 138.
27 **adding that he hoped**: Clements, *From Ice Set Free*, p. 155.
27 **'discretion'**: Kiep, *Mein Lebensweg*, p. 137.
27 **'Germany's contribution to the culture of mankind'**: 'Einstein to Exile Self from Germany Until "Exaggerated Nationalism" Ends', *Indianapolis Star*, p. 17.
27 **His absence would confirm**: Kiep, *Mein Lebensweg*, pp. 137–8.
28 **official German policy**: Ibid., p. 139.
28 **in the name of German decency**: Clements, *From Ice Set Free*, p. 157.

28 **'This company does not honour you'**: Ibid., p. 158.
29 **a room full of Jews**: Ibid.

Chapter 3: The Countess

30 **an enemy of the state**: Schwarte, 'Friedrich Muckermann', pp. 210–11.
31 **drinking game**: Maltzan, *Schlage die Trommel*, p. 80.
31 **the password**: Hans Hirschel to Senator for Social Affairs, Berlin-Wilmersdorf, 21 April 1953, Yad Vashem Archive (hereafter referred to as YVA), M.31/3545.
31 **a small bomb**: Watts, 'Prisoner of Love', p. 51. The incident of the bomb smuggled out under the noses of the Gestapo was recalled by Maria von Maltzan in an interview with the *Observer* newspaper in 1986. But it is not a story she seems to have told other interviewers or included in her autobiography. Maria's nephew, Mortimer, though extremely fond of his aunt and full of admiration for her heroism – which was documented and attested to by many others – suspected that the occasional recollection was 'a little bit exaggerated'. Author interview with Mortimer Graf Maltzan, 15 May 2024.
31 **a broken jaw**: Hans Hirschel to Senator for Social Affairs, Berlin-Wilmersdorf, 21 April 1953, YVA, M.31/3545.
32 **she promptly destroyed**: Ibid.
32 **'Don't! Please! I'm Jewish!'**: Maltzan, *Schlage die Trommel*, p. 102.
32 **Law for the Protection of German Blood and German Honour**: One of the items of legislation known as the Nuremberg laws which were enacted on 15 September 1935 and which sought to protect the supposed purity of the German race.
32 **a riding double**: von Maltza(n)scher Familienverband (ed.), *Maltza(h)n 1945–2019*, p. 30.
33 **His proposal**: Maltzan, *Schlage die Trommel*, p. 107.
33 **yellow velvet frock coats**: Ibid., p. 58.
33 **shot out both of Hitler's eyes**: Ibid., p. 108.
34 **'Don't you recognise me?'**: Ibid., p. 111.

Chapter 4: The Widow and Her Daughter

37 **'cultured Jews' who had proven themselves patriots**: Solf, NMT 3 Justice Case testimony, 16 April 1947, p. 2145.
37 **'this poison has penetrated even you'**: Ibid., p. 2146. Goebbels was apparently undeterred, writing in his diary on 14 May 1933, '[met] with Excellency Solf, who gives me advice on the Jewish question. Otherwise, however, he makes a good impression.' Fröhlich (ed.), *Die Tagebücher von Joseph Goebbels*, part I, vol. 2/III, p. 186.
37 **'medieval methods'**: Becker and Becker (eds), *Hitlers Machtergreifung*, p. 215.
38 **excellent addition to the faculty**: Author interview with Eugen Solf, 20 July 2022. The point is echoed by Rudolf Pechel, who noted how Wilhelm Solf would use his Japanese contacts to save 'various German professors'. Pechel, *Deutscher Widerstand*, p. 90.
38 **She drove almost every day**: Schad, *Frauen gegen Hitler*, p. 173.
38 **emigration affidavits**: Boehm, *We Survived*, p. 133.
38 **forged ones**: Andreas-Friedrich, *Berlin Underground*, p. viii.
38 **inundated with requests**: Hanna Solf to Ruth Andreas-Friedrich, n.d., Institut für Zeitgeschichte (hereafter referred to as IfZ), ED 106/101.
38 **Anni Schulz, living underground, or the Weyl family**: Those names appear in Eugen Solf's application, dated 11 March 2005, to Yad Vashem seeking recognition for his grandmother Hanna Solf as Righteous Among the Nations. Solf interviewed Sabine Weyl on 7 December 2004 and 13 January 2005 for the submission. Private collection.
39 **more about her 'political agitation'**: Boehm, *We Survived*, p. 132.
40 **ostracised**: Schad, *Frauen gegen Hitler*, 172.
40 **'a Jewish Star'**: According to a supplementary RSHA decree, 'from April 14, 1942, the apartments of Jews must be specially marked with a Jewish Star in black print on white paper, which corresponds in style and size to the one to be worn on clothing and is to be put up on the front door next to the nameplate.' Meirer, 'Berlin Jews', p. 95. The text of the decree is in Walk, *Das Sonderrecht für die Juden im NS-Staat*, p. 369.
40 **laundry or vegetables in each hand**: Lagi Ballestrem-Solf mentioned this detail to Eric H. Boehm, in one of a series of extended interviews he conducted soon after the war. Boehm was himself a German-born Jew who had left for the US as a child. He returned as a US serviceman, tasked with interrogating German prisoners of war, and stayed on as

Chapter 5: The Headmistresss

41 **in opposition to the Aryan paragraph**: Meyer, *Elisabeth von Thadden*, p. 481.
42 **staffed by the school's own teachers**: Ibid., p. 480.
42 **displaying the NSDAP party programme**: Irmela von der Lühe, 'Das altadlige Fräulein aus dem Osten', p. 8.
42 **Wieblingen was 'Nazi-free'**: Meyer, *Elisabeth von Thadden*, p. 483.
42 **precious grand piano**: Ibid.
43 **drop the word 'Evangelical'**: Ibid., p. 482.

Chapter 6: In the Room

44 **more than 3,500 princes**: Malinowski, *Nazis and Nobles*, p. 314.
45 **'A new age has begun'**: Clements, *From Ice Set Free*, p. 159.
45 **eyes of a thief**: Ibid.
47 **'politically undependable'**: Ibid, p. 160.
47 **rediscovered its soul**: Ibid., p. 163.
47 **'Now we believe in ourselves again.'**: Ibid., p. 164.
47 **missed her train**: Ibid.
48 **Chiang Kai-shek**: Kiep, *Mein Lebensweg*, pp. 161–4.
48 **alone with their fears**: Clements, *From Ice Set Free*, p. 167.
49 **'If he betrays us'**: Ibid., p. 24.
49 **younger, sceptical self**: Ibid., pp. 33–4.
49 **'my real German homeland'**: Kiep, *Mein Lebensweg*, p. 41.
49 **sons of the Nazi elite**: Roche, *Third Reich's Elite Schools*, p. 35. Ilfeld had become one of the first Napolas, or National-Political Educational Institutions, in 1935.
50 **'Heil Hitler'**: Clements, *From Ice Set Free*, p. 173. In his letter to Otto, the head euphemistically suggested the school's approach was 'too standardised and leaves little room for more individualised educational care'.
50 **millions of others**: Weigel, '"Märzgefallene"', p. 90. The membership freeze of 1933 was lifted in 1937. By the end of the war, the Nazi party had 8.5 million members.

Chapter 7: The Circle

51 **science, culture, government and diplomacy**: Möckelmann, *Hannah von Bredow*, p. 136.
51 **at one time or another**: Solf, NMT 3 Justice Case testimony, 16 April 1947, p. 2174.
51 **mere horror stories**: Boehm, *We Survived*, p. 133.
52 **vent their disgust and despair**: The phrase was Lagi Solf's, explaining the appeal of 'the political oasis' that her mother's home became. Ibid.
52 **involved in preparations**: Klemperer, *German Resistance Against Hitler*, p. 312 n. 199.
53 **back in Cabinet**: Ibid.
53 **almost every day**: Schad, *Frauen gegen Hitler*, p. 171.
54 **'Führer speeches' parodying Hitler's oratory**: Ballestrem-Solf, *Gestapo auf der Teegesellschaft*, 2. Copy in IfZ, ED 106/101, 148–54. In a letter summarising the Gestapo's investigations of the Solf Circle, the head of the SD, SS-Obergruppenführer Kaltenbrunner, noted that, 'At these meetings, speeches by the Führer were parodied and leading figures from the state and the party were held in contempt.' Ringshausen, 'Zwischen Dissens und Widerstand', p. 198.
54 **actively involved in efforts to assassinate the Führer**: Ringshausen, 'Zwischen Dissens und Widerstand', p. 225 n. 47.
54 **a habit of arriving late**: Tuchel, 'Heinrich Himmler und die Vorgeschichte des 20. Juli 1944'. The recollection came from Father Metzger in a statement to the Gestapo dated 30 July 1943 when he was questioned about his links to the Solf Circle. German Resistance Memorial Foundation (hereafter referred to as GDW), BA, NJ 13512.
54 **backed away from Kuenzer**: Klemperer, *German Resistance Against Hitler*, p. 312 n. 199.
55 **simple human decency**: Rothfels, *German Opposition*, pp. 32–3.

Chapter 8: The Night of Broken Glass

56 **Union Club clothing store**: Maltzan, *Schlage die Trommel*, p. 122.
57 **ashamed to be German**: Irmela von der Lühe, 'Das altadlige Fräulein aus dem Osten', p. 7.

57 **joined the Nazi party**: Tuchel, 'Verfolgung, Haft und Tod', p. 185. In his essay on Otto Kiep's arrest, imprisonment and execution, based on notes written by Otto in prison and later passed to his family, Johannes Tuchel mentions that the suggestion in the biography written by his son-in-law Bruce Clements, that Otto only joined the party in 1943, is incorrect. Clements, *From Ice Set Free*, p. 207.

Chapter 9: Someone Must Tell the Truth

59 **a Quaker now devoting herself**: Clements, *From Ice Set Free*, p. 178.
59 **knew exactly what Germany had become**: Ibid., p. 177.
60 **'Someone must tell the truth'**: Ibid., p. 176.

Chapter 10: The Detective

62 **joining the Kriminalpolizei**: Montague, *Chełmno*, p. 16.
62 **involved in the execution**: Ibid., p. 17.
62 **cylinders of carbon monoxide**: Ibid., p. 16.
62 **measuring its efficacy against a German alternative**: Kiep, *Mein Lebensweg*, p. 189.
63 **observe a gassing for himself**: Browning, *Origins of the Final Solution*, p. 188.
63 **its own chauffeur**: Montague, *Chełmno*, p. 17.
63 **'useless eaters'**: The phrase, '*nutzlose Esser*' in German, appears in a post-war deposition by one of the people involved in the T4 euthanasia programme and in the gassing of Jews in extermination camps. Viktor Brack, 'Affidavit concerning the Nazi administrative system, the euthanasia program, and the sterilization experiments', International Military Tribunal (hereafter referred to as IMT), NO-426, 14 October 1946, p. 5.
63 **Kaiser's Coffee Company**: Browning, *Origins of the Final Solution*, p. 189.
63 **through a rubber hose**: Friedlander, *Origins of Nazi Genocide*, p. 139.
63 **forty passengers**: Ibid., p. 140.
63 **As the van drove away**: Ibid., p. 139.
63 **the hammering**: Browning, *Fateful Months*, p. 62.
64 **the 'psychopaths' club'**: Burleigh, *Death and Deliverance*, p. 132.
64 **the rank of SS-Obersturmführer**: Wallis, 'Herbert Lange', p. 92.
64 **1,559 German patients**: Browning, *Origins of the Final Solution*, p. 189.
64 **three hours later**: Friedlander, *Origins of Nazi Genocide*, p. 140.

64 **inscribed amber box**: Montague, *Chełmno*, p. 29.
64 **the Netherlands**: Ibid., pp. 29–30.

Chapter 11: Time to Die

65 **more than 160,000**: Schäbitz, 'The Flight and Expulsion of German Jews', p. 60.
65 **submarines**: Andreas-Friedrich, *Berlin Underground*, p. 180.
65 **yellow badge**: Heydrich's decree, applying to the Protectorate of Bohemia and Moravia, issued on 1 September 1941, was applied to the German Reich on 19 September 1941. *Deutsches Reichsgesetzblatt*, 1941, part I, no. 100, 5 September, p. 547.
66 **'Jews' houses'**: In January 1939, Deputy Führer Martin Bormann circulated a document titled 'Jews' with decisions made by Hitler at the recommendation of Göring: 'It is desirable . . . that Jews will live together in one house, as much as [is] feasible under rental conditions.' *Nazi Conspiracy and Aggression*, III, 069-PS, p. 116.
66 **marked with a star**: Meirer, 'Berlin Jews', p. 95.
66 **side cellar**: Maltzan, *Schlage die Trommel*, p. 150.
67 **on the dot**: Ibid., p. 134.
67 **obstacle was removed**: Maltzan, 'Irgendwie Pack Ich Es Immer!'
68 **Hans did not look**: Leonard Gross interview with Maria von Maltzan, 14 August 1982.
68 **Reichenau Order**: Document NOKW-3411, IMT, *Trials of War Criminals*, XI, pp. 329–30.
68 **1.25 million Jews**: Estimates of the number of Jewish victims of the Einsatzgruppen range from 1.25 to two million. Yad Vashem, https://www.yadvashem.org/odot_pdf/Microsoft%20Word%20-%20216.pdf
68 **he met Professor Schröder**: Gross interview with Maria von Maltzan.

Chapter 12: A Spy in Our Midst

70 **a rented hotel in Tutzing**: Meyer, *Elisabeth von Thadden*, p. 483.
71 **'deficiencies of conviction'**: Ibid., p. 485.
71 **read from the Old Testament**: Heuss-Knapp, *Schmale Wege*, p. 102.
71 **'Rule, Britannia!', no less**: Irmela von der Lühe, 'Das altadlige Fräulein aus dem Osten', p. 9.
71 **'intensive contacts'**: Ibid., p. 10. Lühe quotes a fifteen-page report

on Thadden and her school. 'Landerziehungsheim Wieblingen, private Oberschule für Mädchen, sprachliche Form, Klasse 1-6, Allgemeines; Leitung: Elisabeth von Thadden', Generallandesarchiv, Karlsruhe, 235 no. 42592, p. 14.

72 **'a national socialist education for young people'**: Meyer, *Elisabeth von Thadden*, pp. 486–7.
72 **allowed to stay on**: Meyer, *Elisabeth von Thadden*, p. 487.
72 **'. . . burden my conscience'**: Heuss-Knapp, *Schmale Wege*, p. 102.
72 **some teaching in Tutzing**: In the official proceedings of the Nuremberg hearings, Hanna Solf locates Elizabeth von Thadden in 'Tautzenberg' but every indication points to this being an error in transcription. Solf, NMT 3 Justice Case testimony, 16 April 1947, p. 2169.
73 **unofficial advice clinic**: Ringshausen, 'Zwischen Dissens und Widerstand', p. 196.
73 **On Wednesday evenings**: Irmgard von der Lühe, *Eine Frau*, p. 52.
73 **Pastor Martin Niemöller**: He would find fame after the war for a sermon that became a poem. Delivered in January 1946, it began, 'First they came for the communists . . .'
73 **persecuted souls who were in hiding**: Irmgard von der Lühe, *Eine Frau*, p. 53.
73 **'we're getting the school back'**: Ibid., p. 54.

Chapter 13: Trial Run

74 **a nursing home in Bojanowo**: Montague, *Chełmno*, p. 31.
74 **at the highest levels**: Ibid., pp. 40–2.
75 **with machine guns**: Ibid., p. 41.
76 **a few yards away**: Ibid.
76 **a stinking liquid that smelled of chemicals**: Ibid. The phrase comes from the forester in charge of the Niesłusz-Rudzica forest, Piotr Zalas, who complied with the SS instruction to clear the area but went to see the mass graves for himself a day or two after the first round of killings.
76 **gingerbread and lemonade bottles**: Ibid. That pile was spotted by Zalas.
76 **rank of SS-Hauptsturmführer**: Wallis, 'Herbert Lange', p. 94.
76 **a village called Chełmno**: Though the first place of its kind, Chełmno lacks the infamy of some of the other, larger death camps. Partly that is because there were so few who lived to bear witness. Only seven

Jews are known to have escaped Chełmno. Thanks to the way the camp operated, killing its victims immediately and with next to no permanent population of enslaved prisoners, there were vanishingly few who came out alive. An excellent overview of Chełmno's history has been compiled by the US Holocaust Memorial Museum (hereafter referred to as USHMM) and is included in its online encyclopaedia: https://encyclopedia.ushmm.org/content/en/article/chelmno

Chapter 14: A Secret Funeral

77 **Dr Max Botho Holländer**: Hirschel, Testimony, 30 November 1950, YVA M.31/3545.
78 **a former colleague**: Ibid.
78 **table manners were atrocious**: The recollection comes via the journalist Helene von Bismarck, whose mother is a distant cousin of Maria von Maltzan. Author correspondence, 19 May 2024.
78 **a visit to the barber**: Block and Drucker, *Rescuers*, p. 156.
79 **'You can already trim dogs'**: Maltzan, *Schlage die Trommel*, pp. 166–7.
79 **a state funeral**: Gunkel, 'Sie müssen doch bloß durch die Couch schießen'.
79 **horribly mawkish**: Maltzan, *Schlage die Trommel*, p. 139.
79 **her fur boa**: Hirschel, 'Illegal Life in Berlin', Wiener Library, P.III.d. no. 385, spring 1956, p. 2.
79 **a long, silent embrace**: Gross, *Last Jews*, p. 40.
80 **gold and jewellery**: Maltzan, *Schlage die Trommel*, p. 146.
80 **'The end was pretty bitter'**: Gross, *Last Jews*, p. 40.
80 **'If I survive, he will survive'**: Maltzan, *Schlage die Trommel*, p. 146.
80 **failed to get the papers**: Gross, *Last Jews*, p. 40.
81 **avant-garde intellectual**: Ibid., p. 82.
81 *Shema Yisrael*: Ibid., p. 41.
81 **role of father-to-be**: Ibid., p. 82.
81 **he was a homosexual**: Maltzan, *Schlage die Trommel*, p. 148.
81 **her future husband**: Ibid.

Chapter 15: The Walk to Freedom

83 **food or money**: Wheeler-Bennett, *Nemesis of Power*, p. 594.
83 **escorting them personally**: 'Ein Frauenschicksal im Dritten Reich',

NVZTG, 5 November 1946, Hoover Institution, Julius Epstein Collection, box 58, Hanna Solf folder.
83 **Dr Ferdinand Mainzer**: Schad, *Frauen gegen Hitler*, p. 173.
83 **the 'non-Aryan' writer Annie Kraus**: Möckelmann, *Hannah von Bredow*, p. 138.
83 **she would tremble**: Schad, *Frauen gegen Hitler*, p. 174.
83 **elaborate, and secret, operation**: Boehm, *We Survived*, p. 134.
85 **two deliveries a day**: Sautter, *Geschichte*, p. 161.

Chapter 16: Cast Out

87 **the Jewish section of the cemetery**: Ruppel, *Memories*, pp. 76–7.
87 **rendered in code**: Ibid., p. 78.
88 **'Never carry anything in writing'**: Ibid., pp. 78–9.

Chapter 17: Present at the Creation

89 **modest electric bulb**: Montague, *Chełmno*, p. 203.
90 **any other large, grey van**: 'Testimony of the forced gravedigger Yankev Grojnowski', Ringelblum Archive, vol. 5, pp. 87–115. On 19 January, Szlama Ber Winer escaped from Chełmno and made his way to Warsaw where he gave his eyewitness account, under the pseudonym Yankev or Jakub Grojnowski, to members of the Oneg Szabat group who were compiling evidence about mass killings of Jews. Winer's testimony, sometimes known as the Grojanowski Report, formed part of the Oneg Szabat report 'The Events in Chełmno', dated 25 March 1942. It and much of the Oneg Szabat archive was hidden when the Warsaw Ghetto was liquidated in spring 1943 and was retrieved after the war. Winer was killed in Bełżec in April 1942.
90 **replaced by wooden grating**: 'Testimony of the forced gravedigger Yankev Grojnowski', Ringelblum Archive, vol. 5, p. 91.
90 **falling asleep in his garage**: Browning, *Fateful Months*, pp. 59–60.
91 **keeping the engine running**: This method still required further refinement: 'The application of gas usually is not undertaken correctly. In order to come to an end as fast as possible, the driver presses the accelerator to the fullest extent. By doing that the persons to be executed suffer death from suffocation and not death by dozing off as was planned. My directions now have proved that by correct adjustment

of the levers death comes faster and the prisoners fall asleep peacefully. Distorted faces and excretions, such as could be seen before, are no longer noticed.' SS-Untersturmführer Dr Becker, Riga, to SS-Obersturmbannführer Rauff, Berlin, 'Report on the Functioning of Gas Vans', 16 May 1942, IMT, 501-PS.

91 **Some would be blue**: Browning, *Fateful Months*, p. 62.
91 **others wet with sweat**: 'Invoices for shipments of Zyklon B (prussic acid) and affidavit on the use of the chemicals by the SS [euthanasia and extermination camps]', 30 April 1944, NMT-1 PS-1553, p. 7.
92 **declined an offer**: Browning, *Origins of the Final Solution*, p. 419.
92 **some 44,000 Jews**: 'Chelmno (Kulmhof – Poland)', https://www.jewishgen.org/forgottencamps/camps/chelmnoeng.html
93 **clothing and valuables**: Wallis, 'Herbert Lange', p. 93.
93 **most efficient way**: Ibid.
93 **many of the Jews of Berlin**: Ibid.

Chapter 18: The Path of Resistance

94 **lecture his crew on the merits of national socialism**: Kahn, *Hitler's Spies*, p. 229.
94 **the failed Kapp Putsch**: Wistrich, *Who's Who in Nazi Germany*, p. 29.
95 **identified by the Star of David**: Höhne, *Canaris*, p. 216.
95 **the torching of Warsaw**: Ibid., p. 361.
95 **then set ablaze**: Stewart, *Admirals of the World*, p. 58.
95 **on 12 September 1939**: Höhne, *Canaris*, p. 364.
95 **an even more trenchant opponent**: Müller, 'Structure and Nature of National Conservative Opposition in Germany', p. 162.
96 **a goblet of beer**: Clements, *From Ice Set Free*, p. 194.
97 **granddaughter of John Jay**: Rothfels, *German Opposition*, p. 129.
97 **a moral and spiritual disease**: Clements, *From Ice Set Free*, p. 181.
98 **resistance networks**: Tuchel, 'Verfolgung, Haft und Tod', pp. 186–7.
98 **an envoy for Oster**: Clements, *From Ice Set Free*, pp. 186–7.
99 **'deeply pessimistic'**: Tuchel, 'Verfolgung, Haft und Tod', p. 186. In his essay on Otto Kiep's later life, Tuchel notes that the guest who described Otto's bleak outlook in his diary was Ulrich von Hassell, a fellow diplomat whom Otto saw frequently and Tuchel describes as a 'networker of the resistance'.
99 **'We are surrounded by lies'**: Clements, *From Ice Set Free*, p. 186.

99 **sixty deep-red roses**: Möckelmann, *Hannah von Bredow*, p. 141. The recipient of those flowers was Bismarck's granddaughter, Hannah von Bredow. It presumably happened before Otto Kiep had married Hanna, though Otto was certainly a married man when he sent Bredow what she regarded as 'an overly affectionate telegram'.

99 **bushes of the Tiergarten**: The recollection comes from Otto's grandson. Author interview with Nikolaus Rauch, 1 July 2024.

Chapter 19: The Blonde Poison

101 **green permanent certificates of passage**: Dirks, 'Snatchers', p. 251.
102 **bogus furniture van**: Ibid., p. 259.
102 **food, tobacco or cash**: Grunwald-Spier, *Who Betrayed the Jews?*, p. 120.
103 **she would excuse herself**: Gross, *Last Jews*, p. 216.
103 **over three hundred *U-Boote***: Grunwald-Spier, *Who Betrayed the Jews?*, p. 120.
103 **Blonde Poison**: Gunkel, 'Sie müssen doch bloß durch die Couch schießen'.
103 **Blonde Ghost**: Gross, *Last Jews*, p. 215.

Chapter 20: A Bomb on a Plane

104 **systemic thinker**: Interview with Nikolaus Rauch.
104 **Operation Spark**: Some refer to Operation Flash. Shirer, *Rise and Fall*, p. 915.
105 **press chief**: By his own account, Otto Kiep 'made himself available' to Goerdeler as press chief in 1943. Tuchel, 'Verfolgung, Haft und Tod', p. 187.
105 **the bomb**: Two pairs of British-manufactured Clam limpet mines, each with an 8 oz charge. Hoffmann, *Widerstand, Staatsstreich, Attentat*, p. 334.
105 **thin and small as a pencil**: British-produced 'time pencil' detonators were widely used for covert operations in occupied Europe, and 'the compactness and ingenious construction of these bombs had proved so interesting to the German police that they had turned them over for study to the Abwehr, the German intelligence and counterintelligence service'. Dulles, *Germany's Underground*, p. 2.

105 **disguised as a gift**: John, 'Some Facts and Aspects of the Plot Against Hitler', p. 33.
105 **primed the device**: Schlabrendorff, *Offiziere gegen Hitler*, p. 73.
106 **the bomb remained intact**: Fearing the plot would be exposed, Fabian von Schlabrendorff, one of the conspirators, took a courier plane to the headquarters and retrieved the package containing the bomb. 'When he opened it that night in a private compartment of a train to Berlin, he discovered that the bomb had been properly set, the little capsule containing the acid had been broken, the acid had eaten through the wire, and the firing pin had shot forward. But the percussion cap had not gone off.' Dulles, *Germany's Underground*, p. 67.
106 **'pain over my country'**: Clements, *From Ice Set Free*, p. 189.
107 ***innere Emigration***: Wheeler-Bennett, *Nemesis of Power*, p. 595.
107 **crack down on the enemy at home**: Clements, *From Ice Set Free*, p. 190.

Chapter 21: Closing In

109 **called up for military service**: 'Hubert', Graf von Ballestremsches Firmen- und Familienarchiv (hereafter referred to as Ballestrem), https://www.ballestrem.de/familie-und-orte/einzelpersonen/hubert/
110 **the secret police never made the link**: Ringshausen, 'Zwischen Dissens und Widerstand', p. 199.
110 **nephew of the former German ambassador**: Shirer, *Rise and Fall*, p. 920.
110 **British socialists and trade unionists**: Barnes and Barnes, *Nazis in Pre-War London*, p. 85.
110 **six foot six inches**: Ibid., p. 86.
110 **hid a Jewish family**: Nicolson, 'Marginal Comment', 10 August 1945, p. 126.
110 **In May 1940**: Möckelmann, *Hannah von Bredow*, p. 140.
110 **'No. 1 must disappear'**: Hansen, *Albrecht Graf von Bernstorff*, p. 255.
111 **a new 'Nordland'**: Klemperer, *German Resistance Against Hitler*, p. 293.
111 **the Pius Abbey in Berlin**: Irmgard von der Lühe, *Eine Frau*, p. 67.
111 **Gestapo Group IV B**: Perwe, *Svenska i Gestapos tjänst*, ch. 10.
112 **'Mrs Governor Solf'**: Tuchel, 'Zur vergessenen Vorgeschichte des 20. Juli 1944', p. 11.
112 **taking down car registration numbers**: Ringshausen, 'Zwischen Dissens und Widerstand', p. 199.

Chapter 22: A Secret Mission

113 **the eminent surgeon Ferdinand Sauerbruch**: Shirer, *Rise and Fall*, p. 921.
114 **'There are always people like that'**: Irmgard von der Lühe, *Eine Frau*, pp. 60–1.
115 **travelled to Zurich to see her old mentor**: Ibid., p. 67.
115 **a father figure**: Meyer, *Elisabeth von Thadden*, p. 481.
115 **constantly surrounded by agents**: Irmgard von der Lühe, *Eine Frau*, p. 60.
115 **the Reich Health Office**: Wagner-Nigrin, 'Volksgerichts-Prozess, Berlin, 1. Juli 1944', p. 3.
116 **'Be careful what you say'**: Irmgard von der Lühe, *Eine Frau*, p. 70.

Chapter 23: Go On, Shoot

118 **at the front door**: Hirschel, 'Illegal Life in Berlin', Wiener Library, P.III.d. no. 385, spring 1956, p. 4.
118 **sofa bed**: Ibid.
118 **hooks and eyelets**: Maltzan, *Schlage die Trommel*, p. 140.
118 **codeine**: Ibid., p. 141.
119 **'the Holy Spirit'**: Ibid., p. 153.
120 **onto the sofa bed**: Beyth, Affidavit, 1 December 1950, YVA M.31/3545.
120 **'shoot through the couch'**: Maltzan, *Schlage die Trommel*, p. 154.
121 **'a raggedy piece of furniture'**: Gay Block and Malka Drucker interview with Maria von Maltzan, 29 July 1988, USHMM.

Chapter 24: The Breakthrough

122 **Paul Reckzeh telephoned Bianca Segantini**: Segantini to Elisabeth Wirth, n.d., Landesarchiv Berlin (hereafter referred to as LAB), B Rep. 058 Nr. 7254, p. 3.
122 **at home with her**: Ibid., p. 1.
122 **only child**: Reckzeh statement, 17 October 1952, in ibid., p. 1.
123 **'On the contrary, Frau Segantini!'**: Irmgard von der Lühe, *Eine Frau*, p. 71. Bianca Segantini was, Lühe writes, able to reproduce

whole parts of her encounter with the young Dr and Mrs Reckzeh 'verbatim' two decades later.
124 **peace of mind**: Segantini to Elisabeth Wirth, n.d., LAB B Rep. 058 No. 7254, p. 4.
124 **hidden ear**: Ibid., p. 5.
124 **reveal the badge**: Ibid., p. 4.
125 **'you were a Nazi'**: Ibid., p. 5.
126 **a conversation about religion**: Ibid., p. 6.
126 **'a thousand greetings, from me!'**: Irmgard von der Lühe, *Eine Frau*, p. 73.

Chapter 25: An Invitation to Tea

128 **Bible sessions had been banned**: Meyer, *Elisabeth von Thadden*, p. 488.
128 **a Red Cross tour**: Irmgard von der Lühe, *Eine Frau*, p. 124. Lühe is quoting from the indictment against Thadden and others. 'Anklageschrift des Oberreichsanwalts beim Volksgerichtshof 2 J 243/44 g. Rs./1 L 214/44', 22 June 1944, Bundesarchiv (hereafter referred to as BArch), BStU, MfS AP 12062/76.
128 **a soldiers' home in France**: Meyer, *Elisabeth von Thadden*, p. 488.
130 **leaving before breakfast**: Clements, *From Ice Set Free*, p. 191.
130 **the Kiep house was hit**: the family home, Taubertstrasse 15 in Grunewald, was damaged in the RAF bombing raid of 3–4 September. Middlebrook and Everitt, *Bomber Command War Diaries*, p. 428.
130 **broken windows**: Clements, *From Ice Set Free*, p. 191.
130 **in the Harz mountains**: Hanna Kiep, 'Schilderung Teegesellschaft', apparently May 1944, GDW, NL Kiep.
131 **not to be late**: Maltzan, *Schlage die Trommel*, p. 168.

Chapter 26: Agent Robby

132 **'civil opposition'**: Irmgard von der Lühe, *Eine Frau*, p. 56.
133 **a sense of duty**: '[D]enunciations from the population were crucial to the functioning of the Gestapo'. Gellately, *Gestapo and German Society*, p. 135.
133 **coerced**: Hall, 'Army of Spies', p. 258. Also, OSS Consolidated Interrogation report: Gestapo Linz, National Archives and Records Administration, Washington, DC, 226 EAP 190-6-4-03.

133 **young intellectuals**: Irmgard von der Lühe, *Eine Frau*, p. 60.
133 **forty-six young lawyers**: Ibid.
133 **earlier that summer**: Statement by Walter Huppenkothen, 'Verhaltnis Wehrmacht-Sicherheitspolizei, II.Teil', n.d., IfZ, ZS 249-1, p. 27.
133 **positions of trust**: Ibid.
134 **important for the war**: Irmgard von der Lühe, *Eine Frau*, p. 57.
135 **the Reich Health Office**: Wagner-Nigrin, 'Volksgerichts-Prozess, Berlin, 1. Juli 1944', p. 3.

Chapter 27: An Unexpected Guest

137 **met at the end of the twenties**: Irmgard von der Lühe, *Eine Frau*, p. 62.
137 **'but nothing finished'**: Ibid., p. 61.
137 **a collection of her father's writings and letters**: Ringshausen, *Widerstand und christlicher Glaube*, p. 463, n. 105. In 1912, she published *Giovanni Segantinis Schriften und Briefe*.
138 **perfected her French**: Meyer, *Elisabeth von Thadden*, p. 473.
138 **and also intimate**: Segantini to Elisabeth Wirth, n.d., LAB B Rep. 058 No. 7254, p. 2.
138 **glued to the radio**: Irmgard von der Lühe, *Eine Frau*, p. 62.
138 **'think of each other'**: Segantini to Elisabeth Wirth, n.d., LAB B Rep. 058 No. 7254, p. 2.
139 **conversations with Hitler**: Ibid., p. 3. The book by Hermann Rauschning was *Gespräche mit Hitler*, which became a bestseller in the US and Britain, where it was published as *Hitler Speaks* in 1940. Most historians no longer regard it as a credible document, but its impact on Elisabeth von Thadden was real.
139 **too much for Elisabeth to bear**: Irmgard von der Lühe, *Eine Frau*, p. 63.
139 **and Germans knew it**: Segantini to Elisabeth Wirth, n.d., LAB B Rep. 058 No. 7254, p. 3.
139 **volunteered for duty**: Irmgard von der Lühe, *Eine Frau*, p. 66.
140 **pouring out her heart**: That was how Elisabeth later described the conversation to Hanna Solf. Solf, Witness statement, 14 October 1952, LAB B Rep. 058 Nr. 7253.
140 **to recognise the misfortune**: Schramm, written submission, 12 March 1993, LAB B Rep. 058 No. 7261, p. 1.

140 **a spontaneous addition**: Ringshausen, *Widerstand und christlicher Glaube*, pp. 463–4.
140 **'right thinking people'**: Ruppel, *Memories*, p. 81.

Chapter 28: Kindred Spirits

142 **A member of the SPD**: 'Führerinformation des Reichsministers der Justiz 1944, Nr. 181', 18 July 1944, BArch R 3001/24089, p. 2. Goebbels prepared bulletins for Hitler called *Führerinformationen* summarising key developments.
142 **Hitler would never have been able to start the war**: Ruppel, *Memories*, p. 79.
142 **liaising between**: In 1963, Wolf Stoecker, the nephew of Otto Kiep, wrote an account, 'Bericht über das Verfahren gegen O. C. Kiep vor dem Volksgerichtshof (Juli/August 1944)' (Report on the Proceedings Against O.C. Kiep Before the People's Court (July/August 1944)), with an explanatory note: 'I wrote this report 19 years after the events at the request of Hanna Kiep for her and her children, endeavouring to recount only the facts without embellishment. For the younger generation, it would be helpful to include a description of the overall situation in Germany at the time, to give them at least some idea of the physical and emotional strain and the external and internal pressure we had to live under back then, the constant air raids day and night, the destruction that spread every day, the increasingly untruthful reports from the Wehrmacht – the Allies had landed in Normandy on June 6, 1944, and the Russians were already in Poland – the increasing surveillance and persecution of dissidents by the Gestapo, and much more. The only place where one could speak openly and let off steam was within the closest family or circle of friends.' Stoecker, 'Bericht', p. 2. Courtesy of Gerhard Ringshausen.
142 **the highest-ranked person present**: Mühlen, *Die Angeklagten*, p. 329.
142 **Bismarck's Cabinet**: Marianne Wellershoff, 'You Can't Report Your Own Father!'
143 **managing their household**: Meyer, *Elisabeth von Thadden*, p. 488
143 **cakes and the cream**: Irmgard von der Lühe, *Eine Frau*, p. 77.
143 **bread and bandages**: Ibid., p. 78.

Chapter 29: A Traitor in the Circle

145 **an obliging bow**: Irmgard von der Lühe, *Eine Frau*, p. 79.
145 **the right connections**: Ringshausen, *Widerstand und christlicher Glaube*, p. 466 and n. 118.
145 **volunteered by Arthur Zarden**: Ibid., p. 466.
145 **'Isn't Frau Solf coming?'**: Irmgard von der Lühe, *Eine Frau*, p. 79.
146 **'Not Siegmund-Schultze?'**: Anne and Friedrich were indeed cousins. See Wörmann, *Widerstand in Charlottenburg*, p. 177.
146 **volunteered to open it**: Solf, Witness statement, 14 October 1952, LAB B Rep. 058 Nr. 7253.
146 **Elisabeth swiftly reassured her**: Ibid.
147 **following the discussion eagerly**: Zarden Ruppel, untitled account, 1979, GDW Sammlung Varia.
147 *New York Times*: 'Berlin: Eight Hours After Blasting by RAF,' *New York Times*, 4 September 1943.
147 **circles around each of the targets**: Solf, Witness statement, 31 May 1954, LAB B Rep. 058 Nr. 7257.
147 **'That is quite clear'**: Clements, *From Ice Set Free*, p. 192. Bruce Clements, Otto Kiep's son-in-law, has Otto saying, 'After this, only a miracle can save Germany.' But Hildegard Rauch, who was Otto's daughter, wrote, 'My father's remarks at "tea" have been written down so often, "unless a miracle happens, I see black for Germany", that these were certainly the right words.' Hildegard Rauch to Gerhard Ringshausen, 21 June 2006. Courtesy of Gerhard Ringshausen.
147 **echoed the sentiment**: Schramm, written submission, 12 March 1993, LAB B Rep. 058 No. 7261. Ehrengart Schramm described conversations she had had with her aunt, Marie-Agnes, or Anza, Braune, who remembered that Reckzeh 'took a strong part in this discussion and provocatively reinforced the "defeatist" statements of the other guests'.
147 **stinging criticism of the military leadership**: Ringshausen, *Widerstand und christlicher Glaube*, p. 465 n. 113.
148 **all post sent abroad was censored**: Ruppel, *Memories*, p. 81.
148 **when crossing the border**: Schramm, written submission, 12 March 1993, LAB B Rep. 058 No. 7261.
148 **communications centre near Lucerne**: Clements, *From Ice Set Free*, p. 192.
148 **it had failed**: Ringshausen, *Widerstand und christlicher Glaube*, p. 465.
148 **positively to glitter**: Irmgard von der Lühe, *Eine Frau*, p. 80.

148 **later than the others**: Ruppel, *Memories*, p. 81.
148 **warning glances**: Irmgard von der Lühe, *Eine Frau*, p. 80.
149 **'new men'**: Ringshausen, 'Zwischen Dissens und Widerstand', p. 202.
149 **protect the west against Bolshevism**: Ringshausen, *Widerstand und christlicher Glaube*, p. 466 n. 119.
149 **Zarden had lots to say**: Ibid., p. 466.
149 **Elisabeth remembered**: Schramm, written submission, 12 March 1993, LAB B Rep. 058 No. 7261.
149 **already hard at work in Switzerland**: Ringshausen, 'Zwischen Dissens und Widerstand', p. 202.
150 **he shook his head**: Clements, *From Ice Set Free*, p. 192.
150 **'communications centre' too**: Ibid., pp. 192–3.
150 **Otto dug out his card**: Ringshausen, 'Zwischen Dissens und Widerstand', p. 200. Ringshausen writes that Otto Kiep took up Reckzeh's offer a few days after the party, sending him for delivery 'a letter to a politically uninterested friend in Lucerne', with a view to helping Reckzeh have social contacts in Switzerland. It's possible that he gave Reckzeh two items to deliver, at two different times, but it seems more likely that this non-political friend was in fact the Mr Finkler referred to in Clements's biography of Otto – and that, as Clements has it, the handover of his calling card (rather than a letter) happened at the party itself.
151 **along with Fanny von Kurowsky**: Solf, Witness statement, 31 May 1954, LAB B Rep. 058 Nr. 7257.
151 **late husband's archives**: Solf, Witness statement, 14 October 1952, LAB B Rep. 058 Nr. 7253.
151 **letters to acquaintances**: Ringshausen, 'Zwischen Dissens und Widerstand', p. 202.
151 **the Danish envoy in Bern**: Solf, Witness statement, 14 October 1952, LAB B Rep. 058 Nr. 7253.
152 **to negotiate a separate peace**: Irmgard von der Lühe, *Eine Frau*, p. 82.
152 **everyone would turn out to be a spook**: Ibid., p. 81.

Chapter 30: Secret Listeners

155 **and most committedly Nazi**: Kahn, 'Forschungsamt', p. 12.
155 **fifteen German cities**: 'Diese Haderlumpen', *Der Spiegel*.
156 **34,000 telegrams**: Ibid.
156 **'A' stations**: *European Axis Signal Intelligence in World War II*, vol. 7: *Goering's 'Research' Bureau*, p. 50.

NOTES TO PAGES 156 TO 161

156 **As for 'E'**: there is no mention of 'E' stations in the post-war American report on the *Forschungsamt*. Ibid.
156 **any conversation at any time**: Ibid.
156 **a bulb would light up**: Kahn, 'Forschungsamt', p. 13.
156 **Z-man**: Gellerman, . . . *und lauschten für Hitler*, p. 73.
156 **white paper**: Ibid.
157 **transcript of a vicious joke**: Kahn, 'Forschungsamt', p. 15.
157 **consumer of the Research Office's output**: *European Axis Signal Intelligence in World War II*, vol. 7: *Goering's 'Research' Bureau*, p. 39.
158 **the Führer typewriter**: Gellerman, . . . *und lauschten für Hitler*, p. 74.
158 **Carl Goerdeler, Friedrich Siegmund-Schultze and General Ludwig Beck**: Irmgard von der Lühe, *Eine Frau*, p. 83.
158 **the telephone calls of the Czechoslovak leadership**: Kahn, 'Forschungsamt', pp. 15–16.

Chapter 31: A Mole at HQ

159 **'I'd rather have it back'**: Irmgard von der Lühe, *Eine Frau*, p. 82.
160 **to stand in his way**: Ringshausen, *Widerstand und christlicher Glaube*, p. 467 and n. 123. In Ringshausen's account, it was indeed Reckzeh's father who burned the letter or letters. That does seem the more likely scenario, given that there is little evidence that Reckzeh felt the kind of regret that would have prompted him to destroy the very prize he had secured at such effort less than twenty-four hours earlier.
160 **section 13: Internal Affairs Evaluation**: *European Axis Signal Intelligence in World War II*, vol. 7: *Goering's 'Research' Bureau*, p. 44.
161 **joined the party as early as 1920**: Kahn, 'Forschungsamt', p. 12. The founder was Gottfried Schapper, 'a small, energetic, impulsive redhead' and 'Jew-hater', according to Kahn.
161 **very reliable**: *European Axis Signal Intelligence in World War II*, vol. 7: *Goering's 'Research' Bureau*, p. 60.
161 **discreet sympathy for the German opposition**: Tuchel, 'Die Sicherheitspolizeischule Drögen und der 20. Juli 1944', p. 121.
161 **loose group of resisters around Hans Oster**: Ringshausen, 'Zwischen Dissens und Widerstand', p. 225.
161 **Gestapo surveillance requests**: Ringshausen, *Widerstand und christlicher Glaube*, p. 468 n. 129.
161 **well-timed warnings**: John, 'Some Facts and Aspects of the Plot Against Hitler', p. 40.

161 **a copy of Paul Reckzeh's Gestapo report**: Clements, *From Ice Set Free*, p. 193.

Chapter 32: Sixth Sense

163 **lunch at the Cavalry Club**: Clements, *From Ice Set Free*, p. 193.
163 **closure of many eateries**: Spechler, 'For 115 Years'.
163 **Horcher**: Ruppel, *Memories*, p. 78. Horcher was a clear favourite among the aristocratic classes in particular. In her diaries, Marie 'Missie' Vassiltchikov similarly singled out the restaurant for praise and in part for the same reason as Irmgard: there, one could gorge and 'they scorn the very idea of food coupons'. Vassiltchikov, *Berlin Diaries*, p. 43.
163 **official demands for abstemiousness**: Moorhouse, *Berlin at War*, p. 98.
163 ***Eintopfsonntag***: Rüther, *Hitlers 'Eintopfsonntag'*, p. 40
164 **lobster or oyster**: Vassiltchikov, *Berlin Diaries*, pp. 34–5.
164 **a touring production direct from Italy**: Ibid., p. 49.
164 **danced at fabulous embassy parties**: Ibid., p. 61.
165 **'I wish I had not gone'**: Ruppel, *Memories*, p. 81.
165 **A young man in good health**: Ibid., p. 80.
165 **telltale clicks**: Ibid., p. 82.
167 **pumpkin on her head**: Maltzan, *Schlage die Trommel*, pp. 169–70.

Chapter 33: Be Warned

168 **'absolutely lethal'**: Irmgard von der Lühe, *Eine Frau*, p. 84.
168 **they gasped**: Ibid.
168 **always declined invitations**: Ibid., p. 75.
169 **that little black book**: Zarden Ruppel, untitled account, 1979, GDW Sammlung Varia, p. 4.
170 **the innocent and simple wife**: Clements, *From Ice Set Free*, p. 194.
170 **he expected to be arrested**: Ibid., p. 195.
171 **'I can't sleep any more'**: Irmgard von der Lühe, *Eine Frau*, p. 85.

Chapter 34: Across the Border

173 **an unwitting prop**: Once it became clear to her that she had been duped at the lunch she had hosted in Sils for Paul Reckzeh, Bianca

Segantini gave long and anguished thought to the question of how she had allowed herself to be tricked and especially to the role of Reckzeh's wife, Inge. 'I still ask myself whether she was already aware of her husband's intentions at the time of her visit to me,' Segantini wrote in a nine-page, undated letter to a friend, which replayed the whole encounter. Had the young woman, so passionate in her rejection of Nazism, been in on the deception – or was she another of Reckzeh's victims? Segantini decided that it was almost certainly the latter. Her view was strengthened when she learned that Inge had wanted a divorce as soon as the war ended. But Segantini admitted that she reached her conclusion in part because the alternative was too awful to contemplate. 'I do not dare to pass judgement on Frau Reckzeh today; if she had played his game, she would have been of such human depravity that I cannot or will not believe it.' Segantini to Elisabeth Wirth, n.d., LAB B Rep. 058 Nr. 7254, p. 8.

173 **speak of their plans**: Ringshausen, *Widerstand und christlicher Glaube*, p. 467.
174 **the Swiss police**: Ibid.
174 **owner of the hotel**: Irmgard von der Lühe, *Eine Frau*, p. 86.
174 **'You are making a mess of your life'**: Ibid.
175 **the fondest of old friends**: Ibid.
175 **show of kindness**: Hanna Kiep, 'Schilderung Teegesellschaft', apparently May 1944, GDW, NL Kiep.
175 **were so superficial**: Tuchel, 'Die Sicherheitspolizeischule Drögen und der 20. Juli 1944', p. 121.
175 **a brief written note**: Ibid.
175 **turned him away**: Hanna Kiep, 'Schilderung Teegesellschaft', apparently May 1944, GDW, NL Kiep.
175 **'Let him realise'**: Ibid.
175 **as harmless as possible**: Zarden Ruppel, untitled account, 1979, GDW Sammlung Varia, pp. 3–4.

Chapter 35: Double Bluff

178 **district commander**: Irmgard von der Lühe, *Eine Frau*, p. 99.
178 **faced the interrogators**: Ibid., pp. 94–5.
178 **'It's not about me'**: Ibid., p. 87.
179 **another tea party**: Ibid.
179 **Wirth's political plans**: Tuchel, 'Die Sicherheitspolizeischule Drögen und der 20. Juli 1944', p. 120.

179 **new German government and constitution**: Statement by Walter Huppenkothen, 'Verhaltnis Wehrmacht-Sicherheitspolizei, II.Teil', n.d., IfZ, ZS 249-1, p. 29.
180 **'How many wagons?'**: Irmgard von der Lühe, *Eine Frau*, p. 88.
180 **the war in Asia**: Ibid. The two women cited reports from Indonesia.

Chapter 36: Silk and Lace

183 **tall, fragrant, gorgeous and quite naked**: Irmgard von der Lühe, *Eine Frau*, p. 92.
185 **saving Germany from chaos**: Statement by Walter Huppenkothen, 'Verhaltnis Wehrmacht-Sicherheitspolizei, II.Teil', n.d., IfZ, ZS 249-1, p. 29.
185 **a series of cold shoulders**: Tuchel, 'Die Sicherheitspolizeischule Drögen und der 20. Juli 1944', p. 121.

Chapter 37: Himmler Decides

186 **a special commission**: Statement by Walter Huppenkothen, 'Verhaltnis Wehrmacht-Sicherheitspolizei, II.Teil', n.d., IfZ, ZS 249-1, p. 30.
186 **desk IV A1b**: 'Organisation of the RSHA', vol. 6, section 11.04 (RSHA charts), Donovan Nuremberg Trials Collection, Cornell University Law Library.
187 **he encountered only coldness**: Statement by Walter Huppenkothen, 'Verhaltnis Wehrmacht-Sicherheitspolizei, II.Teil', n.d., IfZ, ZS 249-1, p. 30.
187 **remarkably few calls**: Irmgard von der Lühe, *Eine Frau*, p. 96.
187 **a tea cosy over the receiver**: Heuss-Knapp, *Schmale Wege*, p. 106.
188 **authorised Lange's request**: Tuchel, 'Zur vergessenen Vorgeschichte des 20. Juli 1944', p. 1.

Chapter 38: Dawn Raids

189 **'There's nothing here that could hurt me'**: Clements, *From Ice Set Free*, p. 195.
190 **Albrecht could find no reply**: Ibid., p. 196.
190 **'clear-sighted Kiep'**: Tuchel, 'Verfolgung, Haft und Tod', p. 192.

190 **'a cousin from the front'**: Irmgard von der Lühe, *Eine Frau*, p. 97. The use of this phrase is likely to have been a ruse to encourage Anne to come out of her meeting and into the clutches of the Gestapo.
191 **'an oasis in ruins'**: Ibid., p. 94.

Chapter 39: Free No More

193 **fourth address in two months**: Tuchel, 'Verfolgung, Haft und Tod', pp. 192–3. The observation was made by Helmuth James Graf von Moltke in a letter to his wife, Freya, on 4 January 1944.
193 **came to take Otto away**: This simplest version is the one recalled in ibid., p. 193.
194 **four o'clock in the morning**: Clements, *From Ice Set Free*, p. 197. The dawn raid features in the account written by Otto Kiep's son-in-law.
194 **a third version**: John, 'Some Facts and Aspects of the Plot Against Hitler', p. 38. This account is the one offered by Otto John, a German former intelligence officer involved in the 20 July 1944 plot to assassinate Hitler. After the war, John's career would take an intriguing turn. In 1954, he went missing for three days, only to resurface in East Berlin, where he became a vocal critic of the west. The following year John defected back to West Germany, claiming the move east had been against his will and that he had been abducted by the KGB. That version did not find sufficient takers to prevent John being convicted of treason by a West German court and sentenced to four years in prison.
195 **put her daughters to bed**: Letter from Hildegard Rauch to Gerhard Ringshausen, 21 June 2006.
196 **reported to his superiors**: Irmgard von der Lühe, *Eine Frau*, p. 85.

Chapter 40: The Fall

201 **staff headquarters of Heinrich Himmler**: Tuchel, 'Verfolgung, Haft und Tod', p. 194.
201 **as well as section IV A 2**: Tuchel, 'Die Sicherheitspolizeischule Drögen und der 20. Juli 1944', p. 122.
202 **letter of thanks**: Ruppel, *Memories*, p. 84
204 **washroom window**: Irmgard von der Lühe, *Eine Frau*, p. 102. Others suggest it was, in fact, a stairwell window. See Hank, 'Das abrupte Ende einer Karriere'.

Chapter 41: The First Round

206 **for five hours**: Solf, 'Denkschrift über meine Haft, Genf 1947', 6 February 1947, http://www.arenberg-info.de/htm/Denkschrift-J-S.htm
207 **cut off from the outside world**: Ballestrem-Solf, untitled account of her imprisonment and trial, 6 February 1947, Ballestrem, p. 1. In the letterhead on that document, the countess identifies herself as 'Gräfin Lagi Ballestrem-Solf', her preferred version of her married name.
208 **verbally and in writing**: Ibid.
209 **That night he strangled himself**: Boehm, *We Survived*, p. 137.
209 **severe threats and intimidation**: Ballestrem-Solf, untitled account of her imprisonment and trial, 6 February 1947, Ballestrem, p. 1.
210 **the odd moan**: Boehm, *We Survived*, p. 137.
210 **drab rows of barracks**: Ibid., p. 138.
211 **twenty-four hours without a break**: Irmgard von der Lühe, *Eine Frau*, p. 102.
211 **habit of a Red Cross nurse**: Ibid., p. 103.
212 **word of honour**: Tuchel, 'Verfolgung, Haft und Tod', p. 196.
212 **'the breaking process'**: Ibid., p. 196. The phrase was Otto Kiep's and sounds like a euphemism for torture.
213 **another premature death**: Boehm, *We Survived*, p. 138.
213 **he 'fully understood'**: Tuchel, 'Zur vergessenen Vorgeschichte des 20. Juli 1944', p. 200.

Chapter 42: Ravensbrück

215 **camp for men was added**: Mahn und Gedenkstätte Ravensbrück, '1939–1945 Ravensbrück Concentration Camp', https://www.ravensbrueck-sbg.de/en/history/1939-1945/
216 **Siemens & Halske**: Ibid.
216 **under a programme**: It was classified as Aktion 14f13. Burleigh, *Death and Deliverance*, p. 220.
218 **several valuable privileges**: Eschebach, *Ravensbrück*, p. 35.
219 **finished with life**: Boehm, *We Survived*, p. 139.
219 **a 'cosmopolitan outlook'**: Ibid.
219 **pure suffering**: Irmgard von der Lühe, *Eine Frau*, p. 109.
219 **eyes were bloodshot**: Tuchel, 'Verfolgung, Haft und Tod', p. 201.

Chapter 43: Threats and Menaces

221 **fifteen or thirty minutes**: Hanna Solf testified that the lights would come on every half-hour. Irmgard von der Lühe has it as every fifteen minutes. See Solf, 'Denkschrift über meine Haft, Genf 1947', and Irmgard von der Lühe, *Eine Frau*, p. 107.
221 **the screams of strangers**: Solf, 'Denkschrift über meine Haft, Genf 1947', 6 February 1947.
221 **taken by car**: Solf, NMT 3 Justice Case testimony, 16 April 1947, p. 2151.
221 **always without food**: Ibid.
221 **the letters Reckzeh had delivered**: Solf, Witness statement, 14 October 1952, LAB B Rep. 058 Nr. 7253.
222 **on three grounds**: Solf, NMT 3 Justice Case testimony, 16 April 1947, p. 2152.
222 **'If you are sentenced to death'**: Solf, 'Denkschrift über meine Haft, Genf 1947', 6 February 1947.
222 **we will arrest your sons**: Hanna Solf to Ricarda Huch, 5 July 1946, IfZ ZS/A-26a/3-34.
222 **her youngest son**: Boehm, *We Survived*, p. 140.
222 **seven o'clock in the morning**: Solf, 'Denkschrift über meine Haft, Genf 1947', 6 February 1947.
223 **decaying turnips**: Boehm, *We Survived*, p. 140.
223 **putrefaction in a damp, dark cellar**: Irmgard von der Lühe, *Eine Frau*, p. 107.
223 **barred from speaking**: Zarden Ruppel, untitled account, 1979, GDW Sammlung Varia, p. 10.
223 **four o'clock in the afternoon**: This detail and many of those that follow in the closing pages of this chapter are drawn from Boehm, *We Survived*, pp. 138–40.
225 **execute my mother**: Solf, NMT 3 Justice Case testimony, 16 April 1947, p. 2206.

Chapter 44: Body and Soul

226 **an attempt on his own life**: Tuchel, 'Verfolgung, Haft und Tod', p. 206.
226 **coffee and French cognac**: Ibid., p. 200.
227 **seize power for themselves**: Clements, *From Ice Set Free*, p. 198.
227 **treatment in Ravensbrück**: Ibid., p. 199.

Chapter 45: The Fallout

229 **the Hitler Youth**: Bassett, *Hitler's Spy Chief*, p. 279.
229 **a beauty**: Shirer, *Rise and Fall*, p. 921.
229 **a pagan creed**: Bassett, *Hitler's Spy Chief*, p. 279.
229 *innere Emigration*: Wheeler-Bennett, *Nemesis of Power*, p. 595.
229 **working for the Abwehr**: Sykes, *Troubled Loyalty*, p. 399.
229 **the help of Erich's cousin**: Klemperer, *German Resistance Against Hitler*, p. 336.
229 **secret inks and codes**: Bassett, *Hitler's Spy Chief*, p. 280.
230 **the compartment next door**: Ibid., p. 281.
230 **connected to Otto's**: Wheeler-Bennett, *Nemesis of Power*, p. 595.
230 **'You were coming up to Oxford, I believe?'**: Bassett, *Hitler's Spy Chief*, p. 280.
231 **the Abwehr codebooks**: Shirer, *Rise and Fall*, p. 921.
231 **Abwehr was useless**: Wheeler-Bennett, *Nemesis of Power*, p. 596.
231 **defeatist intelligentsia**: Reitlinger, *SS: Alibi of a Nation*, p. 306.
231 **bundle of reports**: Colvin, *Canaris*, p. 194.
231 **on 18 February**: Shirer, *Rise and Fall*, p. 921.
231 **'a unified German secret intelligence service'**: Colvin, *Canaris*, p. 195.
232 **he would not go**: Ibid.

Chapter 46: The Bridge of Love

233 **flattery and promises**: Tuchel, 'Verfolgung, Haft und Tod', p. 194.
234 **in the garden nursery**: Eschebach, *Zellenbau*, p. 38.
234 **blood sausage for dinner**: Ibid., p. 37.
234 **huntress**: Clements, *From Ice Set Free*, p. 200.
234 **'I saw you'**: Ibid.
235 **a Thermos flask**: Eschebach, *Zellenbau*, p. 39.
235 **forget-me-not**: Ibid.
236 **the request was denied**: Tuchel, 'Verfolgung, Haft und Tod', p. 201.

Chapter 47: The Scourge of Guilt

238 **confessed to everything**: Irmgard von der Lühe, *Eine Frau*, p. 105.
239 **an enchantress**: Ibid., p. 106.

Chapter 48: The Hands of God

242 **'undoubtedly certain'**: Tuchel, 'Verfolgung, Haft und Tod', p. 203.
243 **calmly, rationally and unsentimentally**: Clements, *From Ice Set Free*, p. 201.
244 **13 June 1944**: Kiep, *Mein Lebensweg*, p. 204.
245 **'My Ring, Your Ring'**: Clements, *From Ice Set Free*, pp. 203–4.

Chapter 49: All but a Miracle

246 **listened to the BBC**: Zarden Ruppel, untitled account, 1979, GDW Sammlung Varia, p. 11.
248 **'other people's letters'**: Maltzan, *Schlage die Trommel*, p. 128.
248 **and ate them**: After Maria saw that Count Hermann Keyserling, a noted philosopher and author, had expressed himself on paper – handmade stationery, to be precise – without restraint, she telephoned him, both to alert him to his folly and to urge him to stop using handmade paper, which was especially unpleasant to swallow. Maltzan, *Schlage die Trommel*, p. 131.
248 **a deserter**: Christiansen, *Dommedag*, p. 20.
248 **a secret radio station**: Ibid., p. 21.
248 **organisational genius**: Maltzan, *Schlage die Trommel*, p. 161.
249 **'I can't kill anyone'**: Ibid., p. 166.
250 **'I can't tell you where I've been'**: Ibid., p. 160.
250 **all but a miracle**: Hirschel, Testimony, 30 November 1950, YVA M.31/3545.

Chapter 50: Fate Has Intervened

251 **the guillotine**: Kempner, *Priester vor Hitlers Tribunalen*, p. 278.
251 **'Such a plague must be eradicated'**: In his closing statement,

Freisler said, 'This act is so evil and criminal that the accused must be eliminated. I have never until this moment used the word "eradicate", but I use it here. Such a plague-boil must be eradicated.' Metzger, *Gefangenschaftsbriefe*, p. 125. See also Swidler, *Bloodwitness*, p. 102.

251 **parting words**: In a letter written from Plötzensee prison dated 30 September 1944, Metzger paraphrased Paul's prison epistles, adding, 'like him, I know that I too am supported by the prayers of my loved ones, for which I am very grateful.' Kempner, *Priester vor Hitlers Tribunalen*, p. 278.

252 **the execution of Metzger**: Ibid., p. 286.

252 **air raids on Berlin**: Clements, *From Ice Set Free*, p. 204.

253 **'the success of this effort'**: Tuchel, 'Verfolgung, Haft und Tod', p. 204.

253 **the power to confiscate**: Ibid., 204.

253 **issued charges against him**: Stoecker, 'Bericht', p. 3. The indictment of the chief Reich prosecutor was dated 22 June 1944 and was received by the People's Court on 26 June 1944.

Chapter 51: The Court

257 **Wilhelms-Gymnasium**: See 'König-Wilhelm-Gymnasium', https://berlingeschichte.de/lexikon/mitte/k/koenig_wilhelm_gymnasium.htm Irmgard von der Lühe mistakenly locates the court in the Hotel Eden: Irmgard von der Lühe, *Eine Frau*, p. 117.

257 **150 seats**: Wagner-Nigrin, 'Volksgerichts-Prozess, Berlin, 1. Juli 1944', p. 1. Stoecker puts the figure closer to one hundred. Stoecker, 'Bericht', p. 3.

257 **the cousin's friends**: One of whom was Ruth Wagner-Nigrin, who wrote her brief account of the trial soon afterwards.

258 **the previous afternoon**: Solf, NMT 3 Justice Case testimony, 16 April 1947, p. 2155.

258 **politically reliable**: Stoecker, 'Bericht', p. 4.

258 **considered the case hopeless**: Ringshausen, *Widerstand und christlicher Glaube*, p. 474.

258 **set of handcuffs**: Stoecker, 'Bericht', p. 4.

259 **corralled into a single cell**: Zarden Ruppel, untitled account, 1979, GDW Sammlung Varia, p. 14.

259 **witness for the prosecution**: Ringshausen, *Widerstand und christlicher Glaube*, p. 473.

259 **the low murmur**: Wagner-Nigrin, 'Volksgerichts-Prozess, Berlin, 1. Juli 1944', p. 2.
259 **a raised table**: Stoecker, 'Bericht', p. 4.

Chapter 52: The Hanging Judge

260 **the summer of 1920**: Buchheit, *Richter in rote Robe*, p. 17.
260 **party member 9,679**: NSDAP-Gaukartei, 'Reckzeh, Paul', BArch R 9361-IX KARTEI/33941315.
261 **'Justice is whatever serves the Führer'**: Clements, *From Ice Set Free*, p. 204.
261 **no contact with their clients**: Stoecker, 'Bericht', p. 4.
261 **the indictment**: Indictment of 22 June 1944, p. 2. See Tuchel, 'Verfolgung, Haft und Tod', pp. 205–6.
262 **an acid aside**: Stoecker, 'Bericht', p. 5. Stoecker noted that 'cynical remarks and shouting' were Freisler's stock-in-trade.
262 **glisten and glitter**: Wagner-Nigrin, 'Volksgerichts-Prozess, Berlin, 1. Juli 1944', p. 3.

Chapter 53: In the Dock

263 **skirt and blouse**: Alves, 'Erlebnisse und Gedanken', GDW, NL Kiep.
263 **more of the truth**: Stoecker, 'Bericht', p. 5. The worried ally of Kiep was his nephew Wolf Stoecker, who later described Elisabeth von Thadden as giving answers that 'endeavoured to correspond to the truth even more than was necessary'.
263 **the literature of atheism**: Irmgard von der Lühe, *Eine Frau*, p. 120.
263 **'Say it, say it!'**: Ibid., pp. 126–7.
264 **'defeatist statements'**: Tuchel, 'Verfolgung, Haft und Tod', p. 208.
264 **'Unless a miracle happens'**: Stoecker, 'Bericht', p. 6.
265 **political contact**: Tuchel, 'Verfolgung, Haft und Tod', p. 206.
266 **barely an hour**: Ibid., pp. 208–9.
266 **a secret document**: Solf, Witness statement, 14 October 1952, LAB B Rep. 058 Nr. 7253. Solf referred to Otto Kiep showing the tea-party guests a 'map of Berlin'. Given that no other source speaks of such a map, it seems likelier that what Solf had in mind was the aerial photograph of Berlin published in the *New York Times*.

266 **Just because you are a traitor**: Witness statement by Dr Manfred Stürzbecher, 2 May 1983, GDW, NL Kiep. As a fifteen-year-old Luftwaffe auxiliary, he had been sent to the court as an observer.
267 **three hours**: Clements, *From Ice Set Free*, p. 207.

Chapter 54: 'Anti-State Person'

268 **Hanna was contemptuous**: Clements, *From Ice Set Free*, p. 205.
268 **Small and wiry**: Maltzan, *Schlage die Trommel*, p. 170.
268 **peace negotiations**: Boehm, *We Survived*, p. 141.
268 **she didn't know Wirth**: Solf, Witness statement, 31 May 1954, LAB B Rep. 058 Nr. 7257.
268 **'I did not need a Dr Reckzeh'**: Solf, Witness statement, 14 October 1952, LAB B Rep. 058 Nr. 7253.
268 **Hanna's views**: Boehm, *We Survived*, p. 141.
268 **'liberal in the Goethean sense'**: Maltzan, *Schlage die Trommel*, p. 170.
269 **'. . . we Germans'**: Nicolson, 'Marginal Comment', 10 August 1945, p. 126.
269 **grumbling**: Stoecker, 'Bericht', p. 6.
269 **defeatist, demoralising character**: Hilger van Scherpenberg insisted that he had 'contradicted on several points' the gloomy talk he heard at the tea party. Otto Kiep remained insistent that his colleague had offered no such contrary view, but had instead supplied reasons of his own to be downcast about Germany's prospects. Glumly Otto would conclude that Scherpenberg and his lawyer had constructed a legal defence that identified Otto alone as the guilty man. Ringshausen, *Widerstand und christlicher Glaube*, p. 465 n. 113.
269 **bitter smiles**: Tuchel, 'Verfolgung, Haft und Tod', p. 209.
270 **drawn towards socialism**: Stoecker, 'Bericht', p. 6.
270 **the meaning of 'defeatism'**: Clements, *From Ice Set Free*, p. 206.
270 **'Goerdeler, did I say?'**: Irmgard von der Lühe, *Eine Frau*, p. 128.
270 **have the Kaiser back**: Stoecker, 'Bericht', p. 6.
270 **'Easy for you to say'**: Zarden Ruppel, untitled account, 1979, GDW Sammlung Varia, p. 13.
270 **dark basement room**: Ibid., p. 14.
271 **sitting behind her**: Ruppel, *Memories*, p. 94.
271 **'. . . a Gestapo stooge'**: Boehm, *We Survived*, pp. 141–2.
271 **clearing his throat**: Ibid., p. 142.
271 **'cannot dismiss out of hand'**: Ruppel, *Memories*, p. 94.

271 **dressed all in black**: Irmgard von der Lühe, *Eine Frau*, p. 124.
271 **'heroic death'**: Schramm, written submission, 12 March 1993, LAB B Rep. 058 No. 7261.
272 **how overworked**: Ringshausen, *Widerstand und christlicher Glaube*, p. 473.
272 **since the noon recess**: Solf, NMT 3 Justice Case testimony, 16 April 1947, p. 2157.
272 **slick with pomade**: Witness statement by Dr Manfred Stürzbecher, 2 May 1983, GDW, NL Kiep.
272 **in front of Anza Braune**: Schramm, written submission, 12 March 1993, LAB B Rep. 058 Nr. 7261.
272 **sandwiches, wrapped in paper**: Witness statement by Dr Manfred Stürzbecher, 2 May 1983, GDW, NL Kiep.
272 **amicably he chatted**: Solf, Witness statement, 14 October 1952, LAB B Rep. 058 Nr. 7253.

Chapter 55: Star Witness

273 **volunteer any information**: Clements, *From Ice Set Free*, p. 205.
273 **pulling teeth**: Stoecker, 'Bericht', p. 7.
273 **public attention**: Tuchel, 'Verfolgung, Haft und Tod', p. 209.
274 **'You pig'**: Alves, 'Erlebnisse und Gedanken', GDW, NL Kiep.
274 **submissive and obedient**: Ibid.
274 **ten thousand Reichsmarks**: Ibid.
274 **left side of the courtroom**: Clements, *From Ice Set Free*, p. 207.
275 **ashamed of him**: Tuchel, 'Verfolgung, Haft und Tod', p. 210.
275 **the judge was angered**: Clements, *From Ice Set Free*, p. 208.
275 **the meaning of national socialism**: Ibid., p. 207.
276 **amazed everyone**: Boehm, *We Survived*, p. 142.

Chapter 56: The Verdict

277 **passed a note up to Freisler**: Irmgard von der Lühe, *Eine Frau*, p. 128.
277 **'Defendant Solf'**: Solf, 'Denkschrift über meine Haft, Genf 1947', 6 February 1947.
277 **Sweden's man in Berlin**: Boehm, *We Survived*, p. 142
277 **full dress uniform**: Elisabeth von Gustedt, Diaries, BArch N 1121 18, pp. 13–14.

278 **an act unfriendly**: Schad, *Frauen gegen Hitler*, p. 179.
278 **9 p.m.**: Solf, NMT 3 Justice Case testimony, 16 April 1947, p. 2160.
278 **'That's that fixed'**: Schramm, written submission, 12 March 1993, LAB B Rep. 058 No. 7261.
278 **delivered the verdict**: The quotations that appear in this paragraph and the rest of the chapter all come from the judge's verdict. 'Der Oberreichsanwalt beim Volksgerichtshof 1 D 224/44 2 J 243/44 8 Rs', 1 July 1944, reprinted in Mühlen, *Die Angeklagten*, pp. 328–34.
279 **'her intellectual staleness'**: Mühlen, *Die Angeklagten*, p. 331.

Chapter 57: Killing Hitler

285 **eyepatch**: Marek, 'Failed Plot to Kill Hitler'.
286 **eight o'clock**: Heinemann, *Operation 'Valkyrie'*, p. 252.
287 **Concrete, windowless**: Hasic, 'A Group of German Leaders Tried to Kill Hitler'.
287 **the briefing hut**: Heinemann, *Operation 'Valkyrie'*, p. 252.
287 **diffused and diminished**: Hasic, 'A Group of German Leaders Tried to Kill Hitler'.
287 **pencil detonator**: Dulles, *Germany's Underground*, p. 2.
287 **Plastit W explosive**: 'Der Anschlag', *Der Spiegel*.
287 **frantically closing**: Ibid.
287 **heavy oak**: Heinemann, *Operation 'Valkyrie'*, p. 252.
288 **Wilhelm Keitel introduced**: Marek, 'Failed Plot to Kill Hitler'.
288 **General Adolf Heusinger**: 'Der Anschlag', *Der Spiegel*.
288 **a better look at the map**: Benne, 'Der Fuß an der Aktentasche'.
288 **make a phone call**: John, 'Some Facts and Aspects of the Plot Against Hitler', p. 51.
288 **12.42 p.m.**: Hasic, 'A Group of German Leaders Tried to Kill Hitler'.
288 **leap of flame**: 'Der Anschlag', *Der Spiegel*.

Chapter 58: 'The Führer Adolf Hitler Is Dead'

289 **a massive cloud of smoke**: Marek, 'Failed Plot to Kill Hitler'.
289 **in singed tatters**: 'Der Anschlag', *Der Spiegel*.
289 **choice propaganda image**: Hasic, 'A Group of German Leaders Tried to Kill Hitler'.

289 **'someone tried to kill me'**: 'Der Anschlag', *Der Spiegel*.
289 **talked their way through**: Heinemann, *Operation 'Valkyrie'*, p. 252.
290 **huddled together in the Bendlerblock**: Ibid.
290 **'The Führer Adolf Hitler is dead'**: Jander, 'Coup by Teleprinter'.
290 **explosion of a 15 cm shell**: John, 'Some Facts and Aspects of the Plot Against Hitler', p. 60.
290 **'merely been slightly injured'**: Ibid., p. 58.
290 **and firmly believed**: Ibid., p. 65.
290 **the highest order of priority**: Ibid., p. 59.
291 **in Vienna and Prague**: 'The Attempted Coup of July 20, 1944', Gedankstätte Deutsche Widerstand, https://www.gdw-berlin.de/en/recess/topics/11-the-attempted-coup-of-july-20-1944/
291 **'Do you recognise my voice?'**: The officer, Major Otto Ernst Remer, was in Berlin with Goebbels, who, around 7 p.m., called Hitler. 'Goebbels put through a call to Rastenburg and handed Remer the telephone. He recognized the Führer's voice and came to attention as Hitler briefly explained to him what had happened; he finished by saying, "A clique of lawless, faithless officers have made an attempt on my life, but I am unharmed. I order you to crush this rebellion by any means necessary. You will take your orders from no one but me – your authority is absolute. Do you understand?" "Yes, my Führer."' Galante, *Operation Valkyrie*, pp. 208–9.
291 **radio broadcast had confirmed Hitler's survival**: Hoffmann, *History of the German Resistance*, p. 439.
291 **sequence of teleprinter messages**: Jander, 'Coup by Teleprinter'.
291 **his slow death filmed**: Hasic, 'A Group of German Leaders Tried to Kill Hitler'.

Chapter 59: A Name on a List

292 **at full volume**: Tuchel, 'Verfolgung, Haft und Tod', p. 211.
293 **old, shabby clothing**: Wagner, *Der Volksgerichtshof*, p. 671.
293 **4,980 supposed traitors**: Rothfels, *German Opposition*, p. 16.
293 **'hanged like cattle'**: Kershaw, *Hitler 1936–1945*, p. 693.
294 **one million Reichsmarks**: Boehm, *We Survived*, p. 143.
294 **visiting his parents' grave**: Ritter, *German Resistance*, p. 291. The woman who betrayed him, Helene Schwärzel, had known the Goerdeler family since childhood, but Goerdeler's biographer describes her motives as 'an irresistible love of sensation and a sort of sub-conscious

desire for notoriety'. She later regretted her actions. See also, 'Die Verräterin Goerdelers verhaftet', *Weltpresse*, 19 January 1946, p. 2.
294 **serve in his administration**: Clements, *From Ice Set Free*, p. 209.

Chapter 60: The Butcher's Hook

295 **'The press . . . In prospect was Kiep'**: Tuchel, 'Verfolgung, Haft und Tod', pp. 214–15.
295 **'Some treason plots'**: Ibid., p. 215. Report of the Chief of the Security Police and SD, 8 August 1944, in Jacobsen (ed.), *Spiegelbild einer Verschwörung*, p. 175.
296 **killing the man**: The approach had come in August 1943 from Prussian Minister of Finance Johannes Popitz. 'Die Rede Himmlers vor den Gauleitern', *Vierteljahrshefte für Zeitgeschichte*, p. 376.
296 **'. . . the envoy Herr Kiep'**: Ibid.
296 **spread of defeatism**: Tuchel, 'Zur vergessenen Vorgeschichte des 20. Juli 1944', p. 2.
297 **thick-set SS man appeared**: Tuchel, 'Verfolgung, Haft und Tod', p. 218.
298 **life of the Führer**: According to the leading historian of the resistance, Johannes Tuchel, it is quite possible that Otto Kiep had, in fact, been in contact with Goerdeler but had kept that contact from his wife since the autumn of 1943, 'so as not to endanger her and their children'. Correspondence with Dr Johannes Tuchel, 12 March 2025.
298 **a deplorable state**: Stoecker, 'Bericht', p. 14.
298 **picked up the phone**: Tuchel, 'Verfolgung, Haft und Tod', p. 219.
298 **wrote for twenty**: Clements, *From Ice Set Free*, p. 209.
299 **they did not speak**: Ibid.

Chapter 61: Operation Swedish Furniture

300 **embassy furniture**: Flohr, 'Geheime Fracht'.
300 **encouraged by a bribe**: Block and Drucker, *Rescuers*, p. 154.
302 **longest days of her life**: Maltzan, *Schlage die Trommel*, p. 163.
303 **bitterly cold**: Gross interview with Maria von Maltzan, 14 August 1982.
303 **tapped on the window**: Ibid.

303 **'There's our veterinarian'**: Flohr, 'Geheime Fracht'.
303 **twenty Jews**: 'Maltzan von Maria', Yad Vashem, https://collections.yadvashem.org/en/righteous/4043010

Chapter 62: Death Row

305 **during the breaks**: This detail, and many of those that follow in this chapter, are drawn from the account of Elisabeth von Thadden's final weeks that appears in Irmgard von der Lühe, *Eine Frau*, pp. 130–44.
307 **on the sixth floor**: Ibid., p. 140.
308 **carried out on Fridays**: Ibid., p. 141.

Chapter 63: The Murder Register

310 **That was the signal**: Irmgard von der Lühe, *Eine Frau*, p. 140.
311 **'. . . homeland of love!'**: Ibid.

Chapter 64: The Dead Centre

313 **'a political drawing room'**: Solf, NMT 3 Justice Case testimony, 16 April 1947, p. 2160.
313 **middle of the night**: 'Ein Frauenschicksal im Dritten Reich', *NVZTG*, 5 November 1946, Hoover Institution, Julius Epstein Collection, box 58, Hanna Solf folder.
313 **at the north end**: Solf, 'Denkschrift über meine Haft, Genf 1947', 6 February 1947.
313 **sack of straw**: Hanna Solf to Ruth Andreas-Friedrich, n.d., IfZ, ED 106/101.
314 **'A great deal'**: Boehm, *We Survived*, p. 142.
314 **caught a glimpse**: Ibid.

Chapter 65: Indicted, Again

317 **harassed and humiliated**: Solf, 'Denkschrift über meine Haft, Genf 1947', 6 February 1947.
319 **'treasonous activities'**: For this and subsequent quotations from

the indictment, see 'Anklageschrift des Oberreichsanwalts beim Volksgerichtshof 2 J 243/44 g. Rs./1 L 214/44', 22 June 1944, BArch BStU MfS AP 12062/76.
320 **questioned about it**: Ringshausen, *Widerstand und christlicher Glaube*, p. 478 n. 187.
320 **They were kept apart**: Boehm, *We Survived*, p. 146.
320 **windows had no glass**: Solf, 'Denkschrift über meine Haft, Genf 1947', 6 February 1947.
320 **a bloated rubber doll**: Boehm, *We Survived*, p. 146.
321 **had no strength left**: Solf, 'Denkschrift über meine Haft, Genf 1947', 6 February 1947.
321 **rescheduled for 19 January**: Ringshausen, *Widerstand und christlicher Glaube*, p. 480. Hanna Solf would later say the new trial date was a day earlier, on 18 January.
321 **sausages and smoked bacon**: Maltzan, *Schlage die Trommel*, p. 188.
321 **streaming into the capital**: Ibid., p. 184.

Chapter 66: An Exquisite Deliverance

323 **loud weeping and wailing**: Solf, 'Denkschrift über meine Haft, Genf 1947', 6 February 1947.
323 **great consolation**: Boehm, *We Survived*, p. 146.
323 **Werner Keller**: Maltzan, *Schlage die Trommel*, p. 189. Keller went on to win global fame as the author of *The Bible as History*, published in 1955.
324 **bombers of the United States Army Air Forces**: Carter and Mueller, *The Army Air Forces in World War II*, p. 613.
324 **'Freisler is dead!'**: Boehm, *We Survived*, p. 147.
324 **'No more People's Court!'**: Solf, 'Denkschrift über meine Haft, Genf 1947', 6 February 1947.
325 **crucial file on his desk**: Solf, 'Wilhelm Solf and the Frau Solf Tea Party', p. 16.
325 **falling beam in the basement**: Ringshausen, *Widerstand und christlicher Glaube*, p. 480.
325 **stopped coming to work**: Boehm, *We Survived*, p. 147.
325 **the People's Court had fled**: Solf, 'Denkschrift über meine Haft, Genf 1947', 6 February 1947.
326 **wild desire to live**: Boehm, *We Survived*, p. 147.
326 **in the back of the neck**: Tuchel, '. . . und ihrer aller wartete der Strick', p. 257.

326 **by a firing squad**: Ibid.
326 **beheaded in Brandenburg-Görden**: Klausa, 'Herbert Mumm von Schwarzenstein', p. 1.
326 **beheaded in the same place**: Hassell, *Diaries*, p. 368 n. 96.
326 **'liquidated' on 9 April**: Ringshausen, 'Zwischen Dissens und Widerstand', p. 227.
327 **the group that had formed**: John, 'Some Facts and Aspects of the Plot Against Hitler', p. 27.
327 **Hard evidence had proved elusive**: Hoffmann, *History of the German Resistance*, p. 513.
327 **personal diary was discovered**: Ritter, *German Resistance*, p. 296.
327 **sent to their deaths**: 'The execution was not carried out on the basis of a court order; Himmler ordered the liquidation by hanging on the basis of his own absolute power.' Schlabrendorff, *Offiziere gegen Hitler*, p. 155.
327 **They were naked**: Shirer, *Rise and Fall*, p. 963.
327 **'hanged twice'**: Colvin, *Canaris*, p. 211.
327 **a coded message**: Bassett, *Hitler's Spy Chief*, pp. 287–8.
327 **'duty to my country'**: Colvin, *Canaris*, p. 210.
327 **Dr Ernst Ludwig Heuss**: Heuss would secure the release of all of Fritz Elsas's family, his wife and three children. Just four months later, in August 1945, he and the eldest daughter, Hanne, would marry.
327 **Hagen the historian and Erxleben the priest**: Tuchel, '. . . und ihrer aller wartete der Strick', p. 336.
328 **the last magistrate**: Solf, 'Denkschrift über meine Haft, Genf 1947', 6 February 1947.
328 **ninety pounds**: Hanna Solf to Ruth Andreas-Friedrich, n.d., IfZ, ED 106/101, p. 2.
328 **'cause unrest among the population'**: Ibid.
328 **'oversight' be reversed**: Solf, 'Lebenslauf Frau Hanna Solf, n.d., LAB C Rep. 118–01 Nr. 8173.
329 **a third were uninhabitable**: Some, in an effort to comprehend the scale of destruction, 'imagined the Berlin ruins, calculated as having a volume of 55 million cubic metres, as a wall 30 metres wide and 5 metres high and stretching westwards, reaching all the way to Cologne'. Jähner, *Aftermath*, p. 13.

Chapter 67: Into the Daylight

333 **listened to a speech**: Maltzan, *Schlage die Trommel*, p. 196.
334 **just 1,500 left**: According to Boehm, a further 1,900 Jews would return to Berlin, having survived the camps, joining three thousand others who were mainly *Mischlinge*, the children of mixed marriages, or spouses in 'privileged' marriages who had been able to live legally. See Boehm, *We Survived*, p. ix. Still, the available information is not precise. It is unknown, for example, how many Jews outside Berlin survived, though most estimate it to be as few as two hundred. Correspondence with Professor Moshe Zimmerman, 28 January 2025.
335 **British commanding officers**: Maltzan, *Schlage die Trommel*, p. 212.
336 **twenty hours**: Maltzan, 'Irgendwie Pack Ich Es Immer!'
336 **Pervitin**: von Maltza(n)scher Familienverband (ed.), *Maltza(h)n 1945–2019*, p. 31.
336 **the people's drug**: Ohler, *Blitzed*, p. 1.
336 **merciless towards her**: Maltzan, *Schlage die Trommel*, p. 226.
337 **'. . . other serious damage'**: Rejection of New Application, 6 February 1953, YVA, M.31/3545.
337 **scattering the bones**: Maltzan, *Schlage die Trommel*, p. 223.
338 **at least sixty Jewish lives**: 'Maltzan von Maria', Yad Vashem, https://collections.yadvashem.org/en/righteous/4043010
338 **'such things I really don't care for'**: Block and Drucker, *Rescuers*, p. 157.

Chapter 68: Bearing Witness

339 **a heart condition**: Solf, 'Lebenslauf Frau Hanna Solf', n.d., LAB C Rep. 118-01 Nr. 8173.
339 **on the British**: Nicolson, 'Marginal Comment', 10 August 1945, p. 126.
339 **'It's like a paradise'**: Hanna Solf to Ricarda Huch, 5 July 1946, IfZ, ZS/A-26a/3-34.
340 **'the kindness and moral courage'**: Solf, 'Denkschrift über meine Haft, Genf 1947', 6 February 1947.
340 **financial footing**: Schad, *Frauen gegen Hitler*, p. 196.

340 **ivy and weeds**: Warkocz, 'Die vergessene Widerstandskämpferin'.
341 **ten years in a labour camp**: Schad, *Frauen gegen Hitler*, p. 198.
342 **'magnificent aggressiveness'**: Ibid. The words quoted belonged to Rudolf Pechel, the chaplain who had ministered to both Lagi Ballestrem-Solf and her mother at Ravensbrück.
343 **'. . . a dance of death'**: Boehm, *We Survived*, p. 149.
343 **dishonour on the name**: Solf, NMT 3 Justice Case testimony, 16 April 1947, p. 2189.
343 **'true Germans'**: Hanna Solf to Günther Weisenborn, 8 September 1953, quoted in Schad, *Frauen gegen Hitler*, p. 196.
343 **'shame and disgrace'**: Ibid., p. 197.
343 **'the boundless fatherland of the German spirit'**: Hanna Solf to Ricarda Huch, 5 July 1946, IfZ, ZS/A-26a/3-34.

Chapter 69: Through the Generations

345 **get out of Berlin**: Ruppel, *Memories*, p. 101.
346 ***Mein Kampf* stayed in the toilet**: Ibid., p. 106.
346 **spoke no German**: Ibid., pp. 108–9.
346 **Windham, Connecticut**: See the online obituary for Hanna Kiep Clements at https://hannakiepclements.remembered.com/
347 **the day war broke out**: NSDAP-Gaukartei, 'von Thadden, Adolf', BArch R 9361-IX KARTEI/44320456.
347 **lieutenant in the Wehrmacht**: 'Thadden, Adolf Ludwig', *Neue Deutsche Biographie*, https://www.deutsche-biographie.de/sfz116117.html
347 **dog-whistle neo-Nazism**: Thoma, 'Deutsche Reichspartei', in Benz (ed.), *Handbuch des Antisemitismus*, vol. 5, p. 161.
347 **the National European Party**: 'Von Thadden's Foreign Contacts', *Patterns of Prejudice*, p. 7.
347 **became its leader**: Jaschke, 'Adolf v. Thadden', p. 459.
347 **a TV interview**: Rees, *Biographical Dictionary of the Extreme Right*, p. 387.
347 **intelligence agent**: Hooper, 'Neo-Nazi Leader "Was MI6 Agent"'.
347 ***Widerstehen*: Resistance**: Fox, 'An Opera for My Resistance Fighter Aunt'.
348 **'out of self-interest'**: Schramm, written submission, 12 March 1993, LAB B Rep. 058 Nr. 7261.

Chapter 70: 'The Defendant Is to Blame'

351 **'SMERSH'**: Leide, *NS-Verbrecher*, p. 196.
351 **'I couldn't know that'**: Almut Meyer, 'Der Denunziant Reckzeh', p. 232.
352 **accused him of stealing bread**: Weigelt, *'Umschulungslager'*, p. 90.
352 **'as an informer and denunciator'**: Leide, *NS-Verbrecher*, p. 197.
353 **'severe sentences'**: Ibid., p. 196.

Chapter 71: 'A Congenital Psychopathy'

354 **divorced in July 1951**: Paul Reckzeh, Witness statement, 17 October 1952, LAB B Rep 058 Nr. 7752.
354 **suspended it**: Leide, *NS-Verbrecher*, p. 197.
355 **account from Hanna Solf**: Solf, Witness statement, 31 May 1954, LAB B Rep. 058 Nr. 7257.
355 **two years earlier**: Solf, Witness statement, 14 October 1952, LAB B Rep. 058 Nr. 7253.
355 **'. . . handed me over'**: Dr Fred Dubitscher, Witness statement, 21 July 1954, LAB B Rep. 058 Nr. 7254.
355 **had 'tyrannised' her**: Police Constable Reinhold Plötz, Witness statement, 23 June 1954, LAB B Rep. 058 No. 7254.
355 **he wanted to be heard**: Professor Dr Paul Reckzeh, Witness statement, 11 June 1954, LAB B Rep. 058 Nr. 7254.

Chapter 72: 'Such Dirty Things'

362 **'. . . no further opportunities'**: HA XX/1: Information report on Dr. med. Reckzeh, Paul, 13 August 1965, BArch BStU, MfS, AP 12062/76, p. 113.
362 **'political-operational reasons'**: HA IX/10: Assessment of the unregistered political-operational material of HA IX/11 against Dr Reckzeh, 6 February 1969, BArch BStU, MfS, HA IX/11, AS 190/67, vol. 1, p. 181.
363 **continued to be promoted**: Leide, *NS-Verbrecher*, p. 199.
363 **permission of the responsible ministry**: Ibid., p. 198.

Chapter 73: 'Can You Sleep?'

365 **around Christmas 1944**: Wallis, 'Herbert Lange', p. 98.
365 **security police battalion**: Tuchel, 'Die Sicherheitspolizeischule Drögen und der 20. Juli 1944', pp. 126–7.
365 **Red Army in Bernau**: Wallis, 'Herbert Lange', p. 98.
365 **Hanna Solf was sure**: Irmgard von der Lühe, *Eine Frau*, p. 130.
365 **'in charge of motor vehicles'**: Chief of Base Munich to Chief of Base Berlin, 'Name Trace Request – Herbert Lange', 22 March 1960, p. 1, https://www.cia.gov/readingroom/docs/LANGE,%20HERBERT_0002.pdf
366 **beautiful property on the lake**: Marianne Wellershoff, 'You Can't Report Your Own Father!'
366 **a double garage**: Schad, *Frauen gegen Hitler*, p. 342 n. 38.
367 **the file on Paul Reckzeh**: 'Beiakten zum Vg. AR-Z 2/79. Mehrfertigung StA Berlin 3 P (K) Js 68/62 gg. P. Reckzeh. Bd. 6', BArch B 162/18935.
367 **should be closed**: Irmgard Zarden Ruppel later wrote that the file was closed on different grounds, namely that, in the eyes of the law, there was no crime in which Reckzeh was implicated: since those accused on the basis of his testimony had been represented by counsel before the People's Court, 'it had been a legal trial'. Ruppel, *Memories*, p. 96.

Chapter 74: Betrayal

369 *Ave Maria a trasbordo*: Author interview with Carola Reckzeh, 19 November 2024.
369 **his constant bragging**: Author interview with Dagmar Aßmann, 11 September 2023.
369 **light bulbs and toilet paper**: Interview with Carola Reckzeh.
369 **'Moral weakness'**: Segantini to Elisabeth Wirth, n.d., LAB B Rep. 058 Nr. 7254, p. 2.
369 **would not submit to surgery**: Interview with Dagmar Aßmann.
371 **hiring an escape agency**: The escape organiser was named in the German papers as Julius Lampl. 'Das ist der Arzt, der seiner Tochter ans Messer liefern', *B.Z.*

371 **infiltrated by the Stasi**: According to Dagmar Aßmann, goddaughter to Paul Reckzeh's wife, Ruth, 'Everybody in West Berlin knew that [the Lampl agency] was a Stasi company.' Interview with Dagmar Aßmann.

372 **informed on his daughter**: 'Ein Gestapo-Spitzel der DDR', *Bunte*. Michael Böttcher discovered something else that he suspected had also played a part in Reckzeh's calculations. Professor Paul Reckzeh had left a serious inheritance sitting in a bank account in Hanover. The money was meant for his grandchildren, Barbara and her brother, Paul-Günther, but Reckzeh Jnr had found a way to smuggle the interest to East Berlin so he could use it himself. Böttcher suspected the doctor had feared that if Barbara were in the west, she would have access to the money and that that tidy revenue stream would dry up. That view certainly influenced some of the coverage of the story in the West German press. When the story ran in *Bunte*, the line under the headline read: 'When Barbara is able to get to the west, she'll be a millionaire.' But others close to the family were sceptical, believing that Paul Reckzeh had no reason to worry on that score, since his wife already had the ability, in part via a friend in the west, to access and manage those funds. The friend was Heidrun Voigt, the mother of Dagmar Aßmann. Correspondence with Dagmar Aßmann, 30 January 2025.

372 **less coloured by personal pain**: Historian Harry Waibel concluded, 'In 1978 he betrayed his daughter Barbara to the Ministry for State Security (Stasi) when she wanted to flee to Hamburg.' Waibel, *Diener vieler Herren*, pp. 255–6.

372 **Bautzen**: Interview with Dagmar Aßmann.

372 **safe in the knowledge**: Indeed, so comfortable did he feel in the 1990s, Paul Reckzeh made the case that he deserved financial compensation as a victim of Soviet internment. He even wrote to the family of Elisabeth von Thadden, attempting to enlist their help. Interview with Marianne Wellershoff.

373 **article on their desk**: Interview with Carola Reckzeh.

373 **'knew, but didn't want to know'**: Ibid.

Bibliography

Archives

Berlin Document Centre, Berlin
Bundesarchiv, Berlin
CIA Archive, US National Archives, College Park, MD
Donovan Nuremberg Trials Collection, Cornell University Law Library, New York
Elisabeth-von-Thadden-Schule Archive, Heidelberg
Generallandesarchiv, Karlsruhe
German Resistance Memorial Foundation, Berlin
Graf von Ballestremsches Firmen- und Familienarchiv, Berlin
Institut für Zeitgeschichte, Munich
International Military Tribunal, Nuremberg Trials Project, Harvard Law School Library, Cambridge, MA
Julius Epstein Collection, Hoover Institution, Palo Alto, CA
Karlsruhe Municipal Archives, Karlsruhe
Landesarchiv Berlin, Berlin
National Archives and Records Administration, Washington, DC
Nuremberg Military Trials Collection, Nuremberg Trials Project, Harvard Law School Library, Cambridge, MA
Ringelblum Archive, Jewish Historical Institute, Warsaw
United States Holocaust Memorial Museum, Washington, DC
Wheeler-Bennett Archive, St Antony's College, Oxford
Wiener Holocaust Library, London
Yad Vashem Archive, Jerusalem (YVA)

Primary and Secondary Sources

Andreas-Friedrich, Ruth, *Berlin Underground, 1938–1945* (New York: Henry Holt, 1947)
'Der Anschlag', *Der Spiegel*, 20 July 2004
Atwood, Kathryn J., *Women Heroes of WWII: 32 Stories of Espionage, Sabotage, Resistance, and Rescue* (Chicago, IL: Chicago Review Press, 2019)
Balfour, Michael, and Julian Frisby, *Helmuth von Moltke: A Leader Against Hitler* (London: Palgrave Macmillan, 1972)
Barnes, James J., and Patience P. Barnes, *Nazis in Pre-War London, 1930–1939: The Fate and Role of German Party Members and British Sympathizers* (Liverpool: Liverpool University Press, 2005)
Bassett, Richard, *Hitler's Spy Chief: The Wilhelm Canaris Mystery* (London: Orion, 2005)
Becker, Josef, and Ruth Becker (eds), *Hitlers Machtergreifung: Dokumente vom Machtantritt Hitlers 30. Januar 1933 bis zur Besiegelung des Einparteienstaates 14. Juli 1933* (Munich: dtv Verlagsgesellschaft, 1983)
Bell, George K. A., Bishop of Chichester, 'Die Ökume und die innerdeutsche Opposition', *Vierteljahrshefte für Zeitgeschichte* 5, no. 4 (1957): 362–78
Benne, Simon, 'Der Fuß an der Aktentasche', *Hannoverische Allgemeine Zeitung*, 18 July 2014
Bennet, Ralph, 'Eine Frau kämpft für Recht und Freiheit', *Die Neue Zeit*, 25 April 1946
Benz, Wolfgang (ed.), *Handbuch des Antisemitismus: Judenfeindschaft in Geschichte und Gegenwart*, vol. 5, *Organisationen, Institutionen, Bewegungen* (Berlin: de Gruyter, 2012)
'Berlin: Eight Hours After Blasting by RAF', *New York Times*, 4 September 1943
Bethge, Eberhard, *Dietrich Bonhoeffer: A Biography* (Minneapolis, MN: Fortress Press, 2000)
Block, Gay, and Malka Drucker, *Rescuers: Portraits of Moral Courage in the Holocaust* (New York: Ergo, 1992)
Boehm, Eric H., *We Survived: Fourteen Histories of the Hidden and Hunted in Nazi Germany* (New Haven, CT: Yale University Press, 1949)
Browning, Christopher R., *Fateful Months: Essays on the Emergence of the Final Solution* (New York and London: Holmes & Meier, 1985)
——, *The Origins of the Final Solution: The Evolution of Nazi Jewish Policy, September 1939–March 1942* (London: William Heinemann, 2004)

BIBLIOGRAPHY

Buchheit, Gert, *Richter in rote Robe: Freisler, Präsident des Volksgerichtshofes* (Munich: List, 1968)

Bundesfinanzakademie, *Arthur Zarden (1885–1944): Staatssekretär im Reichsfinanzministerium – Eine Gedenkausstellung* (Bonn: Bundesministerium der Finanzen, 1985)

Burleigh, Michael, *Death and Deliverance: 'Euthanasia' in Germany 1900–1945* (Cambridge: Cambridge University Press, 1994)

Carter, Kit C., and Robert Mueller, *The Army Air Forces in World War II: Combat Chronology 1941–1945* (Washington, DC: Albert F. Simpson Historical Research Center, Air University, and Office of Air Force History Headquarters, USAF, 1973)

Childers, Thomas, 'Hortensienstrasse 50: The Kreisau Circle and the 20th of July' (MA thesis, University of Tennessee, 1971), https://trace.tennessee.edu/utk_gradthes/3110

Christiansen, Robert, *Dommedag* (Copenhagen: Steen Hasselbalch, 1945)

Clements, Bruce, *From Ice Set Free: The Story of Otto Kiep* (New York: Farrar, Straus & Giroux, 1972)

Colvin, Ian, *Canaris: Chief of Intelligence* (London: Victor Gollancz, 1951)

Conze, Eckart, et al., *Das Amt und die Vergangenheit: Deutsche Diplomaten im Dritten Reich und in der Bundesrepublik* (Munich: Karl Blessing, 2010)

'Das ist der Arzt, der seiner Tochter ans Messer lieferte', *B.Z.*, 25 August 1978

Detjen, Marion, 'Fluchthelfer nach dem Mauerbau: Grenzgänger im deutsch-deutschen Beziehungsgeflecht', *Deutschland Archiv* 5 (2002): 799–806

Deutsches Reichsgesetzblatt, 1941, Part I, No. 100, 5 September 1941

'Diese Haderlumpen', *Der Spiegel*, 29 July 1979

Dirks, Christian, 'Snatchers: The Berlin Gestapo's Jewish Informants', in Beate Meyer, Hermann Simon and Chana Schutz, *Jews in Nazi Berlin: From Kristallnacht to Liberation* (Chicago, IL: University of Chicago Press, 2009)

Dulles, Allen Welsh, *Germany's Underground: The Anzi-Nazi Resistance* (New York: Macmillan, 1947)

'Einstein to Exile Self from Germany Until "Exaggerated Nationalism" Ends', *Indianapolis Star*, 16 March 1933

Eschebach, Insa (ed.), *Ravensbrück: Der Zellenbau – Geschichte und Gedenken Begleitband zur Ausstellung*, Schriftenreihe der Stiftung Brandenburgische Gedenkstätten 18 (Berlin: Metropol, 2008)

European Axis Signal Intelligence in World War II, vol. 7, Goering's 'Research' Bureau, https://media.defense.gov/2021/Jul/14/2002762730/-1/-1/0/VOLUME_7_GOERINGS_RESEARCH_BUREAU.PDF

Feldman, Gerald D., and Wolfgang Seibel (eds), *Networks of Nazi Persecution: Bureaucracy, Business and the Organization of the Holocaust* (Oxford and New York: Berghahn, 2004)

Fest, Joachim, *Staatsstreich: Der lange Weg zum 20. Juli* (Munich: Siedler, 1994)

Field, Michael, 'From Vailima to a Nazi Concentration Camp', Invincible Strangers: Samoa's 20th Century, https://invinciblestrangers.wordpress.com/category/nazi/

Flohr, Markus, 'Geheime Fracht', *Die Zeit*, 21 January 2016

Fox, Christopher, 'An Opera for My Resistance Fighter Aunt', *Guardian*, 21 November 2012

Fricke-Finkelnburg, Renate (ed.), *Nationalsozialismus und Schule: Amtliche Erlasse und Richtlinien 1933–1945* (Leverkusen: Leske & Budrich, 1989)

Friedlander, Henry, *The Origins of Nazi Genocide: From Euthanasia to the Final Solution* (Chapel Hill, NC: University of North Carolina Press, 1995)

Fröhlich, Elke (ed.), *Die Tagebücher von Joseph Goebbels, Teil I: Aufzeichnungen 1923–1941 Band 2/III Oktober 1932–März 1934* (Munich: K. G. Saur, 2006)

Galante, Pierre, *Operation Valkyrie: The German Generals' Plot Against Hitler* (New York: Harper & Row, 1981)

Gellately, Robert, *The Gestapo and German Society: Enforcing Racial Policy 1933–1945* (Oxford: Clarendon Press, 1990)

Gellerman, Günther W., *. . . und lauschten für Hitler. Geheime Reichssache: Die Abhörzentralen des Dritten Reiches* (Bonn: Bernard & Graefe, 1991)

'Ein Gestapo-Spitzel der DDR: Wenn Barbara in den Westen kommen könnte, wäre sie Millionärin', *Bunte*, October 1978

'Gestapo-Spitzel geständig', *Tagesspiegel,* 4 February 1953

Graef, Inge, Diaries 1934–64, unpublished

Gross, Leonard, *The Last Jews in Berlin* (New York: Simon & Schuster, 1982)

Grunwald-Spier, Agnes, *Who Betrayed the Jews? The Realities of Nazi Persecution in the Holocaust* (Cheltenham: History Press, 2016)

Gunkel, Christoph, 'Sie müssen doch bloß durch die Couch schießen', *Der Spiegel*, 25 March 2019

Hall, Claire M., 'An Army of Spies? The Gestapo Spy Network 1933–45', *Journal of Contemporary History* 44, no. 2 (2009): 247–65

Hank, Rainer, 'Das abrupte Ende einer Karriere', *Frankfurter Allgemeine Zeitung*, 18 November 2010

Hansen, Knut, *Albrecht Graf von Bernstorff: Diplomat und Bankier zwischen Kaiserreich und Nationalsozialismus* (Berlin: Peter Lang, 1995)

Hasic, Albinko, 'A Group of German Leaders Tried to Kill Hitler', *Time*, 19 July 2019

Hassell, Ulrich von, *The Ulrich von Hassell Diaries, 1938–1944: The Story of the Forces Against Hitler Inside Germany* (Barnsley: Frontline, 2011)

Heer, Hannes, and Klaus Naumann (eds), *Vernichtungskrieg: Verbrechen der Wehrmacht 1941–1944* (Frankfurt: Zweitausendeins, 1997)

Heinemann, Winfried, *Operation 'Valkyrie': A Military History of the 20 July 1944 Plot* (Berlin: De Gruyter Oldenbourg, 2021)

Hendrix, Kathleen, 'Saga Peter Wyden and Stella Goldschlag . . .', *Los Angeles Times*, 21 December 1992

Heuss-Knapp, Elly, *Schmale Wege* (Tübingen: Rainer Wunderlich Verlag Hermann Leins, 1946)

Hilberg, Raul, *The Destruction of the European Jews*, 3rd edn (New Haven, CT, and London: Yale University Press, 2003)

Hoffmann, Peter, *Widerstand, Staatsstreich, Attentat: Der Kampf der Opposition gegen Hitler* (Munich: Piper, 1970)

———, *The History of the German Resistance 1933–1945* (London: Macdonald and Jane's, 1977)

Höhne, Heinz, *Canaris: Hilter's Master Spy* (London: Secker & Warburg, 1979)

Hooper, John, 'Neo-Nazi Leader "Was MI6 Agent"', *Guardian*, 13 August 2002

Huch, Ricarda, *In einem Gedenkbuch zu Sammeln . . .: Bilder deutscher Widerstandskämpfer* (Leipzig: Leipziger Universitätsverlag, 1997)

Jacobsen, Hans-Adolf (ed.), *Spiegelbild einer Verschwörung: Die Opposition gegen Hitler und der Staatsstreich vom 20. Juli 1944 in der SD-Berichterstattung* (Stuttgart: Seewald, 1984)

Jähner, Harald, *Aftermath: Life in the Fallout of the Third Reich 1945–1955* (London: W. H. Allen, 2021)

Jander, Thomas, 'Coup by Teleprinter: The "Valkyrie" Plans to Overthrow Hitler on 20 July 1944', Deutsches Historisches Museum, 19 July 2019, https://www.dhm.de/blog/2019/07/19/coup-by-teleprinter/

Jaschke, Hans-Gerd, 'Adolf v. Thadden (1921–1966): Vom konservativen ostelbischen Landadeligen zum rechtsextremen Parteifunktionär', in Gideon Botsch, Christoph Kopke and Karsten Wilke (eds), *Rechtsextrem: Biografien nach 1945* (Berlin: De Gruyter Oldenbourg, 2023)

John, Otto, 'Some Facts and Aspects of the Plot Against Hitler', n.d., Item 1, Series F, Sir John Wheeler-Bennett Collection, St Antony's College, Oxford

Kahn, David, 'The Forschungsamt: Nazi Germany's Most Secret Communications Intelligence Agency', *Cryptologia* 2, vol. 1 (1978): 12–19

———, *Hitler's Spies: Germany Military Intelligence in World War II* (London: Hodder & Stoughton, 1978)

BIBLIOGRAPHY

Kempner, Benedicta Maria, *Priester vor Hitlers Tribunalen* (Berlin: Rütten & Loening, 1966)

Kershaw, Ian, *Hitler 1936–1945: Nemesis* (London: Allen Lane, 2000)

Kiep, Otto, *Mein Lebensweg 1886–1944: Aufzeichnungen während der Haft* (Berlin: Lukas, 2013)

Klausa, Ekkehard, 'Herbert Mumm von Schwarzenstein: Ein Ex-Diplomat im Widerstand gegen den Nationalsozialismus', *Beiträge zum Widerstand, Neue Folge*, 4 (March 2025), https://www.gdw-berlin.de/fileadmin/bilder/publikationen/Beitraege-NeueFolge/Beitraege-zum-Widerstand_Nr._4-2025.pdf

Klemperer, Klemens von, *German Resistance Against Hitler: The Search for Allies Abroad, 1938–1945* (Oxford: Clarendon Press, 1992)

Körting, Almut E., '"Tödlicher Haß": Zur Beziehung zwischen Haßerziehung und den Morden des Ministeriums für Staatssicherheit in der DDR', *Zeitschrift des Forschungsverbundes SED-Staat* 4 (1997): 126–45

Leide, Henry, *NS-Verbrecher und Staatssicherheit: Die geheime Vergangenheitspolitik der DDR* (Göttingen: Vandenhoeck & Ruprecht, 2007)

Lühe, Irmela von der, 'Das altadlige Fräulein aus dem Osten', unpublished speech, Ravensbrück, 13 September 2014

Lühe, Irmgard von der, *Eine Frau im Widerstsand: Elisabeth von Thadden und das Dritte Reich* (Freiburg: Herder, 1980)

Malinowski, Stephan, *Nazis and Nobles: The History of a Misalliance* (Oxford: Oxford University Press, 2020)

Maltzan, Maria Gräfin von, 'Irgendwie pack ich es immer!', *Veto* 3 (1983)

——, *Schlage die Trommel und fürchte dich nicht: Erinnerungen* (Berlin: Ullstein, 1986)

Maltza(n)scher Familienverband e.V., von (ed.), *Maltza(h)n 1945–2019* (Rostock: Hinstorff, 2020)

Manz, Stefan, 'Migrants and Internees: Germans in Glasgow, 1864–1918' (PhD thesis, Durham University, 2001), http://etheses.dur.ac.uk/1720/

Marek, Michael, 'Failed Plot to Kill Hitler', *Deutsche Welle*, 20 July 2014

Meirer, Albert, 'Berlin Jews: Deprived of Rights, Impoverished, and Branded', in Beate Meyer, Hermann Simon and Chana Schutz (eds), *Jews in Nazi Berlin: From Kristallnacht to Liberation* (Chicago, IL: University of Chicago Press, 2009)

Metzger, Max Josef, *Gefangenschaftsbriefe* (Freising: Kyrios, 1948)

Meyer, Almut A., 'Der Denunziant Reckzeh', in Matthias Riemenschneider and Jörg Thierfelder (eds), *Elisabeth von Thadden: Gestalten, Widerstehen, Erleiden* (Karlsruhe: Hans-Thoma, 2002)

——, 'Elisabeth von Thadden (1890–1944): Pädagogin aus christlichem Geist im Konflikt mit dem Nationalsozialismus', in Gerhard Schwinge (ed.), *Lebensbilder aus der Evangelischen Kirche in Baden im 19. und 20. Jahrhundert*, vol. 5, *Kultur und Bildung* (Heidelberg: Regionalkultur, 2007)

Meyer, Winfried, *Unternehmen Sieben: Eine Rettungsaktion* (Munich: Anton Hain, 1993)

Middlebrook, Martin, and Chris Everitt, *The Bomber Command War Diaries: An Operational Reference Book 1939–1945* (London: Viking, 1985)

Mitcham, Samuel W., Jr, and Gene Mueller, *Hitler's Commanders: Officers of the Wehrmacht, the Luftwaffe, the Kriegsmarine, and the Waffen SS* (Lanham, MD: Rowman & Littlefield, 2012)

Möckelmann, Reiner, *Hannah von Bredow: Bismarcks furchtlose Enkelin gegen Hitler* (Stuttgart: Theiss, 2018)

Moltke, Helmuth James von, *Im Land der Gottlosen: Tagebuch und Briefe aus der Haft 1944/45* (Munich: C. H. Beck, 2009)

Montague, Patrick, *Chełmno and the Holocaust: The History of Hitler's First Death Camp* (London: I B. Tauris, 2011)

Moorhouse, Roger, *Berlin at War* (New York: Basic Books, 2010)

Mühlen, Bengt von zur (ed.), with Andreas von Klewitz, *Die Angeklagten des 20. Juli vor dem Volksgerichtshof* (Berlin-Kleinmachnow: Chronos, 2001)

Müller, Klaus-Jürgen, 'The Structure and Nature of the National Conservative Opposition in Germany up to 1940', in H. W. Koch (ed.), *Aspects of the Third Reich* (London: Palgrave Macmillan, 1985)

Neue Deutsche Biographie (Berlin: Duncker & Humblot, 1949–), www.deutsche-biographie.de

Nicolson, Harold, 'Marginal Comment', *The Spectator*, 10 August 1945

——, 'Marginal Comment', *The Spectator*, 23 November 1945

Office of United States Chief of Counsel for Prosecution of Axis Criminality, 'Document 069-PS', in *Nazi Conspiracy and Aggression*, vol. III (Washington, DC: United States Government Printing Office, 1946)

Ohler, Norman, *Blitzed: Drugs in Nazi Germany* (London: Allen Lane, 2016)

Ottaway, Susan, *Hitler's Traitors: German Resistance to the Nazis* (Barnsley: Leo Cooper, 2012)

Panayi, Panikos, *German Immigrants in Britain during the 19th Century, 1815–1914* (Oxford and Washington, DC: Berg, 1995)

Pechel, Rudolf, *Deutscher Widerstand* (Erlenbach, Zurich: Eugen Rentsch, 1947)

Perwe, Johan, *Svenska i Gestapos tjänst: V140 Babs* (Stockholm: Carlsson, 2011)

———, 'Svensk präst räddade judar i Berlin', *Populär Historia*, 30 January 2024
Pine, Lisa, *Education in Nazi Germany* (Oxford and New York: Berg, 2010)
'Die Rede Himmlers vor den Gauleitern', *Vierteljahrshefte für Zeitgeschichte* 1, no. 4 (1953)
Rees, Philip, *Biographical Dictionary of the Extreme Right Since 1890* (New York: Simon & Schuster, 1990)
Reitlinger, Gerald, *SS: Alibi of a Nation 1922–1945* (London: Arms & Armour Press, 1981)
Ringshausen, Gerhard, 'Zwischen Dissens und Widerstand: Geschichte und Einordnung der Teegesellschaft', in Matthias Riemenschneider and Jörg Thierfelder (eds), *Elisabeth von Thadden: Gestalten, Widerstehen, Erleiden* (Karlsruhe: Hans-Thoma, 2002)
———, *Widerstand und christlicher Glaube angesichts des Nationalsozialismus* (Berlin and Munster: Lit, 2007)
Ritter, Gerhard, *The German Resistance: Carl Goerdeler's Struggle Against Tyranny* (London: G. Allen & Unwin, 1958)
Roche, Helen, *The Third Reich's Elite Schools: A History of the Napolas* (Oxford: Oxford University Press, 2021)
Roon, Ger van, *German Resistance to Hitler: Count von Moltke and the Kreisau Circle* (New York: Van Nostrand Reinhold, 1971)
Rothfels, Hans, *The German Opposition to Hitler* (London: Berg, 1970)
Ruppel, Irmgard, *Memories* (New York: privately published, 2008)
Rüther, Daniela, *Hitlers 'Eintopfsonntag': Eine Legende* (Berlin: Duncker & Humblot, 2021)
'Saltcoats Man Who Played Part in Plot to Kill Hitler Celebrated', *Ardrossan and Saltcoats Herald*, 17 July 2020
Sautter, Karl, *Geschichte der deutschen Post, Teil 3: Geschichte der Deutschen Reichspost, 1871 bis 1945* (Frankfurt: Bundesdruckerei, 1951)
Schäbitz, Michael, 'The Flight and Expulsion of German Jews', in Beate Meyer, Hermann Simon and Chana Schutz (eds), *Jews in Nazi Berlin: From Kristallnacht to Liberation* (Chicago, IL: University of Chicago Press, 2009)
Schad, Martha, *Frauen gegen Hitler: Schicksale im Nationalsozialismus* (Munich: Heyne, 2001)
Schäffer, Johann, 'Maria Grafin von Maltzan (1909–1997): Eine Tierärztin im Widerstand', *Deutsches Tierärzteblatt* 10 (2008): 1332–41
Schlabrendorff, Fabian von, *Offiziere gegen Hitler* (Frankfurt: Fischer Bücherei, 1946)
Schlingensiepen, Ferdinand, *Dietrich-Bonhoeffer 1906–1945: Martyr, Thinker, Man of Resistance* (London: T. & T. Clark, 2010)

Schmädeke, Peter, and Jürgen Steinbach, *Der Widerstand gegen den Nationalsozialismus: Die deutsche Gesellschaft und der Widerstand gegen Hitler* (Munich: Piper, 1985)

Schwarte, Johannes, 'Friedrich Muckermann SJ (1883–1946)', *Die neue Ordnung* 60, no. 3 (2006): 210–16

Shirer, William L., *The Rise and Fall of the Third Reich: A History of Nazi Germany* (New York: Simon & Schuster, 1959)

Sifton, Elisabeth, and Fritz Stern, *No Ordinary Men: Dietrich Bonhoeffer and Hans von Dohnanyi – Resisters Against the State* (New York: New York Review of Books, 2013)

Solf, Eugen, 'Wilhelm Solf and the Frau Solf Tea Party', *Resign!* (January 2021): 4–17

Späth, Tamara, 'Otto Carl Kiep: Als patriotischer Christ dem Nationalsozialismus widerstehen', *Mitteilungen zur kirchlichen Zeitgeschichte* 8 (2014): 117–46

Spechler, Diana, 'For 115 Years, One Restaurant Has Fed the Elite in Berlin and Now Madrid. Nazis included', *Washington Post*, 17 December 2019

Stanuch, Zbigniew, *Ravensbrück: A Story Not to Be Forgotten: The Polish Perspective* (Szczecin: Institute of National Remembrance Commission for the Prosecution of Crimes Against the Polish Nation, 2020)

Stewart, William, *Admirals of the World: A Biographical Dictionary, 1500 to the Present* (Jefferson, NC: McFarland, 2009)

Stiefel, Elisabeth, *Sie waren Sand in Getriebe: Frauen im Widerstand* (Marburg: Francke-Buch, 2013)

Stoecker, Wolf, 'Bericht über das Verfahren gegen O.C. Kiep vor dem Volksgerichtshof (Juli/August 1944)' (unpublished, courtesy of Gerhard Ringshausen, September 1963)

Stutterheim, Kurt von, *Die Majestät des Gewissens: in memoriam Albrecht Bernstorff* (Hamburg: H. Christians, 1992)

Swidler, Leonard, *Bloodwitness for Peace and Unity: The Life of Max Josef Metzger* (Philadelphia, PA: Ecumenical Press, 1977)

Sykes, Christopher, *Troubled Loyalty: A Biography of Adam von Trott* (London: Collins, 1968)

Thadden, Elisabeth von, 'Elisabeth von Thadden: Damals – dann . . . und morgen', unpublished speech, Elisabeth-von-Thadden-Schule, Heidelberg, 7 November 2014

Thadden, Rudolf von, *Trieglaff: Balancing Church and Politics in a Pomeranian World, 1807–1948* (Oxford and New York: Berghahn, 2013)

Thoma, Sebastian, 'Deutsche Reichspartei', in Wolfgang Benz (ed.),

Handbuch des Antisemitismus: Judenfeindschaft in Geschichte und Gegenwart, vol. 5, *Organisationen, Institutionen, Bewegungen* (Berlin: de Gruyter, 2012)

Trebbin, Ulrich, 'Guillotine von Plötzensee: Die verschlungene Geschichte eines Nazi-Fallbeils', *Der Spiegel*, 23 December 2024

Tuchel, Johannes, 'Die Sicherheitspolizeischule Drögen und der 20. Juli 1944: zur Geschichte der "Sonderkommission Lange"', in Florian von Buttlar, Stefanie Endlich and Annette Leo (eds), *Fürstenberg-Drogen: Schichten eines verlassenen Ortes* (Potsdam: Ministerium für Stadtentwicklung, Wohnen und Verkehr des Landes Brandenburg, 1994)

——, 'Zur vergessenen Vorgeschichte des 20. Juli 1944: Der Solf-Kreis', *Die Mahnung* 41, no. 4 (1994): 1

——, 'Verfolgung, Haft und Tod von Otto Carl Kiep', in Otto Kiep, *Mein Lebensweg 1886–1944: Aufzeichnungen während der Haft* (Berlin: Lukas, 2013)

——, '. . . und ihrer aller wartete der Strick.' *Das Zellengefängnis Lehrter Straße 3 nach dem 20. Juli 1944* (Berlin: Lukas, 2014)

Ueberschär, Gerd R. (ed.), *Hitlers militärische Elite: 68 Lebensläufe* (Darmstadt: Wissenschaftliche Buchgesellschaft, 2011)

Vassiltchikov, Marie, *Berlin Diaries 1940–1945* (London: Chatto & Windus, 1985)

'Die Verräterin Goerdelers verhaftet', *Weltpresse*, 19 January 1946

'Von Thadden's Foreign Contacts', *Patterns of Prejudice* 1, no. 1 (1967): 7–8

Wagner, Walter, *Der Volksgerichtshof im nationalsozialistischen Staat* (Berlin: De Gruyter Oldenbourg, 2011)

Wagner-Nigrin, Ruth, 'Volksgerichts-Prozess, Berlin, 1. Juli 1944' (unpublished)

Waibel, Harry, *Diener vieler Herren: Ehemalige NS-Funktionäre in der SBZ/DDR* (Berlin: Peter Lang, 2011)

Wallis, Andrew, 'Herbert Lange – Stralsund's "vergessener" Mann mit einem "unvergesslichen" Leben', in *Stralsunder Hefte für Geschichte, Kultur und Alltag September 2024* (Stralsund: Edition Pommern, 2024): 87–99

Walk, Joseph (ed.), *Das Sonderrecht für die Juden im NS-Staat. Eine Sammlung der gesetzlichen Maßnahmen und Richtlinien. Inhalt und Bedeutung* (Heidelberg: Müller, 1996)

Warkocz, Manuela, 'Die vergessene Widerstandskämpferin', *Süddeutsche Zeitung*, 18 February 2020

Watts, Janet, 'Prisoner of Love', *Observer*, 16 February 1986

Webb, Chris, and Artur Hojan, *The Chelmno Death Camp: History, Biographies, Remembrance* (New York: Ibidem Press, 2019)

Weigel, Bjoern, '"Märzgefallene" und Aufnahmestopp im Frühjahr 1933: Eine Studie über den Opportunismus', in Wolfgang Benz (ed.), *Wie wurde man Parteigenosse? Die NSDAP und ihre Mitglieder* (Frankfurt: S. Fischer, 2009)

Weigelt, Andreas, *'Umschulungslager existieren nicht': Zur Geschichte des sowjetischen Speziallagers Nr. 6 in Jamlitz 1945–1947* (Potsdam: Brandenburgische Landeszentral für Politische Bildung, 2001)

Weitz, John, *Hitler's Banker: Hjalmar Horace Greeley Schacht* (New York: Little, Brown, 1997)

Wellershoff, Maria, *Von Ort zu Ort: Eine Jugend in Pommern* (Cologne: Dumont Buchverlag, 2010)

Wellershoff, Marianne, 'You Can't Report Your Own Father!', *Der Spiegel*, 8 May 2019

Wheeler-Bennett, John, *The Nemesis of Power: The German Army in Politics, 1918–1945* (London: Macmillan, 1964)

Wietschorke, Jens, *Arbeiterfreunde: Soziale Mission im dunklen Berlin 1911–1933* (Frankfurt and New York: Campus, 2013)

Wildt, Michael, *An Uncompromising Generation: The Nazi Leadership of the Reich Security Main Office* (Madison, WI: University of Wisconsin Press, 2009)

Wistrich, Robert S., *Who's Who in Nazi Germany* (London: Weidenfeld & Nicolson, 1982)

Wollenberg, Jörg, *The German Public and Persecution of the Jews, 1933–1945: No One Participated, No One Knew* (Amherst, NY: Humanity Books, 1996)

Wörmann, Heinrich-Wilhelm, *Widerstand in Charlottenburg* (Berlin: Gedenkstätte Deutscher Widerstand, 1991)

Wyden, Peter, *Stella: One Woman's True Tale of Evil, Betrayal, and Survival in Hitler's Germany* (New York: Simon & Schuster, 1992)

Zimmermann, Moshe, *Germans Against Germans: The Fate of the Jews, 1938–1945* (Bloomington, IN: Indiana University Press, 2022)

Index

Abwehr, 53, 94, 201, 229, 231
   resistance cell within, 107, 326–7
Aktion T4 (euthanasia programme), 63, 116
Allied bombing raids, 99
   Berlin, 81, 87, 99, 106, 130, 141, 147, 191–2, 196, 203, 207, 213, 252, 303, 320, 324–5, 328–9
   Brandenburg, 252
   Hamburg, 99
   Oranienburg, 203
Alsenstrasse, Berlin, 15
   9 (Solf family home), 16, 51, 54
Alves, Georg Friedrich (father of Hanna Kiep), 193, 235, 257, 258, 274
aristocracy (nobility), 44, 164, 263–4, 404 n.
Arndt, Ernst Moritz, 307
arrests
   Albrecht von Bernstorff, 110
   Anne Rühle, 190
   Arthur Zarden, 5, 190, 201
   Elisabeth von Thadden, 4–5, 191–2, 210–11
   Elisabeth Wirth, 190–1
   Friedrich Siegmund-Schultze, 114
   Hanna Kiep, 195, 233
   Hanna Solf, 3–4, 190, 206, 317
   Hartmut Plaas, 213
   Helmuth James von Moltke, 212–13
   Herbert Mumm von Schwarzenstein, 109–10
   Irmgard Zarden, 5–6, 190, 201
   Lagi Ballestrem-Solf, 4, 190, 207–8, 317
   Ludwig Gehre, 213
   Max Metzger, 54, 111
   Nikolaus von Halem, 109–10
   Otto Kiep, 193–4, 194–5
Aryan papers, 38
'Aryan paragraph', 41
Ave Maria a trasbordo (Giovanni Segantini), 369

Bach-Zelewski, Erich von dem, 74
Baden, 83
Badoglio, Pietro, 146–7
Ballenstedt, 195
Ballestrem, Count Hubertus von, 51, 109, 175, 208, 321, 341–2, 345
Ballestrem-Solf, So'oa'emalelagi (née Solf; 'Lagi'), 39–40, 51, 146
   absence from tea party, 313
   appointment of lawyer, 323
   arrest, 4, 190, 207–8, 317
   charges against, 319, 320
   death, 342
   detention at Moabit, 320, 324, 325–6
   detention at Ravensbrück, 218–19, 224–5, 313, 314–17, 342
   detention in Munich prison, 209
   discharge from Moabit, 327–9

INDEX

Ballestrem-Solf, So'oa'emalelagi (née Solf; 'Lagi') (*cont.*)
  interrogations, 39–40, 82, 208–9, 313–14, 223–4, 225
  on lessons not learnt from Nazi period, 343
  marriages, 39, 109
  post-war life, 339, 341–3
  postponement of trial, 321, 324, 325
  support for Jews, 39, 40, 82–5, 320
  transfer to Ravensbrück, 209–10
Bautzen prison, 372
BBC, 86, 246
Beck, Ludwig, 149, 158
Będzin, 95
Berlin
  Alexanderplatz police HQ, 36, 233
  Allied bombing raids, *see* Allied bombing raids: Berlin
  Alsenstrasse, *see* Alsenstrasse, Berlin
  aristocratic life, 164
  Barnimstrasse prison, 307–10
  Bellevuestrasse 15 (People's Court building), 257, 325
  Bendlerblock, 290, 291
  Carmerstrasse 12, *see* Carmerstrasse 12, Berlin (Thadden apartment)
  Cavalry Club, 163, 164
  denunciation in, 119, 335
  Detmolder Strasse 11, *see* Detmolder Strasse 11, Berlin (Maltzan apartment)
  food and wine availability, 164
  Foreign Ministry, 46, 48, 51–2, 110, 142, 196–7
  Grosse Hamburger Strasse, 101, 102
  Horcher (restaurant), 163, 404 n.
  Hotel Adlon, 182–3
  influx of refugees, 321
  Jewish population, 40, 56, 101, 334, 422 n.
  Kristallnacht, 56
  Kurfürstendamm 140 (Gestapo building), 5, 194–5, 201, 204, 207, 212, 213
  Lehrter Bahnhof, 328
  Lehrter Strasse jail, 326, 327, 328
  Ministry of Propaganda, 291
  Moabit remand prison, 317, 320–1, 323, 324, 325–6, 327–9
  Nazi parade (1933), 14–15
  Olympics, 34
  Plötzensee prison, 291, 296, 298–9, 310–12
  Prinz-Albrecht-Strasse 8 (Gestapo HQ), 207, 211, 296–7, 298
  Red Army in, 325, 333–4
  Reich Ministry of Justice, 298, 306
  Research Office, 155–8, 160–1, 187
  restaurants, 163–4, 404 n.
  Social Women's School, 20
  Swedish Church, 115, 248, 303
  Taubertstrasse 15 (Kiep family home), 96, 130, 193
  20 July plot, 290–1
  see also Dahlem; East Berlin; Kreuzberg; Wannsee; West Berlin; Wittenau
Bernstorff, Count Albrecht von, 110–11, 111–12, 173, 219, 220, 313, 317, 318–19, 326
Biebow, Hans, 93
Bingham, Captain, 346
Black Orchestra (Schwarze Kapelle), 104, 105
'black swimmers', 165
Blomberg, Werner von, 34
Blonde Poison, the (Stella Goldschlag), 103, 118, 119, 121
blood guilt (*Sippenhaft*), 169, 294, 314, 328
Bojanowo, 74

440

INDEX

Bonhoeffer, Dietrich, 107, 129, 327
Bormann, Martin, 390 n.
Böttcher, Michael, 368–72, 426 n.
Brandenburg-Görden prison, 244, 251, 252, 292, 326
Brandt, Heinz, 288, 289
Braune, Marie-Agnes (née von Thadden; sister of Elisabeth von Thadden; 'Anza'), 24, 129, 171, 197
  absence of charges against, 259
  arrest, 190
  meeting with Paul Reckzeh, 175
  on Paul Reckzeh, 348, 401 n.
  post-war life, 347–8
  tapping of phone, 158
  at tea party, 142–3, 144, 148, 150, 151
  as witness at tea-party trial, 271
braune Blätter (brownsheets), 157–8
Bridge of San Luis Rey, The (Thornton Wilder), 228
Britain
  defection of Vermehrens to, 230–1
  Hanna Solf in, 340
  and Munich Agreement, 52–3, 57–8, 95, 96, 158
  see also London
brownsheets (*braune Blätter*), 157–8
Bülow, Adrienne Gans zu Putlitz von, 174, 178
Bund Deutscher Mädel (League of German Girls), 13, 21, 42
Burschenschaft Rugia, 25

Canaris, Wilhelm, 94–5, 98, 231–2, 327
carbon monoxide, killing by, 62, 63–4, 90
Carmerstrasse 12, Berlin (Thadden apartment), 73, 136, 141, 144, 184, 191
  tea party, *see* tea party (10 September 1943)

Chamberlain, Neville, 52–3, 57, 95, 96, 158
Checkpoint Alpha, 370
Chełmno extermination camp, 76, 89–93, 391–2 n., 393 n.
Christianity, 41, 112
Confessing Church, 41, 107, 139, 178
  see also Quakers
Churchill, Winston, 53
Clements, Bruce (son-in-law of Otto Kiep), 346
Committee of Anti-Fascist Resistance Fighters, 362
Constance, Lake, 165
Conti, Leonardo, 116
Cottbus prison, 317–18
Criminal Police (Kriminalpolizei), 62
Czechoslovakia (until March 1939), 34–5, 52, 60, 96, 158
  see also Prague; Sudetenland; Theresienstadt concentration camp

D-Day landings, 246
Dachau concentration camp, 110, 139
Dahlem, 139–40, 193
Democratic Germany, 173
denazification, 335, 346
Denmark, 98, 147, 280
Detmolder Strasse 11, Berlin (Maltzan apartment), 66, 77–8, 103, 118–21, 248, 321, 333
Deutsche Reichsbahn, 300
Deutsche Reichspartei (German Reich Party), 347
Dirrigi, Christiane, 370, 371
Dix, Helmuth, 258, 269
Dix, Rudolf, 258, 277
Dobberke, Walter, 102
Drögen, 186, 220, 221, 233, 237
  see also Fürstenberg
Dulles, Allen, 179
Dziekanka psychiatric hospital, 64, 74

INDEX

East Berlin, 358, 370, 371
East Germany, *see* German Democratic Republic (GDR)
Eichmann, Adolf, 92
Eidem, Erling (archbishop of Uppsala), 111, 115
Einsatzgruppen, 62, 68, 74, 95
Einstein, Albert, 26, 27, 28, 142
Elliott, Nicholas, 230
Elmau, 171, 177, 180, 191
Elsas, Fritz, 328, 421 n.
Epistle to the Romans (Saint Paul), 308
Ersatzheer (Replacement Army), 285, 286, 290
Erxleben, Friedrich, 319, 327
euthanasia programme (Aktion T4), 63, 116
Evangelical Rural Education Home for Girls, Wieblingen, 20–1, 41–3
    see also Rural Education Home for Girls, Wieblingen
exhaust fumes, killing by, 90–1, 393–4 n.
extermination of Jews by Nazi regime, 75–6, 381 n.
    Chełmno extermination camp, 76, 89–93, 391–2 n., 393 n.
    Einsatzgruppen, 68, 74, 95
    'final solution to the Jewish question', 16, 77, 92, 260–1

Federal Republic of Germany, 354–8
    see also West Berlin
Fellowship of Reconciliation, 113–14
Finkler, Herr, 150, 265–6
Flossenbürg concentration camp, 326–7
Foreign Ministry, 46, 48, 51–2, 110, 142, 196–7
Forschungsamt (Research Office), 155–8, 160–1, 187

Fort VII concentration camp, 62–3
Fox, Christopher (nephew of Elisabeth von Thadden), 347
France, 65, 98, 291
    work of Elisabeth von Thadden in, 128, 184, 191–2
    see also Fresnes; Meaux
Frankfurt an der Oder, 74, 351
Freisler, Roland, 260–1, 264
    death, 324–5
    and Max Metzger, 261, 411–12 n.
    on Solf Circle, 313
    tea-party trial, 259, 261–72, 273–4, 275, 277, 278–82
    trials in aftermath of 20 July plot, 293
Fresnes, 211
Friedländer-Fuld, Milly Antonie von, 16
Fromm, Friedrich, 290, 291
Fürstenberg, 217, 220, 365
    see also Drögen

gas, killing by, 62–3, 63–4, 74, 75–6, 90–1, 92, 216, 393 n.
gas vans, 63–4, 74, 90–1, 92, 393–4 n.
Gehre, Ludwig, 161, 213, 295, 326, 327
Geltungsjuden (people deemed to be Jews), 38–9
Generals' Plot (Oster conspiracy), 52–3, 95–6
German Democratic Republic (GDR), 369
    and Hubertus von Ballestrem, 341, 342
    and Paul Reckzeh, 352, 353, 358, 362, 364
    see also East Berlin
German exiles, 132
    Switzerland, 113, 117, 134, 138, 173
German expats, 22, 39
German Reich Party (Deutsche Reichspartei), 347

442

Gestapo (Geheime Staatspolizei; Secret State Police), 46, 132, 147, 201, 381–2 n.
  assessment of Elisabeth von Thadden, 72
  assumption of responsibilities of Abwehr, 231
  Berlin building (Kurfürstendamm 140), 5, 194–5, 201, 204, 207, 212, 213
  Berlin HQ (Prinz-Albrecht-Strasse 8), 207, 211, 296–7, 298
  capture of 'submarines', 84, 85, 102–3
  importance of Otto Kiep to, 233
  inspection of Rural Education Home for Girls, Wieblingen, 71–2
  Maria von Maltzan shot at by, 249–50
  Munich HQ, 31–2, 206
  recruitment of informers, 132–3
  response to 20 July plot, 293, 295, 296, 297, 313–14, 318
  search of Maltzan apartment, 118–21
  secrecy of arrests of tea-party attendees, 197, 198
  surveillance of Friedrich Siegmund-Schultze, 114
  tensions between Wehrmacht and, 191, 194–5
  see also arrests; interrogations; Lange Special Commission (Sonderkommission Lange); Search Service
ghettos, Jewish, 74, 75, 92–3
Gierke, Anna von, 73, 128
Gniezno, 64, 74
Goebbels, Joseph, 16–17, 37, 163, 291, 328, 333, 386 n., 417 n.
Goerdeler, Carl Friedrich, 52, 148, 149, 295
  and Arthur Zarden, 87–8, 129
  flight and capture, 294, 328, 417–18 n.
  letter to Hanna Solf, 317
  and Otto Kiep, 297, 418 n.
  tapping of phone, 158
  wariness towards Solf Circle, 168–9
Gogalla, Wilhelm, 296–7
Goldschlag, Stella (the Blonde Poison), 103, 118, 119, 121
Göring, Hermann, 16–17, 23, 46, 79, 163
  and Research Office, 155, 157, 158
Görisch, Gerhard, 278
Greifer (grabbers), 102–3
  see also Goldschlag, Stella (the Blonde Poison); Isaaksohn, Rolf; Iskü, Herr and Frau
Grodziec, 75
Gruner, Isa, 73, 128, 158

H., Frau (socialite in Hitler's circle), 182–4
Haeften, Werner von (aide to Claus von Stauffenberg), 287, 290, 291
Hagen, Maximilian von, 319, 327
Hahn, Kurt, 20
Halder, Franz, 179, 184–5, 314
Halem, Nikolaus von, 54, 109–10, 219, 326
Hamburg, 99, 346, 367, 372
Hammerstein-Equord, Kurt von, 53
Hassell, Ulrich von, 314, 394 n.
Hausenstein, Margot (née Kohn), 70, 71
Hausenstein, Wilhelm, 70
Helmstedt border crossing, 370, 371
Heusinger, Adolf, 288
Heuss, Ernst Ludwig, 327–8, 421 n.
Heydrich, Reinhard, 95, 390 n.
Hillbring, Walter, 33
Himmler, Heinrich, 63, 64, 201, 286, 314, 421 n.
  antipathy towards Abwehr, 231
  and arrests of tea-party attendees, 6, 188

INDEX

Himmler, Heinrich (*cont.*)
  expansion of responsibilities, 231
  final days, 345
  interest in Otto Kiep, 242
  response to 20 July plot, 291, 293, 294, 296
Hindenburg, Paul von, 14
Hirschel, Günther, 78
Hirschel, Hans, 66–8, 77, 78, 80–1, 131, 250, 303, 323
  emergence from hiding, 334
  marriages to Maria von Maltzan, 335–6, 338
  and mother, 69, 79–80
  Professor Schröder alias, 68
  risk posed by *Greifer* to, 102
  search of apartment by Gestapo, 118–21
  work with Maria von Maltzan, 335
Hirschel, Luzie (mother of Hans Hirschel), 67, 68, 69, 77, 79–80
Hitler, Adolf (Führer), 13, 16–17, 21
  appetite for war, 95
  appointment as chancellor, 14–15
  circle of female acolytes, 182, 183
  death, 333
  dissolution of Abwehr, 231
  founding of People's Court, 261
  and Franz Halder, 179
  letter from Johann Kiep, 292–3
  letter to Arthur Zarden, 18, 202
  meeting with Arthur Zarden, 17–18
  meeting with Otto Kiep, 45–6
  meeting with Wilhelm Canaris, 95
  Mein Kampf, 13, 22, 47, 80, 345–6
  nationalsozialistische Bewegung, Die, 13
  plots against, *see* plots against Adolf Hitler
  portrait in Brennessel pub, 33

  and Research Office brownsheets, 157–8
  response to Vermehren defection, 231
  response to 20 July plot, 291, 293, 295, 417 n.
  subordination of Wehrmacht to, 195
Hitler Youth, 13, 130, 335
Hodgkin, Henry, 113–14
Holländer, Max Botho, 77–8, 78
Huppenkothen, Walter, 133, 212

Ilfeld, 49–50, 387 n.
Imgart, Dagmar, 111
individuals providing support for Jews
  Albrecht von Bernstorff, 110
  Anna von Gierke, 73
  Elisabeth von Thadden, 42–3, 70
  Erik Wesslén, 248–9
  Friedrich Siegmund-Schultze, 114
  Hanna Solf, 38–9, 83–5, 320
  Isa Gruner, 73
  Lagi Ballestrem-Solf, 39, 40, 82–5, 320
  Maria von Maltzan, 56, 65, 66, 77–9, 165–7, 249
  Wilhelm Solf, 37–8
innere Emigration, 107, 229
International Military Tribunal, Nuremberg, 340
interrogations
  Elisabeth von Thadden, 211, 237–41
  Hanna Kiep, 233–4
  Hanna Solf, 206, 207, 221–3, 318
  Irmgard Zarden, 201–2, 203–4, 270
  Lagi Ballestrem-Solf, 39–40, 82, 208–9, 223–4, 225, 313–14
  Maria von Maltzan, 31–2
  Otto Kiep, 212, 226–7, 242, 297
Isaaksohn, Rolf, 103, 118, 119, 121
Iskü, Herr and Frau, 103
Italy, 146–7

444

INDEX

Japan, 37–8, 277–8
Jehovah's Witnesses, 209, 215, 217, 223
Jews
  acquisition of Aryan papers, 38
  in Berlin, 40, 56, 101, 334, 422 n.
  emigration from Germany, 37–8, 39, 42, 46, 83; *see also* 'submarines' ('U-boats'; Jews in hiding): escape routes
  extermination of, *see* extermination of Jews by Nazi regime
  Geltungsjuden (people deemed to be Jews), 38–9
  in Germany, 65, 422 n.
  in hiding, *see* 'submarines' ('U-boats'; Jews in hiding)
  individuals providing support for, *see* individuals providing support for Jews
  Mischlinge, 42, 422 n.
  persecution of, *see* persecution of Jews by Nazi regime
Josias, Hereditary Prince of Waldeck and Pyrmont, 44–5

Kaltenbrunner, Ernst, 295, 388 n.
Kapp Putsch, 94
Keitel, Wilhelm, 195, 288, 290, 293
Keller, Werner, 323–4
KGB, 364
Kiep, Albrecht (son of Otto and Hanna Kiep), 49, 50, 106, 130, 189–90, 194, 235
Kiep, Charlotte (mother of Otto Kiep), 47, 57, 96
Kiep, Hanna (née Alves; wife of Otto Kiep), 27, 48, 50, 61, 96, 98, 99, 106, 175
  appeal for clemency on behalf of Otto, 292, 293
  arrest, 195, 233
  and 'The Bridge of Love', 228, 235
  detention at Ravensbrück, 233, 234–6
  farewell letters from Otto, 244, 245
  final meeting with Otto, 298
  interrogations, 233–4
  love of Otto for, 99, 170, 227
  post-war life, 346
  response to uncovering of Paul Reckzeh, 169–70
  search for Otto, 298
Kiep, Hanna Charlotte (daughter of Otto and Hanna Kiep), 98, 195, 346
Kiep, Hildegard (daughter of Otto and Hanna Kiep), 96, 195
Kiep, Ida, *see* Westphal, Ida (née Kiep; sister of Otto Kiep)
Kiep, Johann (brother of Otto Kiep), 257, 292–3
Kiep, Max (brother of Otto Kiep), 47, 49, 257
Kiep, Otto Carl ('O.C.'), 22, 44–50, 59–61, 96–100, 129–30
  anticipation of arrest, 189–90
  anticipation of Second World War, 60
  appeal for clemency, 292
  arrest, 193–5, 231
  biography, 346
  and 'The Bridge of Love', 228, 235
  and Carl Goerdeler, 297, 418 n.
  charges against, 253, 261
  conversation with Göring, 46
  conversation with Irmgard Westphal, 107–8
  detention at Brandenburg-Görden, 244
  detention at Gestapo HQ, Berlin, 298
  detention at Plötzensee, 298
  detention at Ravensbrück, 227–8, 234–6
  efforts to frustrate mission of Paul Reckzeh, 185

445

INDEX

Kiep, Otto Carl ('O.C.') (cont.)
and Einstein dinner, 26–9, 142
and Erich Vermehren, 230
execution, 298–9
family home (Taubertstrasse 15), 96, 130, 193
farewell letters to wife, 244, 245
final meeting with wife, 298
and Helmuth James von Moltke, 96–7, 161–2
on Hilger van Scherpenberg, 292, 414 n.
implicated in 20 July plot, 294, 295, 296
importance to Gestapo, 233
informs tea-party attendees of Paul Reckzeh's identity, 168
insomnia, 106
interest of Himmler in, 242
interrogations, 212, 226–7, 242, 297
invitation to tea party, 130
joins Nazi party, 57
joins OKW, 61
Lange on, 193
love for wife, 99, 170, 227
lunch with Elisabeth von Thadden, 163, 164–5
meeting with Hitler, 45–6
meeting with Josias, Hereditary Prince of Waldeck and Pyrmont, 44–5
and Operation Spark, 104–6
refusal to meet Paul Reckzeh, 175
resignation as consul general, 47
resistance activities, 98
response to death of Max Metzger, 252
response to inevitability of death sentence, 242–3
response to Kristallnacht, 57–8
response to Nazi regime, 46–7, 47–9, 50, 57
response to uncovering of Paul Reckzeh, 164–5, 169–71
role in OKW, 94, 95
sentence, 281
signing of confession, 297–8
and Solf Circle, 51–2
strategy for helping end Nazi regime, 60–1
suicide attempt, 244–5, 252–3
tapping of phone, 158
at tea party, 142, 145, 147, 148, 150
on tea party, 232
transfer of case to People's Court, 242
transfer to Gestapo HQ, Berlin, 296–7
transfer to Plötzensee, 296
transfer to Ravensbrück, 213–14
trial, 258, 259, 261, 264–7, 274–6, 278–9, 279–80, 280, 281
on truth, 99
uncovering of Paul Reckzeh, 161–2
visits to London, 59
visits to Switzerland, 150, 265
Kiep Clements, Hanna Charlotte (née Kiep), see Kiep, Hanna Charlotte (daughter of Otto and Hanna Kiep)
Kindt-Kiefer, Johann Jacob, 173, 179
Konin County, 75–6
Kosten, 63
Kraus, Annie, 83
Kreisau Circle, 96–7, 110, 111, 161, 285
Kreuzberg, 338
Kriminalpolizei (Criminal Police), 62
Kristallnacht ('night of broken glass'), 56–7, 57
Kübler, Harry, 341
Kübler, Manfred, 103
Kübler, Stella (née Goldschlag), see Goldschlag, Stella (the Blonde Poison)

446

INDEX

Kuenzer, Richard, 52, 53, 54, 111–12, 220, 313, 318–19, 319, 320, 326
Kunz, Wilhelm, 258
Kurowsky, Fanny von, 23–4
  acquittal, 282
  arrest, 6, 190
  charges against, 253, 261
  tapping of phone, 158
  at tea party, 142, 145, 148, 149
  trial, 259, 261, 270, 279

Lake Constance, 165
Lange, Herbert ('Leo'), 7, 25, 62–4, 74–6, 89–93, 132–5, 173, 213, 220, 298, 315
  expectations regarding tea party, 145, 146
  and Inge van Scherpenberg, 197–8
  interpretation of stalled mission of Paul Reckzeh, 186–8
  interrogations by, 201–2, 203–4, 212, 221–3, 223–4, 225, 226–7, 233, 237–41, 242, 270
  killing by gas, 62–3, 63–4, 74, 75–6, 90–1, 92
  meeting with Professor Paul Reckzeh, 357–8
  on Otto Kiep, 193
  recruitment of Agent Robby, 133–4
  request to Research Office, 158
  response to report on tea party, 160–1
  at tea-party trial, 257, 272
  uncertain fate of, 365–6
Lange Special Commission (Sonderkommission Lange), 186, 187–8, 213, 220, 233, 257, 365
Lange Special Detachment (Sonderkommando Lange), 63–4, 74–6, 89–93
Law for the Protection of German Blood and German Honour, 32

Law for the Restoration of the Professional Civil Service, 53–4
League of German Girls (Bund Deutscher Mädel), 13, 21, 42
Łódź, 74, 92–3
London, 59, 60
Lucerne, 148, 150

MacDonald, Ramsay, 265
Mainzer, Ferdinand, 83
Maltzan, Count Joachim Carl Mortimer von (brother of Maria von Maltzan; 'Carlos'), 13, 14, 30, 32, 68
Maltzan, Countess Maria von, 12–14, 30–6
  apartment (Detmolder Strasse 11), 66, 77–8, 103, 118–21, 248, 321, 333
  and baby son, 81
  conversation with sister-in-law, 247
  decision not to attend tea party, 131
  declared one of the Righteous among the Nations, 338
  denazification work, 335
  drug addiction, 336–7
  final visit to Militsch, 246–7
  and Hans Hirschel, 66–8, 69, 77, 80–1, 334–5, 335–6, 337–8
  interrogation, 31–2
  and Luzie Hirschel, 79–80
  marriages, 33, 335–6, 338
  plan to study veterinary medicine, 67
  post-war life, 334–8
  pregnancy, 69
  preparation for arrival of Red Army, 321, 333
  prowess with a gun, 33, 249
  and Red Cross, 67
  resistance activities, 30–1, 34, 247–50, 300, 301–3, 411 n.
  resists molestation by Red Army, 334

INDEX

Maltzan, Countess Maria von (*cont.*)
  response to Nazi regime, 13, 79
  risk posed by *Greifer* to, 102, 103
  search of apartment by Gestapo, 118–21
  shot at by Gestapo, 249–50
  support for Jews, 56, 65, 66, 77–9, 165–7, 249
  suspicions in aftermath of tea party, 165, 167
  veterinary work, 247–8, 334, 335, 337
  visit to Africa, 32
  visit to Berlin police HQ, 36
  visit to Czechoslovakia, 34–5
  and Walter Hillbring, 33
  and Walter von Reichenau, 68, 79
  and Werner Keller, 323–4
  witnesses Kristallnacht, 56
Marienborn border crossing, 370, 371
Meaux, 4, 191–2
Mein Kampf (Hitler), 13, 22, 47, 80, 345–6
Metzger, Max, 111–12, 115, 220, 251–2, 318, 319, 412 n.
  arrests, 54, 111
  and Roland Freisler, 261, 411–12 n.
Michendorf rest stop, 370, 371
Militsch, 12, 32, 246–7, 337
Ministry for State Security (Ministerium für Staatssicherheit; Stasi), 360–2, 362–3, 363–4, 370, 371, 372
Mischlinge, 42, 422 n.
Mohr, Wolfgang, 39
Moltke, Count Helmuth James von, 96–7, 161–2, 212–13, 213–14, 231, 317
Monte Verità, 339
Mosley, Oswald, 347
Muckermann, Friedrich, 30, 31
Müller, Pastor, 148
Mumm von Schwarzenstein, Herbert, 53–4, 109–10, 219, 326

Munich, 13, 31–2, 33, 206, 209
Munich Agreement, 52–3, 57–8, 95, 96, 158
Mussolini, Benito, 287, 290

National Democratic Party of Germany (Nationaldemokratische Partei Deutschlands), 347
National Socialist German Workers' Party (Nationalsozialistische Deutsche Arbeiterpartei; NSDAP; Nazi party)
  and aristocracy, 44
  ban on new members, 23
  Berlin parade (1933), 14–15
  coming to power of, 12
  entrenchment in German life, 47
  joined by Otto Kiep, 57
  Munich parade (1932), 13
  Nuremberg rallies, 49
nationalsozialistische Bewegung, Die (Hitler), 13
Nazi regime
  and Christianity, 41
  extermination of Jews, *see* extermination of Jews by Nazi regime
  persecution of Jews, *see* persecution of Jews by Nazi regime
  see also Reich Security Main Office (Reichssicherheitshauptamt; RSHA); Schutzstaffel (SS); Sturmabteilung (SA)
Nebe, Arthur, 90
New York, 26, 27, 28, 346
Niemöller, Martin, 73, 139, 140, 391 n.
'night of broken glass' (Kristallnacht), 56–7, 57
nobility (aristocracy), 44, 164, 263–4, 404 n.
NSDAP, *see* National Socialist German Workers' Party

448

INDEX

(Nationalsozialistische Deutsche Arbeiterpartei; NSDAP; Nazi party)
Nuremberg laws, 39, 65
  see also Law for the Protection of German Blood and German Honour
Nuremberg rallies, 49
Nuremberg trials, 340, 343

Oberkommando der Wehrmacht (OKW), 94
  resistance cell within, 97, 98
  see also Abwehr; Wehrmacht
Ohm, August, 310, 311, 312
Olympics, Berlin, 34
Operation Spark, 104–6, 285–6, 396 n.
Operation Valkyrie, 286, 290
Oranienburg, 203
  Sachsenhausen concentration camp, 203, 207, 211, 341–2
Orenstein, Benno, 15, 16, 87
Orenstein, Edithe, see Zarden, Edithe (née Orenstein)
Oshima, Hiroshi, 277–8
Oster, Hans, 52, 53, 95–6, 96, 98, 100, 130, 169, 231, 327
Oster conspiracy (Generals' Plot), 52–3, 95–6

Papen, Franz von, 46
Partenkirchen, 3
Patriotic Women's Association (Vaterländischer Frauenverein), 24
Patschkau labour camp, 35
Paul, Saint, 308
People's Court
  Bellevuestrasse 15 building, 257, 325
  flight of personnel, 325
  founding, 261
  lawyers acceptable to, 258
  response to *Wehrkraftzersetzung*, 242–3, 261

supportive trainee lawyer from, 306
tea-party trial, see trial of tea-party attendees
transfer of case of Otto Kiep to, 242
trials in aftermath of 20 July plot, 293
persecution of Jews by Nazi regime, 65–6
  boycott of Jewish businesses, 37
  deportations, 65, 109
  designated houses, 66, 390 n.
  detention at Ravensbrück, 215
  economic exploitation, 18, 75–6
  ghettos, 74, 75, 92–3
  Kristallnacht, 56–7, 57
  Law for the Restoration of the Professional Civil Service, 53–4
  Nuremberg laws, see Nuremberg laws
  Search Service, 101–3
  Star of David badges, 40, 65–6, 95, 390 n.
  sterilisation, 217
Persilschein, 335
phone-tapping, 156–8
Plaas, Hartmut, 161, 213
Planck, Erwin, 314
Plettenberg, Countess Elisabeth von, see Vermehren, Elisabeth (née von Plettenberg)
plots against Adolf Hitler, 293
  Generals' Plot (Oster conspiracy), 52–3, 95–6
  Operation Spark, 104–6, 285–6, 396 n.
  20 July plot, 286–91, 293–4
Poland, 61, 62, 95, 138, 179
Police Regulation on the Marking of Jews, 65–6
Popitz, Johannes, 314, 315, 418 n.
Poznań (Posen), 62–3, 296
Prague, 60, 291

449

INDEX

Quakers, 149, 269, 280

race defilement (*Rassenschande*), 32, 215
railways, 300–1, 303
Ravensbrück concentration camp, 215–20, 314, 316, 318
Ravensbrück concentration camp detainees, 215, 219
  Hanna Kiep, 233, 234–6
  Lagi Ballestrem-Solf, 218–19, 224–5, 313, 314–17, 342
  tea-party attendees, *see* tea-party attendees detained at Ravensbrück
Reckzeh, Barbara (daughter of Paul Reckzeh), 368–72, 426 n.
Reckzeh, Inge (née Graef; first wife of Paul Reckzeh), 122
  divorce, 354, 357
  meeting with Bianca Segantini, 123, 124, 125–6, 144, 404 n.
  Professor Paul Reckzeh on, 356–7
Reckzeh, Ingeborg (daughter of Paul Reckzeh), 354, 356–7
Reckzeh, Paul, 7, 23, 133–5, 186
  access to father's bequest, 426 n.
  Alfons Sack on, 275, 276
  Anza Braune on, 348, 401 n.
  attempt of Irmgard Zarden to reopen case against, 367, 425 n.
  betrayal of Barbara Reckzeh, 372
  death, 367, 372
  divorce from Inge, 354, 357
  efforts to renew contact with tea-party attendees, 175–81
  and Frau Weber, 355
  frustration of mission of, 184–5
  interpretation by Lange of stalled mission of, 186–8
  introductory visit to Elisabeth von Thadden, 137, 139–40
  legal process for arrest of, 354–8
  meeting with Bianca Segantini, 122–7, 404–5 n.
  meeting with Elisabeth von Thadden after tea party, 177–81
  meeting with Joseph Wirth, 173–4
  meetings with Friedrich Siegmund-Schultze, 115–16, 144, 174
  offer to act as courier for Elisabeth von Thadden, 150, 159–60
  post-war life, 351–4, 358–64, 366, 367, 368–70, 372, 426 n.
  report on tea party, 160, 161–2, 164, 170
  suspicious behaviour, 116, 117, 140, 144, 174
  at tea party, 143, 144–52
  uncovering as Gestapo agent, 161–2
  views of father on, 355–8
  views of relatives and acquaintances on, 369
  visits to Switzerland, 113, 115–17, 122–7, 173–5
  as witness at tea-party trial, 272–4, 278, 280
Reckzeh, Professor Paul (father of Paul Reckzeh), 123, 159, 160, 354, 355–8, 364, 426 n.
Reckzeh, Ruth (née Hensel; second wife of Paul Reckzeh), 368, 369, 426 n.
Red Army, 246, 321, 325, 333–4, 337, 352
Red Cross, 67–8, 72–3, 101, 171–2, 184, 191
Reich Health Office, 115
Reich Ministry of Justice, 298, 306
Reich Security Main Office (Reichssicherheitshauptamt; RSHA), 92, 132, 326, 381 n.
  see also Gestapo (Geheime Staatspolizei; Secret State Police); Sicherheitsdienst (SD)

450

INDEX

Reichenau, Walter von, 68, 79
Reichenau Order, 68
Reichlin von Meldegg, Baroness Martha, 70–1
Reichsgau Wartheland (Warthegau), 64, 89
Reinhardt, Fritz, 18
Remer, Otto Ernst, 417 n.
Replacement Army (Ersatzheer), 285, 286, 290
Research Office (Forschungsamt), 155–8, 160–1, 187
Ribbentrop, Annelies von, 16
Ribbentrop, Joachim von, 16, 158
Richert, Arvid (Swedish envoy in Berlin), 248, 277, 300
Richter, Martha (housekeeper), 4, 207, 208, 209, 340
Roma, 92, 215, 217
Roosevelt, Franklin D., 179
Rosenberg, Alfred, 46–7
RSHA, *see* Reich Security Main Office (Reichssicherheitshauptamt; RSHA)
Rühle, Anne
  absence of charges against, 259
  arrest, 190
  response to Nazi regime, 24
  response to uncovering of Paul Reckzeh, 171
  tapping of phone, 158
  at tea party, 143, 144, 145–6, 148, 150, 151, 152
  visit to Friedrich Siegmund-Schultze, 114
  as witness at tea-party trial, 271
Ruppel, Irmgard (née Zarden), *see* Zarden, Irmgard
Rural Education Home for Girls, Wieblingen, 43, 70–2
  see also Evangelical Rural Education Home for Girls, Wieblingen
Ruspoli, Princess Elisabeth, 314, 315
Rzgów, 75

SA (Sturmabteilung), 13, 56
Sachsenhausen concentration camp, 203, 207, 211, 341–2
Sack, Alfons, 258, 274–6, 280
St Anne's Church, Dahlem, 139–40
Salomon, Alice, 20, 24, 41
Schacht, Hjalmar, 129, 142, 270, 314
Scherpenberg, Hilger van, 23, 171, 363
  arrest, 197
  charges against, 253, 261
  detention at Brandenburg-Görden, 244
  meeting with Paul Reckzeh, 175
  Otto Kiep on, 292, 414 n.
  post-war life, 345
  response to Nazi regime, 23
  response to uncovering of Paul Reckzeh, 172, 195–6
  sentence, 281–2
  tapping of phone, 158
  at tea party, 142, 145, 147–8
  transfer to Ravensbrück, 213–14
  trial, 258, 259, 261, 269–70, 278, 279
Scherpenberg, Inge van (née Schacht), 171–2, 177, 181, 196–8, 257
Schlabrendorff, Fabian von, 396 n.
Schloss Elmau, 171, 177, 180, 191
Schloss Militsch, *see* Militsch
Schönefeld airport, 371
Schramm, Ehrengard (née von Thadden; 'Eta'; sister of Elisabeth von Thadden), 191, 257, 258, 306–7
Schramm, Percy Ernst (husband of Ehrengard von Thadden), 257, 306–7
Schultz, Elisabeth von (sister of Hanna Solf), 4, 207, 208, 209
Schulz, Anni, 38–9

451

INDEX

Schutzstaffel (SS), 13, 25, 381 n.
   economic exploitation of Jews, 75–6
   exploitation of slave labour, 216
   patrols near Berlin, 301–3
   see also arrests
Schwarz, Else (Kiep housemaid), 193, 194, 235
Schwarze Kapelle (Black Orchestra), 104, 105
SD (Sicherheitsdienst), 62, 231
Search Service, 101–3
   see also Greifer
Secret State Police, *see* Gestapo (Geheime Staatspolizei; Secret State Police)
Security Police School, Drögen, 186, 220, 221, 233, 237
Segantini, Bianca, 122–7, 137–9, 144, 145–6, 369, 404–5 n.
Segantini, Giovanni, 122, 369
Shanghai, 39, 208
Sicherheitsdienst (SD), 62, 231
Siegmund-Schultze, Friedrich, 52, 113–16, 134, 145, 146, 149, 158, 279
   and Elisabeth von Thadden, 19, 115
   meetings with Paul Reckzeh, 115–16, 144, 174
   visit of Anne Rühle, 114
Siemens & Halske, 216
Sils Maria, 122, 138
Sippenhaft (blood guilt), 169, 294, 314, 328
Sixth Army, 68
slave labour, exploitation by SS, 216
SMERSH, 351
Social Democratic Party (Sozialdemokratische Partei Deutschlands; SPD), 23, 142, 269
Soldau transit camp, 64
Solf, Johanna ('Hanna'), 82, 109
   account of experiences under Nazi regime, 340
   appointment of lawyers, 258, 323
   arrest, 3–4, 190, 206, 317
   charges against, 253, 261, 318–20
   death, 340–1
   detention at Cottbus, 317–18
   detention at Moabit, 317, 320–1, 323, 324, 325–6
   detention at Ravensbrück, 219, 221, 224–5, 313, 314–15
   detention at Sachsenhausen, 207, 211
   discharge from Moabit, 327–9
   family home (Alsenstrasse 9), 16, 51, 54
   interrogations, 206, 207, 221–3, 318
   and legal process for arrest of Paul Reckzeh, 354, 355
   letter from Carl Goerdeler, 317
   letters to Swiss contacts, 151
   marriage, 11, 12
   mission to demonstrate existence of another Germany, 343–4
   possible sighting of Lange, 365
   post-war life, 339–40
   postponement of second trial, 321, 324, 325
   refusal to meet Paul Reckzeh, 175
   response to uncovering of Paul Reckzeh, 168
   and Richard Kuenzer, 53
   support for Jews, 38–9, 83–5, 320
   tapping of phone, 158
   at tea party, 142, 145, 146, 148, 149, 151–2
   train journeys to Gestapo HQ, Berlin, 211
   trial, 258, 259, 261, 268–9, 277–8, 280, 313
   as witness at Nuremberg, 340, 343
   see also Solf Circle (Solf-Kreis)
Solf, So'oa'emalelagi, *see* Ballestrem-Solf, So'oa'emalelagi (née Solf; 'Lagi')

INDEX

Solf, Wilhelm, 11–12, 16, 37–8, 277–8
Solf Circle (Solf-Kreis), 51–2, 53–5, 109, 110, 111, 112, 220, 277, 318
  detention of members at Ravensbrück, 218–19
  Ernst Kaltenbrunner on, 388 n.
  Heinrich Himmler on, 296
  reputation for poor security, 168–9
  Roland Freisler on, 313
  see also Solf, Johanna ('Hanna')
Sonderkommando Lange (Lange Special Detachment), 63–4, 74–6, 89–93
Sonderkommission Lange (Lange Special Commission), 186, 187–8, 213, 220, 233, 257, 365
Soviet Union, 138, 151–2, 179, 260, 364
  see also Stalingrad
Soziale Arbeitsgemeinschaft, 19, 113
SPD (Sozialdemokratische Partei Deutschlands; Social Democratic Party), 23, 142, 269
Spindler, Leopold ('Poldi'), 370, 371
SS, see Schutzstaffel (SS)
Stalingrad, 99–100
Star of David badges, 40, 65–6, 95, 390 n.
Starnberg, 30–1, 340–1
Stasi (Ministerium für Staatssicherheit; Ministry for State Security), 360–2, 362–3, 363–4, 370, 371, 372
Stauffenberg, Count Berthold Schenk von, 291
Stauffenberg, Count Claus Schenk von, 285–90, 291
Stawiszyn, 74
Steinberg, Colonel von, 274
sterilisation, human, 217
Stoecker, Wolf (nephew of Otto Kiep), 257, 263, 400 n.

Strübing, Johannes, 206
Sturmabteilung (SA), 13, 56
'submarines' ('U-boats'; Jews in hiding), 38–9, 65, 66, 77–9, 83
  capture by Gestapo, 84, 85, 102–3
  emergence from hiding, 334
  escape routes, 83–5, 165–7, 248–9, 300–1, 303; see also Jews: emigration from Germany
  recruitment by Search Service, 101–2
  see also Hirschel, Hans
Sudetenland, 52, 57–8, 158
Svensson, Eric, 81, 119
Sweden, 301, 303
Switzerland
  as destination for 'submarines', 84, 165, 166
  German exiles, 113, 117, 134, 138, 173
  Quakers, 149
  recuperation of Solfs, 339
  visits by Elisabeth von Thadden, 138, 139
  visits by Otto Kiep, 150, 265
  visits by Paul Reckzeh, 113, 115–17, 122–7, 173–5
  see also Lucerne; Sils Maria

tea party (10 September 1943), 128–9, 141–3, 144–52
  invitations, 129, 130, 131, 140
tea-party attendees
  efforts of Paul Reckzeh to renew contact with, 175–81
  Himmler and arrests of, 6, 188
  implicated in 20 July plot, 295
  informed of Paul Reckzeh's identity, 168
  response to death of Max Metzger, 252
  secrecy of arrests, 197, 198
  trial of, see trial of tea-party attendees

INDEX

tea-party attendees (*cont.*)
  see also Braune, Marie-Agnes (née von Thadden; sister of Elisabeth von Thadden; 'Anza'); Kiep, Otto Carl ('O.C'); Kurowsky, Fanny von; Reckzeh, Paul; Rühle, Anne; Scherpenberg, Hilger van; Solf, Johanna ('Hanna'); Thadden, Elisabeth von; Zarden, Arthur; Zarden, Irmgard
tea-party attendees detained at Ravensbrück, 217, 218–19, 220, 223, 237, 246
  Elisabeth von Thadden, 237, 239–41
  Hanna Solf, 219, 221, 224–5, 313, 314–15
  Irmgard Zarden, 246, 366–7
  Otto Kiep, 227–8, 234–6
Thadden, Adolf von, 347
Thadden, Ehrengard von, *see* Schramm, Ehrengard (née von Thadden; sister of Elisabeth von Thadden; 'Eta')
Thadden, Elisabeth von, 18–21, 70–3, 128–9, 347
  anticipation of death, 305, 308, 309
  anticipation of post-war Germany, 143, 149
  apartment, *see* Carmerstrasse 12, Berlin (Thadden apartment)
  appeal for clemency by family, 305–7
  arrest, 4–5, 191–2, 210–11
  assessment by Gestapo, 72
  and August Ohm, 310, 311, 312
  and Bianca Segantini, 137–9
  charges against, 253, 261
  detention at Barnimstrasse, 307–10
  detention at Gestapo HQ, Berlin, 211
  detention at Ravensbrück, 237, 239–41
  detention at Sachsenhausen, 211
  efforts to frustrate mission of Paul Reckzeh, 184–5
  execution, 312
  final letters and testament, 311
  and Friedrich Siegmund-Schultze, 19, 115
  guilt regarding tea party, 238
  and Hans-Hasso von Veltheim, 311
  informs tea-party attendees of Paul Reckzeh's identity, 168, 171–2
  and Inge van Scherpenberg, 171–2, 177, 181
  interrogations, 211, 237–41
  introduction by Bianca Segantini of Paul Reckzeh, 125–6, 127
  introductory visit of Paul Reckzeh, 137, 139–40
  letter to Friedrich Siegmund-Schultze, 150, 159–60
  lunch with Otto Kiep, 163, 164–5
  manacling of, 305, 307
  meeting with Frau H., 182–4
  meeting with Lisi von Thadden, 308–9
  meeting with Paul Reckzeh after tea party, 177–81
  and Red Cross, 72–3, 171–2, 184, 191
  response to Nazi regime, 21, 41–3, 56–7, 70, 71, 139, 141
  response to uncovering of Paul Reckzeh, 164–5
  sentence, 281
  tapping of phone, 158
  at tea party, 141, 143, 144, 145, 146, 148, 149, 150, 151, 152
  train journeys to Gestapo HQ, Berlin, 211
  transfer to Plötzensee, 310
  trial, 258, 259, 261, 263–4, 278, 279–80, 281

INDEX

visit of Arthur Zarden, 177
visits to Switzerland, 138, 139
'Wieblingen teas', 128, 136–7
work in France, 128, 184, 191–2
Thadden, Elisabeth von (née Freiin von Thüngen; wife of Reinold von Thadden; 'Lisi'), 308–9
Thadden, Marie-Agnes von, *see* Braune, Marie-Agnes (née von Thadden; sister of Elisabeth von Thadden; 'Anza')
Thadden, Reinold von (brother of Elisabeth von Thadden), 178, 257, 363
Theresienstadt concentration camp, 69, 79, 101
Thierack, Otto, 298
Third Reich, *see* Nazi regime
Thun-Hohenstein, Count Paul, 181
'Total War', 163, 328
trial of tea-party attendees, 257–9, 261–82
    Elisabeth von Thadden, 258, 259, 261, 263–4, 278, 279–80, 281
    Fanny von Kurowsky, 259, 261, 270, 279
    Hanna Solf, 258, 259, 261, 268–9, 277–8, 280, 313
    Hilger van Scherpenberg, 258, 259, 261, 269–70, 278, 279
    Irmgard Zarden, 259, 261, 270–1
    Otto Kiep, 258, 259, 261, 264–7, 274–6, 278–9, 279–80, 280, 281
Trieglaff, 18, 19, 149
Trott zu Solz, Adam von, 97, 229, 230, 299
Turkey, 229–30
Tutzing, 70
20 July plot, 286–91, 293–4
    execution of purported conspirators, 293, 310
    increase in number of prisoners at Ravensbrück following, 314

interpreted as culmination of wider conspiracy, 295–6
Otto Kiep implicated in, 294, 295, 296
response of Gestapo to, 293, 295, 296, 297, 313–14, 318
response of Himmler to, 291, 293, 294, 296
response of Hitler to, 291, 293, 295, 417 n.
tea-party attendees implicated in, 295

'U-boats', *see* 'submarines' ('U-boats'; Jews in hiding)
United Kingdom, *see* Britain
United States, 22, 46
see also New York

Vassiltchikov, Marie ('Missie'), 404 n.
Vaterländischer Frauenverein (Patriotic Women's Association), 24
Veltheim, Hans-Hasso von, 311
Vermehren, Elisabeth (née von Plettenberg), 229–31
Vermehren, Erich, 229–31
Veronica, Saint, 307
Vienna, 291

Waldberg, Max von, 42
Waldeck and Pyrmont, Josias, Hereditary Prince of, 44–5
Waldheim trials, 353, 354
Wannsee, 77
Wannsee Conference, 77, 260–1
Warsaw, 95
Warthegau (Reichsgau Wartheland), 64, 89
Warthegau mental hospital, Kosten, 63
Weber, Frau, 355
Wedderstedt, 189
Wednesday Group, 295
Wehrkraftzersetzung, 242–3, 261

455

INDEX

Wehrmacht
  Replacement Army (Ersatzheer), 285, 286, 290
  resistance cell within, 285–6
  Sixth Army, 68
  subordination to Hitler, 195
  tensions between Gestapo and, 191, 194–5
  see also Oberkommando der Wehrmacht (OKW)
Wesslén, Erik, 248–9, 300
West Berlin, 354, 368, 370
West Germany, see Federal Republic of Germany
Westphal, Ida (née Kiep; sister of Otto Kiep), 59–60, 99, 106–7, 170–1, 189
Westphal, Irmgard, 106–7, 107–8
Weyl family, 38–9
Widerstehen (Christopher Fox), 347
Wieblingen, 20–1, 41–3, 70–2
'Wieblingen teas', 128, 136–7
Wilder, Thornton, 228
Wirth, Elisabeth, 178, 180, 190–1, 211
Wirth, Joseph, 52, 134, 145, 174, 179
  contact with Arthur Zarden, 202
  meeting with Paul Reckzeh, 173–4
  purported involvement in anti-Nazi plot, 226–7, 265, 279, 280–1
Wittenau, 336–7
Wolf's Lair (Wolfsschanze), 286

Yad Vashem, 338

Zarden, Arthur, 14–15, 16, 87, 219
  arrest, 5, 190, 201
  and Carl Goerdeler, 87–8, 129
  contact with Joseph Wirth, 202
  death, 204–5
  grief following wife's death, 87
  invitation to tea party, 129
  letter from Hitler, 18, 202, 382–3 n.
  meeting with Hitler, 17–18
  meeting with Paul Reckzeh, 175–6
  response to Hitler becoming chancellor, 14, 15
  retirement, 17–18
  suspicion of Paul Reckzeh, 165
  tapping of phone, 158
  at tea party, 141, 145, 148, 149
  visit to Elisabeth von Thadden, 177
  withdrawal from Berlin life, 86, 129
Zarden, Edithe (née Orenstein), 15, 17, 86–7, 87
Zarden, Irmgard, 15–16, 42, 86, 87, 129
  acquittal, 282
  arrest, 5–6, 190, 201
  charges against, 253, 261
  death, 346
  denazification work, 346
  detention at Ravensbrück, 246, 366–7
  detention at Sachsenhausen, 203, 211
  interrogation, 201–2, 203–4, 270
  meeting with Paul Reckzeh, 175
  post-war life, 345–6
  postcards to Paul Reckzeh, 366–7
  response to father's death, 204
  response to Nazi party, 16–17
  suspicion of Paul Reckzeh, 165
  tapping of phone, 165
  at tea party, 141, 148, 150, 151
  train journeys to Gestapo HQ, Berlin, 211
  trial, 259, 261, 270–1
  visit to Germany, 365, 366
Zeuthen, 366, 368–9
Zimmerman, Brigitte (secretary to Otto Kiep), 233, 272
Zyklon B, 62